GOETHE
AND THE
NOVEL

By the same author:

Adalbert Stifter: A Critical Study
The Emergence of German as a Literary Language

GOETHE

AND THE NOVEL

ERIC A. BLACKALL

CORNELL UNIVERSITY PRESS

ITHACA AND LONDON

First published 1976 by Cornell University Press.
Published in the United Kingdom by Cornell University Press Ltd.,
2-4 Brook Street, London W1Y 1AA.

International Standard Book Number 0-8014-0978-0
Library of Congress Catalog Card Number 75-38426
Printed in the United States of America by York Composition Company
*Librarians: Library of Congress cataloging information
appears on the last page of the book.*

For my beloved wife
Jean Frantz Blackall

Contents

Acknowledgments

I would like to express my gratitude to the John Simon Guggenheim Foundation for awarding me a fellowship which enabled me to think my way into this immensely complex subject, to Herbert Dieckmann, Hildegard Emmel, and Heinz Politzer for their constant encouragement, to Loisa Nygaard for her contribution to the composition of the notes to this work, and to Kay Scheuer and Constance Colwell for their careful scrutiny of the final manuscript. I have also benefited greatly from the criticisms offered in such a generous spirit by the two readers of my manuscript for Cornell University Press.

Sections of Chapter 6 represent a reworking of parts of my article "Sense and Nonsense in *Wilhelm Meisters Lehrjahre*," published in the fifth volume of *Deutsche Beiträge zur geistigen Überlieferung* (Berne, 1965). The beginning of Chapter 11 is a reworking of an article in German, "Zur Kontrapunktik von *Wilhelm Meisters Wanderjahren*," which appeared in *Die Ringenden sind die Lebendigen* (Stuttgart, 1969), a tribute to Hermann Leins on his seventieth birthday. The second section of that chapter is a reworking of my article "Wilhelm Meister's Pious Pilgrimage," published in *German Life and Letters* in July 1965. I am grateful to the Francke Verlag of Berne, the Metzlersche Verlagsbuchhandlung of Stuttgart, and Basil Blackwell of Oxford for permission to use parts of these articles in reworked form.

A few points in Chapters 7 and 9 are further developed in my article "Goethe's Silences" in *Geist und Zeichen* (Heidelberg, 1976), a festschrift for Arthur Henkel.

The translations of the passages quoted in this work are in every case my own. There are complete translations of *Werther* by William Rose (London, 1929), Victor Lange (New York, 1949), Bayard Quincy Morgan (London, 1957) and Harry Steinhauer (New York, 1970). The standard translation of *Wilhelm Meister's Apprenticeship* is that by Thomas Carlyle (Edinburgh, 1824; revised edition, London, 1839; reprint available in a paperback published by Macmillan). There are three readily available translations of *The Elective Affinities:* one by Elizabeth Mayer and Louise Bogan (Chicago, 1936), the Penguin Classics edition translated by R. J. Hollingdale (London, 1971) and a translation by H. M. Waidson under the title *Kindred by Choice* (London, 1960). No satisfactory translation of the *Journeymanship* is currently available.

Eric A. Blackall

Ithaca, New York

GOETHE
AND THE
NOVEL

1

Introduction

Goethe has rarely been ranked among the great novelists. However much we may admire *The Sorrows of Young Werther*, this fact alone will hardly place him alongside Balzac or Tolstoy or Dickens. In part this is because he was not primarily a novelist but so much else besides. And yet he did write four remarkable novels. Each is very different from the others, each appeared at a different stage in Goethe's long creative life: *Werther* in 1774, *Wilhelm Meister's Apprenticeship* in 1796, *The Elective Affinities* in 1809, and *Wilhelm Meister's Journeymanship* in 1829. There was therefore no one period in Goethe's life when his preferred artistic medium was the novel; he was not drawn to the novel at one particular time to express one particular stage of his evolving consciousness. He was drawn toward the novel at different points, and never at any of these points did he abandon other literary forms. As a result each of the novels has usually been considered in relationship to works in other genres which Goethe was writing at about the same time. Rarely have all the novels been considered in relation to one another. *Werther* has often been compared with *The Elective Affinities* in its portrayal of passion, and the two Wilhelm Meister novels with each other as novels of education, and *The Elective Affinities* with the second Wilhelm Meister novel as books of renunciation. But rarely have all four been considered together as the *œuvre* of a novelist; and they have never been considered with reference to the general potentialities or the historical development of the novel as a form.[1] Is there any unity here? Did Goethe turn to the novel, rather than to drama or lyrical poetry, to express some particular type of experience? Or was it merely a question of range of experience? (If so, why was *Faust* not written as a novel?) Was it a question of being able to introduce a wide range of characters? (If so, why was *Werther* written as a novel?) Was it a question of considering man not for himself but in relation to society? (If so, why was *Torquato Tasso* written as a play?) Was it the desire to portray society in all its complex texture? Or was it a question not of a different subject matter but of a different structuring theme? Is there a theme common to these four novels which demanded epic rather than lyric or dramatic construction? Is there a perspective in the novels basically different from that of the plays and the poems? If so, what is it? What is the relation between art and reality in these novels?

Goethe's novels are all rooted in the outer world of his time and place. The characters, the settings, the problems, even the terms in which people think are those of that period. The structure of German society with its landed gentry, its urban bourgeoisie, its small courts, and its social outcasts (especially actors) is all there. But Goethe is not a social novelist; he is not concerned with social institutions as such. The fact that Werther deplores the conditions of middle-class existence [*die fatalen bürgerlichen Verhältnisse*], and that Wilhelm Meister spends much time reflecting on the differences between aristocratic and bourgeois life should not delude us into identifying Goethe with his characters and the way in which they try to account for their difficulties. Between *Werther* and *Wilhelm Meister's Journeymanship*, that is to say between 1774 and 1829, great historical events changed the whole social organization of the world. But none of them plays an active part in Goethe's novels, except the foundation of a new society in America (which exception is in itself, as we shall see, significant). Goethe was deeply concerned about the French Revolution and its aftermath, and he treated this subject in other works. But not in the novels. Here historical events fashion the terms in which Goethe's characters express themselves, but only the terms: for the problems treated are not problems which arise or arose from historical events, although the problems manifest themselves in shapes conditioned both by historical events and by the intellectual and social climate of the time. It is therefore misleading to assert, as one recent critic has, that Goethe's novels portray the passage from a feudal to a middle-class society. The society of these novels was indeed in such transition, being the society of Goethe's own day; but social transition is not the theme of these novels. They are concerned with a wider conception of order, of which social order is a part, but only a part.

Werther seems to deal with a hypersensitive temperament at variance with the world. The question is: what is "the world" in this novel? If it were society, then this would be a novel about the individual who fails to find his place in society and commits suicide. It would then fall into the familiar pattern of the novel being used to describe an individual in relationship to society. We must surely immediately agree that this is not true of *Werther* to the extent that it is true of, say, *Tom Jones* or even *Pamela*. If it were true, we would have to ask ourselves whether it is Werther or society that is responsible for his failure. We would also face the question: which society? The rebuff that Werther receives from aristocratic society in the second part of the novel is irritating but not conclusive: the other social obstacle would seem to be that his beloved Lotte is engaged and later married to Albert. But the institution of marriage —usually for some inexplicable reason considered to be middle-class—is obviously not in itself the reason for Werther's suicide. The striking thing about the novel is the unity of its standpoint. It is a novel of obsession, not one of conflict. In form it is a letter-novel without a replying correspondent, and a *roman personnel*. Except for one brief section we never really move outside Werther's mind. That there is an outside "world" is part of the illusion; and because there is no objective reality, Werther is not, cannot be, in conflict with it. The poignancy of his situation is that he thinks he is: but this sense of conflict is as much an illusion as the outside world with which he feels himself in conflict.

Historically *The Sorrows of Young Werther* has been considered as a novel of sensibility, a confessional novel, perhaps even the first Romantic novel; all this is true, and yet does not properly describe the book or account for its individuality and greatness. In form it can be related to the epistolary novel of the eighteenth century, and certain elements in it can be related to other types of eighteenth-century writings; but this does not accurately designate its true form as a literary work. In respect to both content and form it can be placed in a historical perspective, but without being fully accounted for. The same is true of each of Goethe's other novels. My purpose in this book is to assess Goethe's achievement as a novelist and to consider his views on the novel as a form, in relation both to the development of the genre during his lifetime and to the ways in which he went beyond this. In our considerations we should always remember that Goethe was born into the world of Richardson and died in that of Balzac and Stendhal. His life therefore spanned a tremendous range of variety of novels and novelists and witnessed a substantial development of the form, from its emergence as a genre to its attaining a position of preeminence among the literary genres.

It has sometimes been asserted that Goethe considered the novel an inferior form of literature and never said much about it anyway. Nothing could be further from the truth. In fact we find in reviews, letters, and conversations extensive comments on specific novels, and we have one lengthy comment (in *Wilhelm Meister's Apprenticeship*) on the novel as a form, and several notable shorter pronouncements on this topic. Goethe followed the development of the genre throughout his life. His reading of novels was constant and extensive. He read most of the important novels that appeared during his lifetime, and many less important ones. He read not only German, French and English novels, but Cervantes and Manzoni, some Chinese novels and some from Greek antiquity. Towards the end of his life he immersed himself in Scott and James Fenimore Cooper. He was fascinated by the possibilities offered by the genre. And each of his novels is an experiment, reconnaissance into unexplored but infinitely exploitable territory.

Apart from *Werther*, the novels of Goethe hardly belong to the literary experience of the educated general reader. It therefore seems to me advisable to give an analysis of each of them. In my analysis I shall go beyond plot-summary, interpreting each novel as a total structure of meaning, emphasizing themes and recurrent preoccupations, and examining in some detail the more important moments and passages. This is, I believe, essential groundwork for any assessment of Goethe's achievement and his attitude to the novel as a form, and it is my hope that the close readings I offer will also be of interest to those who are already acquainted with these works. Since my intention is to place Goethe's views on the novel and his own novels in a European, and to some extent even a global setting, I shall not assume any knowledge of German on the part of my readers. The translation is in every case my own. In the notes I shall refer the reader who wishes to pursue matters further to the German text of what I quote in translation and to some of the secondary literature which I have found most stimulating, both negatively and positively. I shall not attempt, however, to survey all that has been written about the individual novels.

2

Soliloquy in the Epistolary Mode

It was as a novelist that Goethe first came to the attention of the reading public. For despite the considerable interest that his play *Götz von Berlichingen* had aroused in his own country, it was a novel, *Werther*, that brought him international fame. This is still the most read of his novels, for, although in some ways essentially of its period, it possesses more than historical significance in the quality of its imaginative vision and the subtlety and scope of its writing. Whether we think of it as an epistolary novel, a confessional novel, or a romantic novel, *Werther* is a masterpiece—perhaps indeed the greatest exemplar—of any and all of these genres. How was it that Goethe, at the age of twenty-five, should have achieved at one go such mastery?

Werther was not, however, his first attempt at writing a novel. A few pages have survived from a manuscript which dates from the autumn of 1770 or the succeeding winter, when Goethe was a student at Strassburg.[1] This consists of two complaining letters from rejected lovers to their fickle lady-loves. The fragment gives little indication of what the novel was to be like, except that the tone is sententious and rococo. Like Goethe's own rococo poems of the second half of the 1760s, it suggests the instability of love, representing, as one critic has put it, a stage that had to be worked through before he could write *Werther*.[2] But it is in no way a first shot at what was to become *Werther*, nor does it show any serious thought about the novel as a genre of literary expression. These are fictive letters: and if there is any context to which they might rightly be related, it would be that

of Goethe's own letters of the period and the letter-novels
which he had read.

What novels had he read when he embarked on *Werther?*
What did he say about them? Did he reveal any marked likes or
dislikes?

The answer is that he read those novels which most young
Germans of his class and education were reading. As a child he
read *Robinson Crusoe* and that most famous of German novels
based on it, Schnabel's *The Island of Felsenburg*. He also read
Fénelon's *Télémaque* quite early.[3] Somewhat later he read
Richardson's novels, *La Nouvelle Héloïse*, *The Vicar of Wakefield*, *Manon Lescaut*, *Das Fräulein von Sternheim* (a novel of
sensibility by his friend Sophie von La Roche), and the first important philosophical novel in German, Wieland's *Agathon*, as
well as Wieland's earlier parodistic attack on "enthusiasm," his
novel *Don Sylvio von Rosalva*. All this is attested.[4] He also seems
to have known something of Rabelais at this time, and Jung-
Stilling reports in his autobiography that Goethe acquainted
him with Fielding and Sterne (this must have been in 1770–1771
when Goethe and Jung-Stilling were both students at Strassburg).[5] The extent to which Goethe was acquainted with the
novels of Fielding—both at this time and later—is difficult to
determine; but there are several indications that he knew Sterne's
Tristram Shandy—or knew about it—in these early years.[6] It is
of course likely that he had read other novels by this time, but
we have no documentary evidence beyond what I have stated.
He said very little about those novels which we know him to
have read, and his comments are more concerned with content
than with form. In a letter to a young woman he says that girls
find Sir Charles Grandison "a fine piece of a man" and think they
would like such a one themselves.[7] And in later years, while
looking back on this period of his life, he asserted that his liking
for both *The Vicar of Wakefield* and *Manon Lescaut* at that
time was primarily due to similarity between their characters
and situations and those of his own life.[8] In 1811 Goethe re-

flected on why *Manon Lescaut* had appealed to him so much at the time of his love affair with the Frankfurt girl who is simply called "Gretchen" in his autobiography. He says:

The great intelligence with which this work was conceived and the inestimable artistry with which it was executed were not indeed apparent to me at that time. The book affected me solely by its subject matter: I thought I could be just as loving and true as the Chevalier and, as I considered Gretchen far better than Manon had shown herself to be, I believed that everything one might do for her would be well invested [*wohl angelegt*]. And as it is the nature of novels that the fulness of youth is oversaturated and the dryness of age refreshed by them, so did the reading of this book contribute greatly to making my relationship with Gretchen richer, more pleasing, even more blissful while it lasted and my condition more wretched and my sickness more incurable when it was over.[9]

His reactions to Rousseau's *La Nouvelle Héloïse* are clothed in darkness. Undoubtedly the novel affected him greatly, as we can see from his own novels, but all he ever said about it is the brief note in one of the drafts for his autobiography: "1761. Nouvelle Heloise appeared. I read it later."[10]

We therefore have no evidence at all that the author of *Werther* had thought about the novel as a form and the opportunities that it offered—except of course that he was writing *Werther*. What then does an analysis of the novel itself tell us about his conception of the genre?

There are two versions of *Werther*, both of which were published during Goethe's lifetime. The first appeared in 1774, the second in 1787. These two versions have never been properly compared with each other: certainly not in connection with Goethe's conception of the novel as a form and the problems that it presented to him,. which is our present consideration. Most modern readers know only the second version, and most translations are usually of this final version of the work, and understandably so.[11] But there are differences between the two versions which are important for the particular investigation that we are here engaged in. In this chapter I shall concentrate on the first version of the novel, whereas in the next chapter I shall turn to the second. I believe I can assume that the reader knows the plot of *Werther*, and what now follows is therefore not a recapitulation of the total action but an analysis of the structure, which will proceed by emphasizing the main stages in the development of its theme.

The brief address to the reader with which the work begins is both conventional and individual. It asserts, in conventional eighteenth-century terms, the "reality" of the fiction, but at the same time it requests a very special attitude from the reader:

Everything that I have been able to find on the story of poor Werther I have carefully collected, and now lay before you, knowing that you will thank me for this. You cannot deny his mind and his character your admiration and love, nor his fate your tears.

And you, good soul, who feel the same pressure as he—take comfort from his suffering, and let this book become your friend when you by fortune or your own fault cannot find any closer friend.

The situation at the opening of the novel is one of flight from the world: the mood is that of relief. "How glad I am that I am away!" Werther is escaping a love affair and trying to persuade himself of his innocence in what had happened. His manner is, however, not entirely convincing; nor does he seem to have convinced himself, for there is some gnawing sense of guilt ("Did I not feed her feelings?"). He resolves "no longer to chew over the little evil which Fate has served us, as I always have done. I want to enjoy the present, and the past shall be past for me."[12] This is too determined to be comfortable, too self-justifying to be innocent. The basic theme of the novel is announced in these very first pages: the work is to be concerned with a man's attempt to construct an artificial world as a surrogate for reality. This mind that considers itself put upon by fate because it is so sensitive, which normally "chews over" every setback, feeds on past emotions, is not likely to enjoy any "present," to find itself in what is an attempt to forget or delude itself.

Uncertainty already prevails in Werther's second letter. "A

wonderful serenity has taken hold of my soul, like those sweet spring mornings which I enjoy with all my heart. I am so alone and so much enjoy my life in this district *which is created for souls like mine.*" We should do well to ponder the words which I have italicized, for they represent, *in nuce* and right at the beginning of the novel, Werther's problem. The external world exists for him primarily in relation to his own "soul," and as the novel proceeds it exists ever more exclusively in this relationship, until it finally has hardly any objective existence at all. In this second letter he says that in this spring landscape he feels "the presence of the Almighty who created us all according to his image, the breath of the All-loving [one] who lifts and sustains us in eternal bliss." He wants to express in lines and shapes what he feels, for he is an artist. His art is to be, as he puts it, the mirror of his soul which is the mirror of eternal God. We notice that his art is not an attempt to establish contact with the real world around him, but the expression of ideas in his own soul. In the third letter he expressly considers whether the sense of paradise around him is produced from his own mind or whether this landscape really has these qualities in itself. One thing that disturbs him greatly is that his ecstasy has reduced him to stagnation as an artist: he cannot any longer express what he experiences. He turns away from books which lead, encourage, inflame; he needs "cradle-song," a lulling of his turbulent self toward the lost peace of childhood. In Homer he finds a patriarchal, basic, paradise-like world which provides him somehow with the cradle-song he desires. As he sits and reflects, he feels surrounded by what he calls "the patriarchal idea." Everything becomes transformed by this idea. Girls fetching water from a well become daughters of Old Testament kings. He watches the children and simple rustic people around him, longing for some real contact with a meaningful world outside himself. "I have made all sorts of acquaintances; but have found no society." The fact that he is not one of these people either by class or by temperament, that he is separated from them by sophistication and self-awareness, prevents any real contact. To share their joys he must forget himself; but this is not the enriching relationship he seeks. And so: "I turn back into myself and find a world." This is the first important high point in the book, and it is to be Werther's disaster. Important too is the statement at the end of the same letter (22 May) that he who *fashions his world from out of himself* and is happy yet to be a man—that such a man has a sense of freedom because however narrow his world may be, it is his own world, and he can leave his prison at will.[13] Werther's search for peace and beauty and a meaningful relationship to the world has led him, therefore, back into his own self. What he creates is an artificial order based not on any relationship of the individual to what lies outside himself, but on a total absorption in his own thoughts. This is the tragic theme of the novel, for such activity is bound to lead to disaster. The self-centeredness of the protagonist has sometimes led critics to call this a lyrical novel. But that is not an apt description, for although the work has lyrical moments it is concerned with a temporal progression towards death which, painfully elaborated as it is, stage by stage, constitutes an essentially epic structure.

Werther continues valiantly to try to maintain an outer world independent of his own inner world, to "hold on in future only to Nature," for Nature alone, he thinks, can induce art. He is impressed by a young mother whom he meets and talks with about her children, her husband, and her daily life, and comments that she "treads out in happy serenity the narrow circle of her existence, helping herself through from one day to the next, sees the leaves fall and has no other thought thereby than that winter is coming."[14] In other words he is impressed by this woman who, despite the narrowness of her life, has none of the tension between an outer and an inner world which afflicts him.

The next stage in the developing action seems to represent a real contact with the outer world: namely, the meeting with Lotte. "So much simplicity alongside so much intelligence, so much goodness with so much firmness, and a peace of soul with

real life and activity"—the description is full of significance because it presents Lotte as the harmonious combination of ideals
which so far have appeared to Werther only in tension. So far
he has been unable to establish contact with an outer reality because he has been thinking all the time in abstractions like
"Nature," "Peace," "Paradise," and searching for these rather
than for empirical reality. It is a nice irony that he should immediately dismiss this description of Lotte as "wretched wishy-
washyness . . . miserable abstractions," but his apparent detachment from his own words is a diagnosis which does not suggest
—nor even seek—a cure. He goes on to describe her dancing in
terms of an idea, and it is significant that this idea is harmony, the
very quality that he lacks: "She is so much in it [the dancing]
with her whole heart and soul, her whole body, one harmony, so
carefree, so unconstrained [*unbefangen*], as if this was really
everything, as if she were not thinking or feeling anything
else. . . ." Reality bursts in on abstractions when he learns that
Lotte is as good as engaged to Albert. The dance is invaded by
sounds of a storm which has been threatening all evening and
now breaks. "Disorder became general," says Werther, reporting
the circumstances. But Lotte takes charge of the situation, organizing a game of counting. She admits that she has been as afraid
as anyone else; but, in pulling herself together in order to give
the others courage, she has become courageous herself. As they
look out on the receding storm, her eyes fill with tears; she lays
her hand on his and says "Klopstock!"

This cacophonous outcry is somewhat disconcerting to those
who read the novel in English and are unacquainted with the
literary context of the name. For German readers at the time of
the novel's first appearance it was an allusion charged with meaning, although this is no longer so for general readers in Germany
today. Klopstock is no longer a household word. But in eighteenth-century German poetry Klopstock stood for something
of the greatest importance. He was the poet who gave expression
to states of extreme feeling, states which transcended normal

experience and sometimes approached the inexpressible. Lotte is thinking of a particular ode by Klopstock, *Spring Festival* [*Die Frühlingsfeier*, first published in 1759], which treats of the presence of the Almighty in a storm, in majesty while it rages but as grace to mankind in the refreshing rain. The poem ends in a picture of the storm receding into gentleness. The effect of Lotte's outcry on Werther is to release his pent-up feeling, the surging of his heart which, in trying to "hold on to Nature," he has been repressing, or attempting to forget. As an expression of mutual understanding, her laying her hand on his represents for Werther an indication of affinity, a message—of salvation, as it were—from outside of himself. Werther kisses her hand, his own eyes full of tears, but tears of joy. A further stage has been reached in the development of the theme. Werther now seems to have turned outward from himself.

But the result of this seemingly new-found external reality is conveyed by Werther as follows: "And then I left her [the morning after the ball, having seen her home] with the assurance that I would see her again that same day and I kept my promise and since then sun, moon and stars may calmly get on with their business [*ihre Wirthschaft treiben*], I know not whether it be day or night, and the whole world is lost around me."[15] In other words the effect of this break-out from a self-centered world has been for Werther to lose the external world except for that part of it which pertains to Lotte. But she is dependent on his own world in a way that he here recognizes without fully understanding it. The description of her in terms of "miserable abstractions" had already revealed the extent to which his image of her was dependent on his own preconceived ideals. His first sight of her, surrounded by her six brothers and sisters, to whom she is both housekeeper and mother, had represented his longing for an antipode to his own restlessness; she embodies the same domestic serenity that he had recognized in the young mother earlier. Her taste in novels reinforces this idea: "My favorite author" she says on the way to the ball, "is he in whom I find my world reflected, where things happen as they do to me, and whose tale is as interesting and heart-felt as my own domestic life which is indeed no paradise and yet, taken as a whole, a source of inexpressible happiness." Lotte is therefore the external correlative of his ideals and his frustrations. She is and remains an extension of himself.

In the letter dated 21 June, Werther contrasts man's desire for self-expansion with his deep urge toward self-limitation. He had come to this place—called Wahlheim (literally "chosen home") —with the desire to expand himself into Nature.

It is strange how I came here and looked down from the hill into the beautiful valley that drew me on from all sides. There the copse! If only you could mingle with its shadows [he thought]! Over there the peak of the hill! If only you could look over the whole area from there! The hills ranging into each other and the inviting valleys —if only I could lose myself in them!—I hastened there! and returned, and had not found what I hoped for. Distance is like the future. A huge twilight whole lies there before our soul, our feeling floats about in it as our eye upon it, and how we long to give up our whole being, to let ourselves be filled out with all the rapture of one great glorious feeling—but when we hasten there, when the "there" becomes "here," then everything is as before and we stand there in our poverty, in our limitedness, and our soul thirsts for the assuagement that has slipped away. And so the most restless of wanderers longs finally once again for his fatherland and finds in some cottage, on the bosom of his wife, in the circle of his children and his labors to support them, all that bliss which he had vainly sought in the wide empty world.

Werther is here recognizing that expansion of self into limitlessness involves loss of self because self implies finite limits. To experience a "there," the necessary precondition is a "here." Every "there" becomes in turn a "here," and presents in turn another "there." Everything external always merges again with the self and becomes part of it, leaving a non-self still unattained.

The contrast of the wanderer and the cottage is imagery which recurs constantly in Goethe's early poetry and persists throughout his entire work, appearing even in the last act of

Faust, Part Two.[16] It embodies a basic tension between irreconcilable alternatives of motion and rest. But as enunciated here by Werther it has a certain speciousness because it does not really apply to him. He is not the wanderer in search of self-realization in an expanding horizon of experience, nor does he show any real desire for self-limitation in a settled existence. He may persuade himself that his problem lies in the tension between these two things, but in fact his dilemma is his inability to accept any reality outside of and independent of himself. What he experiences outside of himself is experienced solely in terms of his own "miserable abstractions." He speaks of the "patriarchal" conditions of life around him which he can weave into his life "without affection"—but this whole affection for patriarchalism is itself an affectation, as is also his desire to model himself on children.[17] He is in love with his own vision of Lotte, which is a vision created by his own concepts of paradise, harmony, simplicity, nature, and patriarchalism. Her otherness is therefore also dependent on him, for it is an extension of himself and not real otherness. When Albert arrives, it becomes clear that Lotte is not the externalization of Werther's ideals but has real otherness which is not dependent on Werther at all. And Werther is doomed: for in this self-deluding attempt at experiencing otherness, he has abandoned all other otherness.

The next stage in the development of the novel's theme is represented by two conversations: one on ill humor and one on suicide. At the house of the local vicar, Werther attacks ill humoredness [*die üble Laune*], saying that if one appreciates goodness one should also be able to tolerate what is bad [*das Übel*]. The vicar's wife replies that we do not always have such control over our emotions, for so much depends on the state of our body. Agreed, says Werther: then maybe ill humor is a sickness? Yes, says Lotte, for if she feels upset, she just jumps up and sings, and her ill humor is all gone. Werther then equates it with lassitude [*Trägheit*] to which we are naturally prone, though this is something we should counter and "pull ourselves together" [*sich ermannen*] for it is really a vice [*Laster*] that hurts other people. It springs, he says, from discontent with ourselves and envy of others. Struck by the impassioned nature of his utterance, Lotte urges him, on the way home, to "spare himself." This he does not do, however, and when Albert arrives, he refuses to face the reality of the situation, and explains to the recipient of his letters that he is incapable of decisive action to relieve the situation— although he has moments when he contemplates "going," if only he knew whither.

It is soon after Albert's arrival that the conversation on suicide takes place. The moral justification of suicide was a topic that greatly occupied the eighteenth century.[18] But here the discussion is concerned not merely with the moral question but with what drives men to suicide. Albert—a thoroughly sensible man who avoids exaggeration or extremes and places more trust in reason than in feeling—condemns suicide as foolish, even as vicious: Werther pleads for some understanding of the reasons that drive some people to suicide. The argument moves on to deal with the question whether an evil action or a crime can be excused or justified by its causes. Albert agrees that it may be, because men carried away by passion have lost all power of reflection and can be considered drunk or mad. Werther reacts violently to this: were not all extraordinary people who achieved great and seemingly impossible things always called drunk or mad? Albert objects that suicide is not a "great thing," but an act of weakness, "for it is certainly easier to die than to endure with fortitude a life full of pain." Werther replies that if man, who can bear only a certain degree of joy or sorrow or pain, is forced to bear more than this degree, his position is similar to that of the slave in revolt. There are also diseases which affect nature so much that man is driven by them into death. If this happens in the mind. . . . "Consider a man," says Werther, "who is invaded in his own narrow life by impressions which harden into fixed ideas until finally a mounting passion robs him of all power of sense and destroys him." This is, of course, exactly what Albert had been referring to, and the odd thing is that the terms of Werther's description are not very different from those of Albert's, for both talk of someone who loses his senses. The difference lies in attitude: for Werther such a man provokes sympathy, for Albert disapproval or at most regret.

[Although this is surely not necessary—neither for Albert nor for anyone else—Werther feels that he has to explain his point still further. That he should feel the need to do this, or simply want to, is indicative of his insecurity. His further explanation takes the form of a short narrative which is of great importance in the structure of the novel. It tells of a simple young girl engaged in a narrow round of domestic duties, whose passionate nature, fanned by male flattery, makes her dissatisfied with her life and who, when she finds herself irresistibly drawn toward a certain man, "forgets the world around her, hears and sees nothing but him, the only one, and longs for him, the only one," so that she wants to be joined to him and share everything with him. Led on by promises and displays of affection, she has reached the point where she experiences all joys—and then he leaves her.]

With all her senses petrified she stands before an abyss, everything is darkness around her, no way out, no consolation, no sense of the future, for he in whom she felt her whole existence has left her. She does not see the wide world before her, nor those many people who could make up her loss, she feels herself alone, abandoned by the world—and blind, gripped and squeezed by the terrible grief of her heart, she plunges down into the water, to stifle her torments in an all-embracing death. Look, Albert, this is the story of so many people, and is this not a case of sickness? Nature finds no way out of the labyrinth of confused, conflicting forces—and man must die.

Albert's only reply is that this was a simple girl: he cannot see how a man of intelligence could be excused for such an act. "Man is man," says Werther, "and the little intelligence that one may have does not come much into play—or not at all—when passion rages and when the limits of human existence press in on one."

There is a complex thematic interplay between these two conversations. At the vicarage Werther had called ill humor a "vice"; in the conversation with Albert he had declared that suicide was not a vice. At the vicarage he had stressed that man can overcome ill humor by "pulling himself together," which is what Lotte told him to do on their way home and what he had subsequently proved himself incapable of doing. In a letter to his friend he had described his situation at that time as like that of a man with a creeping sickness who cannot pull himself together: but the vicar's wife had suggested that ill humor was just such a sickness. In that same letter he had been talking about "going," which might mean departure for another place but might suggest departure from life itself. The idea of suicide seems to have suggested itself after the first conversation, and in the second it comes fully into the open. This time it is Albert who talks about "pulling oneself together," and Werther who suggests this may not always be possible. And the story of the young girl is the story of the obsessive directing of all emotion on to one person: when this person fails, the girl has nothing else to fall back on. Like Werther she has given up all else for her emotion: he describes her fate as a "case of sickness," and sickness in this context means the inability to find any way out of the labyrinth.

"Nature" [*die Natur*], he said, "finds no way out." He was here talking of *human* nature, of course. But the next stage in the narrative is an extension of this idea to include the whole of external nature. Werther now observes that his whole attitude to Nature has changed from a sense of one vast living mass of varied productive activity permeated by the spirit of the eternal creator to a view of nature as a monster of destruction in which everything is destroying either something else or itself—an "all-devouring, all-ruminating monster" (18 August). Werther now finds that his active forces are all reduced to lassitude—that same lassitude which he had decried at the vicarage; he cannot do anything, he has no imagination and no "feeling for nature," books revolt him. He longs for some external activity in a different place: but wonders (quite rightly) whether he will not take

with him his "inner, uncomfortable impatience." He finally does
decide to go away, and he does so after a conversation with Lotte
in which she, by talking of death and transience and of her
mother's death and the gap that this had left in her life, is suggesting indirectly what Werther will feel away from her and she
while he is away. But in the account of her mother's deathbed,
describing how the mother had entrusted the other children to
her, and how she died in peace knowing that Lotte would be
happy with Albert, ⌈Lotte is also emphasizing the other pole of
her life, her stable domestic existence, her reality apart from her
existence in Werther's mind.⌉

   The second part of the novel shows us Werther unhappy but
trying to make the best of his new life as an employee of the
Ambassador. But he is soon exasperated by the mechanical punc-
tiliousness of his employer, the general jockeying for position of
those who surround him, and the "wretched middle-class conditions" [*die fatalen bürgerlichen Verhältnisse*] which interfere
with his attempts to make friends with these aristocrats. His
senses, he writes to Lotte, are dried up—"not one moment of
fullness of heart, not one happy tearful hour. Nothing! Nothing!
I stand as if before a peep-show watching the little men and
little horses moving around and ask myself often whether this is
not optical illusion. I play too, or rather I am played, like a
marionette and often grasp my neighbor by his wooden hand and
recoil shuddering."[19] The world outside his own self is fading
ever more into insignificance. His only real involvement with
this world has been his meeting with a certain Fräulein von B.,
who, in her ability to muse with him on "rural scenes of unmixed
happiness," reminds him of Lotte, of the Lotte of his mind. But
not of the real Lotte, for soon after this the news reaches him of
Lotte's marriage to Albert. The style of his letters begins to
become ejaculatory and disjointed. He then receives a social
reproof for staying on, after dining with his sympathetic friend
Count von C., into a reception where only aristocrats are present,
and although the Count explains the situation with great tact and

kindness, Werther rushes away into the country to watch the sunset and read the passage in Homer where Odysseus is entertained by the swineherds. The occurrence is merely an external confirmation of his feeling an outsider in this society, a climactic revelation of his failure to find release from himself. That his reaction is not merely anti-aristocratic is suggested by the fact that he accepts the invitation of a prince to go with him to his country estate. The confrontation with society is over.

The next stage in the developing structure of the novel is an attempt by Werther to turn back the clock. On his way to the Prince's estate, he revisits his birthplace. He presents this journey as a pious pilgrimage, an act of homage to the image that he preserves of past happiness with perhaps the hope of salvation in refinding it. The lime tree—as so often in German Romantic literature—is the symbol of unfulfilled longing. Beneath it Werther as a child had longed for experience of the wide world, but now he returns from that world with broken hopes and finds that the scenes of his childhood have changed too. His childhood dream had been one of losing himself, and his restrictedness, in distant immensities: what has changed is the likelihood of fulfilling such longing. Not self-loss but self-recognition would bring about Werther's fulfillment. But this he never really achieves. He does not stay long with the Prince who, as a "man of intelligence [*Verstand*]" (like Albert) has little respect for Werther's heart which, Werther now says (letter of 9 May), is his only pride, "the source of all strength, all happiness and all misery." One could say that he has lost himself in his own heart.

As he returns to Wahlheim he finds, as with his birthplace, that nothing is any longer as it was: the young mother no longer appears to him as an image of contented domesticity, the road he had traveled to fetch Lotte for the ball provides no flutter from the past, the beautiful walnut trees at the vicarage under which he had sat with Lotte have been chopped down by the crabbed, insensitive wife of a new vicar. The image of simplicity and patriarchalism is no longer suggested by these surroundings:

instead of a sense of lasting values, a sense of loss invades him, the image of a demythified, godless world:

Ossian has supplanted Homer in my heart. What a world this noble man leads me to! To wander across the heath with the storm winds raging, summoning up by the dim light of the moon the spirits of the fathers in steaming mists. To hear from off the mountains, in the roar of the forest stream, the half-faded moaning of spirits from caves and the laments of the maiden, grieving unto death, around the four moss-covered, grass-grown stones of her nobly fallen beloved. And then when I find him, that wandering gray bard, who seeks on the broad heath the footprints of his fathers, and finds—ah!—their gravestones. . . . And then, grieving, he looks toward the loving Star of Evening plunging into the rolling sea, and past times come alive again in the hero's soul, those times when the friendly beam lighted the dangers of the bold and the moon illumined their gar- landed, victoriously returning bark. . . . When I so read the deep sorrow on his brow, see this last solitary hero stumble on in dire exhaustion toward the grave, see how he drinks in one painfully glowing joy after another from the feebly present shades of the departed, and how he looks down on the cold earth, the tall waving grass, and cries out: The Wanderer will come, will come, he who knew me in my beauty, and will ask, where is the singer, the glorious son of Fingal? His footstep passes over my grave. In vain he seeks for me on earth. O my friend! I would then, like some noble- minded squire, draw my sword and straightway deliver my prince from the twitching torture of slowly ebbing life—and then dispatch my own soul after the demigod that I had freed.[20]

In the search for the past, only death has been found. This Ossianic world is peopled only with ghosts, and there is no reply to the laments of those stricken with grief. This second "Wan- derer" is Werther himself. In a post-heroic world he would perform a heroic action.

In the next few letters Werther speaks of the emptiness in his heart. I said earlier that Werther had lost himself in his heart— and not only himself but all that stands outside himself. But now "his heart is dead." Nature has changed because his heart is dead, he has lost "the sacred enlivening power of creating worlds around [him]"—that is, from out of his own heart. Nature lies before him "like a lacquered picture," and he is "like a dried-up well, a leaking bucket" before the face of God, for he has prayed to God for tears like a farmer who prays for rain. But God does not grant rain or sunshine to violent askers, and the former bliss that he, Werther, had felt had come to him because he waited patiently for God's spirit and had received it wholeheartedly and gratefully when it came (letter of 30 October).

An important new stage has been reached in the development of the novel. In his longing for a relationship outside of himself Werther finally turns to God. His vocabulary moves over into that of the Passion, and finally he compares himself with Christ. If life tasted bitter to the Son of God, why should he, Werther, pretend that it tasted sweet to him? Even Christ had that terrible moment on the cross when he cried: "My God, my God, why hast thou forsaken me?" Why should he, Werther, therefore be ashamed of such feelings in himself? Toward the end of the letter of 30 November he likens himself to the returning prodigal son:

Father whom I know not! Father who formerly filled my whole soul and now has turned His face from me! Call me to Thee! Be no longer silent! Thy silence will not hold up this thirsting soul—And would any man, a father, be able to feel angry when his unexpectedly returning son fell on his neck and cried: I am here again, my father. Do not be angry if I break off the pilgrimage which I should have endured longer according to Thy will. The world is all alike, toil and labor, reward and joy; but what is all that to me? I am only well where Thou art, and in Thy countenance will I sorrow and be glad—Wouldst Thou, loving Heavenly Father, turn such a son away?

There is a fallacy in Werther's argument. The prodigal son did not ask his father to receive him; he returned penitent and saying: "Father, I have sinned against heaven, and in thy sight, and am no more worthy to be called thy son." And it was the father who fell on the son's neck, not vice versa. Werther's approach amounts to a demand that he has the right to be received. It therefore seems to me wrong to speak, as Erich Trunz does, of Werther's "religious longing" [*religiöse Sehnsucht*]. It is rather a matter of longing to be free of individual existence, to abandon individuation. Werther describes the Father as someone he does not know: the Prodigal Son, however, knows Him well. For Werther God had been present in Nature, but Nature had changed, and God is silent.[21]

This passage comes after the story of the mad boy whose only happy moments were when he was completely out of his mind. Werther involuntarily compares the boy's seeking flowers for his beloved when there are none with his own lack of hope and purpose; and he comments on the boy's belief that his misery springs from outside causes whereas in fact it derives from his broken heart and mind. On 8 December he likens himself to a man pursued by an evil spirit. At night he watches the flood waters of the river which have invaded the whole of the valley like a raging sea into which he is tempted to cast himself. His desire to plunge himself into Nature and thereby lose his identity, at the beginning of the novel combined with ecstatic love of Nature, is now directed to the all-destructive Nature he had already recognized already in the letter of 18 August, the "all-devouring, all-ruminating monster." For the flood has consumed many places associated with his brief happiness with Lotte. A position of extreme tension is reached: "I am finished. My senses are confused. For eight days now I have no power of reflection, my eyes are full of tears. I am nowhere well and everywhere well. I wish nothing, demand nothing. It would be better if I went" (end of letter of 17 December).

At this point Goethe switches to an external narrator, apparently to achieve some sort of distance from this absorbing—perhaps one might say dangerously absorbing because doomed—character. It is necessary, says the anonymous narrator, to interrupt the sequence of letters in order to communicate the "detailed

account of the last noteworthy days of our friend," the material
for which has been gathered from the mouths of Lotte, Albert,
Werther's manservant and other witnesses. Albert, he tells us,
was beginning to resent Werther's attentions to Lotte, which
increasingly endangered the harmony of the relationship between
her and Albert. Lotte herself was assailed by a sort of melancholy which Albert could account for only as increased passion
for her lover, and Werther as deep concern for the changed attitude of her husband. Mistrust between the two men increased.
Meanwhile the decision to leave this world hardened in Werther's
mind; but he was determined that this should be a considered
act, undertaken with a calm mind from firm convictions. The
beginning of a letter to Wilhelm found among Werther's papers
shows his hesitation because (like Hamlet) he does not know
what lies behind the curtain. Meanwhile Lotte is asking him to
visit her less—"Things cannot go on like this."—She urges him
once again to moderate his feelings and, rather insensitively perhaps, to find someone else on whom to bestow his affections, to
take a trip, etc., etc. It is now that Werther begins his last letter
to Lotte.

"It is decided, Lotte, I want to die, and this I write to you
without any romantic exaltation, completely calm, on the morning of the day that I shall see you for the last time." This letter
is intended to be delivered to her after his death. He will die, for
Lotte's sake, for one of the three of them must go. He views his
death, therefore, as a sacrificial death, and once again we feel the
religious overtones. He breaks off his letter to go to Albert's
house and finds Lotte alone (Albert being away on business).
She is somewhat nervous and induces Werther to read to her his
translation of Ossian. The mood is similar to the earlier passage
about Ossian (see above, p. 33): a nocturnal landscape, stormy
winds on the heath, everything empty in the moonlight save for
Ossian himself, the bard, invoking his departed friends. They
are all dead, but live on in the song of the bards—like all else in
the world of Ossian. It is a tale of lonely maidens bewailing lover

or brother, of the untimely death of young warriors, of those left behind whose lamentations are conveyed by the singers, the poets. A flood of tears from Lotte causes Werther to break off and clasp her hand. Once again a common reaction to literature (as with Klopstock) has revealed their emotional affinity with each other. "They felt their own misery in the fate of these noble persons, felt it together, and their tears united them," says the narrator. They have been listening to the tale of a young girl abducted by the brother of a warrior slain by her lover. She cries out, is rescued by her brother who in turn is slain by her lover who mistakes her brother for the original abductor, and finally both the maiden and her lover are drowned, leaving only the father to lament them. The girl-brother-lover relationship appears to Lotte doubtless as a parallel to her own triangle of wife-husband-lover. It also doubtless appears so to Werther and merely strengthens his resolve.

Lotte begs Werther to continue and he does so with a reference once again to the wandering bard: "The time of my withering is near, near the storm which blows down my leaves! . . . Tomorrow the wanderer will come, he will come who saw me in my beauty, round about in the field his eye will seek me, and will not find me." At this point Werther and Lotte come together in a first and last passionate embrace. She tells him he must never see her again. He wanders around the town for a time, then goes home to continue his letter to her after a good long sleep.

The next paragraph of the letter is his farewell, a farewell that includes a plea for forgiveness but also expresses his joy at the knowledge, after the scene we have just witnessed, that she loves him. Albert has returned in the early morning, and from him Werther requests the loan of his pistols through a written message delivered by his servant. It is Lotte who hesitatingly gives the pistols to Werther's servant, and this gives Werther the impetus for the next paragraph of his letter. "You, Lotte, hand me the implements, you from whose hands I wished to receive death and now receive it." Werther puts his affairs in order, writes brief farewell notes to Wilhelm and to Albert, and then settles down to the last paragraph of his letter to Lotte.

Everything is now calm, both around him and in his soul. Through the wild Ossianic clouds that float past his window he sees the stars of eternity, which will never fall because they are maintained there by God. He asks to be buried beneath two lime trees in the churchyard. After a reference to those "pious Christians" who may not wish to be buried alongside him, a suicide, he mentions the good Samaritan as contrasted to the Levite, again refers to Christ's cup of death, and reasserts that his death is sacrificial, for Lotte's sake. Shortly after midnight he shoots himself, but not very efficiently, for he is still alive when his servant comes to wake him next morning. He is dying by the time the doctor gets there. Albert, Lotte's father, and the children come to pay their last respects. He is buried that night. "The old man [Lotte's father] and his sons followed the corpse. Albert could not. They feared for Lotte's life. Craftsmen carried him. No priest accompanied him."

It is surely significant that Werther should have done such a poor job of shooting himself. He cuts a sorry figure alongside, say, Hedda Gabler, and as a ritual suicide his cannot compare with that of Sappho, Empedocles, or even Madame Butterfly. And yet, as we have seen, he views his death as a moral act of sacrifice, and takes pains to make it quite clear that his action resulted from a considered resolution, a conscious act of will. The contrast between heroic intent and feeble execution becomes all the more striking when we consider how carefully he had himself stage-managed his death scene. He dresses himself up in a blue coat and yellow vest such as he had worn at the ball, and wears the pale red ribbon that Lotte had been wearing on that occasion. Two more things are carefully placed so that all may see that he has acted in full possession of his faculties: the bottle of wine from which he has drunk only one glass (Lotte had been urging him not to drink too much), and the open copy of Lessing's play, *Emilia Galotti*, in which the heroine chooses death in a conscious act of will in order to escape her own emotional weakness. But the act itself does not live up to the expectations aroused by these preparations. It is somehow weak. There is irony here, a conscious and purposeful irony. And irony, as we shall see, was to be a recurrent mode for Goethe the novelist. To miss the irony is to miss the point. Werther is not "god-filled and god-driven" (Korff), not "titanic" (Gundolf), and certainly not a "crucified Prometheus" (Peter Müller). Schiller came closer to the truth when he called Werther's character *sentimentalisch*, one that was sicklied o'er by the pale cast of thought, sick, as the distinguished Italian Germanist Ladislao Mittner has suggested, because "he too much likes to feel healthy, senses too strongly the fascination of any expression of health," a sufferer who admires his own suffering.[22] He is not a tragic, but at most a pathetic figure. We may well be able to give him our "tears" and perhaps even our "love," as the editor requested in his opening address to the reader. But to what extent can we react to his "mind and character" with "admiration"?

Only, I think, if we interpret the word *Leiden* in the title as "sufferings" rather than "sorrows"—which is a perfectly legitimate translation. To some degree one can admire a sufferer simply because he does suffer, has the capability of suffering—but then only if the cause of his suffering is something important. The novel is not just about the "sorrows" of a lover unable to have what he wants, but is concerned with the "sufferings" of a man attempting to find some order of existence into which he can integrate himself without losing himself. This is a quest which can evoke admiration, for it is fraught with dangers and is of universal import. Seen in this way, Goethe's novel indeed transcends its time despite the eighteenth-century mode in which it is written. It deals with man's struggle for self-fulfillment with reference to what lies outside the self, for realization of self without total retreat into the self. Werther fails: he does retreat into

the self and the self disintegrates because nothing outside it really
has independent validity for him. Ultimately the book is about
the quest for order—order not in the sense of social or domestic
order, but as the basic ontological necessity. And this was to be
the theme of all Goethe's novels.

It was the intuitive insight of genius that led Goethe to choose
the epistolary form for his novel. Much had been said, and was
still to be said, in the eighteenth century about the virtues of this
form. Its advantages were, first, that it took the narrator into the
action and thereby achieved a singular degree of unity, and secondly that it produced a state of illusion in the reader akin to that
of drama because the action unfolded as it happened instead of
being recalled retrospectively. These two points were made, for
example, by Montesquieu in his *Réflexions sur les lettres persanes*
(1754), and he added a third, namely that digressions are structurally more viable in an epistolary novel than in other forms of
narrative fiction.[23] The first two points were reiterated by Marmontel in his *Essai sur les romans* of 1758,[24] and Richardson in
the preface to *Sir Charles Grandison* (1753) justified the epistolary form of that novel on the grounds of spontaneity and the
illusion created in a letter that what is to follow is still undecided.[25] On the other hand there were voices raised against the
form—notably that of the German critic Blanckenburg (*Versuch
über den Roman*, 1774), who asserted that the correspondents in
epistolary novels were often in too strong a state of emotion to
be able to account for the causes of events.[26] In other words,
Blanckenburg thought that it was difficult to combine immediacy
with explanation of how the immediate situation was brought
about. For example he declared that Clarissa's flight with Lovelace is accounted for only by external events, and insufficiently
by analysis of Clarissa's inner motives.[27] He thought that the
form does not usually create an illusion of reality because the
author is always "peering through his characters." Thus when
Rousseau's Julie writes a letter on duelling, we may well ask
whether, in view of the impending danger for her beloved, she

is in a fit state to philosophize.[28] In other words digressions, for Blanckenburg and in contrast to Montesquieu, were *not* viable in the epistolary novel, if it was really to achieve the semblance of reality. Blanckenburg's whole approach to the genre of the novel was to demand that it deal not with external occurrences but with the inner development of character—and also with the manners, the *mœurs*, the *Sitten* of the time. A few months after Goethe's *Werther* appeared, Blanckenburg published a long review of it, praising it for its presentation of development [*Werden*] as a clear chain of cause and effect, its interrelating of characters and events by showing how characters are affected by events, and its portrayal of German *Sitten*.[29]

By *Sitten*, Blanckenburg in this context meant "the formalities and pedantries of our German aristocracy."[30] When Goethe himself looked back on *Werther* in the third volume (published in 1814) of his autobiography *Fiction and Truth*, he did not say anything about this aspect of the novel's social scene.[31] He had not been concerned with a portrayal of *mœurs*, that much seems quite clear, though he does not explicitly say so. But we can deduce it from his description, in this passage of his autobiography, of what *had* been in his mind when he was writing *Werther*. He says that his objective had been to portray a *taedium vitae* which was current during his youth among young men of a certain type—that is to say, he had been concerned primarily with a psychological rather than a social problem, with a state of mind rather than with *mœurs*. "All pleasure in life," says Goethe, "is based on a regular recurrence of external things" —so long as we are "open" to them.[32] But if we do not "participate," then this recurrence becomes oppressive. The recurrence of love becomes oppressive, for second love never has that ideality that first love has; the vagaries of fortune and favor in their constant recurrence breed insecurity; and the surprise recurrence of our faults as we consciously cultivate our virtues depresses us perhaps most of all. All this works restrictingly on the hot blood and lively imagination of youth, so that a tendency to

set oneself free from such a clamp [*Klemme*] becomes not unnatural. Goethe adds that in his own particular youth there was
an external factor which exacerbated this state of mind, namely
the influence of English literature, the literature of melancholy,
on the minds of young Germans. Here he does mention social
and political factors: how many noble Britons, he says, had been
banished, imprisoned or expropriated by the changing tides of
historical fortune! This fact had produced in England a strong
sense of the impermanence and worthlessness of earthly things.
Expression of this in literature brought some relief through its
perspectival shaping: but the basic mood remained somber.
Goethe mentions Young's *Night Thoughts*, the English satirists,
Gray's Churchyard, Goldsmith's *Deserted Village* and the soliloquies of Hamlet. Ossian's *ultima thule* had provided the perfect
locale for such moods. Basic to these young Germans of the
1770s, says Goethe, was the frustration of emotions unable to
spill out into satisfying external activity. Essentially Goethe is
here analyzing what Karl Moor in Schiller's first play, *The Robbers* (1781), had called the "corsetting" nature of the "flaccid
castrati-century" [*schlappe Kastratenjahrhundert*], where there
were no more heroes but only talkers about heroes.[33] In this state
of ennui, young men played with thoughts of suicide, and the
great impact of *Werther* on its generation was due, says Goethe,
to its tangible portrayal of the "essence of a sick, youthful delusion" [*das Innere eines kranken jugendlichen Wahns*]. Goethe
emphasizes that he is not talking about suicide as a heroic resolution but about essentially inactive persons who "because of
exaggerated demands [that they place] on themselves" become
disenchanted with life.[34] He then goes on to say that he had experienced all this himself but had liberated himself from its
weight by writing *Werther*.

The moods Goethe describes here were, he says, essentially
the products of solitariness. For such men avoid contradiction,
avoid society, and are "thrown back into themselves." In his own
case, says Goethe, his lonely soliloquies tended to transmute

themselves into dialogues with imaginary partners, sometimes for
the sake of active response, sometimes for the sake of a receptive
listener. This led him to settle on the epistolary form for his
novel,[35]—but although the novel originated in imaginary dialogues
with *various* people, when the letters came to be composed,
they were addressed essentially to *one* "friend and partici-
pant." Goethe does not explain why he did this. The "dialectical exercises" which, he says, had sometimes figured in these
imaginary conversations find no place in the novel, except for the
criticisms by Lotte and Albert as reported by Werther. There
is no real dialogue, and certainly no dialectic, in the novel. This
is conscious artistry, for this monologue character reinforces the
point that no real dialogue is ever possible for Werther. His
narcissism, resulting in those "exaggerated demands" on the self,
makes Werther pathetic rather than tragic, and culminates in
the very serious irony of the death scene. *The Sorrows of Young
Werther* is not really an epistolary novel, it is one extended
soliloquy.[36] The curious fact about its maturation is that it
springs from soliloquy, transposes itself into imaginary, and
therefore internal dialogue, issues forth as fictive external dialogue, but then finally reverts to soliloquy inside the fictive
epistolary mode.

But the final section of the novel is told by a narrator. Why
did Goethe choose to break the hermetic form of Werther's
soliloquy in this way?

3

The Fictive Editor

We have an important piece of evidence that, in composing the last section of *Werther*, Goethe had reflected on what sort of narrative technique to adopt, and had considered various possibilities. Among the papers of Goethe's friend Frau von Stein there was a single sheet in Goethe's handwriting, which is now preserved in the archives at Weimar. On it is the following:

Sie sind durch ihre Hände gegangen, sie hat den Staub davon geputzt, ich küsse sie tausendmal, sie hat euch berührt. Und du Geist des Himmels begünstigst meinen Entschluss. Und sie reicht dir das Werckzeug, Sie von deren Händen ich den Todt zu empfangen wünschte und ach nun empfange. Sie zitterte sagte mein Bedienter als sie ihm die Pistolen gab. O Herr sagte der gute Junge eure Abreise thut euern Freunden so leid. Albert stand am Pultem, ohn sich um zu wenden sagte er zu Madame: Gieb ihm die Pistolen, sie stund auf und er sagte: ich lass ihm glückliche Reise wünschen, und sie nahm die Pistolen und putzte den Staub sorgfältig ab und zauderte und zitterte wie sie sie meinem Buben gab und das Lebe wohl blieb ihr am Gaumen kleben. Leb wohl leb wohl!
Hier hab ich die fleischfarbene Schleiffe vor mir die sie am Busen hatte als ich sie kennen lernte, die sie mir mit so viel Liebenswürdigkeit schenckte. Diese Schleife! Ach damals dacht ich nicht, dass mich der Weeg dahin führen sollte.
Ich bitte dich sey ruhig.[1]

The German is somewhat bumpy but the meaning is clear enough. Here is a literal translation:

They have gone through her hands, she has cleaned the dust from them, I kiss them a thousand times, she has touched you. And thou,

spirit of heaven, dost favor my decision. And she gives you the implement, She from whose hands I wished to receive death and ah! now receive it. She quivered said my servant when she gave him the pistols. O Sir said the good fellow your departure makes your friends so sad. Albert stood at the desk without turning round he said to Madame: give him the pistols, she stood up and he said: I bid [you] wish him a happy journey, and she took the pistols and cleaned off the dust carefully and wavered and quivered as she gave them to my fellow and the farewell stuck in her throat [literally, "on her palate"]. Farewell, farewell!
Here I have the fleshcolored ribbon before me which she had on her bosom when I made her acquaintance, which she gave me with so much friendliness [lovableness]. This ribbon! Ah then I did not think that the path would lead me thither. I beg you be calm.

The passage refers to the pistols, with one of which Werther shot himself. Apart from a few minor substitutions for individual words, every phrase of this passage occurs in the completed novel. But not as here presented. In the novel this material reappears partly in Werther's last letter to Lotte, and partly in the third-person account of the narrator. As presented on this individual sheet, the form is puzzling. It could be part of a letter from Werther to someone other than Lotte, for instance to Wilhelm, the recipient of Werther's other letters. But if so, to whom is the final admonition addressed, "I beg you be calm"? To the recipient of the letter? To himself? Or to Lotte? In the novel the words are addressed to Lotte. It is also possible that this is not from a letter at all, but represents an entry by Werther in his own diary. The style, spelling, and punctuation are those of the young Goethe. And Ernst Beutler has pointed out that the watermark in the paper on which these lines are written is the same as that of the *Mahomet* manuscript, which we can definitely assign to 1772 or 1773.[2] It would seem therefore that this is a first sketch for the climax of the novel; but that it represents a form of communication, probably diary-entry, which was abandoned in favor of the alternation between narration by the anonymous editor of Werther's paper (the *Herausgeber*) and Werther's own last letters.

The reason for this change of form might seem obvious: Goethe needed a third-person narrator to relate the circumstances of Werther's death, because for all his epistolary genius Werther could hardly do this himself. Yet even leaving aside such extreme cases as Moses (who gave a third-person account of his own death) or Schnitzler's Fräulein Else (who dies in the middle of the last word of her stream of consciousness), this argument appears tenuous if not irrelevant. For the novel could have ended with Werther's last letter to Lotte and the announcement in it of his being about to shoot himself. Or the circumstances could have been described in a letter by someone else— by the Magistrate, for instance. The need for a third person to narrate Werther's death does not therefore in itself account for Goethe's abandonment of the epistolary form at this point in the novel, and it becomes even less likely an explanation when we consider the fact that the switch comes some time before Werther's death. Can there be some other reason? Let us examine the structural function of this switch of standpoint in the novel.

In the first published version of the novel the switch occurs after that letter of Werther's which ends with the words: "I am nowhere well and everywhere well. I wish nothing, demand nothing. It would be better if I went" [*Mir wäre besser ich gienge*]. The letter sequence is then broken by the "editor" [*Herausgeber*], who says the break is necessary to provide an account of Werther's last days and proceeds to tell us how Werther's passion had gradually undermined the relationship between Albert and his wife.

So far everything that has been told us could have been conveyed by Werther in a letter. He would probably not have said that he was disrupting the life of the married couple, but a report of Albert's changed behavior would have implied this. Strangely enough, the narrator's account of Albert's behavior is weighted in favor of Werther. Albert is ill-humored, he speaks with "rather dry words" to his wife of Werther's "all too frequent visits." This is hardly dispassionate narration. The narrator then tells us that the idea of leaving this world was taking ever firmer hold on Werther's mind, *but that it was not a new idea to him.* Indeed it was not, as we know from Werther's letters. It would seem probably, therefore, that this "editor" is in fact Wilhelm, the recipient of Werther's letters. But he then offers an explanation for Werther's suicidal tendencies: that his honor had been offended by what happened in the society surrounding the Ambassador. It was this vexation, the narrator suggests, which gave him such distaste for all business affairs and political activity, and this, together with his debilitating passion for Lotte, had extinguished whatever life force there was in him. The attentive reader must question this "explanation": for Werther's suicidal tendency can be attested before the period at the Ambassador's, his distaste for affairs—or indeed for any activity— has been apparent from the very beginning, and he had never spoken of his honor being offended. And Wilhelm, as recipient of the letters, should have known this. Is then this "editor" someone other than Wilhelm?

It would seem that Goethe is here using the anonymous narrator, whether he be Wilhelm or not, to provide a rational explanation of Werther's melancholy and suicide. Or at least to suggest a *possible* explanation. The reason for the switch to the editor appears therefore to lie in Goethe's desire to get outside the standpoint and feelings of Werther. But is this narrator a person at all, or merely a narrative device? Is he intended to be a real reporter (possibly Wilhelm) or is this just a mechanism for ending the story? He asserts that he collected his material from those persons who were closest to Werther. In part this is a switch to the device of the omniscient narrator, but in part it is simulation of reliability through the claim that every available piece of evidence from all available witnesses is being given us. Every detail of the events of Monday, 21 December is indeed meticulously documented by this editor-reporter. Werther starts

writing his letter very early; he calls his servant at 10 to tell him
he is going away, he eats (presumably soon after), visits the
Magistrate, is back at 5, goes to Lotte at 6:30, leaves as the maid
is laying dinner, walks out through the town gate and returns
home without his hat around 11. Each stage has its witness—his
servant, the Magistrate, his maid (who stokes the fire at 5),
Lotte, Lotte's maid, the guards at the town gate, and finally
again his servant. But the only witness who could have given the
narrator the details of what happened in Lotte's house is Lotte
herself. The fiction of the painstaking reporter breaks down
here, and we are back with the omniscient narrator. The person
has yielded to the device.

Many of the details of the death scene and some of those in
the material leading up to it were taken by Goethe from a real-
life occurrence. A young theological student named Jerusalem
had recently shot himself in similar circumstances. He had been
in love with a married woman and, like Werther, had suffered a
social rebuff at an aristocratic gathering and also at the hands of
an ambassador. The great number of details taken over into the
death scene can be seen from Goethe's friend Kestner's long
account of the catastrophe in his letter to Goethe of 2 November
1772.[3] Technically the interesting thing about this letter is that
Kestner (a legation secretary who certainly must have had legal
training) carefully indicates the person from whom he got each
particular piece of information. The effect is of a character as he
appeared to many people. This undoubtedly appealed to Goethe
as a method of getting outside the character of Werther, or at
least of attempting—or pretending—to do so. There is, however,
no information in Kestner's report about the woman whom Jerusalem loved, except that she was the wife of the Secretary H——.
Jerusalem never spoke about this, not even to his closest friend.
But Kestner says he is "reliably informed" (*zuverlässig unterrichtet*) on this point. There is a reference to Secretary H——
taking Jerusalem home after a dinner to drink coffee with his
wife, of Jerusalem's saying that this would be the last coffee

which he could drink with her. But apart from this, "no one knows what happened there," says Kestner. Jerusalem then *seems*, says Kestner, to have made careful preparations for his death; he wrote letters, including *perhaps* one to the ambassador which the ambassador *perhaps* destroyed. Such juridical caution is not maintained by the narrator in *Werther*, for some things in his narrative, notably his description of Lotte's feelings after Werther's last visit, are the work of the fictive omniscient narrator, who also "knows" precisely the several points at which Werther interrupted the writing of his last letter to Lotte.

This oscillation between a person and a device, between a well-informed reporter and the conventional omniscient "narrator" is, however, not the only disturbing feature of the final section of this first version of the novel. If the report of the editor is intended to be a distancing structural feature, then this purpose is belied by Werther's long letter, interrupted and resumed four times, which throws us right back into the tumult of Werther's own struggle for resolution. The letter is given us in five sections: the first contains the decision to die, the second the determination to see Lotte once more, the third his knowledge of her love; the fourth concerns the pistols and the last his farewell. The visit to Lotte comes between sections two and three, and the request for the pistols between sections three and four. But narration and letter are so neatly combined that one hardly notices the transitions. It is as though Werther himself were the narrator. The switch to the narrator in this first version of the novel comes at the point where the tension in Werther is too great for the epistolary fiction to be convincingly maintained. But it is not a switch away from Werther. Almost everything that is reported is colored by Werther's own viewpoint: Albert is unpleasant, Lotte unwilling to commit herself. Only after Werther is dead does the narration become really objective.

Goethe had found himself faced with an interesting structural problem. The final narration, after Werther's death, had to be objective. When was the transition to come? If the letters had

continued right up to his death, the final narration would have
become a coda, a footnote almost. This seems to have been un-
satisfactory to his artistic sense. He breaks at Werther's exclama-
tion that it would be better for him "to go," and moves seemingly into a well-documented protocol of what happened after
that. But the objective unity of presentation is broken by
Werther's letter to Lotte and by the necessity to describe, in
terms that only Werther could have used, his last two meetings
with Lotte, and Lotte's state of mind after the second. And so
Goethe, by rejecting a continuous letter sequence and also possibly the switch to diaries, has not achieved an objective transition to the final narration.

When Goethe came to revise the novel for the second version,
he seems to have realized this. He worked on it in the 1780s, and
it is the revised version of 1787 that most of us read. Most of the
revisions come after the switch to the editor, and those that come
before seem preparatory to the changes in the editor section.
The main addition before the switch is the story of the peasant
lad, his passion for the widow and his committing murder out of
jealousy. This is told in three sections, the last of which comes
after the switch to the editor, which now comes even earlier,
after the letter of 6 December, describing Werther's obssession
with Lotte's dark eyes and the contrast between ecstasy and
reality. And the editor's report begins differently: not with the
cool statement that it is *necessary* to depend, from here on, on
the testimony of others, but with the regretful wish that there
had been preserved sufficient written documents by Werther so
that it would *not* have been necessary to interrupt the sequence
of his letters by narration. He then goes on to say that he has
collected testimony from those who *could* have been acquainted
with Werther's story, but this time gives *no* names and adds
significantly that opinions varied, depending on the moods of
the persons involved. All he can do, he says, is to report conscien-
tiously and insert those of Werther's letters that have remained,
not neglecting the smallest piece of paper because "it is difficult

enough to uncover the real motivating forces in any characters, especially in such unusual persons as these." He begins by describing Werther's inner turmoil: "The harmony of his mind was completely destroyed, an inner heat and violence which drove all forces of his nature into confusion, produced the most unpleasant effects and finally left him only with a certain lassitude out of which he strove to lift himself even more anxiously than he had fought against all evils before." This state of mind made him unjust to others. Albert did *not* change, he was *not* cool towards Lotte or Werther—at least that is what Albert's friends told this narrator.

This narrator seems to be disagreeing with the narrator of the first version. The second narrator emphasizes Werther's mental state, and indicates that it alone was responsible for what followed.[4] Lack of balance, violence, anxiety made him "a sad companion who became more and more unhappy, and more and more unjust as he became more and more unhappy." He was rapidly losing contact with the outside world, and did so completely after his attempt to defend the peasant lad, the final section of whose story comes at this point. In the peasant lad he saw himself. This apparent interest in something outside himself was therefore really just another aspect of self-obsession. In his revision Goethe plays down the idea that external events or persons had any effect on Werther's final resolve. The objective frame of reference, suggested hopefully but very tentatively in this second version (in contrast to the definiteness with which the narrator had begun in the first version), has receded immediately. It is already gone when the narrator describes Werther's lack of harmony, which follows immediately on his statement of the difficulty of ascertaining motives. And when the narrator gives us an account of what Werther was saying to himself as he fetched Lotte from her father's home, the whole spuriousness of the third-person narration is revealed. We have not gotten outside of Werther. The idea of a dispassionate, objective narrator has been abandoned, partly because it didn't work, but mainly

—and this seems to me the really important point—because it was undesirable.[5]

In the first version Goethe may have been attracted to the idea of a narrator in order to seek a transition to the necessary objectivity of the final reportage. He was undoubtedly also influenced by the form of Kestner's report on the death of Jerusalem.[6] It seemed to be a way of getting outside the character of Werther, of breaking the tension in the letters when this had reached a point of climax, of achieving some degree of distance. But the device had not only broken down technically, as we have seen, because of the undistanced material which, for other reasons, Goethe had included in this seemingly distanced section of the novel. It had also resulted in Lotte and Albert emerging as characters outside of and independent of Werther's feelings, and to the transference of some responsibility to them. The result was that the unified, single standpoint of the book had been broken. In his revision Goethe remodeled his presentation of Lotte and Albert, leaving out that certain edginess which both of them were said, in the first version, to have shown towards Werther. He did this partly in answer to protests from his friends the Kestners on the way in which their married life had been presented in the first version of the novel.[7] But not only for this reason, because there is artistic gain in the preservation of a unified standpoint despite the apparent distancing by the narrator. For this *is* only apparent; Werther and his point of view are still dominant. Albert's words to Lotte, definitely called "sharp" [*spizz*] in the first version, now only *seem* "cold or even hard" *to Werther;* it is now Werther who is cold to Albert, not vice versa. If the narrator of the first version may have been intended by Goethe to represent Wilhelm, but emerged as a Wilhelm who became so involved in things which only Werther could know that he ended up as Werther, this second narrator is Werther himself from the very start, a Werther trying, or perhaps we had better say *pretending*, to achieve distance toward himself, to be his own narrator.

At the time of the revision Goethe spoke of his desire to "tighten up" the book.[8] By his treatment of the narrator section he has done this. We are deluded into a sense of having been elevated to a plane from which we can see Werther himself in a wider perspective. We feel that we have dissociated ourselves from this terrifyingly fascinating character. We say that we can now see what was wrong: we can now see how his death stemmed from his absorption in his own mental state: we feel that, now we have achieved this point of vantage, we would not ourselves succumb to such a situation, we would surely be able to rise above it, to work ourselves out of it because we recognize it for what it is. Werther is no model, no ideal character. He is a man gone wrong, but a man destroyed by himself. The "tightening up" of the narrator section in the second version reinforces this picture of Werther. We see that he is *not* badly treated, that he is not even misunderstood: but that on the contrary he is sympathetically understood and loved by both Albert and Lotte. Goethe is most anxious, in this second version of his novel, that we shall see the sickness of Werther and not identify him with his author, nor ourselves with him *totally*. This amount of distance Goethe desires: not, however, so much distance that we shall not identify with Werther *at all*. We must feel the common ground. We must understand and share Werther's anguish to the utmost, and to the very end. But we must also be able to see it as something askew. The second narrator brings us to this viewpoint and, unlike the first narrator, reveals that Werther's situation springs only from inside himself. In order to see Werther's malady we must get outside of him; in order to sympathize with its origins we must to a certain extent remain inside his world. The second narrator serves this double function in that we remain with Werther's point of view and yet see it *as a point of view*, not as absolute. The book now maintains its single-mindedness right through to the end, and thereby gains in strength. This second narrator is no more able to get outside of Werther than Werther was able to get outside of himself. The narrator's inability to achieve distance therefore somehow provokes distance in us.

The fiction of the "editor" is, like that of the epistolary mode, a device to disguise the fictive nature of a novel and give it a semblance of historical truth. As a defense against the widespread assertion that the romance dealt with untruth and improbabilities, many a novelist of the eighteenth century had asserted that he was communicating a "true story," an "histoire véritable." Thus Defoe in the preface to the first part of *Robinson Crusoe* (1719) said of his novel: "The Editor believes the thing to be a just History of Fact; neither is there any Appearance of Fiction in it." We note that this author, like that of *Werther*, describes himself as an "Editor." In the preface to his later novel, *Roxana* (1724), Defoe declared that the work was "not a story, but a history." Many novels appeared at this time in France with titles such as "Histoire de . . . ," "Mémoires de . . . ," "Les Confessions de . . ." or "Lettres de . . . ." The number of such titles seems to have diminished, both in France and in England, after about 1750, but novels purporting to be "Lifestories," "Confessions," or "From the papers of . . . ." still continued to appear in England, France and Germany. To such fictive denials of fictitiousness belong also the countless found manuscripts, unearthed documents, stories overheard on journeys and family secrets finally cleared up at deathbeds. Other favorite narrative modes to simulate real life were the first-person narrative, the novel in dialogue (which some German writers attempted, rather undistinguishedly, to establish) and the epistolary novel. A strong influence on the first-person narrative form was that of autobiographies, particularly the so-called spiritual autobiographies. Thomas Mann is certainly right when he writes that "a work like *Werther* is inconceivable without a long tradition of pietistic introspection."[9]

What Goethe has done in *Werther*, and done brilliantly, is to intensify the sense of reality by combining the three techniques of first-person narration, epistolary exchange, and third-person narration by "informed observer." This observer is the recipient of the letters as well, but, in his function as editor, he suppresses his own answers. What we have is reported first-person narration without the voice of the reporter, and then when the novel later switches to third-person narration, the account given is built around Werther's last letter, so that the confessional aspect is maintained up to the very end. Even the account of Werther's death and burial makes all the points that Werther's ghost would have made.

4

Uncertain Irony

Three years after *Werther* was first published, Goethe was at work on a second novel. On 16 February 1777 his diary records: "In Garten dicktirt an W. Meister"—dictating *at* Wilhelm Meister—which implies that the work was still very much *in progress*. There are various other references to it during the same year. What sort of novel was this to be? From a letter which Goethe's close friend Knebel wrote to Herder that July, it is clear that the novel was to be about the theater, for Knebel refers to it as "Wilhelm Meister's Theatrical Mission."[1]

It is difficult to decide why the successful author of *The Sorrows of Young Werther* should have turned his attentions as a novelist to this subject. We know of course that Goethe had been interested in the theater since childhood. The puppet theater and amateur theatricals of his childhood, the performances by French actors during the occupation of Frankfurt in the Seven Years' War, his own visits to the theater as a student in Leipzig and later at home in Frankfurt, his early interest in Shakespeare, the testimony in *Fiction and Truth* that, when he began to write, his natural mode of dealing with a sequence of actions was drama (hence the autobiographical narrative of Götz von Berlichingen emerges under his hands as a drama), the writing of his own early plays and their performances in Hamburg and Berlin—all this meant that as author, spectator, reader and even actor, he was intimately acquainted and connected with the theater.[2] Since the publication of *Werther* he had accepted the invitation of the Duke of Weimar to settle in that

town, which had a distinct culture of its own and a lively interest
in the theater. But the year before Goethe arrived in Weimar
the theater had burned down. There was therefore, for the
present, no theater-building. But there were court productions
by enthusiastic amateurs, of French plays performed in French
and then later of some plays in German. The French plays seem
to have been acted by members of the court aristocracy, but
some court officials (who of course did not belong to the aristocracy) took part in the German plays, including Goethe. He
played the demon of Pride in a "Temptation of St. Anthony,"
and he played the title role in a German version of Cumberland's
The West Indian. His own *Singspiele* were performed by such
a group. And, as a climax, there was the famous performance of
his *Iphigeneia on Tauris* (in its first, prose version) on 14 February 1779, in which Goethe himself played the part of Orestes. In
due course he became entrusted with the overall direction of
these performances. So in these years he was adding experience
as a director to his knowledge of the theater, thereby attaining
deeper insight into the vagaries of actors and the everyday
chores and frustrations of running a theatrical company. He had
good musicians, scene-painters and carpenters to help him. In
1780 a new theater-building was inaugurated. The players were
still mostly members of the court aristocracy, but professional
actors and actresses were occasionally engaged for particular
performances. Nevertheless this remained fundamentally a theater of amateurs, playing to an invited and exclusive audience.

It could be that these experiences engendered the subject of
Goethe's second novel. But the actors in the novel are not amateurs, they are professionals—traveling actors, for the novel takes
place at a time before the advent late in the eighteenth century
of national established theaters in German cities with salaried
companies of actors performing repertories of dramas (and in
some cases operas and *Singspiele*) for the general public.[3] Before
the establishment of such theaters, Germany had only court
theaters and traveling companies performing wherever they

could. Vienna was an exception because, since the time of the accession of Maria Theresa, it had possessed a court theater of great distinction which became a separate institution outside of the palace compound of buildings, and various suburban theaters which specialized in more popular drama and were frequented by all classes of society, including the aristocracy.

In the course of Goethe's novel Wilhelm Meister becomes a member of a traveling group of actors. The phrase "theatrical mission," which, judging from Knebel's letter quoted above, was part of the title at least as early as 1777, would seem to imply that he has an important task of some sort to perform in connection with the theater.[4] This points to another factor that undoubtedly contributed to Goethe's choice of theme for his second novel. The concept of the theater as a moral institution, an educative force, was by no means dead. Four years before the first reference to Goethe's novel, an article by Wieland had been published in his periodical *The German Mercury*, which contained the following passage:

The art of drama and the art of acting which had been a political institution in ancient Greece have become in our times, thanks to the concerted efforts of the best minds, a moral institution which exerts a beneficent influence on the temperament and customs of a people and, in the hands of wise rulers, is one of the most effective means of educating the minds and hearts of their subjects.[5]

Such ideas were current at the time Goethe arrived in Weimar. The reason for this high view of the stage in the Germany of the second half of the eighteenth century was that theater, more than any other form of literature, *confronts* the public. The author speaks directly to listening ears, and he speaks simultaneously to many persons. On the stage, art becomes practice. This idealistic conception of the theater is an important element in the *Theatrical Mission*, and it is the contrast between this and the sordid reality of the actors' life that constitutes in large part both the charm and the irony of the book. Implicit in this contrast is another—namely that between the different ways the actor appears on the stage and off the stage. This in turn presents the paradox that the theater does not always hold up the mirror to nature but is often a contrast to nature, embodying a world of illusion which nevertheless—and by the very fact that it is not real—affects the world of reality. One thinks necessarily of the scene between Hamlet and the actors: and it is no coincidence that *Hamlet* figures largely in this novel. Acting is the assumption of personality other than one's own, the willing and purposeful assuming of otherness.

There had of course been earlier novels primarily concerned with actors, for example Scarron's *Roman Comique*, and others where actors had made incidental but significant appearances, such as *Don Quixote* and *Gil Blas*. But a comparison of Goethe's novel with these works does not suggest that they influenced the composition of the *Theatrical Mission*. The actors and actresses of the *Theatrical Mission*, petty as most of them are, have little in common with the crude or despicable personages of Scarron and Lesage. Moreover, we have no evidence that he knew the works of Scarron and Lesage by this time, though we do have evidence that he knew about Cervantes.[6] Scarron's characters are for the most part actors, but his work is not really a novel about the theater. Despite some few specific references to dramatists and theatrical events of the day, it does not give a picture of theatrical life of the time, nor do the various events and sentiments spring from the particular nature of theatrical life. It is really an anti-heroic adventure novel and the fact that the characters are actors is coincidental rather than essential. They could equally well be something else. In Scarron's novel there is no trace of any high view of the theater, let alone of a belief that it had a "mission."

A similarly unexalted view of the theater is represented by Lesage, who had, of course, his own disillusioning experiences as a dramatist to build on. In *Gil Blas* the theater is a social meeting place, not a moral institution. In the theater scenes the focus is on the spectators in their relations with the actors, and more especially with the actresses. Practically nothing is said about the plays or the productions. The actors are not considered at all as artists, but presented as conceited, lewd, gluttonous, malicious persons. In fact the theater, far from being a moral institution, is a school of immorality, and as early as the end of the third book Gil Blas severs his connections with it.

In *Don Quixote* there are three places which deal specifically with the theater. After the famous conversation of the Canon of Toledo and his priest on books of chivalry, the two men go on to talk about drama, lamenting the way that modern drama has defaulted from Cicero's moral conception of the theater. Secondly; just before the episode of Master Pedro's Puppet Theater there enters a group of players with a cart, "a parcel of merry wags" according to Sancho, but for Don Quixote they are "below the order of Knighthood" and therefore not worthy of his attention. Thirdly, in the episode of the puppet theater, the theater is used as an image for the tension between illusion and reality which is the subject of the whole novel. The talking ape of Master Pedro confirms that what Don Quixote saw in the cave of Mendocinos was part real, part illusion. But Don Quixote suffers because he cannot distinguish between the two. He takes the play of the oppressed Melisandra as reality and attacks and smashes the puppets—which seems silly, but for Master Pedro those puppets are reality, have been his reality. Kings and Emperors, horses and chests had all been his—but now no more. Don Quixote listens to his lament but accepts no responsibility: he is bewitched, he says, by evil magicians who have placed him in a world where he cannot distinguish between illusion and reality. Now it could of course be that Goethe through his reading of *Don Quixote* had become aware of the theater as a symbol of the tension between illusion and reality. But we do not need to assume this, for it could equally well have come from his reading of *Hamlet* or from his own experiences in the theater. Similarly the fact that Cervantes had a high view of the theater is not really decisive, for this Goethe would also have found in

Hamlet and it was a widespread conception amongst intellectuals of his own day.

Oskar Walzel has pointed out that a great number of the topics uppermost in the minds of persons concerned with the German theater in the 1770s are referred to in the *Theatrical Mission* and that several well-known plays of the previous two decades are specifically mentioned in it.[7] One of these topics was the pariah-like status of the actors. These German companies of traveling actors were social outcasts with reference to the rigid three-class system of eighteenth-century German society. It could be that Goethe, in choosing the subject, was attracted by the idea of a community embracing variety and a community that cut across the rigid class distinctions of society and existed in its own right outside of society. Instead of the traveling hero of eighteenth-century fiction we are to have a traveling community, a community on the move because it cannot, and is not permitted by society, to have roots. It is independent of the factors that condition social living because of its rootlessness: but at the same time by choosing this theme Goethe was maintaining a certain freedom from social norms by providing himself with a medium outside of society for reflection upon society. *Wilhelm Meister's Theatrical Mission* comes closer to being a social novel than any other of Goethe's novels, because it does reflect on society. And yet it is not concerned primarily with society, for in it society exists as representing community and is therefore an image rather than a social reality.

By 1785 Goethe had completed six books of the novel, and he was working at a seventh when he went to Italy in 1786.[8] He then became dissatisfied with it—for reasons which I shall discuss later in this chapter—and dropped it. He did not take it up again seriously until 1794, when the six books already written were radically rewritten and reduced to four, with four more books being added between then and 1796. In the process it became a totally different novel as is indicated by the new title, *Wilhelm Meister's Apprenticeship*, and was published in four

small volumes in 1795–1796. Fortunate circumstances have pre-
served for us a copy of what he had written of the *Theatrical
Mission* before going to Italy, a copy made by a certain Bäbe
Schulthess and her daughter which came to light in 1910.[9]

The protagonist of Goethe's second novel is just as dominant
in the structure of the work as the sorrowing Werther. But in a
very different way. Unlike Werther he is constantly oriented
to otherness, although like Werther he is very much concerned
with the realization of himself. For Wilhelm Meister the realization of self involves the discovery of self—something that
Werther had never contemplated as necessary, so sure was his
sense of self-awareness. Wilhelm Meister has no such self-awareness: he is bewildered and a seeker from the beginning, a seeker
for relief from a sense of restriction every bit as intense as
Werther's, but a seeker for some whole, some community outside
himself in which his individual existence will be meaningful and
productive. The story of his search is not completed in the
Theatrical Mission, for the work breaks off with Wilhelm at a
crossroads in his life, confronting two divergent tendencies in
his nature.

The Theatrical Mission begins as follows:

It was a few days before Christmas Eve in the year 174– that Benedikt
Meister, burgher and merchant in M——, a middle-sized imperial city,
was returning home from his customary stag-group around eight in
the evening. The game of tarok had finished earlier than usual and
he was not exactly in the mood to return so soon to his own four
walls, which his wife did not indeed make a paradise for him. There
was still time until supper and she was not accustomed to fill out
such intervals with sweetness, so that he preferred not to come to
table until the soup was somewhat overcooked.
    He was walking along slowly and thinking about the position of
mayor which he had occupied this last year and about his business
and various small benefits when he noticed in passing that his
mother's windows were brightly lighted.[10]

This is Wilhelm's father. It is with him and his world that the novel begins, for Benedikt Meister and his mother represent the two decisive factors in Wilhelm's development. They do not have much direct influence on it for both soon disappear from the canvas of the novel. But the father represents middle-class life and his mother embodies the flight from this settled existence into a world of fancy. Goethe begins a novel this time with the depiction of the ground from which his hero springs and in which the basic tension that complicates his later existence is already present. At the beginning of the novel the protagonist is still a child, receptive but not yet self-aware. There is narration in this novel such as there was not in *Werther*, narration by an omniscient narrator with no specified relationship to the characters he is describing. He is, on the whole, a rather impersonal voice until he suddenly emerges in the third chapter as a personality with a distinct attitude toward what he is narrating: speaking of Wilhelm's mother, the narrator here "regrets" having to tell us that in later years she "got a passion for an insipid person" [*eine Leidenschaft für einen abgeschmackten Menschen kriegte*].[11] The verb *kriegte* is nowadays a vulgarism (which is why I translate it as "got"), and it was in the eighteenth century, though Goethe did use it several times in his letters. Whether the intention of the narrator is here depreciatory or ironic, or neither, is difficult to determine. But this is true of the whole tone of this narrator in the first part of the *Theatrical Mission*. Before analyzing him further, however, we must recount briefly and in broad outline what he narrates, for the benefit of those unfamiliar with the novel.

Wilhelm Meister is the son of a businessman, and is fascinated by the theater from his earliest years. His grandmother delights him with a puppet show one Christmas Eve. At first it is magic to him but when he discovers the puppets and how they are worked, he realizes this is a practical project and goes on to perform plays and operas with his childhood friends. In vain does Wilhelm's father try to make a businessman out of him as the years pass; his whole enthusiasm remains for the theater. He falls in love with an actress, Mariane, experiences all the joys of first love, decides to become an actor, and voices idealistic conceptions of the public role of the theater. His brother-in-law Werner, more practically minded, tries to puncture Wilhelm's idealism by telling him that Mariane is kept by a rich lover. This is true, but she really loves Wilhelm and is pregnant by \him. At the end of Book One, however, when Wilhelm discovers that Mariane does have a rich lover, he is overcome by despair and falls seriously ill.

As Book Two opens Wilhelm is recovering his health and has long conversations with Werner on certain questions of dramatic art and on the poet's view of life. Parts of his own poetic productions are then given us. He is present at the cross-examination of an actor, Melina by name, who has run off with the daughter of a middle-class family. Melina speaks very negatively about the acting profession but this does not deflate Wilhelm's idealistic view of the theater as an educative institution. Werner talks to Wilhelm about the virtues of the mercantile life. Wilhelm's father then sends him on a business trip, and he is glad to leave.

In Book Three he witnesses on his journey various simpler types of theatrical performances. In a town he encounters a company of traveling actors which Melina and the girl, now his wife, have joined. In their lodging he meets a strange child called Mignon who had been bought from a group of acrobats, the leader of which had mal-treated her, by the manageress of this acting troupe, Mme. de Retti. Wilhelm talks about the present state of German drama with the actors, and reads them his own drama on the subject of Belshazzar, which they decide to perform. Meanwhile he has rescued Mignon from the obtrusive molestations of a stranger, whereupon she kneels before him in gratitude, imploring him to buy her from the troupe.

Book Four begins with Mignon's famous song, "Knowst thou the land where the lemons bloom?", and her request that Wilhelm take her with him to Italy: "I'm cold here." There follows a violent quarrel between Wilhelm and Mme. de Retti, who refuses to pay back the money that Wilhelm has advanced the company. She leaves by night with a lover and Wilhelm is left to pay the bills. He then decides to take the company with him to the town of H***[Hamburg?] where he has a friend, the director of a theater. Two other characters now advance into the forefront of the action: the high-spirited, fickle but attractive young actress Philine, who does her best to seduce Wilhelm, and a strange, melancholy old man, the

Harper, who sings sad songs of ill fate. Philine having made a new conquest in the Master of the Horse at a neighboring count's castle, the company is invited to perform before the Count. The book ends with a memorable scene in which Mignon—half-child and half-woman—is overcome by convulsions in Wilhelm's presence and says to him in tones of anguish: "Will you be my father? I am your child."

Book Five opens with the troupe entering the castle in pouring rain and finding no preparations made for their proper reception. But this is soon put right. Wilhelm meets Jarno, a favorite of the Count's, and Jarno introduces Wilhelm to the works of Shakespeare. A play is to be performed in honor of a visiting prince and Wilhelm is commissioned to write a prologue. Wilhelm and Jarno talk about Shakespeare, and Jarno makes negative remarks about Mignon and the Harper. The actors leave the castle and on their way to H***, as they are encamped in a forest clearing, they are attacked by marauding soldiers. Wilhelm is wounded, loses consciousness and then awakes in the arms of Philine with Mignon moistening his feet with her tears. The picture of the aristocracy given in this book shows the superficial quality of its interest in the theater. But the encounter with Shakespeare is to prove important.

Book Six starts with the sudden appearance of a "beautiful Amazon" accompanying the doctor that the Harper has fetched from the neighboring town, to which the other actors have fled. Wilhelm is taken to them and they upbraid him for his poor management and Philine for her refusal to pawn her possessions so that they may have something to eat. Philine disappears in the night. Wilhelm daydreams about the Amazon, who had seemed like a saint to him. Mignon endeavors to replace Philine in Wilhelm's affections and sings her song of yearning, "He who knows longing / Knows what I suffer." The troupe eventually reassembles in H*** with Wilhelm's director-friend Serlo, the successful practical man-of-the-theater. Wilhelm talks to Serlo and his sister Aurelie about *Hamlet*. Aurelie, an impassioned but temperamental actress, tells Wilhelm about her unhappiness in love and how acting has become a surrogate reality for her. She is always playing with a dagger and in one histrionic outburst she cuts Wilhelm's hand across the life-line. The news of his father's death now reaches Wilhelm, who is therefore free but nevertheless undecided. After considerable hesitation he finally signs the contract with Serlo for the troupe, with himself as a leading

actor in it, but as he does so, the vision of the Amazon appears again
in his mind.

It is clear that Wilhelm is not entirely satisfied with himself at
the point that the novel breaks off. He acts, we are told, in a
daze [*betäubt*], and the Amazon represents the incursion into
his life of some mysterious higher entity which obsesses him but
which he does not understand—except as something he longs for.
At the beginning of this final scene Wilhelm has asserted that he
is "not at the crossroads but hard by the goal and yet does not
dare to take the final step." The situation has been created by
the severence of his bonds with middle-class, mercantile existence
through the death of his father: the "final step" would be the
step out of bourgeois life into the world of the theater. The
vision of the Amazon must therefore represent that undefined
something which makes him hesitate to take this step. She embodies something not contained in the actors' life and the world
of the theater. His horizon has therefore broadened, and in a way
he *is* at the crossroads—faced with a choice not so much between
the limiting sense of bourgeois existence and the wider possibilities of theatrical life, but rather between the limited range of
theatrical existence and the wider horizons opened up by the
Amazon.

Not only has Wilhelm's horizon broadened, but the novel itself has done so in the course of its composition. Goethe's original intention seems to have been to give a broad picture of theatrical life in Germany at that time. But along with this pragmatic,
realistic purpose there was also, from the outset, the idealistic
theme of the theater as an educative institution. These two
themes did not combine well, for the realistic depiction he
sought was bound to be in large part sordid, and the idealistic
message was bound to be rather high-flown. Commentators have
racked their brains trying to decide how the novel was to end,
whether Wilhelm was to find his ideal in the theater or not, and,
consequently, whether the title *Wilhelm Meister's Theatrical*

Mission is serious or ironical.[12] I believe that such speculation is completely futile for it is my opinion that Goethe did not know himself how his novel was to end and this is the main reason why he stopped with Wilhelm's hesitations and vision.

We have already established that Goethe was at work on the *Theatrical Mission* by February 1777. It seemed to be progressing quite well until July 1783 when he expressed some dissatisfaction with it, saying that what he had written fell far short of his "idea."[13] He felt the need to work the whole thing over again before proceeding further, and emphasized that he needed to "make it more sharply and palpably organized" [*schärfer und fühlbaarer an einander rucken*].[14] Then, in October 1784, while he was sketching out the sixth book he wrote to Frau von Stein, his most intimate friend and companion of those years, that "the dear phantom is very kindly helping me on," which can only refer to the Amazon.[15] The significant fact is that he seems to have been stuck until he took up this typical motif of the romance—the coincidental appearance of a *belle inconnue* at a crucial moment. In the next year, 1785, he wrote (also to Frau von Stein) that he was studying *Hamlet* carefully.[16] In September of that year Goethe was stuck again. He never got beyond the vision of the Amazon at the end of the sixth book.

He was "half-way through the fourth book" in 1783 when he voiced his dissatisfaction with the novel. If we assume that this fourth book was at that time more or less as it is in the Schulthess copy, then he had reached the financial troubles of the troupe, had passed through Mignon's song about Italy, had perhaps reached the entry of Philine into the action and maybe even the first mention of the Harper. These three characters— Mignon, Philine and the Harper—represent a broadening out of the original concept, that of a theater-novel. But they are of the greatest importance to Goethe, for at this point he gets rid of Mme. de Retti and her tedious lover, pushes Melina into the background, and indulges his delight in the vitality of Philine, burrows deep into the Harper and makes Mignon's convulsive, passionate nature burst out in the magnificent, moving scene with which this fourth book closes. A new dimension has entered the novel, the dimension of the mysterious unfathomable depths of certain temperaments, a dimension of poetry such as does not naturally belong in a realistic novel of theatrical life though it might be associated somehow with Goethe's intentions in regard to his idealistic theme. The mysterious characters—Mignon, the Harper and the Amazon—are taking over from the others, except for Philine, but then there is something unfathomable and elemental about her too.[17]

The novel, therefore, had begun to split apart. If we take first Goethe's declared intention of portraying "the whole life of the theater" [*das ganze Theaterwesen*], then we can trace an upward line from the puppet theater of the opening scenes through Wilhelm's early theatricals, his first contact with professional theater (Mariane), the conversations with Werner, the theatrical experiences of the journey, the troupe of Mme. de Retti and the performance of *Belshazzar*, the conversations with Jarno about Shakespeare, up to the meeting with Serlo and Aurelie and the planned performance of *Hamlet*. This is a consistent upward line of development. But if we consider the other theme, the idealization of the theater as a moral institution, then no such progressive development can be traced, but neither is there a clear downward disintegration under the impact of experience of the everyday realities of the theater. Instead we have a curiously ambivalent adumbration of this basic idea. When Wilhelm first meets Mariane off the stage it is in a convivial gathering of the actors, and to them he expounds in ecstatic terms his high view of the theater where the actor assaults the "hard breast" of man with a series of emotions, thereby awakening him to a sense of kinship and love for his fellow-men, and, by his portrayal of virtues and vices in their "nakedness" and his keen sense of beauty and ugliness, has a moral effect on the spectators.[18] The narrator comments: "How happy this concept of the actor was which Wilhelm praised in his heart. . . . He thought of their [the actors'] domestic life as a series of worthy actions and occupations of which their stage appearances were but the upper glint on the silver."[19] But the ensuing conversations of the actors present a somewhat confusing picture, for although they talk about trivial things and express trivial opinions, "the conclusion was always the public and its attention and contentment, and also the great and important influence of the theater on the culture of the nation and the world."[20] Wilhelm, so the narrator tells us, does not know how to resolve these contradictions. But what he has heard does not seem to affect his idealizing attitude. A little later on he says to Mariane: "My soul glows at the thought of one day appearing on the boards and speaking into men's hearts, telling them what they have long been yearning to hear."[21] The questioning of the moral nature of the theater would therefore seem to belong to the narrator but not, at this point at least, to Wilhelm, who is being gently ironized as a youthful enthusiast. The narrator has already told us that Wilhelm's love of the theater is really a flight from the restrictedness of bourgeois existence. But the life of these actors reveals itself as just as petty and sordid as the mercantile existence which he has fled, and this is true even of their concept of the theater, as we see from the actions and opinions of the Melinas and Mme. de Retti. Wilhelm certainly does not share their low opinions of that institution, but by the middle of the fourth book—that is to say at the very point where we have shown that the novel takes on a new dimension—he begins to have doubts. These people are becoming tiresome to him; they have taken his money, his vision is dissipating. " 'Oh,' he cried, 'if only many a foolish youth who chases such a will-o-the-wisp, who is enticed by this siren from his predestined path, might grow wise by my example.' "[22] It is his affection for Philine and his sense of responsibility for Mignon and the Harper that prevent his breaking off from the actors at this point. (Notice that these are the three characters of the "new" dimension that the novel is taking on.)[23]

The important point about this stage in the narrative is that the questionings previously voiced by the narrator are now raised by Wilhelm himself.[24] But his idealistic conception of the theater receives a new boost from his encounter with Shakespeare in the fifth book. This, Wilhelm tells us, spurs him on to a greater activity "in the real world" [*in der würklichen Welt*].[25] But this activity is to be in the theater—activity in a fictive world, with the assertion that this is profitable to the real world. The dubiousness of this ideal constitutes Wilhelm's problem: he is too immersed in the fictive to be effective in the real. The narrator tells us that Shakespeare aroused feelings and capabilities in him of which he had previously had "no conception or awareness": but Wilhelm tells Jarno that Shakespeare had strengthened *existing* feelings and resolves in him.[26] Wilhelm is wrong here on two counts: he overestimates both his affinity with Shakespeare and the influence of art on his own life. Despite all that he says, and he is an impassioned talker, art is for Wilhelm not an interpretation of life but a substitute for reality. This is what Aurelie tells him later:

Nothing comes into you from outside! I have never seen anyone who so thoroughly misjudges [*verkennt*] the people he lives with. Allow me to tell you that when one hears you explaining your Shakespeare one would think you had just come from a council of gods creating men in their own image, but in your relations with people you appear to me like the first-born child of creation.[27]

He fancies himself as Hamlet, but the fictive duel that he jokingly fights with another actor (whose name, significantly, is Laertes) is interrupted by the incursion of real violence in the persons of the marauding soldiers. This incursion of unpleasant reality is in turn transfigured, however, by the ideal appearance of the Amazon, who is both vision and reality. Her head may seem to him surrounded by a halo in his feverish delirium, but she does cover him with a very real cloak which he retains. The important thing is that she comes to him when he is wounded—both physically, and in his self-esteem. His further attempts to probe the character of Hamlet are invaded by recollections of the Amazon, but also by the sounds of Mignon's singing. A connection between these two women is suggested at this point of the *Theatrical Mission,* and was to emerge more clearly in *Wilhelm Meister's Apprenticeship.*

It is immediately after Aurelie has cut the life-line on Wilhelm's palm that he receives the news of the death of his father. This is also a break in his life-line, for he is now relieved of all responsibilities toward the mercantile world. It is significant that a short time before he was trying to decide what Hamlet's state of mind was before the death of his father. Now that his own father is dead, how will Wilhelm react? Is he really free of what his father had represented? Will he, like Hamlet, postpone active decision? Will he turn his back on his family heritage, the mercantile life and its values, for the theater? Is this his "mission"? "His heart was inclined towards it," says the narrator, "but a nameless something opposed his desire."[28] And in his hesitation before agreeing to join Serlo's company, he finds it "strange" that when faced with the possibility of realizing his "mission" he had paused. Goethe too seems to have paused before proceeding to what would appear to be the climax of his prime intention in this novel, the fulfillment of a "Theatrical Mission." The lifeline of the novel is also cut. Wilhelm does sign up but the Amazon hovers over the end of this fragment as a questioning, doubting presence.[29]

For all its indecisiveness the *Theatrical Mission* is a splendid novel. Some critics, among them Gundolf, have considered it a greater work than the *Apprenticeship.* It is bursting with vitality, full of colorful detail, variety of moods, interesting and vividly drawn characters (especially the women), and it contains in Mignon one of Goethe's richest and at the same time most elusive creations. It ends with the portrayal of the tension between fulfilled obligation and unfulfilled longing, and perhaps the most satisfying thing about the *Theatrical Mission* is that this tension is not resolved. The ending was, as we have seen, not intended to be an ending, but it is a good ending. For what is most impressive about this novel is its presentation of human indecision in the face of the conflicting demands put upon all of us, and particularly on those of us who are young—demands stemming from the self and demands coming from the world in which we must live, unless, like Werther, we evade the issue. In this novel Goethe has artistically recreated—for the first but not for the last time—the great impressions of his childhood, the disturbances of his adolescence, and his longing for security and fullness. It is a poem of growth out from childhood and home, growth also from the world of fancies into that of reality. To portray this, the loose and inclusive form of the novel was eminently suitable.

And yet the *Theatrical Mission* remains a flawed work because of its uncertain narrative voice. The narrator of the beginning of the novel does not just relate, he comments. And his comments stem from his own concept of what childhood is, so that he generalizes from individual episodes. Because of his alienation from his mother and the severity of his father, the child Wilhelm retreats into himself as the only course left open to him, "a fate which with children and old people is of great consequences,"[30] adds the narrator. And when Wilhelm discovers the puppets packed away in a box, the narrator compares his resultant combination of quiet and disquiet with children's first awareness of difference between the sexes. Sometimes he even adds an "I cannot fail to observe" (*ich kann nicht unbemerkt lassen*) to indicate what he is doing. He introduces his account of the onset of Wilhelm's puberty with a general comment on the "mixed" quality of this stage in human development—half-childhood, half-manhood—and then proceeds to apply this as a metaphor to the state of the German theater at the time: "The German stage was then in the same state of crisis: it had thrown away its child's shoes before they were worn out and so had to run barefoot."[31] At this point in the novel things are getting mightily confused: the story of Wilhelm is becoming combined with theatrical history, the narrator's commentary is becoming digression, and the narrator's voice is no longer contributory to the narrative texture but has become that of the author.

The fiction of the narrator has therefore broken down, not in conscious artistic intention (as in the second version of *Werther*) but because it has not been properly managed. Even when the narrator is not indulging in extrinsic commentary his attitude to Wilhelm is inconsistent, alternating between intense identification and critical detachment. Goethe is insecure, in the *Theatrical Mission*, in his use of irony. As always he was attracted to irony as a mode that gives that *Heiterkeit* (an untranslatable word; perhaps "serenity" or "clarity" might come closest) which he considered essential to all great art. But, for all his desire to maintain distance—at least aesthetic distance—from the hero of the *Theatrical Mission* he was unable totally to withhold from him his heartfelt sympathy. The result is a curious vacillation in narrative voice which mars the novel. This voice ironically points out that experience of life in a theater is a more comfortable excitement because you have a roof over your head in all weather; and that artistic aspirations are often erotic as well; and that women who know they are attractive play cat and mouse with men who think they are the recipients of particular attention, but are not; that Mariane praised the delivery, but said nothing about the content, of Wilhelm's *apologia* for the actor's life. In this last example we notice that the ironic detachment, though reported by the narrator, is expressed, albeit implicitly, by another character in the novel, Mariane. And indeed once Wilhelm has passed out of childhood, ironic commentary is provided either by other characters or by his own self-questionings, so that the ironic narrator is no longer needed. All we need now is the impersonal narrator.

But unfortunately Goethe did not recognize this fact, and the narrator keeps on butting in with supererogatory commentary, often *à la* Fielding or Wieland to introduce a new chapter, but egregiously when compared with those two great commentators. There is also too frequent resorting to such tedious devices as

"I'm sure the reader is wondering what happened to X," or "we will not bore the reader with more details about this." As the novel proceeds, the conscious insistence on the presence of a story-teller becomes an obstacle rather than a gateway to the characters. My point is that authorial intrusions often disturb rather than enrich the texture, and that ironical reflection in the narration is too inconsistently maintained to be a structurally organizing element.[32] In *Tom Jones* the contributions of the author as author are clearly distinguished from those of the author as narrator: not so in the *Theatrical Mission*, where Goethe endows Wilhelm with an analysis of the poetic mind and with views on Corneille which are hardly consonant with the restricted intelligence of his protagonist, and even introduces the shoddy device of Wilhelm's communicating parts of an essay by an "unknown friend" on the pleasurable emotions aroused by tragedy. Fielding mostly keeps such direct communication by the author-as-author to the introductory chapters to the individual books of *Tom Jones*. His narrator is a commentator like the narrator of the *Theatrical Mission*, who ironizes as he tells his tale. His irony extends not only to what is told but to the process of telling. It may well be that Goethe was trying to emulate the author of *Tom Jones* in his use of general commentary to begin a new chapter, and he does occasionally mock the devices and conventions of narrative fiction. But the difference is surely that the narrator of *Tom Jones* interprets what he narrates and is therefore the central organizing element in the structure, whereas in Goethe he is merely a machine.

There are, however, certain moments in the *Theatrical Mission* where the ironic narration *is* eminently effective and becomes a poetic prism breaking up the reflection of an experience into a myriad of constituent colors. For instance, the narrator has been commenting on the fact that in any pair of young lovers, one is usually more experienced than the other, leading the other on to ever greater pleasure for which he is grateful, whether or not he perceives the cunning intention. He then proceeds from this observation to describe what happened to Wilhelm and Mariane:

The lightness, liveliness and wit with which at the onset of their passion for each other they had striven to capture and entertain each other and spice every caress, grew daily less. At first they often joked in little scenes from this or that play, mocked each other with the loving teasings of this or that poet, and when he finally fell on her neck after such teasings and punished her with a kiss and they through such a blissful catastrophe declared all that had gone before to be falsehood, then those were the highest moments of their love. But now, when they indulged themselves to excess in these joys, this had an effect on Wilhelm's head as if he were intoxicated by beer, he became sullen and uncomfortable in his desires and lapsed into various petty jealousies and teasings, which one may well pardon him, for he was worse off than a man chasing a shadow, because he held in his arms and touched with his lips something that he could not enjoy, could not sate himself with. Mariane was not unaware of his torment and at times could well have shared with him the joy he so passionately desired; she felt he was worth more than she could give him, but his confusion and his love obscured his advantages and her silence, her restlessness, her tears, her fleeing embraces (the most pleasant tones of devoted love) cast him distractedly and overwhelmed by sorrow at her feet, until they both at last in twilight moments of tumult lost themselves in those joys of love which Fate reserves for the children of men, to compensate them in some degree for so much pressure and pain, grief and want, waiting, dreaming, hoping and yearning.[33]

Such a passage shows in its intercalation of the playful and the deadly serious, of wit and passion, teasing and torment that Goethe is aware of the power of irony as a means to delineate the full complexity of anguished experience. But nevertheless the use of the ironic mode in *Wilhelm Meister's Theatrical Mission*, when the work is considered as a whole, remains indecisive, insecure and uncertain.

5

Search for a Definition

When Goethe came to rework the *Theatrical Mission* into *Wilhelm Meister's Apprenticeship*, he made sure that the irony should be all-pervasive, consistent, and firmly handled. To obviate the problem of how to deal with Wilhelm's childhood without a constantly interpreting narrator, he lets Wilhelm himself recount his childhood to Mariane in her dressing room. And she is bored, and falls asleep.

Earlier in this study, it was asserted that Goethe's novels are concerned with a quest for order; three things should be clear now from my analysis of the *Theatrical Mission*. First, the work is concerned with an outwardly directed search for order that is both personally satisfying and communally viable, whereas Werther's search is too much inwardly directed to be lastingly viable. Secondly, Wilhelm's quest is born, like Werther's, out of a sense of restriction, is aimed at finding a form of existence in which restricted faculties may find unrestricted, or less restricted, expression, but with Wilhelm the desire for useful activity plays a much larger part. Thirdly, Wilhelm's quest also involves coming to terms with himself and with the tension between middle-class stability and imaginative restlessness, as represented by his father and his grandmother at the beginning of the novel, a tension between obligation and longing which is unresolved, but reaches a climax at the point where the novel breaks off.

It is significant that the first working-out of this material is dominated by the concept of "mission," and that the final version of the novel speaks not of a "mission" but of "apprentice-ship." The change of focus is very revealing. What the Wilhelm of the *Apprenticeship* experiences is far more concerned with coming to terms with himself than his counterpart in the *Theatrical Mission* ever conceived, for the latter was obsessed with the concept of a "mission" from the outset, and vitiated by it. When the Wilhelm of the *Apprenticeship* talks to Mariane about his childhood experiences he is already interpreting them as what he conceives to be an ordered development: he is already seeking order by imposing it on the past and reinterpreting that past as an orderly, logical process leading to the present and to what he has decided is to be his future. The search for meaning and shape in the temporal sequence of events is an important new facet of the search for order in Goethe's novels, and it is a recurrent element in the complicated texture of *Wilhelm Meister's Apprenticeship*. It appears in Wilhelm's own meditations but not only there. For the narrator of this novel reflects Goethe's desire to distill some shape or pattern from the manifold variety and conflicting claims of occurrences, encounters and attitudes which make up the seeming chaos that is life in its totality. Whether there is such a thing as fate or whether there is only chance is one of the prime questions raised by this novel.

By 1795 Goethe had reached an important stage in the composition of *Wilhelm Meister's Apprenticeship*. He had by then completed the transformation of the six books of the *Theatrical Mission* into the first four books of the *Apprenticeship* and was pressing on into new terrain.[1] Sometime in the first six months of 1795[2] he composed a passage summarizing a conversation between Serlo, Wilhelm and the other actors, which contains an attempt to define the novel as a genre by delimiting it from the drama. This passage is generally considered to be Goethe's only extended statement about the novel. It runs as follows:

> One evening the company debated whether precedence of rank should be accorded to the drama or to the novel. Serlo asserted that this was a futile and ill-conceived argument, since each could be

excellent in its own way, so long as it kept within the bounds of its genre.

"I myself am not quite clear about that," said Wilhelm.

"Who is?" said Serlo. "And yet it would be worth while going into the matter more closely."

They all talked back and forth a good deal and the final result of their conversation was roughly this:

Both in the novel and in the drama we observe human nature and action. The difference between the two genres lies not merely in their external form, that is to say that people talk in the one and are usually told about in the other. Unfortunately many dramas are only novels in dialogue, and it should be perfectly possible to write a drama in letters.

In the novel it is predominantly sentiments and events that are to be presented; in drama, characters and deeds. The novel must move slowly and the sentiments of the main personage must, in some way or another, hold up the progression of the whole toward its resolution. Drama must move quickly and the character of the main personage must press towards the end, and only be held up [i.e., not *hold up* this progression]. The novel hero must be passive, or at least not active to a high degree; from the hero of drama we demand effective action and deeds. Grandison, Clarissa, Pamela, the Vicar of Wakefield, Tom Jones himself are, if not passive, yet retarding personages, and all events are to a certain extent fashioned after their sentiments. In drama the hero fashions nothing according to himself, everything resists him, and he either clears obstacles or pushes them aside, or he succumbs to them.

And so we agreed also that we could very well give Chance free play in the novel, but that it must always be guided and controlled by the sentiments of the personages; whereas Fate which, without any action by men on their part, drives them through outside circumstances unrelated to themselves toward an unforeseen catastrophe, can have its place only in drama; and that Chance may indeed produce pathetic situations but never tragic situations; whereas Fate must always be terrible and becomes tragic in the highest sense if it brings guilty and innocent deeds which are not connected with each other into some dire connection.[3]

The passage acknowledges the novel as a genre with its own characteristics, and as a genre worthy of serious consideration as literature, so much so that it can support comparison with drama, and by "drama" it is clear that Goethe means tragedy, which was generally considered the highest form of literature in the eighteenth century. The comparison cannot but recall Aristotle's between tragedy and the epic, and might suggest that the novel had replaced the epic as narrative literature, were it not for the delineation of the characteristics of the genre which suggest something quite different from the epic; for the epic cannot be said to be dependent on sentiments and events rather than on characters and deeds. The novel is not presented, therefore, in this passage as the modern representative of or correspondence to the epic. Our first observation on analyzing this passage would therefore be that Goethe accepts the novel as an important genre with its own particular characteristics, which are not those of the epic.[4]

If we now look at the characteristics of the genre as here listed, they add up ultimately to one assertion—that the novel is controlled by sentiments [*Gesinnungen*] which fashion the events [*Begebenheiten*] and retard the action. This presupposes a relatively inactive main personage (I purposely avoid the word "hero" or "protagonist," which would suggest more will and action) and results in a plot characterized by chance rather than by fate, and these chance happenings are produced by what the characters *are*, rather than by what they *do*, by their states of mind rather than their actions. The sentiments are central because they result in chance events, reveal the character of the main personage and hold up the action. As an aesthetic of the novel this assertion is questionable, even if we apply it only to the genre as it had developed up to 1795. If we assume that by "deeds" [*Taten*] Goethe means things one does and that by "events" [*Begebenheiten*] he means things that happen independently of an active agent, then there is a contrast here of some meaning although not perhaps of absolute precision: but what is the distinction between "characters" [*Charaktere*] and "sentiments" [*Gesinnungen*]?

The distinction goes back to Aristotle, who in the *Poetics* distinguishes between *ēthē* and *dianoia*.[5] The former, usually translated as "characters," refers, according to S. H. Butcher, to "the moral element in character . . . an expression of moral purpose, of the permanent disposition and tendencies, the tone and sentiment of the individual," whereas *dianoia*, usually translated as "thoughts" or "sentiments," "is the thought, the intellectual element, which is implied in all rational conduct, through which alone *ēthos* can find outward expression." Butcher continues: "Wherever moral choice, or a determination of the will is manifested, there *ēthos* appears. Under *dianoia* are included the intellectual reflexions of the speaker; the proof of his own statements, the disproof of those of his opponents, his general maxims concerning life and conduct, as elicited by the action and forming part of a train of reasoning."[6] O. B. Hardison emphasizes that *ēthos* refers to something constant (compare Butcher's phrase "permanent disposition"), whereas *dianoia* refers to a specific individual situation, "is related to contingencies."[7] The first would seem to refer primarily to active will, while the second refers to reflection and denotes primarily the embodiment of such reflection in spoken words. In Dacier's famous French translation of 1692, the distinction was explained thus: *dianoia* does not mean "the inner concepts of the mind . . . but the speeches by which one explains these concepts whether they have [already] produced some action or are [merely] preparing for such."[8]

These terms were widely used in the eighteenth century and not only in discussions of tragedy. Aristotle had also employed them in his discussion of the epic, and we find them used with reference to the epic in essays and treatises of the eighteenth century, for instance by Addison in his essays on Milton, by Pope in the preface to his translation of the *Iliad*, and by the German critic Gottsched in his *Critische Dichtkunst* of 1730. In turn Fielding applied them to the novel conceived as "comic epic," and they reappear in this passage from *Wilhelm Meister's*

Apprenticeship. When Goethe here speaks of "characters" [*Charaktere*] he means *ēthē*, not characters in the sense of personages, for which he uses *Personen* or *Figuren* in this passage; when he says "sentiments" [*Gesinnungen*] he means, in part at least, *dianoia*. But there is an important difference from Aristotle, in that Aristotle considers both *ēthē* and *dianoia* as constituent elements of both tragedy and epic, whereas Goethe assigns *Charaktere* to drama and *Gesinnungen* to the novel. Goethe's concept *Gesinnungen*, although it is undoubtedly based on Aristotle's concept *dianoia*, is somewhat wider. In the eighteenth century the plural *Gesinnungen* was used to denote individual expressions or embodiments of one's *Gesinnung*, the way one is "minded," or, if I may be allowed the term, one's "mindedness." Elsewhere Goethe distinguishes between *Gesinnungen* and thoughts [*Gedanken*]. One of his *Maxims and Reflexions* reads: "Everything depends really on the *Gesinnungen:* where these exist, thoughts appear, and even afterwards, the thoughts are still there."[9] He also distinguishes between *Gesinnungen* and opinions [*Meinungen*]. In 1813 he wrote in a letter:

Men are united by *Gesinnungen* but divided by *Meinungen*. The former are something simple, in which we find ourselves together; the latter represent something manifold, in which we find ourselves scattered apart. The friendships of youth are based on the former, the divisions of age are the fault of the latter. If only one realized this earlier, if one could acquire in developing one's own way of thinking a liberal view of that of others, even of those ways of thinking directly opposed to one's own, then one would be much more tolerant and seek to gather together again by *Gesinnung* what had been splintered by *Meinung*.[10]

Obviously the word *Gesinnungen* has more of an emotional quality for Goethe than does the word *Gedanken*, and a more positive, productive quality than *Meinungen*. It seems to me that Goethe's use of *Gesinnungen* is close to the English eighteenth-century use of *sentiments* to designate, I quote the Oxford Dictionary, "a mental feeling," a "thought or reflection coloured by or proceeding from emotion." *Gesinnungen* are not therefore only *spoken* sentiments.

There is another point that must be emphasized. When Dr. Johnson in a famous utterance said one should read Richardson "for the sentiment, and consider the story as only giving occasion to the sentiment," he was implicitly setting up an opposition of story (or plot) and sentiment.[11] But for Goethe, we notice, plot is not the "occasion" for sentiment, but is "fashioned after [or according to] the sentiments" [*nach den Gesinnungen gemodelt*]. Goethe distinguishes within a novel between events [*Begebenheiten*] and sentiments, but says that the novel should include both and that there should be a close connection between them. In fact: the external action or plot of a novel is the events, and the internal action or plot is the sentiments. And this is where chance comes into the argument. For Goethe's conception of the external action that a novel should have was much closer to that of the romance where, according to Sir Walter Scott, "the interest . . . turns upon marvellous and uncommon incidents" than to that of the novel as it distinguished itself from the romance in these years, namely as a genre that feigned real-life truth, eschewed the marvelous, and presented an external action dealing on the whole with credible personages and incidents such as might commonly occur to such persons, given their personalities and motivating forces as portrayed in the novel.[12] Except in *Werther* Goethe never disdained the "marvellous" and "uncommon" in his novels. He had, as he once said, a *Lust zu fabulieren* —a delight in spinning tales—and he liked surprises, unexpected encounters, strange coincidences.[13] All this belongs in large part to the realm of chance: and perhaps the most important statement in this passage in the *Apprenticeship* is the recognition that the novel can deal with chance whereas tragedy cannot (or should not). This is, however, no mere kowtowing to the tradition of the romance, but an asseveration of chance as an experiential fact, and the desire to express this fact in that literary genre where it could legitimately and meaningfully be rendered, namely the novel. The novel deals in its external action with chance events—things that befall the characters—and in its internal action with the reactions or sentiments of the personages towards these events. And these sentiments retard the progress of the action, often constituting in themselves the main interest of the narrative fiction.

Werther, one could say, consists almost entirely of such "sentiments," and Goethe's prescription is moderately applicable to the novels of Richardson—though only moderately so, for they do contain "characters" in the Aristotelian sense who certainly, when occasion demands, perform "deeds." And neither Pamela nor Clarissa nor Tom Jones is really "passive." Goethe's description would seem to best fit *The Vicar of Wakefield*, for the second half of that novel (though only the second half) shows retardation of the action by expansive treatment of Dr. Primrose's sentiments—but also by inset narratives (such as that of George's adventures) and the development of subordinate characters (such as Jenkinson or Arabella Wilmot), all of which, however, do contribute to the final resolution. But there are other novels that we know Goethe had read by this time which do not fit his attempt at a definition of the genre and are not mentioned in this passage in the *Apprenticeship*. This fact has been little noticed by critics, if indeed at all, but it is highly significant.

What novels, then, had Goethe read between the publication of the first version of *Werther* and the composition of this passage in the first half of 1795? We have evidence that in these years he read Friedrich Heinrich Jacobi's *Woldemar, Don Quixote*, Diderot's *La Religieuse* and *Jacques le Fataliste*, and Karl Philipp Moritz's *Anton Reiser*. He also read Rousseau's *Confessions*, which some of his contemporaries, notably Friedrich Schlegel, considered a novel.[14] There were special reasons why he should have read these particular novels: Jacobi was his friend, Moritz he became acquainted with in Rome, *Don*

Quixote he read in the translation by his Weimar friend Bertuch, the two works by Diderot were circulating at the time in Weimar in a copy of Grimm's *Correspondance Littéraire*, and he read Rousseau's masterpiece in the Geneva edition of his works, a copy of which was given him as a present in May 1782.[15] No such personal reason suggests itself for his reading of Lesage's *Le diable boiteux*, a novel which he refers to several times over the succeeding years, the first such reference being in his version of the *Birds* of Aristophanes in 1780.

Goethe did not like *Woldemar:* Sophie von La Roche reported to Wieland in the summer of 1779 that she had heard that Goethe had climbed an oak tree, given a witty speech attacking the book and then nailed it by both covers to the tree,[16] and in October of that year Goethe's friend Johanna Schlosser reported to Jacobi himself that Goethe had found good things and fine ideas in the novel but "couldn't stand the smell of the book."[17] What was this "smell" and why did Goethe find it so distasteful? *Woldemar*, like Jacobi's earlier novel *Eduard Allwills Papiere*, deals with the problem of the subjectivism of the man of intense feeling, viewed, as Roy Pascal has said, "from the point of view of normal burgher life, in the framework of normal social and domestic relations."[18] Woldemar marries into domesticity but simultaneously maintains a "soul-friendship" with a woman who is emotionally and intellectually more his equal, Henriette. His last words in the novel are: "He who relies on his heart is a fool," and she replies "Trust in love. Love takes all, but also gives all." And in this sentimental, histrionic climax order is restored. Pascal suggests that Goethe would have been roused by the implications "that friendship demanded this continual discharge and sharing of emotions," that he may well, in the light of his own friendship with Frau von Stein, have found this portrayal of a "soul-friendship" repulsive, and that Jacobi's presentation of the problem, which Pascal defines as "how to escape from *Sturm und Drang* subjectivism while retaining the richness of emotional experience the *Sturm und Drang* had discovered," would have seemed superficial to the Goethe of these years who was seeking some worthy practical activity for his emotional and intellectual powers. Jacobi's solution of "submitting to middle-class environment and standards," says Pascal, would hardly have appealed to the Goethe of the Weimar court.[19] Pascal may have somewhat overstated the sociological point, but the psychological problem is certainly one that was uppermost in Goethe's mind, and Jacobi's solution must have seemed ludicrous to the man wrestling with the *Theatrical Mission*. His objections to *Woldemar* were therefore probably to its content, as the metaphor "smell" also suggests, not to anything connected with Jacobi's use of the novel form, which presents a fairly standard combination of narration, letters and conversations.

Lesage's *Le diable boiteux* is a much more interesting novel than *Woldemar*, especially in the use that it makes of a structural frame to give a panoramic view of the world. In gratitude for being temporarily rescued from a magician's power, Asmodée, the demon of lust and Cupid under another name, who makes ridiculous marriages and has introduced into the world "luxury, debauchery, games of chance and chemistry," who is "the inventor of carousals, dancing, music, plays and all the new fashions of France," who limps because he came off the worse in a fight with the "devil of [self-] interest," takes his liberator, a young scholar, up to a high tower at night and removes the roofs of all the houses to show him all that is happening in the city and to "uncover the failings of men." In Goethe's version of Aristophanes' *Birds* (1780, first published in 1787), there is talk of an eagle-owl called Kriticus, satisfied with nothing and therefore deemed to have great knowledge, who each day thinks over what people had done the day before: "We assume that he will have seen all towns only at night like the limping devil."[20] Later, in the first book of *Fiction and Truth*, describing the various houses and gardens of Frankfurt as they appeared from the city wall, Goethe compares himself with the limping devil:[21] likewise in the *Campaign in France* (1796) as, unseen, he

watches a gathering in a hostelry.[22] In his introduction to the
autobiography of a soldier called Mämpel (published in 1826 as
Der junge Feldjäger), Goethe speaks of this soldier's being introduced through billeting into the heart of various and contrasting households "as if by the hand of a limping devil."[23]
From all this we gain nothing more than that the initial idea of
Lesage's book was known to Goethe and retained its appeal
for him throughout his life, for the idea of the devil as a mediator
of experience would obviously have appealed to the man writing
Faust. Nothing more is said about the book, nothing about its
progression through various spheres of life, with scenes in the
prison and the madhouse, reflections on the sleeping dead, investigation of the dreams of the sleeping living and the past his-
tories of ransomed slaves, nor of its structure, which loosely
aligns short narrative vignettes, interrupting this occasionally by
longer life-stories, two of which are full-length novellas and one
other purposely left unfinished. In its panoramic form the novel
is closer to *Faust* than to any of Goethe's novels; but its use of
novellas inside the panoramic framework may well have shown
Goethe the effectiveness of this type of novelistic structure. It is
basically the medieval structure of a series of adventures, such as
we still find in Cervantes and Rabelais, and, like those two greater
exemplars, shows the passage from anecdote and novella to the
novel as a panorama and interpretation of society.

As for *Don Quixote*, there are brief references to it in letters
to Frau von Stein in 1780 and 1782, and the diaries show that he
was reading it again in 1799 and 1800, this time perhaps in
Tieck's famous translation which began to appear in 1799. But
for the moment Goethe made no comments.

Goethe was deeply affected by Moritz's autobiographical
novel *Anton Reiser*, which is a powerful study of the development of a neurotic, introspective and masochistic temperament
out of a childhood atmosphere of tortured pietistic religiosity.
At the time he met Moritz and read his novel Goethe was on the
Italian journey that was to be the turning point in his life. He

was in flight from Weimar, thirty-seven years old, taking stock
of his life and considering how best to engage his immense creative energies and unify his wide-ranging intellectual interests into
a total picture of art, nature, and society with himself as the
mediator-poet. In Anton Reiser he saw his former self with all
the nervousness that he had not yet fully contained and never
was fully to overcome. Anton Reiser too was turned inwards,
over-sensitive, endangered. On 16 December 1786 Goethe wrote
to Frau von Stein of Moritz: "He is like a younger brother of
myself, of the same ilk, but abandoned and bruised by Fate
where I was favored and preferred. This gave me a strange
retrospect into myself,"[24] and one week later he urged her to
read *Anton Reiser*, "a psychological novel . . . valuable to me
in many senses."[25] It was just about this time (the end of 1786)
that Goethe broke off his work on the *Theatrical Mission*. The
Wilhelm Meister of that novel had hoped, like Anton Reiser and
like Moritz himself, to find in the theater a liberation from
middle-class narrowness and fulfillment of a passionate self.
But none of the three found what they sought where they sought
it. It was also at about this time that Goethe set to work on the
revision of *Werther*. It could therefore well be that the encounter with Moritz and his novel gave Goethe a greater detachment toward the characters of Werther and Wilhelm Meister,
those two mirror-images of his earlier tense self.

The reading of Rousseau's *Confessions* must also have worked
in this direction. Goethe must have been affected by Rousseau's
power to write about himself. "How wonderful it is, and how
pleasant [*angenehm*], to find the soul of a deceased man and his
innermost tender affections [*seine innerlichsten Herzlichkeiten*]
lying open on this or that table," he writes to Frau von Stein in
July 1784[26]—a clumsy tribute to a book that is surely "wonderful" and yet anything but "pleasant"! Nevertheless what Goethe
is pinpointing here is a great writer's ability to present meaningfully to the public at large, "on this or that table," the secret
places of the heart. As with Anton Reiser a good deal of what is

thus revealed is frighteningly pathological. The same was true of much of *La Religieuse*. Whether Goethe was equally attracted by the extraordinarily successful narrative distance that Diderot achieved in the last section of his novel, we shall never know. Leaving aside the epistolary exchange of the *Préface-Annexe* (which appeared in the *Correspondance Littéraire* in 1770 whereas the text proper did not appear there until 1780, when Goethe and others at Weimar read it), *La Religieuse* is a first-person narrative from beginning to end, but the swift and sketchy account of the heroine's life after she leaves the cloister produces a sort of emotional relaxation in the reader, so that not only the nun herself but also the reader becomes involved in a sort of catharsis after the fierce dramatic confrontations that she and the reader have participated in. We know that Goethe thought highly of this novel and that he and Schiller wanted to publish a German translation of it.[27] But whether Goethe was attracted by its sophisticated form or merely by its sensational content cannot be definitely established. One can, however, reasonably speculate that here, as with Moritz and Rousseau, he was impressed by a novel which presented intensely emotional experiences without losing detachment. In giving his manuscript to Meister, who succeeded Grimm as editor of the *Correspondance Littéraire*, Diderot said of *La Religieuse*: "It is the obverse of *Jacques le Fataliste*. It is full of pathetic scenes. It is very interesting and all the interest is concentrated on the person who is speaking. I am quite sure that it will affect your readers more than Jacques makes them laugh, whence it could happen that they will sooner wish to get to the end."[28]

As for *Jacques le Fataliste*, Goethe declared in a letter of April 1780 that it was "a very delicious, big meal prepared and served with great understanding for the mouth of a single idol. . . . I sat myself down in the seat of this Bel and in six uninterrupted hours consumed all the courses and side dishes according to the order and intention of this artistic cook and table-decker. Since then it has been read by many readers but unfortunately all of them, like priests, have divided up the meal, nibbled here and there and carried away, each for himself, his favorite kind of food."[29] What Goethe is here admiring, is Diderot's ability to combine very disparate parts into a satisfying whole. In 1805 he was to single out this same quality with reference to another work of Diderot's, *Le Neveu de Rameau*, speaking on that occasion of Diderot's talent for "knowing how to combine the most heterogeneous elements of reality into an ideal whole" [*ein ideales Ganze*], that is to say, a whole which embodies an idea or proceeds from an idea.[30] In another reference to *Le Neveu de Rameau* Goethe said: "I had always been extremely attracted, not by Diderot's sentiments and manner of thinking, but by his manner of presentation as an author, and I found this little work most excellent and exciting. Hardly anything was for me more impudent and controlled, more witty and bold, more immorally moral than this. . . ."[31] Judging from this passage, written considerably later than the period we are at present considering, we can say that it was the artist rather than the thinker that he admired in Diderot. And let us notice what it is that Goethe particularly admires: it is the ability to present conflicting things in an artistically satisfying whole.

The structure of *Jacques le Fataliste* is indeed brilliant. Basically a dialogue between Jacques and his master, the book presents opposing points of view on the subject of chance and fate, and on free will and determinism, and by demonstrating that an extreme, one-sided belief in either of the opposing points of view is absurd and inconclusive, it establishes the limitations of human cognition. The debate, like the story (if one may call it such) is inconclusive, and the author ironically provides two conclusions. One cannot be sure that Goethe got to the end, for Roland Mortier tells us that the text of *Jacques* was not complete in the *Correspondance Littéraire* until June 1780,[32] and Goethe's statement about it was made in a letter of 7 April (which might explain how, for all his good command of French, he could read it in six hours). But he certainly read enough to

appreciate the structural force of exposition through polar oppositions. He would surely also have noticed the ingenious and
novel use of intercalated stories which, even if it is true, as
Robert Niklaus asserts, that "they never illustrate the views of
either the master or Jacques," nevertheless enrich, by their real-
life quality in contrast to the cerebrations of the two disputants,
the total texture of the novel. These undoubtedly were the "side
dishes" to which Goethe referred. Their contribution to the
whole, contrapuntal as it often is, and the fact that some overlap
with each other and that some of the characters in them (for
instance the Marquis des Arcis) also appear in the framework
dialogue—all this was to be revelatory and stimulating to Goethe,
who went on to produce the *Conversations of German Emigrants*,
a collection of novellas with a discursive dialogue framework,
and, much later, *Wilhelm Meister's Journeymanship*. There is
no doubt in my mind that Goethe learned a lot about the potentialities of the novel as a form from reading *Jacques le
Fataliste*. And the whole argument about determinism and free
will—transformed in the alembic of Goethe's own poetic mind
(for Diderot was no poet)—was to be built in to *Wilhelm
Meister's Apprenticeship*. That this was a delayed reaction need
not surprise us: for Goethe's creative imagination, like that of
other great poets, often worked in this way. The fact that he
returned to *Jacques le Fataliste* some fifty years later and read it
again with admiration shows the lasting hold that it had on his
mind.

   In his judgment on *Jacques le Fataliste* Goethe had spoken of
a "cook" and the "preparation" of the meal, *Zurichtung*—a primarily culinary word in German which denotes skillful combination of ingredients, devices to heighten flavor, and probably
the use of spices. There was also mention of a "table-decker,"
the *Tafeldecker*, the "officer in a prince's household who has
charge of the table-linen, who lays the table, etc.," as the Muret-
Sanders dictionary defines him (the second edition of Adelung's
German dictionary, 1793–1801, defines the word in similar

terms). One might be tempted to deduce from this metaphor that by 1780 Goethe recognized that the most important constituent element in a novel is the author, both as artist and personality. But this would be unwarranted, for although the statements we have been considering do indicate a greater awareness on Goethe's part of the importance of the personality of the author-narrator and of a certain distancing of the narrator from the author as structural features in a novel, there is not a word about either author or narrator in the passage in the *Apprenticeship*, which is entirely concerned with action and sentiments without any consideration of the mediating agent and the various forms the mediation can take. There is no mention of a cook in this passage, and nothing about laying the table except for the demand that the manifestations of chance shall be guided and controlled by the sentiments of the personages, that the "events" shall be "fashioned" after or according to these sentiments, and that the action shall depend on retardation.

And the strictures do not entirely fit the examples. It can hardly be said that the workings of chance in the life of Tom Jones are guided and controlled by his sentiments (whatever they may be), and the "events" in *The Vicar of Wakefield* are certainly not "fashioned" after the Vicar's sentiments. It would seem necessary to distinguish between events in the sense of happenings and events in the sense of reactions by the personages to such happenings. One may well grant that Pamela's marriage and Clarissa's death are fashioned by their sentiments: but Clarissa's elopement, which starts the whole external action rolling, depends not just on her sentiments but on the will of Lovelace, and is a deed such as the excursus in the *Apprenticeship* would assign to drama. There remains the concept of retardation. The point at issue is not that the ultimate crisis or resolution is delayed in a novel but not in drama, but how and by what it is delayed, namely by the sentiments. As we have already observed, this prescription fits *The Vicar of Wakefield* best out of the novels which Goethe names. It also fits *Agathon, Robin-*

son Crusoe, Télémaque, and *La Nouvelle Héloïse*—in fact the
description applies best to those discursive novels where plot is
of less significance than ideas, and where characters are sub-
servient to the discussions they provoke and the sentiments they
express. It also applies to *Werther,* which is significant. It would
apply preeminently to *Tristram Shandy,* but we cannot be sure
that Goethe had read that novel by this time; if he had, why then
is it not mentioned in this passage? It is indeed curious that there
is no mention of Sterne in the whole passage.

There are, however, novels that we know Goethe had read
and admired, which the definition (if one may call it such) does
not fit. It does not fit *Anton Reiser,* it does not fit *La Religieuse,*
and it fits *Manon Lescaut* only in a very special sense. For although sentiments play a large part in Prévost's novel they do
not retard the development of the action, nor are the events
fashioned according to them. Just the opposite: this novel depicts
the conflict between actions and sentiments. There are plenty of
"events," but it is also much concerned with actions. Prévost
described his hero as a combination of vice and virtue, one whose
thoughts are good but whose actions are bad: "un jeune vicieux
et vertueux tout ensemble, pensant bien et agissant mal, aimable
par ses sentiments, détestable par ses actions."[33] The events (in
the sense of external happenings) are a series of reversals of
fortune: good turns to bad, bad turns to temporary good. These
reversals are often brought about by violent occurrences—abductions, imprisonments, pirate attacks, flight, murder, death—incidents such as had characterized the older romance, and are here
more often than not presented as the workings of malevolent
fate (or chance). In the central conversation of the novel, at the
prison of St. Lazare, Tiberge reproaches Des Grieux with a
"contradiction d'idées et de conduite" which Des Grieux attempts to rebut by asserting the steadfastness of his love, for
which Heaven will surely reward him. When Tiberge replies
that his friend should be prepared to sacrifice earthly gratifica-
tion for heavenly reward, Des Grieux admits that he should act

in accordance with his beliefs but that action is not always within his power. It is only at the end of the novel, after the death of Manon, that events bring him back to his beliefs and sentiments. Chance plays its part in *Manon Lescaut;* it does not have much part in *La Nouvelle Héloïse* or *La Religieuse.* And surely, even if one might hesitate to call the situations in these novels "tragic," they approach very closely to this quality, are more than just pathetic.

The terms of this famous passage in the *Apprenticeship* are therefore somewhat imprecise, and their application is limited. This is immediately recognized in the novel, because the definition of drama that the participants in the conversation had arrived at is found not to fit *Hamlet.* "The hero [*of Hamlet*]," they said, "really only has sentiments and it is only events that affect him, and therefore the play has something of the extended, expansive quality [*von dem Gedehnten*] of the novel; but because Fate has marked out the plan, because the play begins from a terrible deed, and the hero is always being pressed toward a terrible deed, it is in the highest sense tragic, and admits of no other than a tragic ending." One may well object (and I think we as attentive readers are meant to) that any theory of drama that does not apply to *Hamlet* is suspect. One could also object that the interpretation of *Hamlet* offered here is patently false, for the play does not begin from a terrible deed, nor has fate marked out the plan, which remains undecided; it is this preeminently that gives the play its dramatic tension. But such an objection would be irrelevant. Goethe may have thought thus; or the characters in this scene of *Wilhelm Meister's Apprenticeship* may have thought thus. But that they should argue themselves into agreement on a theory of drama which does not fit *Hamlet,* the play they so much admire and are about to produce, is amusing and should make the reader pause. It would, I think, be right to say that this passage does not represent Goethe's formulated view on the distinction between novel and drama. But it would also be true to say that he is here playing with a concept—retardation—which he had deduced particularly from *The Vicar of Wakefield* and which he thinks might be useful in some such final statement, but that possibly he already sees its limitations as a working concept. He was to return to it during the next few years, as we shall see; but he finally discarded it, not as untrue but as unusable. That irony may have been at play here, and that he may already have had his doubts in 1795 is suggested by a letter to Schiller dated 8 July 1795, where Goethe jocularly took up the terms "sentiments" and "events." He had just arrived in Carlsbad and had "started a little romance" [*Roman*] in order to get himself out of bed in the morning. "I hope," he wrote, "that we shall be able to moderate our sentiments [*Gesinnungen*] and control events [*Begebenheiten*] sufficiently, so that it may last a couple of weeks."[34]

   In October of this same year 1795, while working at the seventh book of *Wilhelm Meister's Apprenticeship*, Goethe produced his translation of Mme. de Staël's *Essai sur les fictions* (which had been first published in France in that same year). Goethe's title was *Versuch über die Dichtungen*, and the essay was published in Schiller's periodical *Die Horen* in 1796. Fiction, said Mme. de Staël, by moving the heart, has a great influence on our moral ideas, for it uses the passions with philosophy as the invisible guiding principle directing their effects; but if this philosophy should reveal itself too soon, it will lose its power.[35] Her purpose was to prove that fiction which "portrays life as it is with subtlety, eloquence, depth and morality [*finesse, éloquence, profondeur et moralité*—Goethe's equivalents are *Feinheit, Beredsamkeit, Tiefe und Moralität*] is the most useful of all forms of fiction."[36] Goethe adds a phrase to this sentence, saying that the intention is to write in praise of novels. Fiction of the Marvelous (to which belongs the epic) demands, according to Mme. de Staël, a simple childlike state of mind and credulity and can be conceived as a series of allegories. But as an interpretation of human actions and emotions it tends to be inconsequential and unconvincing, because the Gods are "personified Chance" and *Chance should not play any such part in fiction* (my italics). "Everything invented must have verisimilitude . . . everything that is to arouse our amazement must be explicable by a chain of moral causes; only then will one perceive in such works a philosophic result" [*résultat plus philosophique; ein philosophisches Resultat*].[37] The most admirable parts of works dealing with the Marvelous are those independent of the Marvelous: in Milton's Satan it is the man we admire, what remains with us of Achilles is his human character, one would wish to forget the magic in the passion of Rinaldo for Armida, and the power of the *Aeneid* consists in its expression of such feelings as belong to all hearts at all times. Mme. de Staël does not deny talent to these epic writers, but hopes that future writers will avoid the supernatural, because we can really comprehend only what is compatible with our own experience of men and things. As for allegory: "if its purpose [i.e., the moral idea] be too clearly stated, it becomes tiresome; if concealed, we forget it; if our attention is to be divided [between image and idea] the work tends not to hold our attention at all."[38] The upshot of all this is that the novel—here regarded as the literary form of the future—should concentrate on the depiction of real characters, events and emotions, presenting these as conditioned by and explicable from themselves without reference to outer forces (such as fate or chance) or abstract ideas, and embodying meaning without saying so. The "philosophic result" should be drawn by the reader and emerge from the novel which must be self-contained and self-sufficient, not dependent for its full comprehension on references outside the framework of its action.

"Only the modern novel," the treatise continues, "is able to act usefully on our education by the portrayal of our accustomed feelings" [*sentiments habituels; gewohnten Empfindungen*]. Some have posited a special class of "philosophical novel" but all novels should be philosophical in the sense that, "created from the inner nature of man, they speak back to that

inner nature" (this phrase is Goethe's addition and does not appear in the French original)[39] and this is hardly achieved by
relating all parts of the story to a central idea, because this tends
to lessen verisimilitude in the connection of events (Mme. de
Staël writes *situations*), and "each chapter becomes a sort of allegory, its events being an illustration of the principle which is to
follow." She cites Voltaire's *contes* as examples which, she
thinks, would be more effective if they eschewed the supernatural, if they offered examples rather than parables and if the
whole plot were not so forcibly directed to one and the same
end: "Such novels are like tutors whom children do not believe
because everything that happens must fit in with the lesson they
wish to inculcate: whereas the children have some sense that
there is less orderliness in the true course of events."[40] But the
novels of Richardson and Fielding which keep close to life
[*côtoyer la vie; sich an der Seite des Lebens halten*] in order to
show the "gradations, developments and inconsequences of the
history of the human heart" and at the same time to show "the
continual return from the results of all experience to morality of
action and the advantages of virtue," use fictitious events but
feelings natural to all men. "Only the authority of great masters
could raise the status of the novel," for its low esteem derives
from its portraying ugly vice rather than assembling what may
serve men as a model.[41] The novel affects the morality of individuals, from which public morality derives. The novel as a genre
is held in low repute partly because it has tended to concentrate
on the portrayal of love, a passion which influences youth but
inspires little interest at other stages of life. And yet love is the
basis of all deep and tender feelings. Nevertheless the novel could
and should also deal with other emotions such as ambition, pride,
avarice or vanity. Such emotions are portrayed in historical
writings, but the novelist can probe deeper into the human heart,
so that the moral effect deriving from the "development of inner
movements of the soul" may be even stronger than that of history, since the novelist includes only what is necessary to his

desired effect—a selectivity which history and memoirs cannot maintain.[42]

The moral effect of the novel lies in its power to work through the emotions, a procedure not approved of by some strict philosophers but nevertheless one that corresponds to the way in which human nature works. Virtue must be "animated" if it is to combat the passions. Fiction "exercises the soul in noble passions and thereby accustoms it to them."[43] More morality can be derived from good novels than from many moral treatises. Novels can indeed be even stricter in morality than ethical treatises because by working on our feelings they bring us to accept moral positions which are convincing when demonstrated by example, but which might seem dry or extreme in an abstract treatise; and by portraying dangerous passions the novelist makes the reader aware of their symptoms and growth and therefore more able to recognize and combat such passions.

Mme. de Staël concludes with a tribute to certain novels which cannot be assigned to any class, mentioning *Werther* and *La Nouvelle Héloïse*. Although the purpose or aim is often moral, what remains with the reader is the sense of the omnipotence of the heart. These are isolated, individual works of genius, expressing every motion of passionate characters, books for "burning, sensitive souls" who cannot themselves express what they feel, who would be alone in the world and curse their natures, were it not for such books as these, which "bring them in their loneliness some rays of that joy which evades them in the world," books to give them respite from disappointed hopes, books that become their understanding friends. Such books arouse respect for the suffering heart. "In this life which one traverses better if one feels it less, we should try to detach man from himself, halt the effect of passions and replace them by independent pleasure."[44] This the novelist of genius can do.

In the course of her argument Mme. de Staël makes an assertion which is directly opposed to a claim made in the passage we have been analyzing from the *Apprenticeship*. As we have seen she rejects chance as an element in the novel, on the grounds that chance conflicts with the principle of verisimilitude, for she demands from the novel the same iron logic of cause and effect that drama should have. Her criteria for the structure of a novel are derived from classical French drama of the seventeenth century. The novel, she believes, should follow the pattern of drama, the only difference being that the novel allows more time "to distinguish shadings" [*die Schattierungen abzustufen*, Goethe translates].[45] Life is not so restricted, not presented so much in contrasts, "theatrically," as it must needs be in a play. In other words: whereas the passage in Goethe's novel distinguishes the novel from drama, Mme. de Staël asserts there is no basic distinction. Throughout the eighteenth century there had been considerable debate on whether the structure of the novel should follow that of the epic or that of the drama. Mme. de Staël came down firmly on the side of drama. Not so Goethe who, at least in this passage, saw the novel as an opportunity to express chance, and was therefore, as regards external action, much more in line with the tradition of the romance which, because of its lack of both verisimilitude and dramatic logic, was rejected by Mme. de Staël. To this type of external plot the passage in the *Apprenticeship* adds sentiments, whereas for Mme. de Staël the important thing was characters, which Goethe assigned to drama. And her concept of the "philosophic result" represents a moral demand of which there is no mention in what the actors had arrived at in Goethe's novel. On these four points—the role of chance, the relation to drama, the relative importance of characters and sentiments, and the "philosophic result"—the argument of Mme. de Staël's essay is directly opposed to the passage in the *Apprenticeship*. And yet the passage was composed in the first half of 1795 and the essay translated in October!

Why then should Goethe have been sufficiently interested in this essay to translate it so soon after composing that passage for his novel? The pessimism of the essay's beginning and end represents the residue in Mme. de Staël's mind of the events of The

Terror. Literature was to distract, and to restore one's faith in moral values. All this would have appealed to Goethe, especially at this particular time when his own view of human nature was equally gloomy and his horror at the march of public events equal to hers. The essay is a justification of the writer in such times, particularly of the writer of fiction and specifically of the novelist. Goethe must have been attracted by the envisagement of the novel as the genre that keeps close to ordinary life. There was in him a strong realist trend, but along with it, at least in the Goethe of the middle and late years, went an equally strong belief that art should be something more than mere depiction. He disliked realism that became banal or repulsive; on the other hand he disliked the fanciful which severed all contact with reality. He believed that great literature could and should inculcate ideas, but he disliked outright didacticism. Goethe must therefore have been attracted by the idea that a novel should have a "philosophic result" but without explicit philosophizing, and will have a "moral effect" without moralizing.[46] In like manner he would stand his ground against Schiller's suggestion that he should make more explicit the relation of the various elements in *Wilhelm Meister's Apprenticeship* to the philosophic idea of the whole. And the assertion at the end of the essay that a novel like *Werther* has its own special kind of moral effect must have appealed to him greatly just at this time when he was revising the novel so as to obviate too great an identification with Werther on the part of readers. He recognized, in his letters to Schiller of October 1795, a certain disunity in Mme. de Staël's essay[47] and although he did not specify where he sensed this, the praise of the personal novel at the end may well have seemed to him inconsistent with the general thesis of the novel as a positive force in development of public morality, as it has to certain modern critics. But, in fact, Mme. de Staël was implying that the personal novel, by demonstrating the great power of passion, can help passionate people to detach themselves from themselves and that this is a moral effect. Most important of all considerations was perhaps the high place that she accorded to the novel. It was in her opinion the genre of the future. We must remember that Goethe while translating her essay was also completing a novel on the grand scale, of deeply serious content, on which he had been working for nearly twenty years, a novel that was to become the most important novel in German literature.

Goethe had been much occupied, at least since the Italian journey of 1786–1788, with the problem of how to present reality in art so that prosaic reality may acquire the greater truth of poetic reality by embodying ideas. Art must be rooted in the real incidents of experience but it must also express meaning, Goethe believed, not directly by abstract philosophizing or interpretative commentary, but through consequential form such as life itself does not possess, and by symbolic vistas. On a journey to Frankfurt in August 1797 Goethe expressed in a letter to Schiller his puzzlement that certain real impressions of the journey tended to induce in him a reflective frame of mind which he could account for only by suggesting that such momentary impressions connected up somehow with his general, total experience. These impressions were, says Goethe, "what a felicitous subject is for the poet, namely felicitous objects for the observer and since in the mere fact of recalling them one cannot give them poetic form, one must needs give them an ideal form, a 'human' form in the highest sense—and this [process] has been connoted by that much misused expression 'sentimental' "[48]—so that his journey might be termed a "sentimental journey." Goethe is here using the term "sentimental" in Schiller's sense of the relating of the objects of direct personal experience to ideas, and is punning on Sterne's title. Schiller replies to Goethe with a notable statement (letter of 7 September 1797):

The sentimental phenomenon in you does not disturb me and it seems to me that you have yourself explained it adequately. It is a need of poetic natures, or perhaps one should say of all human minds, to tolerate as little emptiness as possible around them, to appropriate to themselves through feeling as much world as possible, to seek out the depth of all appearances and to postulate everywhere that humanity is a whole. If the object is individually empty and hence without poetic content, then one's faculty for ideas [*Ideen-vermögen*] will try to grasp it from its symbolic side and thus make language for humanity out of it. But the sentimental (in the good sense of the word) is always an effect of the poetic striving which, from reasons either in the object or in the mind, is not completely fulfilled. This poetic demand, without a true poetic mood and without a poetic subject, seems to be your situation, and consequently what you are experiencing is merely the general story of the sentimental mode of feeling and corroborates everything we agreed on together about it.

But I must remind you of one thing. You express yourself as though all this depended on the object—which I cannot grant. The object must of course *mean* something, just as the poetic object must *be* something, but in the last resort it depends on the *mind* whether an object means anything to it, and hence emptiness or richness of content [*das Leere und Gehaltreiche*] lies more in the subject than in the object. It is the mind which sets the bounds here, and it is in the treatment, not in the choice of material, that I feel, here as everywhere, something to be either commonplace or interesting [*das Gemeine oder Geistreiche*]. What the two places you mention were for you, any street or bridge or ship or plough or any other mechanical tool would perhaps have been to a more open poetic mood [*Stimmung*]. Do not therefore dispel these sentimental impressions: give them expression as often as you can. Nothing but the poetic so cleanses the mind of the empty and commonplace as such observation of objects, a world is placed thereby into the individual thing, and flat appearances take on thereby a boundless depth. If this is not poetic, it is, as you yourself say, human; and the human is always the beginning of the poetic which is but the peak of the human.[49]

Schiller returns to the topic a week later (letter of 17 September):

Two things belong to the poet and artist: that he rise above the real and that he remain within the sensual [*innerhalb des Sinnlichen*, i.e., that perceptible by and that belonging to the senses]. When both these things are combined we have aesthetic art [*ästhetische Kunst*]. But in unfavorable, formless nature it is all too easy for the artist to leave the sensual as well as the real, to become idealistic and, if his understanding is weak, maybe fantastic: or if, compelled by his own nature, he will and must remain within the sensual, then he also tends to remain with the real and becomes narrowly realistic or, if he lacks imagination, slavish and banal. In either case he is therefore not aesthetic.

It is the reduction of empirical forms to aesthetic forms which is the difficult operation and here it is usually either body or spirit, either truth or freedom that is lacking. The ancient models, both in poetry and the plastic arts, seem to me preeminently to have demonstrated the value of presenting empirical nature already reduced to aesthetic nature and, if we study them deeply, they can provide us with hints on the process of this reduction. From despair at being unable to reduce to aesthetic nature that empirical nature which surrounds him, the modern artist of lively mind and fancy prefers to leave this empirical reality and seek help in the imagination against it, placing a poetic content into his work which would otherwise be empty and meagre because the content which must be drawn from the depths of the [real] object is lacking.[50]

The problem of how to be realistic without being banal was, for both Goethe and Schiller, that of how to transcend the real and yet remain within reality. Given Mme. de Staël's statement of the nature of the novel, it was obviously the most fundamental problem for any novelist.

The year 1797, in which this exchange of letters took place, was one in which Goethe was much concerned with matters central or tangential to a definition of the novel as a genre. Earlier in that year, on 19 April in fact, he had returned to the concept of retardation, suggesting that retarding motifs were essentially "epic." He no longer made any distinction between retardation of the action by sentiments of the main character (in the novel) and retardation of the action by factors outside of the main character (in the drama), which had been advanced in the passage in *Wilhelm Meister's Apprenticeship*; he was now concerned with retardation as a general feature of narrative, with what he termed "retarding motifs."[51] Schiller approached the matter from a somewhat different angle: action, he said, is only the means in the epic, whereas it is the end in drama. Hence epics should avoid subjects which arouse such strong feelings that the action becomes too absorbing to serve as a means towards a more general aesthetic purpose. Each part of an epic should have its independent value, each point in the action should be equally interesting. At this time Goethe was planning a second epic (*Hermann and Dorothea* was already completed), to be entitled *The Hunt*. It was never written, but the subject became that of the *Novella* of 1827. Goethe was concerned by the fact that the action of *The Hunt* would move consistently towards the resolution and therefore contain no retarding motifs. Schiller replied that retardation can be conveyed not merely by the nature of the action but by the nature of its progression [*Art des Wegs—Art des Gehens*, letter of 25 April]; but that the element of surprise included in the plan (presumably at the climax) was more proper to comedy and would be hard to integrate into an epic poem. Goethe's plan has not survived, but from letters of Schiller and of Wilhelm von Humboldt (both of whom knew about it) we learn that the poem was to be concerned with a German prince, just returned from the wars, and a group of noblemen who set out to hunt wild animals, especially a lion and a tiger, which have escaped from a village circus during a fire. There is no indication in these letters of what the surprise was to be but we can probably assume that it was somewhat similar to the end of the *Novella* of 1827, where it is the innocent fearlessness and faith of a child that conquers danger and passion. We can, I think, assume this because Goethe himself told Eckermann that although in detail the *Novella* was a totally different work from what *The Hunt* was to have been, "the action and the course of the development remain unchanged."[52] In 1797 Goethe took seriously the objections of Schiller, and apparently also of Humboldt, to the subject and let it drop. When he took it up again in 1826, it became a prose work, and specifically a novella in accordance with the conception he had developed of that genre as centering on "something unusual that has happened" [*eine sich ereignete unerhörte Begebenheit*], on an individual motif which has something striking and surprising about it.[53] The ending of the *Novella* is lyrical and symbolic, with the ultimate climax in a song; but the beginning is quite realistic. This has disturbed and still disturbs many readers. To Eckermann's criticism that the ending was "too lonely, too ideal, too lyrical" and his question whether some of the other characters should not reappear to give the conclusion more breadth, Goethe replied that this would have made the ending *prosaic*, and that he wanted it to rise to a final, single climax like a solitary flower produced from a whole mass of leaves and stem—this flower to represent the idea-content of the work, namely that the untamed and invincible is controlled better by love and piety than by force. The "real" exposition was there solely for the sake of this "ideal" climax. "For what value has the real *per se?*" Goethe continued to Eckermann, "We are pleased if reality is presented with truth, and this may give us a clearer knowledge of certain things: but the actual gain for our higher nature lies only in the ideal [*dem Idealen*] which has proceeded from the heart of the poet."[54] This was perhaps his final word on the relationship between idea and reality in fiction. To remain within reality and yet rise to poetic truth, to transform (in Schiller's words) empirical into aesthetic forms, Goethe moved in the course of the *Novella* from prose through rhythmic prose into verse.

The *Novella* is not a novel, but there are several important points made in this conversation which bear on Goethe's attitude to the novel. First: in wrestling with the subject of his *Novella* Goethe clearly delineated the novella as a form, distinguishing it from the epic and, implicitly, from the novel. Secondly: for Goethe surface realism is insufficient; it must culminate in some expression of the "idea" perceived in the subject matter. That this expression is symbolic rather than direct and abstract keeps the work inside poetry and preserves the contact with real things. Thirdly: the lyric poem is often the necessary means to express this symbolic dimension because it represents in language a similar elevation from the ordinary to that of the "ideal" in the content. Similar considerations had already affected the form of all Goethe's novels, without his being able or wishing to present them in such conscious theoretical formulation as here.

It is instructive to look back from this conversation of 1827 to the year 1797 when Goethe was searching for a concept and definition of the novel that would justify his affection for the form and solve the problem of how to produce a poetically satisfying work out of what was essentially "prosaic" material. On 20 October 1797 Schiller had written to him that the novel-form was "decidedly not poetic" [*schlechterdings nicht poetisch*]:

It lies solely and entirely in the sphere of reason [*des Verstandes*], is subject to all the demands and partakes of all the limitations of the reason. But when a truly poetic spirit [like Goethe's] has made use of this form and expressed the most poetic states [*die poetischsten Zustände*] in this form, then a strange vacillation between prosaic and poetic mood arises which I find difficult to describe. I might say that Meister (I mean the novel) lacks a certain poetic boldness, because, as a novel, it always has to satisfy the reason, and yet on the other hand that real sobriety [*Nüchternheit*] which it itself to a certain extent invokes as an expectation, is lacking because the work has emanated from a poetic mind. . . .

Since you now have reached the point where you must demand the very highest of yourself and the objective and the subjective must absolutely coalesce, then it is above all necessary to make sure that what your mind puts into a work shall always employ purest form and nothing get lost in an impure medium.[55]

In his polite, but somewhat testy answer, Goethe wrote:

What you say about Meister I understand full well. It is all true and more besides. It was its imperfection [*Unvollkommenheit*] which gave me most trouble. A pure form helps and sustains, whereas an impure form is always hindering and dragging. But let it be what it is: it will not easily happen to me again that I make a mistake [*mich . . . vergreife*] both as regards subject and form, and let us wait to see what genius may grant us in the autumn of our lives.

Good luck with Wallenstein.

There is heavy irony here, for Schiller was to have equal trouble fusing the poetic with the prosaic in *Wallenstein*.

This exchange of letters has often been used to prove that Goethe had a low opinion of the novel as a genre.[56] But this is wrong. When Goethe speaks of "impure form" [*unreine Form*] he does not mean inferior or inadequate: he means that it is not a pure (i.e., completely) *poetic* form like that of a tragedy or an epic, but a mixed form because it is part prose, part poetry. He recognizes that this must be the case because, as Schiller had pointed out in his own terms, a novel is necessarily subject to the formal, structural demands of prose, which are not those of poetry. There is, however, an element of confusion in this exchange of opinions: for we should note that Schiller talks of "purest *form*" but of "impure *medium*." Medium is not form; and Goethe, in his reply, is implying this, for his contrast is between "pure form" and "impure form." The problem is how to achieve pure form in an impure medium. "Pure" here means poetic, and "impure" means non-poetic or prose. Schiller seems to suggest that this is impossible to achieve—the most one could arrive at was a vacillation between poetry and prose. Goethe was to prove that it was possible: the novel could, and would in his hands, combine poetry and prose.

During this same important year, 1797, Goethe and Schiller returned to the concept of retardation in the essay "On Epic and Dramatic Poetry," of dual authorship. This essay (which was not published until 1827) attempts to distinguish between the two genres with reference to the various types of motif that they employ. Motifs are classified into five categories: progressive, regressive, retarding, recalling and forestalling. Progressive motifs (those furthering the action) are used especially in drama; regressive motifs (those preventing the action from reaching its goal) are used almost exclusively in the epic. Retarding motifs (those slowing up progress towards the goal), recalling motifs (introducing what happened before the work begins) and forestalling motifs (anticipating what will happen after the time covered by the work) are common to both epic and dramatic writers. The real distinction between the two genres is, therefore, in the use of progressive or regressive motifs. Retarding motifs are here, in contrast to the passage in the *Apprenticeship*, no longer considered as belonging primarily to the epic, or the novel. Elsewhere in the essay we read this passage:

> The world of fancies [*Phantasien*], presentiments, apparitions [*Erscheinungen*], chance and fate occurrences [*Zufälle und Schicksale*]. These are open to both [the epic and the drama], but they must of course be related to the sensually perceptible [*sinnliche*] world, which creates a difficulty for modern [poets], for it is difficult to find a correspondence to the wondrous beings, gods, prophesiers and oracles of antiquity, desirable as that would be.[57]

The contrast between fate and chance, so basic to the passage in the *Apprenticeship*, has therefore also been abandoned, and we now find them lumped together. In a letter to Schiller of 23 December Goethe expressed his regret "that we moderns are so inclined to mix genres, and that we are not even able to distinguish them from each other," and then went on to observe that the categories worked out in the essay "On Epic and Dramatic Poetry" did not fit his epic *Hermann and Dorothea*, which contained no exclusively regressive motives; nor did the events between the death of Hector and the departure of the Greeks from Troy, the subject of a second epic poem on which he was at work at that time (the *Achilleis*, which was never to be finished).[58] Goethe in this essay was primarily concerned with justifying the epic as a form of modern literature, but much of what the essay says about the nature of plot in a narrative work has reference also to the novel. Goethe concludes this particular letter to Schiller with a gesture of despair at all theory of genres: "So much on what I perceive at present, *salvo meliori* [for lack of something better] for, if I am not mistaken, then this material, like so much else, cannot really be expressed in theoretical terms. What genius has achieved, we can see; who is to say what it may or should achieve."

So far Goethe. But the impassioned theoretician Schiller was not to be put off so easily. Three days later he replies to Goethe's letter saying that, as for him, he had found the categories worked out in the joint essay very useful in determining what sort of subject was suited to each of the two genres. And he then goes on to suggest a new contrast, which concerns the manner of presentation in drama and the epic.

> Dramatic action moves before me. I myself move around epic action so that it seems to stand still. . . . If an event moves before my eyes then I am riveted to the physical here-and-now and my imagination has lost all freedom, there is a continual unrest in me. I must remain with the object, no looking back or thinking over is possible because I am following an outside force. But if I move *around* the event, which cannot evade me, then I can break step, linger for a longer or shorter time according to my subjective need, take steps backward, or forward, and so on. This accords very well with the concept of the Past [*Vergangensein*], which can be thought of as static, and the concept of narration [*Erzählen*], for the narrator knows the end already at the beginning and in the middle, and hence every moment of the action is of equal value to him and he maintains calm freedom throughout.
>
> The epic writer must treat his event as completely past, the dramatist as completely present. . . .[59]

Important is the recognition here made that a narrator can pause, delay, look back, look forward, offer reflections and commentary, and that Schiller considered this desirable. He has therefore transmuted the concept of retardation of *plot* into that of the reflective *narrator*. In the same letter he remarks that all poetry tends to give actuality to what has happened, and the epic poet strives to make past happenings present without obliterating the sense of their being past. Also that poetry tends to make what is actually present—the here-and-now—recede by *Idealität*, transposing the real into an idea, so that the dramatic poet "holds at a remove from us that reality which impinges on us as individuals and thus endows the [spectator's] mind with poetic freedom towards material" [*Stoff*]. But each of the two genres tends naturally towards the other—the epic towards ideality, the drama towards actuality. But this, Schiller asserts, does not imply or justify mixture of genres.

Yet even Schiller was not satisfied with this frantic but, one must admit, brilliant search for definition. For in his next letter to Goethe he wrote: "In order to exclude from a work all that does not belong to its genre [*Gattung*], one must be sure to include all that does belong to it. And this is just what is lacking. Because we cannot assemble the conditions governing each of the two genres, we are compelled to mix them." Goethe's reply to this (30 December 1797) was: "I share your opinion that one should strictly separate only in order that one may then permit oneself later the introduction of extraneous elements [*fremdartiger Teile*]. One works quite differently from principles than from instinct, and a deviation of whose necessity one is convinced cannot become a fault. These theoretical reflections cannot occupy me any longer, I must get back to work."

If we put the passage from the *Apprenticeship* alongside all this, it is clear that most of the points made in the former have now been abandoned. It has proven impossible to distinguish clearly between the novel and the drama. There is no more talk about the sovereign importance of sentiments, and the distinction between deeds and events, as well as that between fate and chance, is no longer used as a means of differentiation. And the concept of retardation is first modified and then abandoned. But we must never forget that the passage we have so thoroughly examined is a passage in a novel, and is the result of a fictitious discussion between fictitious characters preparing to perform *Hamlet* and trying to understand it better.[60] It is obviously not Goethe's final word on the novel as a form, for, as we have seen, most of its points have been abandoned by the end of 1797—two years later. But in its delineation of the genre and in what it says about sentiments and plot, it is a perfect justification of one

particular novel, namely the novel in which it occurs. And in
what it says about the novel hero, it is a perfect description of
Wilhelm Meister himself, who fully believes that events are
fashioned after his sentiments and that he guides and controls
the workings of chance. But the narrator, as we shall see, thinks
otherwise.

6

Fate and Chance

The reworking of the six books of the *Theatrical Mission* into the first four books of the *Apprenticeship* was extensive, radical, and masterly. Everything is pared down to essentials, and much colorful detail has been lost in the process. Wilhelm's childhood, now related by him to Mariane, is presented not as a process of development but solely in relation to his idealization of the theater. Everything that was part of Goethe's aim of giving a broad picture of contemporary theatrical life is cut out: the debate on Corneille, *Belshazzar*, Mme. de Retti, and the financial squabbles are completely gone. On the other hand, everything is structured anew around the organizing idea of Apprenticeship, and this is apparent from the start. There is a much greater security evident in the handling of the plot, and the narrator maintains from the beginning an ironical stance toward his hero, now characterized as a "young, affectionate, unfledged merchant's son" by Mariane's rather mercenary maid on the second page of the novel. There are also additions which serve to clarify the emerging outlines of the general theme. The most important of these are two conversations of Wilhelm with mysterious strangers, the earlier entry of Philine into the action and a new character, the Countess,[1] an impassioned, endangered person whose aristocratic beauty and grace arouse tender emotions in Wilhelm and in whom he sees the positive side of high social life. This latter had not been presented in the *Theatrical Mission* but is important for the counterpoint of the *Apprenticeship*.

The fourth book of the *Apprenticeship* ends with the cutting

111

of Wilhelm's lifeline by Aurelie, and the fifth begins with the
news of the death of Wilhelm's father, his hesitations whether
or not to join the acting troupe under Serlo's direction, his decision to do so, and the vision of the Amazon. Here is a summary
of the rest of the action for the sake of readers who are not well
acquainted with the novel:

In a letter to his brother-in-law Werner, Wilhelm defends the theater as the only place where he, as a burgher and not an aristocrat,
can be a public person and yet develop his inner self. It is only
after this that he signs the contract with Serlo and Mignon tries to
draw his hand away from signing it. Preparations now begin in
earnest for the performance of *Hamlet,* with Wilhelm to play
Hamlet and Aurelie to play Ophelia. The question is: who is to play
the Ghost? Wilhelm receives a mysterious message that the Ghost
will appear and at the right moment, and he and Serlo decide to
rely on this. Meanwhile there are extensive discussions about the
play, one of which leads in to the passage on novel and drama that
was discussed in the last chapter, and the performance finally takes
place. It is a great success and the Ghost does appear at the right
moment, with a voice that sounds to Wilhelm like that of his own
father. During the night after the performance an unidentified
woman caresses Wilhelm in his bed. He is uncertain whether this is
Mignon, whose development into a woman he has recently become
aware of, or Philine; but it turns out to be Philine. The person who
played the Ghost has left behind a veil embroidered with the words:
"For the first and last time! Flee, young man, flee!." Preparations for
a second performance are prevented when the theater catches fire.
This seems to be the work of the Harper, who is now close to mad-
ness. The Harper threatens a boy named Felix, who is apparently
the child of Aurelie, during the ensuing confusion, but the child is
saved by Mignon's appeal to Wilhelm who thereby acquires a
strong sense of responsibility for Mignon and Felix, "the children,"
as he calls them. Aurelie gives one last impassioned performance, as
the Countess Orsina, the cast-off mistress of the prince in Lessing's
Emilia Galotti, and then declines and dies. But while she is on her
deathbed Wilhelm reads to her a manuscript which the doctor has
given him to read her. As she dies Aurelie gives him a letter to carry
to her lover Lothario, who had abandoned her.

At the end of Book Five Wilhelm is already veering away from the ideal of the theater as a form of life. The actors drift out of the novel at this point, leaving only Mignon and Felix as Wilhelm's inheritance.

Book Six consists of the manuscript that Wilhelm read to Aurelie. It is entitled *Confessions of a Beautiful Soul* and is the spiritual biography of a woman who had found respite from the torments of her passionate nature in a practical, pietistic form of religion.

At the beginning of Book Seven, Wilhelm journeys to Lothario's castle to deliver Aurelie's letter. He again meets the second of the two strangers he had encountered in the early part of the novel (in the *Apprenticeship*, but not in the *Theatrical Mission*), who is now an Abbé. He tells Wilhelm not to feel that his past activity with the theater was wasted time, and to press on to "the next thing." At Lothario's castle Wilhelm finds both the Abbé and Jarno, and the bag of a doctor attending Lothario looks strangely like that of the surgeon who had attended Wilhelm when he was wounded and first saw the Amazon. Conversations take place about living one's life according to an idea, and the danger of extreme fixed ideas, such as the Harper's sense of being pursued by evil fate. A contrast is now provided to the excessive inwardness of the Harper's internal disorder and the internal order of the "Beautiful Soul" of the sixth book, in the person of Therese, a neighboring landowner, who lives according to an excessive sense of external order. Wilhelm is attracted by Therese's clarity and orderliness and decides that she is the right person to be entrusted with the care of Mignon and Felix. In the castle of Lothario there is a mysterious tower to which no one is allowed access, and Wilhelm tries to find out more about it. Meanwhile he has been told that Felix is not the child of Lothario and Aurelie as he had suspected, but his own child by Mariane, who had remained faithful to him and died in miserable circumstances. Wilhelm therefore now decides to keep Felix with him and send only Mignon to Therese. But Mignon does not wish to be separated from Wilhelm and says that she longs for the Harper. "No one knows what I owe to him," she says. She agrees to go to Therese only if Felix may go as well. Wilhelm therefore sends both children to Therese. He now takes his official departure from the theatrical profession and writes to Werner that he is associating himself with a group of men who will lead him to "pure and secure activity." Next day he is taken into a hall where he meets again, one by one, the mysterious strangers who have intervened at various points in

his life. Finally he is given his indentures as testimony to the successful completion of his apprenticeship. He now asks whether it is
really true that Felix is his son, and is told that by asking that question he has shown that his apprenticeship is completed: "Nature has
declared you free." The various persons we have encountered in this
seventh book are all members of a Society of the Tower which
guides men's lives by bringing them to self-knowledge, or says
it does.

At the beginning of the eighth and last book of the novel we find
Wilhelm no longer relating life to himself nor to preconceived ideas
but experiencing the world anew through the eyes of Felix. He
begins to plan his life with reference to Felix, and decides to offer
his hand to Therese. Mignon is with Lothario's sister. Wilhelm has
already discovered that the Countess is Lothario's sister and assumes
this will be she. But when he gets to the house where Mignon is,
he discovers that this sister is none other than the mysterious "Amazon." Her name is Natalie, and she is Lothario's other sister. Mignon
is ailing. Wilhelm talks to Natalie about the education of children,
and she expresses her belief in allowing personalities to develop
through error, but only if one also imparts to them certain "laws"
which give a certain security to hold on to. Wilhelm feels intellectually and emotionally drawn towards Natalie, but he has already
offered his hand to Therese, and a letter arrives from her accepting
his proposal. But when Therese arrives in person, Mignon collapses
and dies, with her hand on her heart, at Natalie's feet. Wilhelm is
deeply affected by the loss of Mignon, and in his thoughts she is
somehow connected with Natalie: "In his spirit all was bare and
empty; only the images of Mignon and Natalie hovered like shadows
before his imagination." Throughout the novel Natalie, as the Amazon, has been the unrealized goal of his aspirations. Natalie, not
Therese, is the necessary companion for him, as Mignon's death at
her feet indicates. For Mignon represents man's desire for fulfillment
despite her inability to say what this fulfillment shall consist in.
Wilhelm now inveighs against the Society of the Tower for their
interference in human lives, and all he wants to do is to go off alone
with Felix and wander through the world. But he is held back by
the exequies of Mignon and his concern about the fate of the
Harper. He is full of uneasiness, haunted by a sense of fragments of
experiences which do not connect into a meaningful whole. The
funeral of Mignon takes place in a hall with the inscription *memento
vivere* and at this occasion he is bidden back into life, with a chorus

describing her as the "formative force" [*bildende Kraft*]. Nothing was clear about Mignon, says the Abbé, except her love for Wilhelm, but that consumed her. We are then told that Mignon was the child of the Harper, who had been a monk, and his sister Sperata, whom he at first had not known to be his sister. Hence his oppressive sense of guilt. The Harper now has in his possession a glass of opium, so that the knowledge that he can at any time himself end the sorrows of life gives him the strength to bear these sorrows. But Felix falls ill and the Harper, believing that Felix has drunk the opium, kills himself. Concern over Felix brings all the characters close together, and especially Wilhelm and Natalie. But it is not Providence nor fate nor education nor character, nothing sublime or moral, that brings the final resolution of the action of the novel: Felix is saved from death because he had always drunk out of the bottle instead of using a glass, and has therefore not consumed the opium as the Harper thought, and Wilhelm is finally brought to a union with Natalie by someone eavesdropping and hearing that she desires such a union. The eavesdropper is one Friedrich, a young man who lives life to the full and has never been held back in so doing by ruminations. It is he who points to the fact that Wilhelm is in love and that the union with Natalie is the keystone to his years of apprenticeship, so that like Saul the son of Kish, he "went out to seek his father's asses, and found a kingdom." "I do not know the value of a kingdom," says Wilhelm in the last words of the novel, "but what I do know is that I have found good fortune [*Glück*, in the sense of both "luck" and "happiness"] which I do not deserve and would not exchange for anything in the world."

The striking thing about the plot-line of *Wilhelm Meister's Apprenticeship* is that it is full of coincidences—unexpected meetings, mysterious occurrences, sensational events and an admixture of supernaturalism only partly accounted for rationally by the hocus-pocus of the Society of the Tower. Chance seems to be rampant and even though the activities of the Society of the Tower are, in the Society's own assertions, *guided* chance, the two events that bring the novel to its conclusion—Felix's bad drinking habits and Friedrich's eavesdropping—are completely outside their control. So are Philine, Mignon and the Harper. So also is Natalie who, as we shall see, represents a higher force than the rationalistic pedagogics of the Society. As a plot this is essentially in the tradition of the romance: and, as Marianne Thalmann and Hildegard Emmel have shown, many elements of it are in keeping with popular, sensational fiction of the time. Readers of such literature, for instance, would not have been a bit surprised by the appearance of the unrehearsed Ghost in the performance of *Hamlet:* it was exactly what they, from their reading, would have expected to happen.[2] Goethe liked such surprises: they were for him the stuff of the novel. Events had, for him, their own place and appeal; he delighted in the unexpected, his novel is intended to hold the attention by mystifying and finally leading up to the revelation of secrets. There are also plenty of sentiments to occupy us on the way, although the novel never degenerates into discussion for its own sake. The mysteries of the novel are ultimately rooted in the question whether fate or chance is operative.[3] If a succession of incidents is to be anything more than a disconnected number of occurrences, there must be some rhythm or shape discernible—in a plot, though this is not necessarily so in life. In *Wilhelm Meister's Apprenticeship* Goethe was wrestling with the whole problem of plot. Basically the novel is concerned with development, and how development takes place.[4] Of primary concern therefore is the impact of external factors upon an inner development, of events on sentiments. Partly because of his delight in the unusual and the unexpected, but more because of his acceptance of the existence and the importance of such events in the texture of human experience, he worked into the structure of his novel much that does not have clear psychological or rational grounding, much that does not belong "to the realm of reason," to use Schiller's phrase.[5] And throughout the novel Wilhelm is made to ponder these things. His sentiments are much concerned with events, though events are not fashioned after his sentiments, even though he would like to think that they were.

The novel works through oppositions, and the most important of these is that between fate and chance. Wilhelm at the beginning is prone to believe in fate. When his father sends him on the journey he perceives "the beckoning hand of guiding fate" in this circumstance.[6] It is also, he thinks, fate that leads him through Mariane to the theater. There was even fate in the sale of his grandfather's paintings, which, he asserts to the Stranger at the end of Book One, led him away from lifeless pictures to the living theater. The Stranger objects that young men are apt to explain their own desires in terms of the workings of external forces. The texture of the world, he says, is woven of necessity and chance, man's reason stands between and can control them by treating necessity as the basis of existence and manipulating chance to his use: but if man imputes arbitrariness to necessity and sense to chance, this is the abandonment of reason and indulgence in inclination; it is mistaken piety to assign pleasant chance-phenomena to the workings of divine guidance. But, says Wilhelm, do not chance-phenomena sometimes set one on a path towards a goal one had hardly envisioned, and is not this conducive to a belief in fate? The Stranger replies that each of us has his fortune [*Glück*] in his own hands as does the artist his raw material, to which he and only he can give form. But: "This art [of shaping one's fortune, one's *Glück*] is like all others: only the capacity [*Fähigkeit*] is inborn in us, the art must be learnt and carefully practised."[7]

This parallel between life and art now links up with Wilhelm's defense of the artist to Werner in Book Two, which had seemed more Goethe than Wilhelm in the *Theatrical Mission*. Wilhelm praises to Werner the higher vision of the poet by means of which he works over and transforms into meaning the raw material of life: "the poet lives the dream of life as a man who is awake, and the strangest of occurrences is for him both past and future alike."[8] Wilhelm works himself into the belief that the break-off from Mariane was "organized by fate for his advantage."[9] Despite the talk with the First Stranger, he has therefore in no wise abandoned his belief in fate. And his view of the poet, here advanced, as a bird soaring above the sordid pressures of life, nesting in treetops and feeding on buds and fruits, is patently false in its insistence that "fate" has thus elevated the poet above all other men. For what the First Stranger had said was that the ability and indeed necessity to give form to experience is innate in *all* men. When Wilhelm encounters the Second Stranger on a boat trip (the incident occurs in the ninth chapter of the second book), the conversation begins with art and only then broadens out into some comments on fate. The two conversations therefore proceed in opposite directions, and we should notice this. To Wilhelm's question whether a "fortunate temperament" is not all that the artist needs, the Stranger asserts that "cultivation" [*Bildung*] is the necessary correlate and underlines the formative value of external conditions. Wilhelm immediately starts talking about fate again, but the Stranger objects to the idea of education through fate, because fate must needs work through the clumsy medium of chance: take the case of someone destined by fate for the theater who is brought by chance into contact with a puppet theater and is thereby hamstrung in his histrionic development. To Wilhelm's surprise at this example he replies that it was given him by chance. The reader may well be puzzled that to illustrate the clumsiness of chance the Stranger has been given by clumsy chance an example which is not at all clumsy but extremely apposite. Such is the complex irony of this book. Wilhelm speaks of being "warned" by his experience with Mariane. It is clear that Wilhelm can only find meaning by accepting the concept of fate. Hence his statement to the Harper that the latter's song had released everything that was pent up in his, Wilhelm's, heart. This song,

> Who never ate his bread with tears,
> Who never sat upon his bed
> Weeping through anguished nights of grief,
> He knows you not, you heavenly powers.
>
> You lead us into life, and then
> Leave the poor man to become guilty,
> And then abandon him to pain;
> For all guilt is repaid [*rächt sich*] on earth,

recognizes suffering and assigns it to the workings of fate or destiny. But the song of Mignon, whom after the news of Mariane's pregnancy he accepts as a substitute child and an embodiment of responsibility, is one of longing for fulfillment with the suggestion that the path of longing leads out of this world:

> Knowst thou the mountain and its path of clouds?
> The mule seeks out in mist its way,
> In caverns dwell the ancient brood of dragons,
> The rock falls sheer and over it the flood;
> Knowst thou this place?
> Thither! Thither
> Goes our way; o father, let us go!

"Dahin *geht* unser Weg"; there is no choice; and it is fraught with danger and possibly involves death.

Although Willhelm is aware that he ought to move on, he is held back by his newly acquired sense of responsibility for Mignon and the Harper. The outer forces are already working, although so far only through people. For he agrees (with Philine) that people mean more than things: "Man is the most interesting thing for man. . . . Everything else that surrounds us, is either just element in which we live, or instrument which we use."[10] This is a clear reference back to the two conversations with the two strangers. And the question is whether to accept a concept of circumstances as "element in which we live" (in the terms of the Second Stranger) or as "instrument which we use" (in the terms of the First). The opposition of fate and chance has become interwoven with that of inner or outer form-giving. The narrator emphasizes the ambiguity of his theme in the last sentence of Book Three. Speaking of the parting of Wilhelm from the Countess he says: "Unhappy pair! What strange warning of Chance or Fate was it that tore them apart?" In other words, is chance so clumsy after all? Is this also a warning, as Wilhelm had tried to persuade himself of his break with Mariane? Is it chance, or fate? Does it point to some meaning, some sense in life—or not?

Meanwhile as Wilhelm reads Shakespeare in a room "to which only Mignon and the Harper were willingly allowed access"[11] (significant fact), he asserts that he stands before the open folios of fate in which the howling storms of action blow the pages back and forth. Reading, in these circumstances, must have been rather difficult; but it is not so much a question of reading Shakespeare as of reading into Shakespeare an external confirmation of what Wilhelm wants to believe. For, as we have seen, having first asserted that he experiences new emotions, Wilhelm then begins to see in this experience the workings of some outside force, and claims that he finds fulfilled and developed here all the presentiments [*Vorgefühle*] he had ever had about men "and their fates."[12] He interprets Shakespeare therefore as a confirmation of his belief in fate, and the immediate effect is to arouse in him a stronger desire to plunge into the world of action. Jarno encourages him, but at the same time makes derogatory remarks about Mignon and the Harper. Wilhelm is "dismayed," "deeply wounded," and breaks out in reproaches against Jarno as a "moribund man of the world" who represents "the apparent sagacity" of the world.[13] What Jarno has to offer cannot outweigh what binds Wilhelm to Mignon and the Harper. For although Jarno had given him the book, it is read in a place consecrated to Mignon and the Harper.

Book Three had ended with the question: what strange warning "of Chance or Fate" [*des Zufalls oder der Schickung*] had torn Wilhelm from the Countess? The phrase recurs in the first pages of Book Four: the Harper, Wilhelm decides, is one who "by Chance or Fate" [*durch Zufall oder Schickung*] had loaded great guilt upon himself. The Harper feels that he does not "belong to himself" but to an inexorable fate [*einem unerbittlichen Schicksale*]; in terms of the tension between inner force and outer force, he represents the extreme standpoint of recognizing only outer force. He wanders so that his unhappy *Genius* may not catch up with him. Wilhelm asserts that the Harper lives "in a presentiment of strange connections and premonitions,"[14] which is exactly what he feels too, as he has told us with reference to Shakespeare. Hence his sense of kinship with the Harper. But Wilhelm's view is optimistic: "we will see whose genius is stronger, your black one or my white one." The same ambiguity that pervades the poem *Wanderer's Storm-Song* as to whether *Genius*—the driving and pursuing force—is internal or external, is here apparent. At this point in the novel Wilhelm is caught in the ambiguity, whereas the Harper accepts only external fate:

> And the beautiful image of the whole world
> Breaks to pieces around his guilty head.
>
> [*Und über seinem schuld'gen Haupte bricht / das schöne Bild der ganzen Welt zusammen*].

The sense of any meaningful order in life has departed from the Harper. Wilhelm self-confidently thinks he has it, though he is still confused by the words of the two strangers and by his growing self-identification with Hamlet. This latter develops after his failure in responsible action against the robbers. And immediately before the *Hamlet* analysis, Wilhelm takes stock. The "protecting spirit" in which he hopefully believes has so far produced confusion. The threads of his "Fate" are tangled into knots and he longs for some "Chance" to unravel or cut them, he says.[15] In other words he looks to some external force to solve his problem. But none comes. Instead he grows increasingly aware of the failure of his inner force, but puts the blame on external circumstances. He broods on Hamlet's "The time is out of joint; O cursed spite, / That ever I was born to set it right!" and he explains Ophelia to Aurelie in similar terms: "The whole structure of her existence breaks at the joints . . . and the lovely building collapses completely."[16] Ophelia is therefore linked with both Hamlet and the Harper. And Wilhelm would like to identify himself with Hamlet.

Wilhelm's conception of Hamlet is that of a prince deprived of his expected destiny, a tender vessel into which an oak tree is planted, a soul unable to cope with the action demanded of it, "die der Tat *nicht gewachsen ist*."[17] In the immediately preceding chapter Wilhelm has been talking of the inability of himself and the actors to ward off the marauding robbers, "es ergriff sie eine Gefahr, der sie *nicht gewachsen waren*."[18] He knows that his fault is inactivity and finds consolation in identifying himself with Hamlet, as the echoing phrase clearly indicates. In his own life he is disturbed by the fact that his one self-reliant assumption of responsibility for the fortunes of the troupe has ended in failure: in the play he imputes Hamlet's misfortunes to fate. In both cases responsibility is transferred from character to external circumstances. This is consoling, but not for long. Wilhelm, having so far interpreted the play in terms of the character of Hamlet, exhorts the actors not to base an interpretation of the whole on any individual character. He does so because he is becoming increasingly unable to identify himself with Hamlet. The truth is that Wilhelm has come to see that Hamlet *did* move out of his inactivity. It is highly significant that, having first been violently opposed to any cuts, Wilhelm produces an acting version which omits Fortinbras entirely and changes the external action so as to avoid Hamlet's journey to England. Gone therefore is the contrast with the man of action, gone the fourth soliloquy ("How all occasions do inform against me") with its turn towards action, gone the assumption of action in Hamlet's boarding of the pirate ship and his dispatching of Rosencrantz and Guildenstern. The parallel with Wilhelm's own inactivity has been artificially restored by excising all that interfered with it.[19]

In *Wilhelm Meister's Apprenticeship* Goethe employs polar contrasts such as that between fate and chance to build up a constantly evolving picture of the complexity of truth and experience. What seems to have validity at one point is modified or denied by something else at another. Life is presented as an intricate texture of glaring contrasts and surprising connections. As in others of his works Goethe uses pairs of contrasting characters to develop his theme. Consider for instance in the first book the contrast between Wilhelm and his father, between Wilhelm and Werner, between Wilhelm's father and Werner's father. Later we have an elaborate pattern of interdependent oppositions, especially in the women characters: Philine and Mignon, Aurelie and Mignon, Aurelie and Therese, Therese and Mignon, Therese and Natalie. The most fundamental of these oppositions have some basis of similarity: thus both the "Beautiful Soul" and the Harper are turned in upon themselves, but whereas his inner life is a "hollow, empty self" [*hohles, leeres Ich*],[20] hers is full of strength and light. Both Mignon and Serlo are concerned about Wilhelm's affection for the theater, but whereas Mignon tries to dissuade him, Serlo encourages him. Serlo is arguing from the head, Mignon from the heart: but their common concern reveals divergent attitudes, each of which is justified by its own terms. The characters themselves often experience life as contrast. Compare Aurelie's "We can always attain to the light of understanding; but no one can give us fullness of heart," with Mignon's "Reason is cruel, the heart is better" [*Die Vernunft ist grausam, das Herz ist besser*].[21] The very sentence structure often embodies such contrasts. When the child discovers the puppets in the box, he is, we are told, "more quiet and more unquiet than before" [*ruhiger und unruhiger als vorher*];[22] when the actors discuss the limitations of the theater they become "more or less agreed and not agreed" [*mehr oder weniger einig und uneinig*].[23] The fact that in these two examples the opposites are connected by *und*, suggests that they may add up to a higher term. "More quiet and more unquiet" implies a higher state than being just more quiet or just more unquiet: but how about "agreed and not agreed"? The first example seems to express real subsumption, the second is ironical. The fact that the terms contrasted are sometimes mutually exclusive on one level is important for an understanding of the book, as is the observation that a higher term is sometimes suggested which may be real but may sometimes be ironic. If ironic, the effect is to emphasize not only the opposition but the co-existence of the opposites; if the higher term is real, it represents the opposites as polarities of a greater unit.

Another facet of this conception of a higher term is the revelation of unapparent similarities. Connections are constantly establishing themselves between the most disparate elements of experience. Certain images and ideas recur like leitmotifs throughout the novel: the figure of a young officer (Mariane's costume, Jarno's friend, Friedrich's disguise), the painting of the sick prince which Wilhelm had first seen at his grandfather's, Mariane's necklace and scarf. Both Mignon and Therese adopt men's clothes. Both Serlo and Wilhelm have rebelled against their fathers. Both Aurelie and Wilhelm have embraced the theater out of a patriotic desire to educate their countrymen. Much of Wilhelm's later activity is prefigured in his youth. Thus in the play of David and Goliath he imagines himself as a hero (as later in *Hamlet*) and shows a taste for grandiloquent speeches (as later in his planned philippic against Lothario—the faithless seducer of Aurelie, as he thinks). Tasso's heroine Clorinda, who had figured in one of his childhood theatrical ventures, recurs to his mind, together with the female figure in the painting of the sick prince, when he is brooding on the Amazon. It is at this point in the novel that Wilhelm expresses the following thoughts: "Do not, in youth as in sleep, images of our future destiny surround us and become visible as presentiments before our unbiassed gaze [*unserm unbefangenen Auge*]? Are not the seeds of what is to befall us already scattered by the hand of Fate, is it not possible to have a foretaste of the fruits which we someday hope to gather?"[24] Let us note that these sentiments are phrased as questions. This is not a statement of fact, but an expression of hope. Wilhelm wants to believe this, but the reader sits back and smiles. For Wilhelm had said much the same about Shakespeare. There is irony here. Wilhelm, in his search for a pattern of experience, is persuading himself into a texture of connections which may or may not be real. He is constructing his own plot.

Ambiguity pervades the connections as well as the contrasts, and sometimes the connection is interwoven with contrast. Mariane's scarf and the Ghost's veil are mentioned in close proximity as Mignon packs Wilhelm's trunk. The marble statues in Natalie's house remind Wilhelm of those in Mignon's house in the song about Italy. But for Mignon the statues deplore the present from the standpoint of the past, whereas for Wilhelm they represent the fulfillment of the past in the present. They look at him not with pity as on Mignon ("*Was hat man dir, du armes Kind getan?*"), but "with grave seriousness" [*mit hohem Ernst*], for Wilhelm has rediscovered the "life-joy" [*Lebensfreude*] of his grandfather who had collected these works of art.[25] The connection is overt, the contrast implicit. Similarly the Harper's cry in the last chapter of the novel—"Save the child!"—reminds us that Mignon had used the same words with reference to the same child in another situation. Then it was to save the child from the Harper. But in each case it was to save him from an evil fate. Aurelie's wounding of Wilhelm with her dagger is paralleled by Mignon's bite. Aurelie's dagger represents for her the same possibility of escape as does the opium for the Harper. Then there is the contrast between Philine's knife and Aurelie's dagger. Philine's knife bears the inscription "Remember me!" and as Aurelie cuts Wilhelm's life-line she exclaims: "One must make a sharp incision on you men, if you are to notice."[26] The words "Remember me!" are, of course, used by the Ghost in *Hamlet* and are recalled in the scene of Wilhelm's appearance before the Society of the Tower. Through this intricate motion of contrasts and connections a pattern of connected contrasts is gradually establishing itself. Goethe often used the terms "polarity" and "intensification." It is essentially a dialectical pattern, but it results not in synthesis but in a higher term which is higher because it perceives and maintains the tension rather than resolving it.

It is highly significant that the burgher's son should seek his

literary image in the Prince of Denmark. The opposition of
aristocracy and *Bürgertum* is another important tension in the
novel, presented not merely as a difference of life-styles but as
one of differing opportunities. In a letter to Werner Wilhelm
says that from earliest youth he had felt the need to develop
himself harmoniously.[27] Such harmony is normally possible only
for aristocrats, who do not have to develop one particular faculty in order to earn their livelihood. To present this polarity
more forcefully Goethe has expanded the account of the sojourn
of the actors at the Count's castle given in the *Theatrical Mission*, in particular by elaborating the figure of the Countess and
thereby motivating Wilhelm's subsequent expressions of enthusiasm for the aristocratic mode of life. In his first encounter with
aristocrats in Chapter Two of Book Three Wilhelm expatiates
in an enthusiastic monologue on the advantages of wealth and
high birth in promoting growth, good judgment and the ability
to recognize what is necessary, useful and true. The narrator
comments ironically: "Thus did our friend proclaim good fortune for those who dwell in higher regions," for such "advantages" are in no wise apparent in what Wilhelm experiences at
the castle. And yet he persists in his idealization, obviously trying to find some satisfying obverse in this higher social sphere
to what he feels as restricting in the life of a burgher. But it is a
world of intrigue in which people's feelings are played on and
played with in a dangerous manner, the outstanding example of
which comes when Wilhelm is persuaded to surprise the Countess by masquerading as the Count, and is then surprised by the
Count unexpectedly returning home, so that the Count receives
a psychological shock in apparently seeing himself seated in a
chair in his own room and interprets this as a portent of death,
which drives him to join a religious community. Wilhelm
should have learnt from this experience that this world is no
valid alternative to that of his father and brother-in-law, and
indeed after the troupe has left the castle he begins to talk about
the *disadvantages* of high birth which precludes real intimacy,

sincerity and "inwardness" [*Innigkeit*]. It is just after this that he writes to Werner about aristocrats developing many faculties and burghers exploiting one faculty to a higher level. The latter is indeed not conducive to broad, harmonious development, but the spread of interests entailed by aristocratic life also has its disadvantage in that it neglects the concentrated development of inner force, of *Innigkeit*.

In the second half of the novel the opposition of fate and chance is subsumed with that of aristocracy and bourgeoisie to the general theme of order. Part and whole had been an operative tension in the novel from the very beginning. As a child, Wilhelm was either obsessed by the parts without any sense of the whole, or (as in the play based on Tasso) dimly conscious of a whole but forgetful of the parts. Both these theatrical performances and his vision of his future life with Mariane prove to be based on a false sense of order because they are rooted in fancy and not in reality. Against this Werner holds up the image of true order as he sees it. In his words there vibrates this tension of parts and whole. Order in business life "allows us always to survey the whole without being confused by details."[28] What a wonderful invention is double book-keeping! Wilhelm objects that in adding and balancing the parts, one may nevertheless neglect the true sum total of life. He is unprepared to accept this mercantile view of order: for, having inhaled it at home from his earliest years, he finds the disorder of Mariane's dressing room particularly appealing.

Serlo is also a man who respects order. But he has a broader concept of order than Werner, for in his early life he had fallen in with some people known as the Children of Joy, "intelligent, witty, lively people, who well understood that the sum of our existence divided by reason never comes out exactly but there is always a wondrous remainder."[29] These are important words: they recognize the insufficiency of double bookkeeping, and they suggest the possibility of some higher order in which those elements which elude rational accounting will have their place.

The fact that Wilhelm's father on his death had left his affairs "in best order" causes Wilhelm to reflect on the disorder of his own life, where intentions are not matched by achievements. Trying to find some excuse for this he again transmutes himself into what he conceives to be Hamlet, talking now about "inner circumstances" and "outer circumstances" in the play, claiming that by his cuts he is reducing the outer circumstances.[30] But this would surely put more emphasis on inner circumstances and personal responsibility. Wilhelm can only say that the hero has no plan but the play has. He has now reached the point where he is confused by the play. The Ghost in the performance, like the Ghost in the play, is an outer agent, but the message left by the Ghost in the novel is that Wilhelm should flee, which is exactly the opposite of what he says in the play. Wilhelm is being directed away from his "theatrical mission," but as he tries to question the Ghost in a dream he is encompassed by a pair of arms which might be Mignon's or might be Philine's but prove to be Philine's. Wilhelm is at the turning point, directed back into life but to a life whose pattern is more complicated than his categories of fate and chance, aristocracy and bourgeoisie, inner force and outer force can account for. Double bookkeeping doesn't work.

The paradox is that this broader conception of order involves limitation. "One does not become poorer," says Serlo with reference to the stage, "when one restricts one's household."[31] This is at the end of Book Five, the last chapter of which abounds in references to order. As a producer Wilhelm wants more order in his production; a priest speaks of the necessity in treating the mentally deranged of accustoming them to order. The counterforce that works against order is obsession, such as the guilt feelings of the Harper, and the doctor who is treating the Harper says that man's greatest misfortune is having some idea so take hold of him that it withdraws him from active life. But Wilhelm too is obsessed by an idea. Melina laughs at his "presumption" in aiming at educating the public instead of allowing himself to be educated by them. What finally drives him away from the idea of his "mission," however, is not the Ghost's exhortation nor a change of heart but the letter entrusted him by the dying Aurelie.[32] She had written a letter to Lothario, the lover who had abandoned her, which was meant to wound him just as the Countess Orsina's dagger, which Aurelie manipulates in her last great performance, had been intended to wound the prince in Lessing's play. But as Wilhelm reads to her the "Confessions of a Beautiful Soul," calm descends on her troubled spirit and she replaces the letter with a message of forgiveness.

In reading this sixth book of the novel we should do so with reference to Wilhelm and Aurelie, for only then does its structural function become apparent. The temperament of the *schöne Seele* is as emotional and imaginative as Aurelie's, and like Aurelie she withdraws into an ordered world of her own construction. But her world has the sanction of divine communion and can therefore claim greater truth. Like Wilhelm she believes in higher guidance, but whereas his belief in fate is confusion, her faith in God is strength. Her strength, however, comes to her only through the avoidance of emotional tangles such as that which had sapped Aurelie. Aurelie has no strength because she has no sense of guidance, but the *schöne Seele* only feels guidance because she had avoided Vanity Fair and the Valley of the Shadow of Death. She knows the attractions of the world but shrinks from them into a cultivation of her moral self and that only. She tells her story entirely from the standpoint of what she has persuaded herself to believe. It is a consistent—and, at times, frantic—piece of self-justification: and the statement at the end that she knows no pride is hardly convincing. Nevertheless it is an ordered world—but ordered only because it omits what is disruptive of its calm. It is her uncle who points this out. He distinguishes between the unity that comes from limitation and the harmony that comes from integration. She has resolutely followed her self-appointed goal. True mastery of life consists in determining its circumstances, not in being determined by them. But her life had been determined by circumstances. The image of the artist with which the uncle continues, the architect fashioning form out of the chance materials of nature [*zufällige Naturmassen*] recalls the words of the First Stranger. "Everything outside us is only element, and also, I may say, everything of us [*an uns,* i.e., pertaining to us], but deep within us lies *schöpferische Kraft,* creative force." This should recall to the reader Wilhelm's conversations with both Strangers and his words to Philine quoted above on page 119. Neither Aurelie nor the *schöne Seele* has created form out of the elements of nature; they have merely constructed from the elements of their imagination. Important also is the envisioning of a goal. This the *schöne Seele* had, but Aurelie had not, and Wilhelm only in the vaguest terms. Cultivated people are apt to strive for knowledge of many things and this must lead to superficiality, says the uncle; some limitation by an active goal is necessary. This is a restatement, though not in purely social terms, of Wilhelm's distinction between aristocracy and bourgeoisie. What the uncle advocates, however, is limitation of goal, not limitation of personality such as the *schöne Seele* had shown in the cultivation of her moral self. He himself is an art lover and collector, and he objects to her exclusively moral orientation, asserting that active application of the sensual faculties of man is also a worthy ideal. Indeed the person who strives for moral culture should not neglect to refine simultaneously his sensuality, or else he will be in danger of "slipping off his moral height by following the enticements of unregulated imagination." Indeed the *schöne Seele* finally reaches a stage where she feels her soul entirely detached from her body, and experiences external things only as reflections of the God she worships within. This, we are presumably to understand, is not the operation of "creative force," because it does not create order out of variety, but reduces variety to unity by rejecting what is not consonant with that unity.

In giving this manuscript to Wilhelm, the doctor had said that

overemotional natures such as Aurelie's can be helped by en-
couraging religious feelings within them. Goethe referred to
this part of his novel as "the religious book." We know that in
composing this section he was influenced by the memory of a
pietistic friend of his mother's, a certain Susanne von Klettenberg,[33] and we have ample evidence that between 1769 and 1775
he was in close contact with pietistic circles in Frankfurt. In his
final conception of the *Apprenticeship* the religious life had to
have its place, as one form of order.[34] What we have here is a life
totally controlled from a spiritual center. Goethe respected this
as something exceptional, but he also presented it as limited
though self-contained—limited because although the *schöne Seele*
does engage in active good works, she has suppressed sensuality
instead of integrating it into an ordered whole. Goethe never
denied the importance and positive value of sensuality as a force
which must be involved in any attempt at the mastery of life.
This was to become the basic theme of the great Classical Wal-
purgisnacht of the Second Part of *Faust*.

The first chapter of Book Seven is both prelude and key to
the last two books of the novel. It is spring, the time of com-
mencing fruition. Observing a brilliant rainbow against a dark,
stormy sky, Wilhelm reflects on the antagonisms of experience.
But the quality of experience depends, he says, on an inclination
[*Neigung*] in man to meet the external object [*Gegenstand*].
Every such inclination needs an external object on which to
focus for its realization: and, we are presumably to infer from
the image of the rainbow, every object requires such an inclination in the observer. It is in this form that the tension between
inner force and outer circumstance emerges in these last books.
And the theme of order is steadily developed further. Wilhelm's
first impression of the house of Lothario is one of disorder—
"strange," "irregular," without symmetry. This is because the
object is not yet accompanied by inclination, for Wilhelm is still
full of the devastating reproof that he intends to administer to

Lothario for his treatment of Aurelie. But when he meets Lothario he finds him disconcertingly agreeable and attractive. As he unpacks, Wilhelm comes across the Ghost's veil and indignantly rejects its admonition. What should he flee and whither? Would it not have been better if he had been told to "return to himself"? He then has a dream in which he revisits his childhood. Just before arriving at Lothario's house he had again encountered the Second Stranger, who had told him to think of the future and not lament the past. But the dream is a reckoning with both past and future. In it Mariane is walking with his father whereas Felix is pursued by the Harper but rescued by the Amazon. Wilhelm is torn between a sense of responsibility toward Mariane and his father (the past) and concern for Felix (the future). That the Amazon should rescue Felix and make him grow, like a plant, into two, is significant for Felix-Wilhelm.

Lothario converts the tension of "inclination" and "object" into one between idea and object. Cultivated people, he says, tend to be too much concerned with ideas. An idea had driven him to America; now *das Nächste*—what is nearest at hand—seems to him most important, he says. "Hier oder nirgends ist Amerika"—here or nowhere is America.[35] The intellect [*Verstand*], rational comprehension, is an insufficient guide to life, for its order does not encompass the extra-ordinary, and it is this latter which is demanded of us by "every indifferent day." This recognition of an order greater than that comprehensible by reason is directed against the rationalist Jarno. But Wilhelm too has been interpreting life from ideas, as his antinomies of fate-chance, aristocracy-bourgeoisie and part-whole have indicated. Life, we are being brought to see, is not reducible to categories. There is always the "wondrous remainder," which Serlo had referred to, to reckon with. A spirit of wider tolerance begins to enter the novel just at the very moment when the rationalist Society of the Tower seems to be occupying the center of attention—tolerance for variety and difference, abandonment of categories, even of categories of oppositions. The *schöne Seele* may be limited, but she was the inspiration for Natalie. Therese's addiction to order is too rigid, too unimaginative and inflexible, but it is productive of many good things. Lothario's friend Lydie is passionately impulsive, but she too commands respect for her outspoken criticism of the self-satisfied pedagoguery of the Society of the Tower. She stands aligned with Philine and Friedrich in protesting on behalf of life itself against any attempt to regiment it or interpret it. Impressed by Therese's clarity and order, disturbed by the news of what had happened to Mariane and of the Countess's melancholia, embarrassed by the knowledge that Felix is his natural responsibility, Wilhelm seeks clarification from the Society of the Tower. But all that happens in the scene in the hall, at the end of which his apprenticeship is declared over, is that the categories in which he has so far been thinking are all firmly and ironically rejected. The First Stranger offers to continue the conversation on fate and chance, but disappears before Wilhelm has time to answer. The Second Stranger then disclaims education and asserts the importance of error. A friend of Jarno's reappears to tell Wilhelm that he should find people he can trust. The man who played the Ghost, still sounding like Wilhelm's own father, appears to tell him that he is nearing his goal and his past follies are not to be regretted, nor repeated. And the indentures which he is handed consist of a series of general reflections which do not add up to much more than that life is a very complicated business. The climax is therefore anticlimactic and, to some extent, parodistic: for it seems to point to the inadequacy of all abstract theorizing about life. It is Wilhelm's question about Felix, a question of concern about another human being which implies intimations of responsibility, that signifies the attainment of maturity.[36]

But there still remains Mignon. In the scene in the hall there has been no mention of her. And yet immediately before entering the hall Wilhelm had affirmed that his two protecting spirits were Felix and Mignon. These are his guides to life, for the

Society of the Tower has now absolved itself of any further
responsibility, even though it is questionable whether it had ever
had any real influence on Wilhelm's development. But Mignon
leads Wilhelm to Natalie by dying at her feet. What then is
Natalie?

When Wilhelm first meets Natalie, they establish contact
through their common admiration for the *schöne Seele*. Throughout the book Natalie, as the "Amazon," has represented Wilhelm's uncertain aspirations. In her affection for the ideal in the
schöne Seele, in the fact that, as we are told, she has never known
confusion, that she acts naturally to fill the needs of others and
believes in imparting general principles so as to save men from
unnecessary error, she represents the part played by an ideal in
human life. Some critics of Goethe's novel have objected that
Natalie is colorless in comparison to the other female figures of
the novel. But this seems to me totally wrongheaded in that it
fails to recognize that Natalie plays a different part from the
other female characters in the total structure of *Wilhelm Meister's Apprenticeship*. We are told very little about Natalie because she represents a potentiality rather than a fact. Therese
recognizes in her something higher than clarity and intelligence
[*Klarheit und Klugheit*]; she perceives in Natalie that "noble
seeking and striving for what is better" which she also senses in
Wilhelm.[37] This is why Mignon associates herself with Natalie,
for both represent longing, though with a difference: Mignon
embodies the anguish of longing whereas Natalie represents its
transfiguring power. But Natalie represents a dimension rather
than an achievement. Natalie is the guardian, the "priestess" of
Wilhelm's grandfather's paintings, that precious heritage from
his family past. She therefore directs Wilhelm backwards as well
as forwards. Among these paintings is that of the sick prince,
which is referred to three times in the course of the novel, the
image of man's intangible longings which are somehow connected with love. Ladislao Mittner has directed our attention to
the fact that each time this picture is described, the focus of the

description is centered on a different person in the painting.[38] In the conversation with the First Stranger the spotlight is on the prince consumed by love for the bride of his father; in the context of Wilhelm's vision of the Amazon, the focus is on the woman who approaches the prince's sickbed; in Friedrich's reference to the picture in the last chapter of the novel we learn that the father and the doctor are also in the picture. Friedrich says the picture portrays a case similar to Wilhelm's. The most obvious explanation of what Friedrich means by this remark is that Wilhelm is in love and has been for some time. But there is more to it than that, for as Friedrich describes the picture, he ironically suggests that all four persons in the painting have their correspondences:

"What's the name of the King? [he asks] What's the name of that old goatee with the crown, pining away at the foot of the bed of his sick son? What's the name of the beauty who enters with poison and antidote simultaneously in her demure, roguish eyes? Who is that botcher of a doctor who suddenly sees the light and for the first time in his life can prescribe a sensible remedy, give medication which is a complete cure and is as tasty as it is effective?"

The parallel with Wilhelm and Natalie, united by concern at the sickbed of Felix, and with Friedrich making the right diagnosis is therefore also part of the sense. Note that the prince is not only Wilhelm but also Felix, and that Wilhelm is both father and love-sick prince. But not the Prince of Denmark— the self-image that Wilhelm had worked so hard and for so long to foster. No; he is more like Saul, the son of Kish, "a choice young man and a goodly" as the King James version has it, but no prince. Hamlet had a destiny thrust upon him, a mission to fulfill: Wilhelm had created for himself a mission and tried to persuade himself that, like Hamlet, he was fated to fulfill it. But in fact he was more like Saul whose only "mission" was to locate his father's asses, and who yet found a kingdom. The point is that Saul found something that he was not looking for, and something far more valuable than what he was looking for. His destiny came to him unexpectedly, and not of his own seeking.

The conclusion is therefore ironical. The irony of *Wilhelm Meister's Apprenticeship* is not merely a narrative voice, it is the subject of the book.[39] An ironic standpoint, sometimes light-hearted, but sometimes deeply serious, is indeed consistently maintained throughout the novel. For what more ironic illustration could there be than the story of Mignon's incestuous parentage for the inadequacy of taking "Nature" as one's guide, a prescription delivered to Wilhelm when, at the end of the scene in the hall of the castle, he is told that because he recognized the claims of nature his education was complete? The whole system of conflicting attitudes, the polar structure of the novel, is there to demonstrate the irony of life itself. Nothing is certain, nothing universally valid. Irony is built into the book just as the opposition of fate and chance had been. It is an ironic book about irony, with a plot that portrays a hero desperately trying to make a plot for his own life, past, present and future, only to find out that all his attempts at self-realization and self-expansion are fruitless, and that what really matters is what comes to one by chance—or by fate? For this is the final unresolved irony, and this prototypical *Bildungsroman* seriously questions the whole concept of *Bildung* as a rationally explicable process.

7

The Novel as Poetry

For the German Romantics the novel became the vehicle of extended poetic expression. "The novel is a Romantic book" [*Der Roman ist ein romantisches Buch*], declared Friedrich Schlegel,[1] and what he meant by that assertion was that, of all the larger and longer forms of literary expression, the novel was best suited to the romantic spirit. By "romantic" he meant poetic, and the importance of these German Romantics for our present context is that they raised the novel for the first time from its second-class status and declared it a *poetic* form; for some it was the poetic form *par excellence*. This total change of attitude toward the genre was in large part induced by the publication of *Wilhelm Meister's Apprenticeship*.[2]

Schiller, as we have seen, had talked about the uneasy combination of poetry and prose in the novel, asserting that a novel, by nature, must have a structure deriving from rational organization rather than from poetic freedom. Novalis made a similar point, but came to the opposite conclusion.[3] He did not, like Schiller, demand "sobriety" from a novel but, to use Schiller's other phrase, *only* "poetic boldness." He found Goethe's novel "thoroughly prosaic," "a poeticized bourgeois, domestic tale," pervaded by "artistic atheism"; it was a "Candide against poetry."[4] Schiller's objection had been that both poetry and "prose" had been shortchanged in Goethe's novel: Novalis' objection was that the poetry was sacrificed to the prose—"prose" being for him a totally negative quality embodying the anti-poetic spirit, whereas Schiller's "sobriety" was non-poetic and rationalistically ori-

137

ented but not completely negative, for it was something that, as he said, there should have been more of in the *Apprenticeship*. Novalis conceived of all poetry as being essentially a world which is contrary to what he called "history"—contrary, he said, and yet similar, "as chaos to the completed Creation."[5] By "chaos," Novalis here meant the original, unitary state as opposed to the differentiated, individuated world of the Creation. It was for poetry to recapture this "chaos," this "golden age" that preceded the dichotomies under which modern man labors and which are essentially dichotomies of consciousness. This applies to the novel, which Novalis unquestioningly accepted as a poetic form:

A novel must be poetry through and through. For poetry, like philosophy, is a harmonious attunement of the spirit [*harmonische Stimmung des Gemüts*] in which everything is beautified, every object acquires its right perspective [*Ansicht*], everything finds its proper accompaniment and environment. In a truly poetic book everything appears quite natural and yet so wondrous. One has the sense that it couldn't be otherwise and that one has only been slumbering till now—that only now one has a right sense of the world. All recollection and presentiment seem to come from this same source.[6]

The conflict between poetry and non-poetry is one of the "Unities" of a novel, said Novalis, using the term "Unities" in the sense of classical aesthetics, and referring here particularly to the Unity of Action. The novel hero has a "passive nature," for he is the "organ of the poet inside the novel." The novelist works "to produce poetry by events and dialogues, reflections and descriptions, as the lyrical poet does through feelings, thoughts and images." A novel should be "mythology of reality" [*Geschichte*], mythology in the sense of free, poetic invention which "manifoldly symbolizes reality" [*die Wirklichkeit sehr mannichfach symbolisirt*].[7]

The novel as poetry which expresses mythologically and symbolically the contiguity and connections of the phenomena of experience, the novel as the form that integrates the natural and the wondrous or supernatural, that conveys a "right sense of the world" and combats the non-poetic and anti-poetic—this was a totally new view of the genre. Goethe's novel did not satisfy Novalis's prescription, but it had revealed to him the potentialities of the genre as a poetic, romantic form. These potentialities were elaborated upon by other German Romantic writers, notably by Friedrich Schlegel, who was much more positive in his judgment of *Wilhelm Meister's Apprenticeship* and wrote the first notable essay on Goethe's novel.[8] It was, he said, more than a novel of characters and events, it contained what he called a "true, systematic instinct, sense of the universe, presentiment of the whole world" [*Vorempfindung der ganzen Welt*].[9] He praised the connections constantly being established within the work, the "irony which hovers over the whole work," the "spirit of reflection and return into one's self," the "portrayal of a nature observing itself constantly as if into infinity." In short: what Schlegel singled out for comment about Goethe's novel was its integration of what is individual and what is universal by the constant establishment of connections through recollection and presentiment and by ironical reflection upon and within itself. Schlegel was intimating the sovereign importance of the personality of the author as the structuring force, but the extreme individuality that he demanded of the novelist was, curiously enough, at the same time the expression of universality for Schlegel. He once defined a novel as the "unification of two absolutes—absolute individuality and absolute universality" [*der absoluten Individualität und der absoluten Universalität*].[10] He used terms like "compendium," or "encyclopaedia of the whole spiritual life of an individual" to describe the genre. He also spoke of novels (those he approved of) as "socratic dialogues" which emphasized the relativity of all statements by playing one off against the other.[11] Hence the central importance of irony in Friedrich Schlegel's aesthetic and its interpretation as the means by which poetry conveys the universal through the particular. And the way Goethe's poetry in *Wilhelm Meister* was shot through with prose, and his prose with poetry, was for Schlegel, in contrast to Schiller, not vacillating uncertainty but purposive, ironic richness.

The German Romantics had their own specific answers to the basic questions raised by eighteenth-century critical discussion of the novel as a genre. To the question whether the novel should follow the structural pattern of the epic or that of the drama their answer was that it should do both—indeed it should combine all genres within itself, it should be a "mixture of the dramatic, the epic and the lyric," according to Friedrich Schlegel.[12] As regards the problem of how the novel may keep close to life and yet also be poetic, how to combine what Schiller called "sobriety" and "poetic boldness," their answer was that the novel should not portray "manners," *mœurs*, but "world," *Welt*. Schelling objected that *Tom Jones* was a picture of manners [*Sittengemälde*] but not of the world.[13] By "world," the Romantics meant a sense of the total structure of experience, that "sense of the universe, presentiment of the whole world" which Friedrich Schlegel had admired in *Wilhelm Meister's Apprenticeship*. It implied the transmutation of individual, dissociated experiences into an associative pattern by the author's mind —a process of form-giving which involves understanding and interpretation. To a large extent this was a process of re-creation, a "poeticization" as Novalis called it, in which the familiar becomes marvelous and the marvelous familiar.[14] Hence this "world" that the German Romantics demanded from the novel is really an inner world, what Schlegel called "the whole spiritual life of an individual," produced by an individual consciousness and yet possessed of universality, a compendium, an encyclopaedia, with an order created by what Schlegel called "combinatory wit," with a structure that is independent of and transcends "the process and laws of rationally thinking reason."[15] The question of whether the supernatural should have a place in the novel therefore became irrelevant: the marvelous is the Infinite which shimmers through the finiteness of the plot. The question of whether digressions and reflections are legitimate in a novel also became irrelevant because, since the novel represents inner consciousness, it must needs reflect on itself and by raising questions indicate the merely relative nature of all that it narrates, describes or asserts, in order that we may sense or imply an absolute beyond the relative. Hence the presence of the narrator inside the novel became for the German Romantics no longer a narrative device of debatable validity but the organizing center from which everything radiates and by which everything is connected to everything else, and also a destructuring force emphasizing the relativity of all statement.[16] The author-narrator thereby became the essential objectifying force structuring and destructuring material into a poetic statement in which individuality and universality, restricted confines and wide perspectives, finite definiteness and infinite mystery are combined.

We know that Goethe read Friedrich Schlegel's essay on *Wihelm Meister*, and we also know that he occupied himself with the Fragments published in the *Athenäum*, from which many of the statements I have quoted above are taken.[17] Some of these Romantic formulations—the novel as poetry, the novel as encyclopaedia, as compendium, as socratic dialogue, the praise of irony as a structuring principle, the defense of the supernatural, the conscious contrasting of reality with idea or ideal—seem to have had some effect on his work as a novelist and his judgments on other people's novels. Despite his fruitless attempts at a definition of the novel during the year 1797, and perhaps precisely because of their negative results, his fascination with the genre persisted and his understanding of its potentialities increased. And it could well be that the theoretical pronouncements of the German Romantics, and their novels, imperfect as they were in Goethe's eyes, contributed to this broader understanding. For the Romantics were trying to do something new with the novel, and it was what they were trying to do, rather than the degree of their success, that was important.

In the period between the completion of the *Apprenticeship* and the publication of *The Elective Affinities,* that is to say between 1797 and 1809, Goethe read many of the more important novels that were just coming out, and also read or reread several older ones. In 1799 and 1800 he returned to *Don Quixote,* probably reading it this time in the famous translation by the German Romantic Ludwig Tieck, which began to appear in 1799. But, as during his previous reading of this book, Goethe made no substantial comments.[18] Indeed the only significant references that he ever made to *Don Quixote* are two statements much later in his life. The first is reported by Chancellor von Müller, one of Goethe's closest associates in his later years, who tells us that on 1 February 1819, Goethe said that "the third and fourth parts of *Don Quixote* were first written by someone else and then later written by Cervantes. He had the good sense to want to end with these two parts [i.e., presumably Parts One and Two], for the real motifs are exhausted by then. While the hero has illusions, he is romantic; when he is merely fooled and mystified, all real interest ceases."[19] Secondly, in a review dated 1823 of a collection of Spanish romances, Goethe expressed his admiration in very general terms for the union of an idea with the real world in *Don Quixote* and for Cervantes' ability to maintain some relationship between the lofty and the ordinary.[20] None of this, however, adds up to a detailed criticism of this important novel. There is no discussion of the intricate interdependence of the characters of Don Quixote and Sancho Panza, none of the highly ambiguous nature of our responses to Don Quixote himself. Nor is there any reference to the extremely interesting structure of the book, with its pattern of related conversations and its episodic narratives which have relevance to the main theme (as do those of *Wilhelm Meister's Journeymanship*). One might have expected Goethe, sensitive as he was to Shakespeare, to have said more about the splendid imagination of Cervantes. One can indeed argue, as Goethe did, that the second volume of the novel is inferior: the scenes at the Duke's court are indeed tedious and contain too much ridicule for the balance of the book. But what about the Cave of Mendocinos, Master Peter's puppet show, and Sancho's governorship? The creative union of ideas and reality surely continues right up to Don Quixote's deathbed; and of the great death scene Goethe also said nothing.

With the exception of these two comments on *Don Quixote*, Goethe in fact said little or nothing about narrative literature before Richardson. We have evidence that he was acquainted with the work of Rabelais from quite early on (he spoke of Rabelais as one of his "friends" while he was a student at Strassburg)[21] and in 1792 he used motifs from Rabelais to describe the state of Europe after the French Revolution.[22] He praised Rabelais in the notes to his translation of Diderot's *Neveu de Rameau*,[23] but was not specific, either there or elsewhere, about what he admired in his work. There are passing references to Scarron and to Fénelon's *Télémaque*, but nothing in the nature of critical comment.[24] In 1825 he had the works of Mme. de La Fayette in his hands, but we have no indication of what he thought about *La Princesse de Clèves*, if indeed he read it—though one might have expected him to do so, for he was well informed about and, on the whole, well read in what was important in French literature.[25] In December 1809 we find Goethe reading the great novel of the German seventeenth century, Grimmelshausen's *Simplicissimus*. At that time he was working on material for his own autobiography, and among the jottings for the seventh book, which begins with a long statement about German literature at the time of his birth, there are some reflections on seventeenth-century literature that include a mention of *Simplicissimus* as an adventure novel with good motifs.[26] On 12 December of that same year he remarked to his friend Riemer that *Simplicissimus* was more skillful and more agreeable in its layout [*in der Anlage tüchtiger und lieblicher*] than *Gil Blas*, but couldn't come to a proper end and so became a "collective" (Goethe was referring to the various continuations of the book).[27]

Gil Blas would seem to have been one of Goethe's favorite novels, for we have evidence from his diaries that he read it at least three times—in November 1799, in August 1807, and between May 1813 and April 1814. At the time of his second reading of the book Goethe was concerned with the "novelistic motifs of the [*Wilhelm Meister's*] *Journeymanship*" and with two of the novellas contained in it, "The Man of Fifty" and "The Foolish Pilgrim," as the diaries show:[28] at the time of his third reading he was occupied with the climactic last books of *Fiction and Truth*. This, as we shall see, may have its significance. Goethe also made several statements about this novel. In 1807 he observed the relationship between it and collections of tales like the *Heptameron* of Margaret of Navarre, the *Decameron* and the *Arabian Nights*.[29] In 1809 comes the statement (already quoted above) that Grimmelshausen's *Simplicissimus* was more skillfully and agreeably laid out than *Gil Blas*, which would seem to suggest some notion of the picaresque as a basis of comparison, if nothing more—and yet, perhaps, a good deal more. On 29 May 1814, presumably stimulated by his third reading (at least) of the book, Goethe took up Schiller's comparison of it with *Wilhelm Meister's Apprenticeship*, in a conversation that day with Chancellor von Müller: "Meister had to appear so fermenting [*gärend*], vacillating and flexible so that the other characters could unfold through and around him, for which reason Schiller compared him to Gil Blas. He is like a post on which tender ivy climbed."[30] Finally, speaking of his *Faust* to Eckermann on 13 February 1831, Goethe referred to its various scenes as separate small spheres which affect each other but have little to do with each other, and then proceeded to the following general statement: "The poet's task is to express a manifold world and he uses the tale of a famous hero merely as a kind of continuous thread on which to hang what he chooses. This is true of the *Odyssey* and *Gil Blas*."[31] These various statements seem to testify to an increasingly positive attitude toward a "loose" form of the novel, such as was represented for Goethe by *Gil Blas*, in which the poet's fancy has free play and both the main character and the succession of incidents are designed for variety and for the indulgence of this free play of fancy. They make interesting reading when considered together with Goethe's admiration for Diderot's ability to weave disparate strands into a meaningful whole. Are we to deduce that this conception of loose structure, evolved from his reading of *Gil Blas*, also constituted a meaningful whole? In other words did Goethe consider its seeming lack of form as form in its own right?

I say "seeming" lack of form, for although some critical opinions have imputed this to Lesage, the novel is in fact very well constructed. The individual episodes often have the character of anecdotes, and in this respect the novel does have affinities with collections of tales in a framework, like the *Heptameron* or the *Decameron* or the *Arabian Nights*, the framework here being the character of Gil Blas himself and the people he meets. On this level *Gil Blas* is structurally akin to *Le diable boiteux*: but it goes beyond this level in that the central character develops and is therefore interesting in himself, and also because each book of the novel illustrates both a separate phase in Gil Blas' development and a different part of the social scene. Book One is dominated by the highwaymen; Book Two by the doctors; Book Three by pleasure-loving young noblemen and actresses; Book Four by more distinguished aristocrats; Book Five by the life-story of a real rogue, Don Raphael; Book Six by Gil Blas' brief period of collusion with this rogue, from whom he parts on moral grounds; Book Seven first by the Church (in the person of the Archbishop of Granada), and then by actors, with a lead-over to Book Eight, which deals with Gil Blas' life at court as secretary to the Duke of Lerma. Book Nine is concerned with his fall from favor, imprisonment, and determination to live a simpler life in the country; Book Ten with his attempt to ac-

quire a simpler life and with the life-story of his valet Scipion
(a real picaro who has lived by stealing and deceiving and has
now reformed); Book Eleven with his audience with the King
and his second period at court, this time in the service of Lerma's
successor, the Count of Olivares; and Book Twelve with the dis-
grace of Olivares and Gil Blas' return to the country. The structure represents an upward progress in that we reach the King of
Spain only in the last book (though Gil Blas has assisted him
in his amours earlier, when he was Prince); but this is not a
straight progression, since it is interrupted, as we can see, by
reverses—which makes the book (and its form) all the more interesting. Interesting too is the use of parallel or mirror figures
to Gil Blas, especially Don Raphael, the outright and evil rogue,
and Scipion, the good-natured picaro who becomes the perfect
valet. For Gil Blas himself is neither of these. He is gullible but
not wicked: indeed it is his innocence and piety which make him
gullible and allow him finally to work his way through to moral
goodness.

This undeniably moral tone without overt didacticism, the
demonstration of mistaken orientations through a rich train of
experiences, the fundamentally appealing character of Gil Blas
himself, appealing because of its human truth both in his moments of baseness (as in his indifference to the poverty of his
parents when he himself is at the height of riches) and in his
generosity towards the unfortunate once he has learnt the results
of his own ambitiousness—these things are probably enough to
account for Goethe's affection for this novel, but there was
much more about it to attract him. Above all there is the book's
tremendous sense of life, the many incisively drawn portraits and
the detailed delineation of settings of all kinds, the broad picture
of society, partly realistic and partly satirical, from princes and
bishops down to innkeepers and strolling players: a vast panorama of manners, in its breadth recalling Cervantes and anticipating Balzac and containing certain specific themes particularly
close to Goethe's artistic interests, such as the life of actors and

the depiction of aristocrats, and even the relations of aristocrats to the bourgeoisie. Structurally the book must have interested him because of its leitmotif-like use of characters appearing and reappearing at significant moments in the action, its use of mirror-characters to set off the hero, the irony of situations as well as of occasional author's commentary, and its use of interpolated novellas in the tradition of Cervantes, one of which, "Le mariage de vengeance," is concerned with a painting that functions similarly to certain pictures in *Wilhelm Meister's Apprenticeship* and *The Elective Affinities*. As regards these novellas it seems significant that Goethe reread the book while working certain novellas into the framework of *Wilhelm Meister's Journeymanship*, for the novellas in *Gil Blas* are mostly life-stories told by characters appearing in the novel, which means that the characters of the novellas also in large part appear in the framework—a structural device of which Goethe made striking use in *Wilhelm Meister's Journeymanship*. He may even have observed how Lesage stops a tale at a certain point and gives us the conclusion as part of the framework, for this is exactly what Goethe did with "The Man of Fifty." I think it also not unlikely that the structure of *Gil Blas* was a conditioning factor in the sense of guiding pattern which Goethe was trying to introduce into *Fiction and Truth*, since he was again reading it while working toward the last books of his autobiography. In his references to Gil Blas himself as "fermenting, vacillating and flexible" and as a "continuous thread" Goethe is implying not that Gil Blas is characterless but that he is more inactive than active. This is not true, for Gil Blas is constantly performing acts of choice and in this he differs from Wilhelm Meister. He is, however, a character to whom things are always happening, a fact which allows a variety of outside forces to operate and which therefore brings him closer functionally, though not psychologically, to Wilhelm Meister. It is difficult to see why Goethe thought the layout of *Simplicissimus* "more skillful and more agreeable," and one cannot tell whether he was referring

to the general tone of the book or to its construction. The remark remains mystifying, for it seems clear that Goethe was
more drawn to *Gil Blas*. I believe that this novel had a deeper
influence on him than has been generally recognized, and it is for
this reason that I have treated it at such length.

In the years we are at present considering (1797–1809) several
new trends were visible in the novels appearing in England and
France. But Goethe had nothing to say about the Gothic novel
and the reactions against it, nor about the socially propagandistic
English novels of the closing years of the eighteenth century.
He also said nothing about Fanny Burney or Jane Austen, and
nothing about the Marquis de Sade.[32] He did, however, com-
ment on the novels of Mme. de Staël, and on *Paul et Virginie* and
Atala. And there was some shadow-boxing with Restif de la
Bretonne.
    Early in 1798 Schiller had written to Goethe:

Have you perhaps seen or heard of the strange book by Rétif:
Coeur humain dévoilé? I have just read what there is of it [*Ich hab
es nun gelesen, soweit es da ist*], and despite much that is repulsive,
banal and revolting I enjoyed it. For I have never encountered such
a violently sensual nature and the variety of characters (especially
women) one is introduced to, the vivid actuality of the descriptions,
the specific quality of the manner and the portrayal of the French
character in a certain class of the people—all this cannot fail to be
interesting. For me, who have so little opportunity to draw material
from outside and study people from life, books such as this and
Cellini, have inestimable value.[33]

Schiller was here referring to Restif's autobiographical—perhaps
in part pseudo-autobiographical—novel *Monsieur Nicolas ou le
coeur humain dévoilé*, which had begun to appear in 1796. The
complete novel runs to nearly 5000 pages in a modern edition,
and Schiller seems to be saying that he had not seen all of it. It
narrates a series of seductions, mostly of lower-class provincial
and Parisian girls, in which real emotion, and sometimes a degree

of sensibility, plays its part, frankly and vigorously told, so that the book becomes a combination of adventure novel, erotic novel and social novel. In modern times it has been heralded as a precursor of Zola and of Proust, though its social aspect is closer to the former than to the latter. For a time it was decried and sequestered as pornography. Restif defended himself against the charge of obscenity in his "Note de l'auteur," dated 1796, by claiming that he was depicting not credibility but reality, life as it really was—"Je montre la marche des passions, non dans la vraisemblance, si souvent trompeuse, mais dans la réalité"—and in so doing was tracing the course of his own life. "I will dissect an ordinary man, as Rousseau dissected a great man" [*Je disséquerai l'homme ordinaire, comme J.-J. Rousseau a disséqué le grand homme*], he wrote in the dedication of his novel, which is addressed to himself as his best friend. His book, he declares, is a novel made out of real life, his own life. The dedication concludes with these thoughts:

It is, then, a novel that I give you, worthy reader; but be assured that you will find in it only true facts truly written. I have no need to invent anything. My life was full of interesting events, because I was always free of those vices which consume and brutalize other men, namely gluttony, gambling and indolence. Every moment of my life has been filled up with work and with that noblest of all passions, the only interesting passion—love. I loved my family, I loved virtue and truth. Sometimes I was too much addicted to pleasure, but never to vice.[34]

Modern critics have cast doubt both on Restif's veracity and on his virtue. But the fact remains that this "Rousseau of the gutter" [*Rousseau du ruisseau*], as Grimm called him, depicted a whole sphere of human society that was almost certainly unknown to Schiller.

Goethe replied that he had not yet seen the book but would try to get hold of it. His diaries indicate that he did so and was reading it in June of that year, 1798. In March of the next year Wilhelm von Humboldt wrote to Goethe from Paris, telling him that

Schiller had asked for information about Restif. Humboldt then
went on to report in considerable and very interesting detail on
a visit he had made to Restif—describing his appearance, his
violent and uninhibited talking, his persecution mania and his
curious philosophic and physical theories. Concerning *Monsieur
Nicolas*, Humboldt said he doubted whether any other book
contained "so much, such true and individual life." He mentioned that Restif had been charged with having invented a good
deal of his own "life" and believed it afterwards to be true, but
went on to say that, even if this were so, what was told was true
to life and intensely experienced albeit only in the imagination,
and that if one did not know this book, one had an imperfect
knowledge of the French character.[35] Goethe was so impressed
by this account that he asked Humboldt's permission to publish
parts of it.[36] But he never followed through with this plan, and
never expressed any opinion of his own on Restif's novel. This
may be significant, and a sort of test case. For ultimately the
reason for Goethe's silence was that, interested as he had been in
Humboldt's vivid portrait of this extraordinary man, and interested as he *may* have been generally in the documentation of
manners and perhaps of national character, he was not interested
in such matters as a novelist. Other novelists might use the genre
as a vehicle for such things, but not Goethe, and he was therefore not moved to enthusiasm for the "reality" of such a novelist.
He never wrote novels to depict society.

In October 1803 Goethe wrote to the editor of the Jena
Allgemeine Literaturzeitung, saying that he would like to review
Mme. de Staël's novel *Delphine*, which had appeared in the preceding year.[37] We have reports by two different people that this
novel interested him greatly and aroused his admiration.[38] It was
a somewhat qualified admiration, but he singled out for praise the
intelligence of the book and the "lively portrayals" in some parts
of it, though he considered it uneven in quality. "Intelligent"
[*geistreich*] was a word that he had used several times to characterize the writings of Mme. de Staël, though he usually paired

it with "passionate" [*passioniert* or *leidenschaftlich*].[39] Writing some years afterwards of the effect made by the appearance of her second novel, *Corinne*, in 1807, Goethe wrote (in his *Annals*): "we honored this fine mind and this warm heart." In the same passage he went on to speak of "the highly individual unity and manifold perspectives" [*die individuelle, ganz eigene Einheit und die vielfache Richtung nach allen Seiten*] of *Corinne*.[40]

These two novels are little read today, so perhaps a few words about their content might be in place here. *Delphine* is concerned with the desperations of a woman educated in the spirit of the *philosophes* whose highly passionate temperament comes into conflict both with her own intellectual convictions and with the prevailing social mores of the declining *ancien régime* (the action takes place in the years 1790 to 1792). *Corinne* deals with a similar conflict between mind and heart—this time in a woman who is a poet—and between freedom of feeling and the need to adjust somehow to the demands of society. In both novels the personal fulfillment of an intelligent and passionate woman is vitiated by public opinion and by the ironies of fate. In both, a striving to escape from society and the need nevertheless to belong to it are played off against each other. These novels were for Goethe imperfect books, but he liked them for their combination of intelligence and emotion.

Three years later, in 1806, and in this same journal, the Jena *Allgemeine Literaturzeitung*, Goethe published a review of three German novels, all forgotten today but all—like the novels of Mme. de Staël—somehow connected with the position of women in society.[41] They are entitled *Confessions of a Beautiful Soul written by herself; Melanie, the Foundling;* and *Wilhelm Dumont.* All of them had been recently published; the last two were written by women and the first purported to be by a woman, though Goethe saw through the pretense without much trouble, claiming that its heroine was "a girl as thought up by a man." Goethe made no great claims for any of the three novels, but he did make some interesting general points in his review. These novels, he wrote, "are all intelligently rather than passionately written [*mehr verständig als passioniert geschrieben*], no violent passions are portrayed, the authors do not wish to arouse fear or hope, pity or terror, but to present us with persons and events which shall interest and occupy us in a pleasant way"[42]—in which passage we feel the residue of Schiller's statement about the novel belonging to the realm of the intelligence and his claim elsewhere that the epic should avoid arousing too strong feelings. In all three books there is, says Goethe, to a greater or lesser degree, "a free view of life" [*eine freie Ansicht des Lebens*]. We observe that here, in his first extended statement about novels since the passage in the *Apprenticeship*, Goethe begins with the attitude of the author, the mind shaping the material, that all-important element of which there had been no mention in the passage in the *Apprenticeship* but which had formed the center of his brief comment on *Jacques le Fataliste*. Now it stands first: and the discussion of events, personages and sentiments comes second. Of the first of these novels he says that the main character is unreal but the structure is rationally cohesive [*verständig zusammenhangend*]. He is interested by the way the main character develops partly through conflict and partly through concord with the setting and events. He is interested in the subject of a woman struggling to maintain her individuality amid social conditions of an aristocratic world. But he criticizes the way in which this woman, despite her independence of character, is always subordinating herself to other women. In other words Goethe found the idea of the book interesting but had reservations about the way this idea was worked out. He thought that the solution to the problem was that of a man; a woman would have dealt with the problem differently.

This novel is by Friedrich Buchholz, a well-known publicist of the time.[43] Its central figure is a girl called Mirabella who grows up in ignorance of the identity of her parents, is carefully educated, and develops into a woman of moral seriousness and great intelligence. She becomes friendly with a girl of her own age, Adelaida, who is the very opposite of her in character: restless, violent, witty, with a taste for music and versifying. Mirabella falls in love with Adelaida's brother Moritz, but he is killed at the battle of Zorndorf in the Seven Years' War, fighting for his idol, Frederick the Great of Prussia. Adelaida then inherits some wealth and marries a member of the landed gentry, but the marriage breaks up and Adelaida starts to wander in search of distraction—and wanders out of the book. It is made clear by the author that Adelaida represents fancy and Mirabella intellect. Mirabella gets a position as companion to the daughter of a neighboring prince, and the novel now becomes concerned with the question of how an intelligent and serious-minded woman such as Mirabella can preserve her individuality and yet adapt to the social forms of court life. The young princess makes an unhappy marriage of convenience, and for a time she leaves the court and her husband and takes up a sheltered life with Mirabella in the country, relieved at being removed from the imbroglio of court intrigue. But this is only during the summer, and when winter comes they have to "leave their paradise and return to court." Eventually the princess achieves some *rapprochement* with her husband, but Mirabella becomes increasingly alienated from court society. She refuses a position at court, but remains full of concern for the princess. The two women go on a journey which takes them to Switzerland and then Italy. In Florence they encounter the Countess of Albany, wife of the Young Pretender (the erstwhile "Bonnie Prince Charlie") and Alfieri, the famous Italian poet, whose mistress she is. It is curious to find such famous real contemporaries in a novel, and still more curious to find the countess dying in this novel of 1806 whereas in fact she was very much alive when it appeared and did not die until 1824! The portrait of Alfieri is interesting: he "unites the spirits of Tacitus, Macchiavelli and Rousseau" and represents "the aristocracy in its greatest force," we are told.[44] The princess dies as he is reading his latest tragedy to her. At the outbreak of the French Revolution, Alfieri and the countess leave for Paris, but return horrified after the Terror. First the countess dies, and then Alfieri himself, a man, the author says (through his mouthpiece Mirabella) who should have wielded sword and lance rather than the pen, but lived at the wrong time for that.[45] Mirabella then finds a new friend in one Eugenia, married at seventeen to a worthy man of fifty, who had died extracting from her a promise that she would never marry again, a promise which she has kept. In Vienna both Mirabella and Eugenia fight to maintain their individuality in an environment of immoral wit, sarcasm, charm and corruption. They leave Vienna and settle in the country in Germany, reading recent German literature (including Goethe's *Natural Daughter*, which Mirabella characterizes as a worthy representation of "feudal society in its decay and impending collapse"),[46] shunning society and maintaining poise and serenity.

The main interest of this novel lies, as Goethe rightly said, in its portrayal of the difficulties of a woman, who has been educated to the use of her mind and to respect for moral integrity, in maintaining her standards in a disintegrating feudal society. This theme had interested him in *Delphine*, and it appears in his own play *The Natural Daughter* (completed in 1803).

The second of these books, *Melanie, the Foundling*, has an intensely complicated plot, proceeding, like that of Buchholz's novel, from an initial situation of ignorance of true parentage. Melanie is brought up by a prince and princess, but is soon made aware that she is not their child, suffers possibly well-meant advances from the Princess's brother-in-law, is consequently sent away from court, is pursued by the brother-in-law, but eventually joins up with a theatrical company. She is fêted by various admirers but remains virtuous, then falls in love with a count, but retains her virtue. The count's intention of marrying her is thwarted by his mother, who has other plans for his future. After an unfortunate period as companion to a countess who treats her as a servant, Melanie lives first in the house of a baroness, and then with a middle-class widow of literary pretensions who treats her degradingly. There is much talk about literature, much discovery of identities, much coincidence and adventure, and much sentimentality in this novel. There are also several inset life-stories of the characters. Melanie's father turns out to be the prince of the beginning of the novel, and her mother a lady-in-waiting at the court. Melanie's problem in being both noble and poor is solved when she happens to win a prize in the "English lottery." Eventually she marries her count and all ends happily. The book provoked this general comment from Goethe: "Characters and events are novelistic [*romanhaft*] in the best sense. The characters are always in a state in which real persons rarely find themselves: the events are chosen from reality and compressed" [*zusammengedrängt*].[47] Goethe is here expressing his view that the materials of a novel should be both more unusual and more formed than the events of life. In this particular novel he finds some of the characters less well drawn than others; but the author shows "adequate knowledge of the world." The structure is "skillful enough in a novelistic way," the exposition being pregnant and promising, the development arousing expectation and holding one's interest right up to the surprise of the *dénouement*. In his critique of *Confessions of a Beautiful Soul* Goethe had regretted that "such a novelistic motif" as ignorance of one's real parents should not have been exploited up to the revelation of their identity. In *Melanie*, on the other hand, this motif is used for the development and eventual resolution of the action, Goethe notes.

Wilhelm Dumont is an epistolary novel and consists almost entirely of letters from Adelaide to Clara, though letters from other characters are reported in these. It begins in the present, then moves back in time as Adelaide tells of her life and relates Wilhelm Dumont's, in order that Clara may understand the present situation. The novel begins with Adelaide announcing that she is going to H—— to make inquiries about someone who had gone to America with her brother and had never been heard of since, and Clara asking Adelaide to contact her, Clara's, lover

Ferdinand, who has just arrived in H——. Adelaide goes to H——, reports meeting Ferdinand, but then starts her life-story, the first section of which lasts from page 23 to page 103 of the novel (which consists of only some 350 small pages), and contains a bitter diatribe against the enslavement of women in marriage, their loss of "moral individuality" and the "suppression of feminine humanity."[48] Wilhelm Dumont, who entered her life as a *bel inconnu* soon after she met her husband, seems much less egotistical to her than her husband. There then follows, curiously enough, from page 106 to page 138, Dumont's account of *his* early life, reported by Adelaide in a letter to Clara, a tale of frustrated love for the daughter of his foster-parents (Wilhelm is an orphan), told up to the point of his meeting with Adelaide. She now continues the story of *her* own life, telling of the mutual love between her and Wilhelm, her brother's attempts to break up her marriage so that she might be united with Wilhelm, a dream in which her dead mother appeared and told her that only "a higher hand" should end the marriage tie, and her own resolve to practice renunciation, which she had later regretted in her unhappiness. The husband dies and she sets out in search of Wilhelm. The action reels from one coincidence to another—disguises, false reports, unexpected revelations—and every now and again there is talk of literature, including a passage praising *Wilhelm Meister's Apprenticeship* for its real-life characters, and contrasting it with those more recent (Romantic) authors whose "sluggish imagination reposes on old tales and legends."[49] By page 190 we have at last stopped reminiscing and have returned to the present time. Adelaide finally ascertains (through Ferdinand) that her brother Gustav and Wilhelm (who, as we will have guessed by now, was the friend from whom nothing had been heard) have returned from America to Paris, and Adelaide now searches for both of them. At Paris she finds herself surrounded by emotional and political intrigues. But finally everything is cleared up and Wilhelm and Gustav are found.

Goethe criticizes this novel for not sufficiently exploiting the full possibilities of its main motif—a girl seeking her lover and brother. "Adelaide travels too calmly," he says. "There should be portrayed a passionate effort, a hastening back and forth, a missing and misunderstanding, an unknown approaching, an accidental receding and all else that arises from the situation. But unfortunately there is none of this."[50] Nevertheless he thinks the novel has good qualities: the events do develop out of the characters and throughout one feels a pleasant personality, even though at times it is divided in itself, which creates confusion. All three of these novels, says Goethe, make the mistake of putting reflections on literature, and even literary criticism, into the mouths of their characters; it is not the novelist's business to transmit opinions nor even to present them, especially opinions on individual authors or individual works of literature.

Why exactly Goethe should have chosen to write a review of these three particular novels is not absolutely clear. It is obvious that there is some similarity among them, both in the general theme of women in society and in the overall adventure-novel structure, and we know that Goethe was attracted by such a structure and can surmise from his reactions to the novels of Mme. de Staël that he was interested in such a theme. But there were personal reasons as well. Buchholz's novel was brought out by the publisher Unger, who was one of Goethe's own publishers (he had published a collection of Goethe's works between 1792 and 1800), and whose wife, Friederike Helene Unger, was the author of *Melanie.* And *Wilhelm Dumont* was the work of the wife of the man who taught Goethe Arabic, Professor Paulus of Heidelberg. Both these women were personal friends of Goethe's. There also seems to be some suggestion that Buchholz's novel, which has, of course, no author's name on the title page, was considered by some to be the work of Friederike Unger (who by this time had published several volumes of novels and stories).

In this review, we notice, Goethe is constantly talking of the importance of characters in a novel. On this point he seems to have come full circle from the passage in *Wilhelm Meister's Apprenticeship*, and sentiments are now admitted if they are reflections which are "profound, clever or surprising," but not if they are merely opinions. The element of surprise, acknowledged here in reflections, is also recognized as structurally effective. In fact one of Goethe's persistent contentions now is that the novel should contain something novel. This may be in sentiments, character or plot; but in any case a novel should be more interesting than life—yet not divorced from life, for the author must show "knowledge of the world and of human nature," situations must be "persuasive" though such "in which real persons rarely find themselves," characters "well enough drawn" and not "thought up." Above all, it would seem, the novelist should maintain a "free view of life," a quality that Goethe was later to praise in Goldsmith and Sterne.

And now let us consider briefly Goethe's reactions to the novels of the German Romantics. He had little good to say about them. In June 1795 he was reading Jean Paul Richter's *Hesperus*, his second novel to be published and his first major work, in which his bizarre combination of sophisticated wit and emotional intensity was already very much apparent. Schiller had said of this novel that, although Goethe had called it a "mythological beast" [*Tragelaph*], it was not without imagination and whim and contained many a crazy idea so that it made amusing reading for long nights.[51] Goethe replied that he was glad Schiller had taken pleasure in the book and expressed his regret that Jean Paul lived in such isolation [in a small town in Bavaria] that, despite his many good qualities, he was not able to purify his taste.[52] When Jean Paul visited Weimar some time after this, Goethe's impression of him was of a strange, complicated creature with a good heart but lacking in cultivation. It was because of some "arrogant utterance" of Jean Paul's in a letter to Knebel, of which Goethe became cognizant, that Goethe directed an epigrammatic poem (*The Chinese Man in Rome*) against him, in which reference is made to the enthusiast who compares "his airy web with the eternal carpet of solid Nature" and who calls the healthy man sick, so that he alone, the sick one, may be called healthy.[53] We already seem to be not far from Goethe's famous utterance that the classic is healthy and the romantic is sick. In other epigrams of this period directed against Jean Paul, Goethe charged him with squandering his riches, with having talent but with sight only for grimaces, with lack of culture. By 1807 Goethe's attitude would seem to have become quite negative, for in December of that year he told Riemer that he considered Jean Paul "the personified nightmare of the age."[54]

In 1798 Goethe had read Tieck's novel, *Franz Sternbald's Wanderings*, which is about a German painter of the early sixteenth century who seeks an ideal strangely connected with an encounter in his childhood. Goethe told Tieck that he was "in general agreement" with the novel but opposed to certain particulars, and that he intended to express his opinions on the novel "publicly."[55] This he never did, but we possess certain marginal comments that he wrote into his copy of it.[56] In the first chapter, at the point where Sternbald is taking leave of his friend Sebastian before setting out on his journeyings, Goethe comments: "Too much morning sun . . . sentimentality." In the fourth chapter, where there is a conversation about the works of Dürer and how they compensate for "all the misery of this earth,"[57] Goethe comments: "empty." Sternbald's reflections in the fifth chapter he considers "very pretty, but not artistic" (i.e., not those of an artist). In this particular passage Sternbald has returned to his home, and is sitting beneath a tree, invaded by memories of his childhood and comparing himself with the birds who have no *Heimweh* and also "no school . . . no strict teachers," lamenting the fact that he has forgotten his parents and his past for so long, that "art has hardened him against his best and dearest feelings."[58] Goethe is right: these are "pretty" thoughts compared with Werther's soul-searchings beneath the lime tree. Goethe's point is that this man is supposed to be an

artist, but doesn't talk like one.[59] Later on Goethe objects to
Sternbald's aspiration to "portray nature exactly as it is" as "false
praise of nature in contrast to *dem Idealen*" (i.e., praise of the
real in contrast to ideas or ideals). On the other hand he objects
equally strenuously to Tieck's dedication of the second book of
the novel to young people who still delight in the figures of their
own fancy and "dislike being disturbed in their dreams by the
world of reality"—which Goethe castigates as "false tendency"
[*falsche Tendenz*]. He is right; but what he has not grasped is
that Tieck was portraying in Sternbald an unsuccessful artist—
unsuccessful because he is too overwhelmed by experience of
the world of nature and by his own feelings, to possess that
formative power essential to all artistic representation.

Goethe never expressed any opinion on the other novels of
Jean Paul and Tieck, he did not react to Schiller's devastatingly
negative opinion on Friedrich Schlegel's *Lucinde*, and he never
mentioned Hölderlin's *Hyperion*, Novalis' *Heinrich von Ofter-
dingen*, Brentano's *Godwi* or either of the two novels by Hoff-
mann.[60] He quoted a few lines from a song in one of Eichendorff's novels as representative of the "characterless and talentless
yearning" of the new age.[61] Lack of character, lack of control,
lack of culture and of taste—these were his charges against the
German Romantics and their novels. In a letter of 30 October
1808 to his close friend, the musician Zelter, Goethe granted
that these young Romantic writers (he mentioned specifically
Arnim and Brentano) had great gifts but declared that they did
not know how to use them:

Everything results in formlessness and characterlessness. None of
them understands that the highest and only operation of nature and
art is forming and shaping [*Gestaltung*] and specification in the
form [*in der Gestalt*] so that everything becomes, is and remains an
individual thing of significance [*ein besonderes Bedeutendes*]. It is
not art to let one's talent range humoristically according to one's individual convenience; something must emerge from this, as from the
scattered seed of Vulcan a wondrous snake-boy arose.

It is in addition a very serious matter that the humorous, having no security or law in itself, sooner or later degenerates into melancholy, as we see from the terrible examples of Jean Paul and Görres. And there are always enough people to marvel at and respect such things, for the public will always thank anyone who turns its head for it.[62]

Two months earlier, he had expressed his objections to romanticism in a conversation with his close friend and adviser Friedrich Wilhelm Riemer, in which he emphasized what he felt to be its forced, artificial nature—"a garishly lit masquerade," part humorous, part absurd, with an intellectually fabricated supernatural (in contrast to the "natural" supernatural of the Greeks) —art that is "unreality, impossibility which is given the illusion of reality by fancy" but is too arbitrary to have any general validity.[63]

This conversation, a momentous one for Goethe, took place on his birthday, 28 August 1808. It had begun with their talking about "the new novel, especially his" [*den neueren Roman, besonders den seinigen*]—that is to say, *The Elective Affinities*. In the preceeding May, Goethe had worked out a scenario for the novel and in June and July had dictated the first eighteen chapters, which, in the original chapter numbering, would have extended up to Ottilie's "Letter to my friends" and perhaps slightly further,[64] and sketched out the rest. This first version has not survived. But we know that there was some pause in the composition and that Goethe did not take it up again until the *end* of August, in fact at the very time of the conversation with Riemer which we have just been considering. In this same conversation he told Riemer that his idea in the novel was "to portray social conditions and their conflicts symbolically"—[*soziale Verhältnisse und die Konflikte derselben symbolisch gefasst darzustellen*]. We should note that Goethe does not say *symbolisch darzustellen* but *symbolisch gefasst darzustellen*. The word *gefasst* is the past participle of the verb *fassen* meaning "to seize, to grasp, to comprehend." Goethe is therefore referring to the way this empirical material has been transformed into aesthetic shapes in his mind. He is not talking about symbolic expression but about symbolic intellection. But the novel was far from achieving final form. He worked at it again from April till October of the next year, 1809, rewriting the whole of the first part and completing the second part, and during that time he must have thought through the basic idea again, for the novel as we now know it is no longer concerned with social conditions and conflicts.

8

Novella into Novel

We know that *The Elective Affinities* was orginally planned as a *novella*.[1] We also know that since the completion of *Wilhelm Meister's Apprenticeship* Goethe had become increasingly interested in the expressive possibilities offered by the genre of the novella. He was reading various collections of novellas in these years, including the *Exemplary Novellas* of Cervantes, the *Heptameron*, Boccaccio, and the *Arabian Nights*. He was increasingly attracted by the idea of novellas within a framework and had already tried it out in his own *Conversations of German Emigrants* (1795). In fact, having already decided to write a sequel to *Wilhelm Meister's Apprenticeship*, he was during these years slowly feeling his way towards the structure that *Wilhelm Meister's Journeymanship* would ultimately acquire, namely that of a novel with inset novellas, a form he had already experienced and admired in *Don Quixote*, *Jacques le Fataliste* and *Gil Blas*. It is possible, but not certain, that *The Elective Affinities* was originally intended to be an inset in *Wilhelm Meister's Journeymanship*.[2] Be that as it may, the novella origin is still visible in the completed novel, for it plays with an idea that was new at the time—the concept of elective affinities[3]—and it revolves around a startling incident, the so-called "double adultery" as the hero of the novel himself calls it. This is in accordance with Goethe's later definition of the novella as centering on "something unusual that has happened" [*eine sich ereignete unerhörte Begebenheit*].[4] But out of this attractive idea and this piquant incident there developed a probing psychological novel about fate and chance, necessity

163

and choice, the comprehensible and the unfathomable. In its concentration on four characters, its single-stranded action and its extensive use of dialogue, it seems dramatic rather than epic; but it is epic by virtue of its narrator and its structural use of reflections, even of extracts from a diary. And over it all there broods something that is totally independent of these four characters and of the narrator, something higher and deeper, something daemonic, something that might be explained, or explained away, as being beyond our control and supernatural, and yet something that is not "beyond" at all but terrifyingly immanent, and not supernatural but rooted in nature.

Here is a brief summary of the action:

Baron Eduard and his wife Charlotte, recently married, are leading a comfortable secluded life on their country estate. It is for each of them a second marriage though they had been friends in their youth. Eduard is concerned because an old friend of his, an army captain, is presently without a suitable occupation for his talents, and he suggests that they invite him to come and stay with them to help in the replanning of the gardens and park of the estate, on which they are both working. Charlotte instinctively feels that two is better company than three, but Eduard persists in his request and the Captain arrives. Meanwhile Charlotte expresses concern on her part for her niece Ottilie, a quiet, withdrawn young girl who does not seem to be developing as she should in the boarding school where Charlotte has placed her. Eduard suggests that Ottilie also be invited to stay with them. Charlotte hesitates to do this. Soon after the Captain's arrival, the concept of "elective affinities" is mentioned and Charlotte asks what it means. Eduard and the Captain explain to her that it refers to natural affinities between chemical substances, according to which two compounds when brought together dissolve into component parts, each of which realigns itself with a component of the other compound with which it has natural affinities. A parallel with human relationships is somewhat jocularly suggested.

Since the Captain and Eduard seem to be spending more and more time together, Charlotte decides to invite Ottilie after all, and she arrives. The result is that Eduard and Ottilie grow ever closer to each other, a development which becomes particularly apparent when on an excursion to a mill Ottilie gives Eduard the medallion with a picture of her father which she always wears around her neck, at the request of Eduard who fears that the glass case may break and wound her. Meanwhile Charlotte and the Captain are finding a natural affinity for each other in their work on the grounds. It is planned to build a *Lustgebäude* or pavilion on the top of a hill from which the main house, where they normally live, is not visible. The foundation stone for this is laid on Charlotte's birthday. Soon afterwards a Count and a Baroness, who are each married to someone else but enjoy intimate relations with each other, arrive to visit Eduard and his wife. Their frivolous talk about marital relations serves to disturb the four others, as striking too close to home. It is when the Count tells Charlotte that he could get the Captain a suitable position that she realizes the depth of her feeling for the Captain. But that night something very strange happens: Eduard, reminded by the Count of an occasion years before when he paid a nocturnal visit to Charlotte, decides to repeat the adventure, to Charlotte's surprise. But as they come together, Eduard is thinking of Ottilie and Charlotte is thinking of the Captain.

Next day Eduard tells Ottilie that she loves him and embraces her, whereas Charlotte, out in a boat with the Captain, admits her affection for him but decides this cannot go on. They realize what is happening to the other two and decide to send Ottilie back to her *pension*, but for the time being Eduard and Ottilie, sensing that they are being forcibly kept apart on the estate, become more passionately involved than ever in each other. Eduard is determined to make a great show out of Ottilie's birthday, culminating in a fireworks display. But just before the fireworks are to begin, the lake bank gives way, people fall into the water and a boy is saved from drowning by the Captain. Despite admonitions to cancel the fireworks, Eduard insists in setting them off in a wild display of whirring light and color, but only he and Ottilie are there to see it.

The Captain leaves and Charlotte has a straight talk with Eduard, recognizing what has happened to them both and insisting that they should not behave like children but prove themselves worthy of coping with the situation. Eduard will not give up Ottilie, however. He does agree to go away to gain time for reflection, but only on the condition that Ottilie stay on the estate with Charlotte instead of returning to the *pension*. Ottilie, perplexed at Eduard's departure, becomes increasingly sullen and suspicious. Eduard declares to a family friend, Mittler, an ex-parson who meddlesomely intervenes

in marital conflicts, that his love for Ottilie has given his life meaning. Charlotte announces to Eduard that she is pregnant, reminding
him of that second nocturnal adventure. Eduard draws up his will
and leaves for the wars.

The novel is divided into two parts, and the second part begins
with the arrival of an architect entrusted with the redecoration of
the chapel. There is an important conversation between him and
the two women in which Charlotte explains how and why she had
tidied up and beautified the churchyard cemetery. From here on
we are given several series of excerpts from Ottilie's diary, the first
of which links up with the conversation just mentioned. Ottilie helps
the architect at his work, and the faces he paints all come to resemble hers. On the eve of Eduard's birthday she has a strange
experience of losing her own identity as she sits in silent contemplation in the chapel. The peace of their lives is now invaded by the
arrival of Charlotte's boisterous and socially oriented daughter
Luciane, with a mass of luggage and a train of attendants. Ottilie
withdraws ever more into herself. Then the Count and the Baroness
return, and since his wife has died, they announce their plan to
marry in the near future. The company amuse themselves by arranging various *tableaux vivants*, in one of which, but only after
Luciane's departure, Ottilie appears as the madonna with a child.
The architect, having finished his work, leaves, but a new visitor
comes, the assistant master at Ottilie's *pension* who has always taken
an affectionate interest in her and is now hoping to make her his wife.
   Charlotte gives birth to a son whose eyes strike Ottilie as like her
own, whereas Mittler is surprised by the resemblance to the Captain.
At the baptism the presiding pastor collapses and dies. Ottilie takes
care of the child and, as spring comes, she resolves to transform her
love for Eduard into something unselfish. An English lord and his
companion arrive. The companion tells a story entitled "The Wondrous Neighbors," about a girl torn between affection for someone
she had loved in her youth and commitment to the man she is to
marry. Charlotte is deeply perturbed by this story, which is supposed to resemble something that had happened to the Captain in
his youth. It involves a rescue from possible drowning. The war is
now over, the Captain is now a major, and Eduard, released from
service, urges him to marry Charlotte so that he, Eduard, may have
his Ottilie. He sends the Major to ask Charlotte to divorce him but

she is not at home, and meanwhile Eduard, walking through the grounds, comes on Ottilie with the child by the lake, tells her his plan, observes the child's strange eyes and speaks of "double adultery." He frightens Ottilie by a passionate embrace, and as she tries to hasten home by boat with the child, the child is drowned.

Charlotte feels this is the hand of fate, and agrees to a divorce. But Ottilie, overcome by a sense of guilt, threatens to kill herself if Charlotte agrees to any such thing. Full of remorse and resolved on renunciation, she decides to return to the *pension* and never to speak to Eduard again. But as she stops at an inn on her way, she accidentally encounters Eduard, who has gone to give her a letter saying that she belongs to him. Observing her promise to Charlotte, she refuses to speak but indicates her resolution by gestures. In despair she then returns to Charlotte, still maintaining silence, but declaring in a letter to her friends that she is attempting to regain her equilibrium and asking to be left in peace. Eduard's birthday is approaching and it seems clear that Ottilie will perform some ritual act or declaration on that day. But the tactless Mittler chooses that occasion to discourse on the Ten Commandments and particularly on the prohibition of adultery, which leads to Ottilie's withdrawal and fasting until she dies. The funeral is festive and the burial takes place in the chapel. Some believe she is a saint with healing powers. But Eduard has not the strength to view her in her glass coffin. He lives on, desolate and desiccated, until one day he is found dead. Charlotte has him buried alongside Ottilie in the chapel. "And so the lovers rest beside each other. Peace floats above their place; serene, kindred angels look down on them from the vault of the roof, and what a friendly moment that will be when they someday wake again, together"—thus the narrator concludes his story.

This mere recounting of the "plot" of *The Elective Affinities* conveys little of the atmosphere, texture and interest of the novel. It sounds like a highly improbable succession of coincidences, bordering at times on the absurd and elaborately contrived in order to illustrate the general idea contained in the title, which is itself not particularly convincing as an explanation of human relationships. Chance plays an even larger part than in the plot of *Wilhelm Meister's Apprenticeship,* and in addition there are motifs that point to mysterious, rationally inexplicable elements of experience, motifs and images taken from contemporary romantic natural philosophy—from electricity, magnetism, mesmerism and even graphology. To the realm of chance belong such incidents as the preservation of a goblet engraved with the letters E and O when it is thrown into the air during the laying of the foundations for the *Lustgebäude* (which, following H. G. Barnes, I shall call the "pavilion"), Eduard's dropping Ottilie's letter within sight of Charlotte, the collapse of the lake bank at Ottilie's birthday festival, the arrival of the English lord and his companion's painfully relevant conversation, Eduard's encounter with Ottilie at the lake and the subsequent drowning of the child—all this seems arbitrary, things that happen without any reason. Not assignable to chance are the rationally inexplicable facts that Ottilie's handwriting becomes more and more like Eduard's, that she accompanies him on the piano better than Charlotte does, that both of them suffer from similar headaches. These are not just unusual incidents to spice up the novel, but metaphors, images of sympathetic kinship. And Ottilie's demonstrated ability to detect the presence of metals by some kind of divining rod (actually a suspended metal pendulum) is more than a reference to contemporary scientific experiments, for it too is a metaphorical statement. It indicates that there is some kind of elemental affinity between Ottilie and what lies hidden both in the earth and in the human soul—forces to which we stand in some relationship and some of us in closer relationship than others, forces that affect us perhaps more than we are willing to acknowledge. But what sort of forces are these? Are they forces of nature, working according to natural laws? Are they benevolent, malevolent, or indifferent? Is the sense of affinity that we feel with these forces something which we must necessarily accept, or can we oppose them? In other words: are we bound by affinities or is there such a thing as choice? Are affinities natural, or "elective"?

But these analogies with natural science are not just illustrative metaphors. For the whole question whether an analogy exists between human life and the workings of nature is one of the predominant themes of the novel. Chance comes in here too. Chance is a "malevolent daemon," according to Ottilie. But if there really is a parallel between human relationships and chemical relationships, then the whole notion of chance becomes dubious. If *Wilhelm Meister's Apprenticeship* raises the question whether there really is such a thing as fate, then *The Elective Affinities* is concerned with whether there is such a thing as chance. This question is raised by the very title of the novel: *Die Wahlverwandtschaften*. For *Verwandtschaft* means kinship, both familial and general—*Wahl* means choice, and yet one does not choose, one cannot choose one's kinship, elect one's affinities.[5]

It was certainly no sudden whim, no chance impulse that caused Eduard to invite the Captain and Charlotte to invite Ottilie. But it could perhaps be considered chance that both husband and wife independently but almost simultaneously decide to invite somebody. Eduard is concerned about the Captain's being without an occupation to engage his talents fully; Charlotte is concerned to educate Ottilie "*up into* a splendid creature" [*zu einem herrlichen Geschöpf heraufbilden*]. Ottilie is at school in a *pension* but seems withdrawn and is not making satisfactory progress, and we deduce that Charlotte's intention is to develop Ottilie's social accomplishments, to "bring her out," so to speak. The Captain, who, Eduard tells his wife, is living in inactivity "through no fault of his own, like so many others"—presumably because there is no need for soldiers in a time of peace—is fully developed (whereas Ottilie is not) but unemployed, and he could be useful to them both as a surveyor of their estate. This, Eduard says, would be suitable work for the Captain's abilities—a curious statement, surely, for one might have expected a military man to be better suited to some more vigorous form of activity. But the whole conception of what constitutes satisfying activity is strange in this novel from its very beginning. For how do Eduard and Charlotte spend their time? He, we are told, is "fixing fresh grafts on to young trees," whereas she is covering a garden hut with moss. In other words he is artificially reinforcing youth, she is artificially fabricating nature. There is something odd, something forced about this marriage. There is a strange formality about the initial conversation, with Eduard thanking his wife for listening to him so nicely and promising in turn not to interrupt her.[6] Charlotte reminds Eduard that they had loved each other when young, had both married other people, then become free again and, at Eduard's instigation, married, and that she had sent her daughter Luciane and her niece Ottilie to the *pension* so that she and Eduard could live for themselves and "enjoy their late acquired happiness undisturbed" on this country estate, she looking after the park and he taking care of the garden, he arranging his travel diaries and she helping to copy them, "and we thought it would be so comfortable, nice, friendly and cosy [*so bequem, so artig, so gemütlich und heimlich*] to travel in recollection through the world which we were not able to see together." Being together involves cataloging the time when they were not together—the present is to be spent in making up for the past. Charlotte declares that this is the first really happy summer she has spent, but Eduard is already restive. He wants the Captain, for the Captain belongs to his past and can help in its cataloging and restoration. Charlotte fears the presence of a third person, appealing to the authority of her subconscious, but Eduard says they are both experienced and fully conscious of everything they undertake. To which Charlotte replies: "Das Bewusstsein, mein Liebster . . . ist keine hinlängliche Waffe, ja manchmal eine gefährliche, für den, der sie führt"— consciousness is not an adequate weapon and often dangerous for him who wields it.

   This is more a maxim than an answer. And we should notice that Charlotte tends towards generalized statements.[7] Just before talking about the past, she had made the following remark, prefacing it by saying "Let me begin with a general observation":

Men think more about the particular and the present, and rightly so because they are called upon to act and work [*zu tun, zu wirken*], whereas women are more concerned with how things are connected [*was im Leben zusammenhängt*], and rightly so because their lot and the lot of their families is bound up with such connectedness and it is this very job of connecting and correlating that is demanded of them.

Zusammenhang—context, connections, overall correlation, integration—this for Charlotte is more important than the independent value of separate, individual things. Her concern is essentially communal. She thinks in social terms, and her maxims are not ethical statements but statements about what is advantageous or expedient to preserve equilibrium, to avoid rocking the boat. Thus she does not say that consciousness is *bad* but that it is "dangerous" for him who trusts in it as his defense, dangerous for his relations with others. With Charlotte everyone and everything is viewed with reference to its interaction with other persons and other things. This is what I mean when I say that she thinks *socially*. Her essential concern is prudence. She favors compromise, avoiding awkward situations, playing for time.[8]

But Eduard is quite different. He has something absolute and uncompromising about him, a determination to get his way, if needs be by flirtatious wheedling, which leads to his suggestion that, since Charlotte has confessed her concern about Ottilie, they should invite both Ottilie *and* the Captain. Charlotte expresses her doubt whether one should bring together the Captain who, like Eduard, is "of the age when a man is first capable of love and worthy of love" with a sensitive young girl like Ottilie. And the narrator then proceeds to tell us that some time previously Charlotte had tried to bring about a union between Eduard and Ottilie, that the Captain was to facilitate this, but that Eduard had been interested only in marrying Charlotte. From which two things emerge: that Charlotte is concerned not so much about the Captain's effect on Ottilie as about Ottilie's on

Eduard, and secondly that the Captain is not someone that she knows slightly but a man who has enjoyed her strict confidence.

Which brings me to the subject of the narrator in *The Elective Affinities*. In the second chapter the narrator gives us his view of Eduard:

Eduard was not accustomed to deny himself anything. The spoilt only child of rich parents who managed to persuade him into a strange but very profitable marriage with a much older woman who coddled him in every way by always seeking to repay his good behavior toward her by the greatest liberality, he became his own master after her death, traveled at will, enjoying change and variety, not desiring anything excessive but plenty of different things, free-minded, generous, decent, even courageous if required—what was there that could fail to accede to his wishes!

After having listened to the first conversation between Eduard and Charlotte, we now have the sense of someone interposing himself between us and the characters. But actually this indeterminate presence had intruded itself into the very first sentence of the novel, which reads: "Eduard—for so we shall call a rich baron in the best years of a man's life—Eduard had spent the nicest hour of an April afternoon in his tree nursery." Why the parenthetic phrase? We shall find out only later, for the baron's name is really Otto; and what that implies is purposely withheld from us for the present by this obtrusive narrator who is shaping events according to some purpose of his own from the very first sentence. The narrator is much more of a presence in this novel than in Goethe's other novels, and we must guard against being taken in by him completely. Not that he is wrong; but throughout the novel he is trying to describe something that is really beyond him.[9]

The second conversation between Eduard and Charlotte is interrupted by the arrival of Mittler. They go to meet him through the old churchyard, which Charlotte has cleaned up and beautified. The fact that Eduard is surprised at the way his wife has rearranged the tombstones in order to create a sight "pleasing

to the eye and the imagination," as the narrator puts it, shows
how little he knows about what she has been doing. We are told
that he usually avoided going through the churchyard. It was the
shorter path, but went through Charlotte's terrain. Also it is
understandable that a man of his age would not wish to be reminded unnecessarily of mortality. This is why he is so pleased
that the churchyard has been made beautiful, and he draws
Mittler's attention to the improvement. But Mittler says the dead
should be left in peace. His name means "mediator" and he
prides himself on settling disputes, especially marital disputes.
Like Charlotte he wishes to avoid friction.[10] He is interested only
in the living, and rigidly avoids any contact with the dead.
Hence he refuses to enter the churchyard. Charlotte gives in to
Eduard and the invitation is despatched to the Captain, though
the question of inviting Ottilie is postponed for the moment.
And the chapter ends with this curious passage:

Charlotte played the piano very well: Eduard was not so comfortable with the flute, for although at times he made great efforts, he
did not have the necessary patience and endurance [*Ausdauer*] for
the development of such a talent. He therefore executed his part
rather unevenly. Some sections were good, though perhaps too fast,
but he hesitated over others because he had not mastered them, and
it would have been difficult for anyone else to get through a duet
with him. But Charlotte could adapt: she would stop and then let
herself be hurried on by him, fulfilling thereby the double duties of
a good conductor and a clever housewife, both of whom know how
to keep the general beat [*Mass zu erhalten*] even though the individual passages are not always in correct time.[11]

Realistically viewed this is about music-making; looked at from
the standpoint of idea-content it is about life, marital life. Charlotte plays the piano "very well"—in the sense that she accompanies well, for nowhere in the novel does she play solo. Her
good playing consists in keeping the general beat, the measure,
Mass, and *Mass* means not only "measure" but "moderation."
She does this even though the details are not right, she knows
how to *get through* a duet, *ein Duett . . . durchzubringen*.

This is the narrator speaking. But in the first chapter of the novel Charlotte had said to Eduard: "And then in the evenings you got out your flute again and accompanied me on the piano" [*und begleitest mich am Klavier*]. According to her, then, he accompanies her. Thereby the whole tension in their relationship is revealed, a relationship not of equal voices but of solo with accompaniment. The question is: who plays the accompaniment? Obviously Charlotte, for she allows herself to be hurried on by him whereas he never slows down to keep pace with her. Eduard's playing, the narrator says, lacks the patience and endurance needed for the development of talent. Later, in a notable passage, Eduard is to speak of his "talent for love" [*Talent des Liebens*]. In his love he shows endurance but not patience. For there is endurance without patience and this can be characteristic of any developed talent, even of a talent for love. So the narrator is wrong here. But is he aware of the symbolic dimension of his words?

When the Captain arrives there is much talk of spent youth. His name is Otto, which is also Eduard's real name, the name of his youth, the name Eduard associates with the idea of youth. When he takes the Captain up to a height from which they survey his present estate, the conversation focuses on one particular stand of trees, plane trees and poplars that Eduard had put there in his youth, having rescued them from being cut down and transferred them to this particular location, and this year he hopes that they will again put forth new shoots. The two men talk a lot about the past, and Charlotte joins in. But the Captain's adverse comment on the way she is laying out the park is intrusive and begins to give her a sense of isolation. She listens to the Captain and acts on his suggestion that they get a medicine chest for the house, remove all things that might cause lead poisoning, and have apparatus at hand to deal with the possibility of someone falling into the lakes, which the Captain and Eduard had also viewed from the hill. The idea is to remove everything that is potentially dangerous and to be prepared for whatever dangerous eventualities may arise. But the book shows us that life cannot be disinfected and neutralized this way, and that chance remains a force whose workings cannot be foreseen or forestalled.

The conversation on elective affinities is concerned with the operation of chance in human relationships, and in it the attempt is made to invalidate the concept of chance by adducing the laws of natural science. But the argument is not entirely convincing for, as Eduard points out, the "unity" [*Einung*] of a chemical compound is broken only by a force from outside, that this agent is another chemical compound, and that the coming together of these two compounds is a matter of chance. The conversation begins with Charlotte's questioning whether one can apply the term "affinity" [*Verwandtschaft*], which belongs to the human realm, to inanimate things. She is first told that this is just a metaphor, but Eduard then begins to develop the metaphor into an assertion of real parallelism, speaking of chemical substances as "friends" and "acquaintances" who meet and combine, and then the comparison is reversed and human beings are talked of as though they were chemical substances. "For am I not in your eyes," says Eduard to Charlotte, "the chalk which, affected by the sulphuric acid of the Captain, is withdrawn from your charming company and turned into refractory gypsum?" To which Charlotte objects that this is amusing conversation but human beings are higher than elements and words like "choice" and "affinity" should not be bandied around too lightly. The fact is that the conversation is not amusing, or is no longer so. It has become too serious for Charlotte, who had simply wanted to know what the term "elective affinity" meant so that she would not make a gaffe in society. She expresses a similar objection to the word "separation" [*Scheidung*], used here in its chemical sense, because she is essentially oriented towards the opposite. The chemistry, like the music-making, has become symbolic. But this time the speakers are fully aware of the symbolic dimension.

Charlotte for her part is not prepared to accept the analogy: people are not chemical elements, they have the faculty of choice whereas elements do not, and if there is any factor of choice in the natural world, it lies in the hands of the chemist who brings the substances together. The Captain responds by suggesting that the way substances "flee and seek" each other does seem to suggest some "higher purpose" and justifies talking about "elective affinities." His response is not very convincing, for fleeing and seeking imply free will but offer no evidence of any higher purpose. The conversation has ended in a blind alley of confusion.[12]

Charlotte has not taken this conversation very seriously, or she would not have sent the invitation to Ottilie. But Eduard continues to develop its implications, talking of Charlotte as A, himself as B, the Captain as C and Ottilie as D. If C and D combine, then B, deprived of the company of C, will return to A, "his A and O" as he tells Charlotte. But this is no joke, for B and C have already moved in together, so as to be able to use their time more profitably—presumably in cataloging Eduard's mementos of his past. Charlotte is becoming increasingly isolated but agrees to this arrangement, presumably in order to avoid friction. Very soon after Ottilie's arrival, Eduard's *rapprochement* to her is indicated by a series of metaphorical motifs: that she can look over his shoulder at the book he is reading without disturbing him (as Charlotte does in the same situation), that she accompanies him better than Charlotte does, that her handwriting becomes more and more like his. In this process of approachment the descent to the mill is of central importance. According to Walter Benjamin the mill is an ancient symbol of the underworld. I would add that, as we know from so many German folksongs, it is also a symbol both of love and of time.[13] At the mill Ottilie surrenders to Eduard the picture of her father she wears around her neck. Thereby she surrenders to him the talisman that protects her, and she does so with a glance towards heaven, asking Eduard to keep it for her "till we get home." She has been seduced out of her inner protectedness, is surrendering and entrusting herself to this invading force, until they get "home," whenever that may be.

The narrator tells us that while growing older Eduard had retained something childlike that particularly appealed to the youthful Ottilie. At the laying of the foundation stone of the pavilion—which is to be something new and different from the old, established *Schloss*—it is a goblet engraved with the entwined letters E and O, "one of the glasses made for Eduard in his youth," that, by a fortunate chance, is preserved from destruction. We have noted already how much Eduard is concerned about his youth and its preservation—about the preservation of youth even by artificial means such as grafting or cataloging. It is the memory of a nocturnal visit to Charlotte *in his youth* that prompts Eduard to try it again now, much to Charlotte's surprise, for it is clear from what she says that he has not done this for a long time. Earlier, we remember, Charlotte had talked of Eduard's middle age as the time when a man becomes capable of love and worthy of it. On this particular night this happens because of the renewed vitality that has come to Charlotte as well as to Eduard, through love of another person. The birth of the child is the outward sign of this renewed vitality, but its appearance reveals the ambiguity of the union from which it sprang.

On the very next day Eduard tells Ottilie that she loves him. She returns no answer. On the same day Charlotte breaks off her friendship with the Captain, recognizing the crucial importance of her action and expressing the hope that they may both respond worthily to the challenge and responsibilities that it represents. On the day after the catastrophe on Ottilie's birthday, she makes equal demands on Eduard, namely that he should recognize the situation in which he is, and respond worthily to it, thinking of the welfare of "all the members of our little circle."[14] But he rejects Charlotte's objections to the "extremity" [*das Äusserste*] of his passion, and her argument that they are too old to give

way thus to their emotion, and people would think them "ridiculous" if they did. For he does not care what people think, he
is not ashamed of the "extremity" of his passion, he is excited by
the new youthful vitality that Ottilie has awakened in him. The
only thing he agrees to is to go away, to give himself time to
think what to do. But he never renounces his love for Ottilie.

This is apparent in what he says to Mittler toward the end of
the first part of the novel. Now that he is separated from Ottilie,
he says, she is always in his dreams, but as an embodiment of the
idea of absolute love though always attached somehow to the
real individuality of Ottilie. Now, at a distance, the physical
presence has transmuted itself into an omnipresent idea. This is
his only joy. Many persons would laugh at him, he says, for this
foolish lovesickness. But he is experiencing love for the first time,
and this experience is the crown of his life. This ability to love
is the best thing he has ever achieved:

Everything else in my life up to now was but a prelude, marking
time, passing time, wasting time, until I came to know her, until I
loved her, until I loved her completely and absolutely. People have
said of me—not exactly to my face, but behind my back—that I was
a bungler, just a dabbler in most things. That may well be: but I
had not yet found that thing in which I could show myself a master.
I would like to see anyone who surpasses me in the talent for loving.[15]

This passage has been much discussed and often misinterpreted.
It is undoubtedly a crucial passage for any understanding of
Eduard's character. He is here telling us that in his love for Ottilie
he has discovered his real self, and that this love is the only positive
product of his otherwise bungling existence. Ordinary people
will find him ridiculous and sentimental, but he himself is not
ordinary, nor is the nature and extent of his love.

What we have here is the impassioned, anguished declaration
of an aging lover frantically clinging to his miraculously renewed youth and vitality. It is quite wrong to interpret this
passage as the rhetoric of a dilettante wishfully projecting himself into the role of the great lover, or as the speech of a trifler

for whom love is just another occupation for which one requires a certain skill. The passage is not satirically ironic, it is deadly serious. Eduard is not deceiving himself: what he says is true. Only with the faculty of loving has he become somebody. Only in the act of having to justify himself has he acquired faith in himself. Many things are not clear in *The Elective Affinities*, but the one thing that is quite clear is Eduard's love for Ottilie.[16] Once he himself comes to this realization and this affirmation to Mittler, he is resolute in all that he proceeds to do. Neither Mittler nor the narrator can fully comprehend Eduard. The narrator suggests that in going to the army he is seeking escape through death, that "life threatened to become intolerable to him," that by his death he could "make his loved ones and friends happy."[17] But there is not a word of all this in what he had said to Mittler. He tells the Captain later that he hopes to live—for Ottilie.

The first part of *The Elective Affinities* begins as a *pas de deux* and develops into a *quadrille* that breaks up into confusion. I use these terms advisedly, for the movement of the action is carefully patterned, with a great deal of formal stylization consisting of groupings and regroupings. However, for all this stylization, of which the formal conversations and the importance attached to social formalities and formal occasions such as birthdays are a part, the action is swift, eventful, intensely real—and concentrated on the four principles. Reflections have their part in this texture, conversational exchanges are used to bring out the basic tensions, and set speeches such as Eduard's confessional declaration to Mittler are used to reveal the innermost workings of a character. As a result we have considerable insight into how Charlotte and Eduard think, and some insight into the mind and concerns of the Captain. Both Charlotte and Eduard are eminently articulate, and the Captain, though less talkative than they, tells us enough for us to understand him. Not so Ottilie: her natural mode is silence and almost everything we know about her is told us by others. That she should be so is essential to the organization and balance of this most carefully constructed novel. But her silence presents an interesting problem for the novelist, for Ottilie is to dominate the second half of the novel, must do so, and yet how is she to be made to do so?

When she learns of Eduard's departure she is overcome by feelings of surprise, distress and suspicion, watches Charlotte's every movement, and withdraws ever more into herself. When she learns that Charlotte is pregnant, her withdrawal becomes intense: "She had nothing more to say. She could not hope and dared not wish. And yet her diary, from which we intend to communicate certain excerpts, allows us a glance into her inner life."[18] So says the narrator, who has read plenty of novels and is aware that he is himself constructing a novel. For at the beginning of the second part he comments on the fact that he has reached the point when novelists usually introduce secondary characters, when the main characters "remove themselves, conceal themselves, or are reduced to inactivity." The secondary characters of the second part of the novel—the architect, Luciane, the Count and the Baroness, the English lord and his friend, the teacher from the *pension*—broaden the scope of the novel, bring variety instead of concentration and afford relief from the feverish tension of the first part. But these are not episodic but truly secondary characters, illuminating the primary characters and contributing to the development of the primary theme. This is apparent from Ottilie's diary, the articulate expression of her withdrawal and of the sentiments aroused in her by these various persons.

There was a time when critics objected that the sagacity revealed by Ottilie's comments in her diary is not that of a young, inexperienced girl, and that here, as in the Walpurgis Night Dream of *Faust, Part One* and later in *Wilhelm Meister's Journeymanship*, Goethe has shoveled in a number of maxims that he had thought out for himself over the years and were perhaps lying in his desk drawer unused. This is not the case.

Goethe is concerned to show that Ottilie's inner life is much richer than her external behavior would suggest, that speech is for her (as for Mignon) inadequate and that what for her is most meaningful is not communicable to others. H. G. Barnes has convincingly demonstrated that Ottilie's diary is a commentary on conversations and events in the action of the novel and that it shows a definite development in her attitudes. It is not just an accompaniment to the development of the action; it prefigures what is to come, and it represents the essential action of Part Two of the novel, namely the development of Ottilie.[19]

The narrator asserts that there is a "thread of affection and devotion" that connects and relates everything in Ottilie's diary.[20] This clearly refers to her love for Eduard, and the first excerpts we are given from the diary deal with absence and death, with whether the personality survives after death, with "thinking beyond life" [*über das Leben hinausdenken*], thoughts aroused in Ottilie by her conversation in the churchyard with Charlotte and the architect. The second set of excerpts follows on the strange scene where Ottilie, lost in contemplation in the chapel, becomes for a moment dissociated from herself; in the diary she likens the experience to death and speaks of "inner light" that makes all other light unnecessary.[21] Her reactions to Luciane and her entourage result in statements that she must try to adapt herself to society, to control her feelings; to "present one's self as something" seems to her what society demands, as she observes the Count and the Baroness.[22] It is clear that this is hard for Ottilie and that it is not what she wants to do, that it goes against her nature. She is not interested in appearing well in society, for she is not interested in society, and when she is in society she compares it unfavorably with Eduard. In the seventh chapter we are told that during the Count's second visit, Ottilie had tried to appreciate the claims of the "world," fully realizing that in her love for Eduard she is excluding all that is "world." By this attempt to understand what motivates society, Ottilie does attain to some understanding of interplay, of relations, of

Zusammenhang, of Charlotte's ethos. But her conception of *Zusammenhang* is different from that of Charlotte. Whereas Charlotte aims at maintaining equipoise of conflicting demands and attitudes, Ottilie faces a dissociated world which only comes into shape with reference to one focal point, her love for Eduard.[23] The next stage in her development is her attempt to dissociate her love for Eduard from personal desire for the object of this love. This is embodied in the diary excerpts at the end of the ninth chapter, the chapter dealing with the reawakening of life in the garden and the growth of Charlotte's child. Ottilie is at last able to envision a state of equilibrium:

> Beneath this clear sky, in this bright sunshine it suddenly became clear to her that her love, to become complete, must become completely unselfish [*uneigennützig*], and at some moments she believed she had already reached these heights. She desired only the well-being of her friend, she believed herself capable of renouncing him, even never seeing him again, if only she knew him to be happy. But she was quite determined never to belong to anyone else.[24]

Thus the narrator. But Ottilie's diary reveals that this is a resolve, and not an accomplishment, for she realizes that to fulfill her resolve she will have to transcend her nature: "All perfection of a nature [*Art*] means going beyond one's nature, becoming something incomparable."[25] The initial thought presented by these diary excerpts, that of *thinking* beyond life, has therefore become that of *going* beyond one's nature, one's self.

When Eduard reenters the action of the novel in the twelfth chapter, he declares to the Captain (now a major) that although they are no longer masters of what has happened, they are nevertheless still able to ensure that no harm results. But from this point on no action leads to its intended goal. Eduard's attempts to get Charlotte to agree to a divorce and to gain Ottilie's approval for this, are both thwarted by chance and lead to the death of the child and to Ottilie's collapse. It is when she regains consciousness that Ottilie speaks the words: *Ich bin aus meiner Bahn geschritten, ich habe meine Gesetze gebrochen—*"I have stepped out of my path, I have broken my laws."[26] And it is now, and only now, that she enters on a new path, the path of renunciation and selfless love which she had envisioned in the garden, but had been deflected from by Eduard's violent approaches. She now talks of her love for Eduard as a crime that she must expiate, but her attempts at expiation are again foiled by Eduard. It is now that she speaks of the "malevolent daemon" [*feindseliger Dämon*] that prevents her.[27] This daemon works through various acts of chance—Eduard's coming upon her with the child by the lake, Eduard's unpremeditated meeting with her in the inn. She now resolutely withdraws into silence, but in her letter to her friends she asks them to help her "over this time" through their patience and forebearance. "I am young," she declares, "youth will reestablish itself imperceptibly" [*unversehens*]. It would therefore seem that Ottilie views her withdrawal as something she will, or hopes to, pass through and then reemerge. What form this emergence is to take, is never made clear. But it is to happen on Eduard's birthday. Again the "malevolent daemon" intervenes. In his interpretation (if one may call it such) of the seventh commandment Mittler also uses the word "unselfishness" [*Uneigennützigkeit*]—which becomes for Ottilie the death-summons. But we should note that she never renounces her love for Eduard, she looks at him "full of life and full of love" [*lebevoll und liebevoll*] as she dies, and directs him back into life. He is urged to live on.[28]

But this Eduard cannot do. His renewed youth deserts him, his senses dry up, and "One day they found him dead." Since his thoughts were always of Ottilie, the narrator thinks he may be termed "blessed" [*selig*]. The narrator feels himself called upon to narrate something that extends beyond the confines of normal experience. He can only use religious terminology to describe it. And this is what he is doing in the last sentences of the novel. Only in the Beyond will Eduard and Ottilie find their fulfillment. They rest beside each other in the grave *"und welch ein freundlicher Augenblick wird es sein, wenn sie dereinst wieder zusammen erwachen."*

On first reading this seems an unsatisfyingly flat ending. In a way we all rebel against it. How could Goethe, we ask ourselves, end a highly unconventional novel with such a conventional platitude? One can of course dismiss such a conclusion, as Thomas Mann did, as a mere polite curlicue, a concession to what polite society might say.[29] But why should Goethe end with such a cliché? Why end a novel that makes so few concessions to polite religiosity with such a concession? Or is Goethe here being distantly benevolent toward these two misfits? One could, I suppose, interpret this ending, as Flaubert described the end of *Candide*, as being a "conclusion tranquille, bête comme la vie" which is nevertheless "la preuve criante d'un génie de premier ordre."[30] But these interpretations seem to me somehow inadequate—the products of mystification, frustration or even exasperation. It is indeed a *conclusion tranquille*, but there is no need to drag in "the peace that passeth all understanding," as Hans Reiss does.[31] This is not the peace of the blessed. The tragic tale comes to rest, the narrator lays down his pen, and Goethe casts one last loving glance on those finally at rest. Walter Benjamin interprets the last sentence not as a future fact but as a future hope that the narrator utters in order to reconcile himself to what has happened, the hope that the lovers will awaken in the realm of the blessed. Benjamin has perceived the tentative tone of the narrator's diction. But he has overlooked the fact that the narrator does not use the word "blessed." The moment of awakening is not described as blessed [*selig*], but as *freundlich*, which can mean not only "friendly," but "pleasant," "pleasing," "cheerful," or "propitious," according to the context. Most translators render the phrase as "what a happy moment. . . ."[32] But that is not what Goethe says. If he had wished to, he could have written *welch ein glücklicher Augenblick*. But he did not. The moment is neither blessed, nor blissful, nor happy, nor beautiful (like Faust's). It is *freundlich*. Goethe consciously employs a muted word. Or rather he makes his narrator do so.

The use of the narrator in this novel is very skillful and effective. His "explanations" of what is, ultimately, inexplicable emphasize by ironic contrast the unfathomableness of what he blithely "describes." The lengthy space he allows for the conversation on elective affinities is an attempt to explain by coding what nevertheless cannot be codified, and what emerges is a hypothesis but not an analysis. For what happens in the end is not accounted for by the laws of chemistry. The narrator also has another function: by his suggestions of explanations he keeps the extremely disturbing nature of the subject at a certain distance. For what this novel is really about is the ebbing of vitality, the decaying of human relationships and the attempt to graft new life on to them by injecting youthful energy, which then destroys all else and finally itself. The Austrian dramatist Grillparzer said this is a novel that one cannot fully appreciate until one is fifty, and then one understands it only too well.[33] The really tragic figure of the novel is Eduard, but Ottilie loses her youth as well. She hopes it will return. But this happens only in that she is removed from time and raised above it.

Ottilie is the moral center of the novel, but only in a very special sense. She does not attain sainthood, as some critics have suggested, and the "miracles" produced by her corpse are products of credulity, as the narrator is careful to tell us. And yet this credulity was induced in certain people by the fact that they recognized something apart, something unusual, something almost sacred about Ottilie. The architect feels this, the teacher feels it, Eduard celebrates it and even poor Nanny, the maid, has some dim sense of the same quality about her. There is the sense of her being dedicated to something, her silence, her constant gestures of refusal and yet her being a "closed fruit," as the teacher says, a fruit destined to future unfolding into richness and beauty. She seems to open out silently at the touch of Eduard's love, but then to close up again as she realizes what loving him must necessarily mean in the context of human order. In this novel, Goethe's most mysterious work, the marvelous appears in the form of the incommensurable—that which cannot be encompassed by any finite concept of order because what is here conveyed transcends all finite limits and points towards infinity. Here too, then, the novelist is concerned with the search for order, but this time with a keen sense of what must needs defy and transcend any attempt to incorporate it into an interpretation of life as a rationally ordered whole.

To convey this Goethe has used a narrator who does interpret from a sense of an immanent, and on the whole rational, ordering of life. And although he never admits his incompetence, his powers fail at the crucial moments and his very failure points up the unnarratability of what he is narrating. The irony of this novel is therefore more implicit than explicit. Goethe uses every device known to him to maintain a consciously uneasy balance between perspicuity and opaqueness, rationality and mystery. Charlotte and Eduard argue with each other from clearly established positions—they argue well, convincingly, in terms we can readily understand and identify with. The conversations, though stylized, are real. The actions of Charlotte, Eduard and the Captain are all clearly motivated, sensibly conceived and intended. But none of the three can really measure Ottilie. They believe they can, and that is why they think and act as they do. But she defies all rational comprehension, even by herself, for even her own rationalization of her situation and her conception of the way out fails, because she believes like the others in the power of the human will and does not reckon with those forces beyond human control that are symbolized in what Staiger calls the "romantic intarsia" of the novel.[34] It can indeed be maintained that the novel embodies a tension between the classical conception of man determining his own fate and the romantic conception of his inability to do so. And this is true not only as regards content but also in the tense combination of rationality and irrationality of motifs, to which the title of the novel itself bears eloquent testimony.

There is also the tension between what is being told and the manner of the telling, a tension that adds to the powerful effect of the work. This is another function of the narrator: not only does he by his commentary indicate that what is being commented on allows of no commentary, and by his analysis that what he is analyzing is unsusceptible to analysis, but by the very contrived, formal, sometimes even ponderous tone of the narrator's sentences Goethe achieves an extraordinary distancing effect. It is as though we are looking at something from over a wall, a protecting wall to some degree, for it allows us to hold things at bay, to keep our distance. It may be that this mediation was Goethe's avoidance of full, frank expression of the daemonic nature of his subject. It can, I suppose, be interpreted as part of Goethe's "unwillingness" to accept the frightening nature of the elemental, of his self-delusion culminating in the virtual happy ending with its hoped-for pleasant moment of reawakening. It has been suggested that in *The Elective Affinities* Goethe creates order and logic where there is none—and some would say where Goethe knows that there is none but cannot bring himself to admit that fact. Such an interpretation is possible, however, only if we believe that Ottilie's death is expiatory and regenerative of order, and if we accept the narrator's voice as factual narration without mediating commentary, which it is obviously not.

It seems quite clear to me that in this novel Goethe has realized how the import of a novel can be conveyed through the style of the narrator, and that a narrator can be consciously given a definite style in order to create an expressive tension between what is told and the telling. For despite all the talk of Goethe's having an old-age style [*Altersstil*], the style of *The Elective Affinities* is markedly different from that of, for instance, *Fiction and Truth*. It has indeed a conscious artificiality and formality that put some readers off. But formality is an important constituent element in the total atmosphere of the book. Both space and time tend to appear in formalized manifestations—the gardens, the churchyard, the card-indexing, the *tableaux vivants*, the birthdays, the laying of the foundation stone, the baptism, the funeral. But even the informal and casual takes on a strange forced quality through the tone of the narrator, as in the highly stylized conversations that he reports, the carefully patterned rhetoric of Eduard's declaration to Mittler and the excessively balanced *sententiae* of Ottilie's diary. All this suggests the general tone of trying to keep things in order, to stop them from running away with themselves, and us. Here too belongs the widespread use of *style indirecte libre* in the novel, to which Ludwig Kahn has recently drawn attention.[35] The narrator's intention of establishing a pattern, or of imposing one, is seen in other elements in the novel: for instance in the use of various leitmotifs such as drowning or music-making or headaches, in the use of symbols such as the asters that symbolize death, or Ottilie's medallion, or the casket that Eduard gives her or the fireworks. Also in the use of parallel situations, of mirroring characters such as the Count and the Baroness, or the English lord, or the characters in that strange novella which the latter's companion tells. This tale of "The Wondrous Neighbors" concerns two childhood sweethearts who fall out of love but then are brought back together by unusual circumstances that involve the girl's rescue from drowning by her childhood friend who thereby wins her, for whom he is really destined, from her fiancé. We are told that Charlotte is very upset by this story; we are also told that something similar happened to the Captain and a young woman, but not exactly as in the story. Goethe obscures the relationship of this novella to the main action, for the man who finally wins the girl is at times like Eduard and at others like the Captain. It would seem that Goethe has purposely left the tale ambiguous and capable of multiple interpretations, for any one of the four main characters of the novel can be read into the novella. This is what we are meant to do, and this is what the characters did when they heard the story. The crucial fact about the novella is that it ends happily and order is restored. As a mirror-image, therefore, it represents the opposite of what happens in the novel. But it belongs to the manifold instances of order being sought for, wished for, whether sincerely or forcedly, in which the novel abounds.

9

Subjective Epic and Tragic Novel

Goethe continued to think seriously throughout the last decades of his life about the nature of the novel as a form. Among the *Maxims and Reflexions* (written down mostly between 1800 and 1832) there are three important statements on the novel as a genre.[1] These are:

1. "The novel is a subjective epic, in which the author requests permission to treat the world in his own way. The only question is whether he has a way; the rest will look after itself."
2. "Fairy tale [*Märchen*]: that which portrays for us impossible events in possible or impossible conditions as possible.
   Novel: that which portrays for us possible events in impossible or almost impossible conditions as real."
3. "The novel hero assimilates everything to himself; the theater hero must find nothing similar in all that surrounds him."

In the first of these statements Goethe arrives at a new formulation of the distinction between epic and novel: the novel is not a modern epic, not a bourgeois epic, but a subjective epic—epic in the sense of portraying a world, subjective in the sense of a personal view of the world. As in the earlier statement about *Jacques le Fataliste* and like the general tenor of the 1806 review of the three novels for the Jena *Allgemeine Literaturzeitung*, the emphasis is on the attitude and personality of the novelist. In the second of these maxims Goethe proceeds from the premise that art deals with possible as well as real worlds and that its function is to endow the possible with reality: the novel, however, aspires towards a greater degree of reality than the fairy tale, which is concerned merely with the possible. The third maxim presents a new delimitation of novel from drama: the concept of the novel hero as "assimilating" is more apt than the description of him as "passive" in the passage in the *Apprenticeship*, for it connotes more precisely the relation of the hero to his environment.

In the Jena review article Goethe had spoken of a "free view of life" as desirable in a novelist. This idea is related to the implication in the first of these maxims that the novelist should have a personal view of the world, but Goethe demanded a certain liberality of outlook as well. He returned to this concept and this adumbration of it at various times and in various contexts. For instance he once said that Wieland had a "measured, intelligent joy in life" [*gemässigte, geistreiche Lebensfreude*].[2] We have no specific evidence of Goethe's ever having intensely occupied himself with Wieland's novels, which are among the most interesting and important German novels of the eighteenth century, but he did mention most of them. His view of Wieland (embodied particularly in the seventh book of *Fiction and Truth* and in the obituary speech of 1813)[3] was that of a man who, having first dwelt in those "ideal regions" where youth likes to dwell, became disillusioned and turned back to the real world, presenting in his works the conflict between the real and the ideal in an interplay of the jocular and the serious, and opposing both fantastical idealism and philistine realism. There are points of contact here with what Goethe had said, or was to say, about English disillusionment, about Sterne's combination of the jocular with the serious and about Cervantes' fusion of the ideal and the real. Speaking of Wieland's verse-tales, Goethe said, in *Fiction and Truth*, that they were acknowledged to have a cheerful revulsion against lofty sentiments, which, when falsely applied to life, approach *Schwärmerei* (extravagance or fanaticism), and that, by their very mockery of excess, they reaffirmed true values. Here, we may observe, is a point of contrast with Goethe's view of Voltaire: one of the *Maxims* reads: "Where Frenchmen of the eighteenth century are destructive [*zerstörend*], Wieland is teasing [*neckend*]."⁴ In the obituary speech Goethe praised Wieland's serenity, his *Heiterkeit:* indeed it would seem that he had both the "inner serenity" and the "outer pleasingness" which Goethe demanded of the poet.⁵ Wieland fused morality with sensuality, he possessed what the obituary calls "moral sensuality" [*sittliche Sinnlichkeit*]. "Only in what a man does and continues to do, does he show character, and in this sense there was no firmer, no more stable man than Wieland. By abandoning himself to the variety of his feelings and the mobility of his thoughts without allowing any one single impression to govern him, he showed the firmness and sureness of his mind. This intelligent and ingenious man liked to play with his opinions, but, as all his contemporaries will testify, never with his sentiments."⁶ With all its playfulness, Wieland's art remained rooted in reality despite the fanciful worlds of his compositions: "For his poetic and literary striving was directly aimed at life and, although he did not always have a practical aim in mind, it was somewhere in his vision. That is why his thoughts were always so clear, his expression pellucid and tangible, and because he with his widespread knowledge always kept to the interest of the day, followed it, and exercised his wits on it, his entertainment was manifold and enlivening."⁷ At the beginning of the ninth book of *Fiction and Truth* Goethe said that during his student days the works of Wieland's "second brilliant period" (which would include the verse-tales and the novels *Don Sylvio von Rosalva* and *Agathon*) strengthened in him and his young companions their revulsion from abstract philosophy and their turning toward an active, agitated life and the cultivation of feeling.⁸ This attitude Goethe maintained in himself, and it had certainly played a part in the fashioning and refashioning of *Wilhelm Meister*.

In his review of the volume of Spanish romances, which I mentioned above in connection with his attitude to Cervantes, Goethe had stated that a "high view of life" appeared in these poems as irony, and in a letter to the musician Karl Friedrich Zelter of 25 December 1829 he spoke of this same quality, here called "high, benevolent irony," as a salient characteristic of Goldsmith and Sterne.[9] Sterne's humor, he said elsewhere, "liberated the soul"[10]—(unlike that of Voltaire, which he considered of little use to the world because it was a type of humor that provided no foundation on which to build positively).[11] The letter to Zelter just mentioned goes on to make a distinction between Goldsmith and Sterne. Sterne, says Goethe, tends towards formlessness, whereas Goldsmith is "all form." He notes that the Germans had confused real humor with formlessness, the implication being that Sterne, or facile imitation of Sterne, was partly responsible for this. There is some truth in Goethe's assertion. In the particular context of this letter to Zelter Goethe seems to have been referring to the German Romantics rather than to the earlier German imitators of Sterne, and he may also have had Jean Paul in mind. But his attitude toward Jean Paul had become more positive with the passage of years. He had always liked him as a personality even though he charged him with bad taste and lack of cultivation, as we saw above. But now, in the notes to the *West-Eastern Divan* (composed between 1816 and 1818), he came out with a remarkable tribute to the imaginative power of this weird, but great, novelist.[12] The tribute amounts to a recognition also in Jean Paul of a free-ranging spirit. Here he states that Jean Paul is a gifted author who, in truly oriental fashion, "looks around in his world, gaily and boldly, creates the strangest connections, unites the incompatible, but in such fashion that there is always a secret ethical thread running through by which the whole is led towards a certain unity." Whereas the oriental poets worked in a relatively simple world, Jean Paul works in one that is "cultivated, over-cultivated, miscultivated, distorted" [*ausgebildet, überbildet, verbildet, vertrackt*], a world divided into many capsulated parts by technology, science, politics, wars, arts and various degenerations. We exercise our wits on the strange riddles he sets us and we take pleasure in finding entertainment, excitement, edification and emotion in and behind his motley interlocked world. From the vantage point of this statement we can now better understand Goethe's earlier declaration that Jean Paul was the "personified nightmare of the age" (see above, p. 159). Perhaps this was not a negative judgment at all! In this same note to the *Divan*, Goethe says that Jean Paul not only extends our imagination but "flatters our weakness and firms up our strengths." Goethe here recognizes that there is more to Jean Paul than ingenuity and virtuosity—there is moral strength, and a "benevolent, pious spirit." It is basically the same quality which he had called "free view of life" and is related to the "high, benevolent irony" that he had praised in Goldsmith and Sterne.

It may seem strange that, given his emphasis on this quality in Wieland, Goldsmith and Sterne, he should have said nothing about the irony in Fielding.[13] But it is not irony as such that he praised in Sterne and Goldsmith, it is a particular brand of irony—*hohe, wohlwollende Ironie*—whereas the irony of Fielding in *Tom Jones* is surely neither lofty nor benevolent. The irony in Fielding's *Amelia* is a different matter and to my mind much closer to Goldsmith, but there is no evidence that Goethe read this novel. Indeed I believe that if he had read it and reflected on its moral center, namely Dr. Harrison, Goethe might well have included Fielding along with Goldsmith and Sterne in his praise of this higher type of irony. One must add that, for all the talk about the influence of Fielding on the *Theatrical Mission* and despite Jung-Stilling's assertion that Goethe had introduced him to Fielding, there is no evidence at all that Goethe liked Fielding's novels or was well acquainted with them. Perhaps this was because Fielding was essentially interested in the real, whereas Goethe, as we have seen from his 1827 statement to Eckermann on his own *Novelle*, was primarily interested in "the ideal [*dem Idealen*] which has proceeded from the heart of the poet." And of this there is little in Fielding, especially in the Fielding of *Tom Jones*.

This may also account for his silence on Smollett, whose works were well known in Germany at this time, all the major novels having been translated—indeed if one judges from the number of German editions in the eighteenth century his works were almost as well known as Fielding's and he is often mentioned alongside Fielding as a humorist and a portrayer of manners (for instance, by Blanckenburg).[14] *Humphry Clinker* first appeared in translation in 1772, but Goethe told Kestner that year that he had not read it.[15] This novel has one feature in common with *Werther:* the letters of which it consists are never answered (in the novel, at least) so that, as in *Werther,* we have letters but not a correspondence such as we have in *Clarissa* or *La Nouvelle Héloïse.* But, unlike those in *Werther,* the letters are from various contrasting characters, so that the novel does not have a single perspective. What we are given in *Humphry Clinker* is a polyperspectivist account of life and manners in eighteenth-century England. That Goethe could appreciate this sort of thing is attested to by his interest in various travel accounts and his explicit reference to an incident in this novel while describing a similar experience he had in Göttingen on a journey in 1801.[16] In 1827 he told Eckermann that he had often heard praise of *Roderick Random* but had never read it. He then went on to ask Eckermann whether he knew *Rasselas.*[17] These two statements have often been quoted as Goethe's only recorded remark on Smollett and his only recorded mention of *Rasselas.*[18] What has not been observed is their conjunction. Eckermann had been praising the realism, the *"ganz entschiedene Realität"* of *Roderick Random,* but Goethe referred him to *Rasselas,* which is a novel of a totally different order, dealing with a group of characters who indulge in conversations, either with each other or with persons they meet on their journey, about the relative happiness of various modes of life—a philosophical dialogue with an advancing argument but the barest narrative outline. What Johnson gives us is not *ganz entschiedene Realität* but what one might call *ganz entschiedene Idealität*, voices but never

realistically delineated characters. Something similar would account for Goethe's silence vis-à-vis Schiller's praise of the realism of Restif de la Bretonne's *Monsieur Nicolas* in 1798. For
what Schiller described as admirable was not enough for Goethe
the novelist. Is it not significant that it was the *combination of
reality and ideas* that he singled out as the overriding excellence
of *Don Quixote? Rasselas*, on the other hand, is more ideas than
reality, but there are also more precise reasons why that book
would have appealed in 1827 to the man at work on the final
shaping of *Wilhelm Meister's Journeymanship*. The narrative
framework has elements of the romance such as always appealed
to Goethe (mysterious chambers, caverns, robbers, abductions),
a worldly-wise *raisonneur* with points of similarity to Goethe's
character Montan, an astronomer (though here one whose reason is deluded by imagination), a self-contained, isolated province, and its two main characters seeking a form of life that will
ensure happiness—but, above all, a tone, as Bertrand H. Bronson
has said, "of tested wisdom, sympathetic forbearance and ironic
compassion."[19] I am not suggesting that *Rasselas* was a formative
influence on the final shape of the *Journeymanship*, but that
Goethe's encounter with it may have clarified what he already
knew, namely that his novel should be more like *Rasselas* than
like *Roderick Random*. On the other hand it was to be not a
fantasy but the transformation of realistic material into ideal
essences.

The Vicar of Wakefield was undoubtedly one of the novels
that appealed most strongly to Goethe, and he returned to it
repeatedly in the last decades of his life. He had been acquainted
with it since Herder had read it to him (in a German translation)
in 1770, and fully forty years later he wrote this tribute:

The portrayal of this character in its progress through joys and pain,
the increasing interest of the story with its combination of the
natural with the unusual and the strange, makes this novel one of the
best ever written, and it has the added excellence of being totally

moral, even Christian in the purest sense, portraying the rewarding of goodwill and of persistence in the right, confirming complete trust in God and attesting the final triumph of good over evil—and all this without a trace of religiosity or pedantry. From both these the author is preserved by his noble spirit, which reveals itself as irony, through which this work becomes both wise and pleasant. The author, Doctor Goldsmith, has great insight into the moral world, into its value and its imperfections; but at the same time he can be glad to be an Englishman and appreciate the advantages of belonging to that land and nation. The family with whose depiction he is concerned is on one of the last [i.e., lowest] levels of middle-class comfort and yet it comes into contact with the highest; its narrow circle, which becomes even narrower, enters by the natural and middle-class course of events into the big world; on the rich and troubled tide of English life this little bark floats, and in good and ill it can expect damage or help from the huge fleet which sails around it.[20]

There are three points here: Goethe's interest in the character of Dr. Primrose in its real setting of time and place, his admiration for the moral tone of the book, and his equal admiration for the superior spirit of the author, which hovers with benevolent irony over the characters and incidents. The plot combines "natural" and "strange" elements in an exemplary fashion: in a word, the novel is both true and novelistic, mimesis and fiction. This passage (from Book Ten of *Fiction and Truth*) was almost certainly written in 1811 or 1812; it certainly found its final form in those months. In April 1811 Goethe borrowed a copy of the English text and his diary indicates that he was reading it on 9 and 10 April. On 30 March 1812 he borrowed a German translation of the novel and his diary indicates that he was still reading it on 4 May of that year. Goethe was reliving an important experience of his youth and recreating it in literary form. To recapture the experience he reread *The Vicar of Wakefield*. It still retained its power over him, a power which he was now more able to analyze than he could have been when he first became acquainted with the book at the age of twenty. The analysis bears the mark of Goethe's experience as a writer of novels, of his evolving attitude to the novel as a form, and of his own disappointments in life. For Dr. Primrose had become for him the image of a man who maintains his equanimity in the face of irritations. "By such unpleasant little episodes we were however disturbed as little as Doctor Primrose and his lovable family in the serenity of our life," he wrote of certain incidents in his own life at another point in *Fiction and Truth*.[21] As late as 25 December 1829 he referred, in the letter to Zelter, to himself as a true disciple of Dr. Primrose:

The inhabitant of a big city [such as Berlin, where Zelter was living] is, as it were, a guest at one continuous feast where he only needs to nibble to be fully nourished. But we others have to warm ourselves at the fireplace of necessity [*am ernsten Kamine*], looking from time to time to see whether our homegrown potatoes are cooked or not, which our grandchildren wait eagerly to know, trying to temper their impatience and that of their grandfather by cleverly smacking their lips. From this picture you will recognize the true disciple of Dr. Primrose.[22]

One could say that *Tom Jones* advocates prudence whereas *The Vicar of Wakefield* presents a concern with deeper moral values. If Dr. Primrose had been prudent, he would not have refused submission to Squire Thornhill until the news (later proved false) of Olivia's death. His very imprudence is a refusal to compromise on moral issues, and is therefore a moral quality. It was for Goethe an indication of a "noble spirit" that Goldsmith could create a Dr. Primrose respectfully. Goethe was apparently not disturbed by Dr. Primrose's moral sentiments, nor by his sermon to the prisoners in jail. To us nowadays these may seem disturbingly didactic: for Goethe they were probably a natural expression of the character and therefore true and artistically justified. Goethe's emphasis on the irony of the book indicates, however, that he is aware of a difference between Goldsmith and Dr. Primrose, a difference which, in his view, obviated "religiosity or pedantry." For the novel is full of situations where the author laughs—or, rather, smiles—at his characters (such as that of Dr. Primrose being cheated at the fair by a man expressing admiration for his pamphlet against second marriages for clergymen, the same man having previously cheated his son Moses there; or that of the grand family portrait which, when finished, is too large to fit into any room), as well as those conversations, situations or comments in which one character smiles at another, or even at himself. Irony is therefore displayed both by the narrator, Dr. Primrose, and toward the narrator. This complex ironic tone is set at the very beginning of the novel:

I was ever of opinion, that the honest man who married, and brought up a large family, did more service than he who continued single, and only talked of population. From this motive, I had scarce taken orders a year, before I begun to think seriously of matrimony, and chose my wife, as she did her wedding-gown, not for a fine glossy surface, but such qualities as would wear well. To do her justice, she was a good-natured, notable woman; and as for breeding, there were few country ladies who could show more. She could read any English book without much spelling; but for pickling, preserving and cookery none could excel her. She prided herself also upon being an excellent contriver in housekeeping; though I could never find that we grew richer with all her contrivances.

The final chapter, with the argument on which couple should have social precedence at the altar which then provokes Dr. Primrose to exclaim: "I perceive that none of you have a mind to be married; and I think we had as good go back again, for I suppose there will be no business done here to-day," is in the same general mood, as is the gently humorous final sentence: "It now only remained that my gratitude in good fortune should exceed my former submission in adversity."

An enveloping irony, therefore, holds everything in place, and in this sense is form. What we have between this beginning and this end is a plot full of sensational elements (sudden impoverishment, abductions of daughters, house burning, imprisonment), surprise elements (revelation of the true identity of "Mr. Burchell," restoration of fortune, the fact that Olivia is properly married to Squire Thornhill) and innumerable coincidences. The incidents befall the characters rather than being for the most part induced by them (except by Squire Thornhill), and the characters are tested by these incidents, and remain steadfast rather than changing because of them. The characters are realistically drawn and the settings, whether in the country, in wayside inns or in the prison, are also real. The structure is tight up to the abduction of Olivia but is then subject to retardation by inset narratives or discourses or conversations. This combination of sensational plot with realistic characters and setting is what Goethe meant by the book's combination of the "natural with the unusual and the strange." The easy way in which the middle classes mingle, and eventually marry, with the aristocracy constituted the sense of a "big world," for it presented a society much less narrowly class-bound than that of Germany in Goethe's day. And the fortitude, gentleness and persistence of Dr. Primrose established for Goethe the moral tone, giving the book substance as the benevolent but distanced viewpoint of the author gave it form.

In Goethe's review (written and published in 1827) of Ludwig Gall's *Emigration to the United States*, he compares the main character of this work with Dr. Primrose and refers to the latter's "ruling passion" (using the English words) which drives him on without any clear knowledge on his part of what he is doing.[23] The phrase "ruling passion" comes not from Goldsmith but from Sterne. These ruling passions, or *Eigenheiten* as Goethe also calls them, "are what constitutes the individual, the general is specificated by them, and in the utmost strangeness [*in dem Allerwunderlichsten*] some sense, reason and goodwill peers through, which attracts and captivates us." This passage is from his brief tribute to Sterne published in 1827, in which he also speaks of Sterne's great knowledge of human nature and his great influence on the humanitarian and sentimentalist age of the second half of the eighteenth century.[24] But because the Germans lacked Sterne's compensating humor, his culture of feeling tended to appear in Germany as sentimentality. Elsewhere

Goethe had distinguished between Sterne's mind and his feelings: the former had had little influence on Germany but the impact of his feelings had led to "a sort of tenderly passionate asceticism which, from lack of the humorous irony of the Briton, degenerated into paltry self-torture."[25] In a series of comments, included finally in the section "From Makarie's Archive" in *Wilhelm Meister's Journeymanship*, Goethe is more explicit on what he admired about Sterne's mind. He praises his clear distinction between the true and the false, his rapid transitions from the serious to the jocular, his sagacity and penetration, his serenity, contentedness, tolerance [*Heiterkeit, Genügsamkeit, Duldsamkeit*].[26]

Goethe's acquaintance with Sterne's work began, as we have seen, quite early, but there is no record of his having read *Tristram Shandy* before 1817, although he used phrases like "shandyish" or "shandyism" earlier, in Sterne's sense of, as Goethe himself explains, in the *Maxims and Reflections*, "the impossibility of thinking for two minutes about a serious subject."[27] On 16 September 1817 the diary reads: "Yoricks Sentimental Journey finished. Tristram Shandy begun." On 1 October 1830, speaking specifically of *Tristram Shandy*, Goethe referred to Sterne as "the first to lift himself and us from out of pedantry and philistinism"[28]—terms similar to part of his tribute to Goldsmith in *Fiction and Truth* quoted above. The phrase recurs in the conversation with Riemer on the same day. In both places Goethe spoke of Sterne's freedom and his influence on German youth. Four days later, on 5 October, Goethe wrote to his friend Zelter: "I have been looking again into Sterne's Tristram these last few days, which, when I was a wretched little student, was making such a sensation in Germany. My admiration has increased and is increasing with the years. For who else in 1759 perceived pedantry and philistinism so clearly and portrayed them with such gaiety" [*Heiterkeit*].[29] As for the *Sentimental Journey*, Goethe called this "inimitable" in his notebook for 1789. It had had many imitators but was nevertheless inimitable.

What Goethe most admired in Sterne was his freedom of spirit. To comprehend him, Goethe said, one must consider the moral and ecclesiastical climate of his time and remember, for instance, that he was a contemporary of Warburton, the opponent of deistic freethinking. This freedom of spirit lay, according to Goethe, at the heart of all Sterne's hatred of dogmatic seriousness, his dislike of rigid terminology, his volatility and his wisdom. Sterne's nobility of character prevented his freedom of spirit from degenerating into arrogance or insolence—even his lewdness was an element in which he moved with grace and sense [*zierlich und sinnig*]. It was hard to absorb anything from him: he was "in nothing a model, in everything an indicator and awakener" [*Andeuter und Erwecker*].[30]

Of the English novelists of the eighteenth century it was Goldsmith and Sterne who most appealed to Goethe. Goethe was fully aware of the impact of Swift on his (Goethe's) generation, for he had seen it in that friend of his youth Johann Heinrich Merck, who was thoroughly Swiftean and seems to have contributed something to the delineation of Mephistopheles. Swift seemed to be Herder's favorite author, said Goethe—understandably so in view of what Goethe termed Herder's "teasing and scolding." As for Merck, his letters were sometimes full of "Swiftean gall."[31] But Goethe himself was never temperamentally attuned to Swift. There is also no discussion anywhere of Defoe, nor, as we have seen, of Fielding or Smollett. But there are a few interesting comments on Richardson. Goethe must have known Richardson as well as most Germans of his generation, and read him early in his life, certainly by 1765 when, as a sixteen-year-old student in Leipzig, he wrote to his sister on the eve of her fifteenth birthday: "You are crazy about Grandison. . . . But take note, you shall read no more novels except those which I approve. I have thought over the matter and consider it my duty to tell you what I think about it. I will send you a little essay soon that I shall write on this topic. But don't be afraid. Grandison, Clarissa and Pamela will perhaps be excepted."[32] He adds that *Grandison* is a book to be read "not lightly, but thoughtfully" (*nicht obenhin sondern bedächtig*). On the whole he is against her reading novels, with the sole exception of *Grandison*. He seems to have been concerned in a big-brother way with the effect of Richardson's novels on tender minds. The promised "little essay" never materalized (or is lost). But Goethe's sister apparently retained her affection for these novels and it is interesting to observe that the memorial which he thought of writing about her after her untimely death in childbirth at the age of twenty-six was to have taken the form of a Richardsonian novel, for, says Goethe in the sixth book of *Fiction and Truth*, "only by exact and numerous details which embody the character of the whole and, arising from strange depths, give an idea of this depth, only in such a manner would it have been in any way possible to convey an impression of this strange personality."[33] He recognized elsewhere the effect of Richardson on the development of tender sensibility.[34] And he justified Richardson's use of dialogue by reference to the overall "dramatic" quality of his novels—this when long past his youth, in a letter to Schiller dated 23 December 1797, one year after the appearance of the last part of *Wilhelm Meister's Apprenticeship*.

Goethe showed great interest in the work of Sir Walter Scott, exchanged letters with him in 1827 and also enquired about him from time to time through other people. The first mention of Scott's work is in 1821, when, speaking specifically of *Kenilworth*, he referred to Scott's great talent for turning historical material into graphic, living experience [*Historisches in lebendige Anschauung zu verwandeln*].[35] This ability to translate the past into a living present was the quality that he most admired about Scott. "I have always admired," Eckermann once told Goethe, "Scott's ability to unravel complicated conditions and present them with such great clarity that everything separates itself into masses and firm pictures, which gives us the sense of having viewed from above and all at once what is taking place at the same time in different places"; to which Goethe replied that Scott's artistic sense [*Kunstverstand*] was very great, "which is why those of us who are particularly interested in *how* something is made have a double interest in his works and derive such extreme benefit from them" (9 October 1828). As with Victor Hugo he admired the painstaking historical studies that lay behind Scott's novels, but he also admired the artistic refashioning of such material, the way in which the fruits of historical research were used to produce a work of art. Thus, speaking this time of *Rob Roy*, he said: "Everything about it is great: subject, content, characters, treatment. There is also infinite pains taken in preliminary studies and great truth of detail in the execution" (to Eckermann, 8 March 1831). Of *The Fair Maid of Perth*, which he thought not as good as Scott's earlier novels but still good enough, he said: "Here there is still the great talent of extracting from rich material [*Stoff*] the human content [*Gehalt*], working through the most pertinent details and intensifying every situation to the utmost" (to Riemer, 17 August 1828).

This skill in constructing a narrative by full use of characterizing detail and by complete artistic exploitation of situations is something that Goethe constantly attributed to Scott—even admitting that it sometimes led him into mistakes. Goethe mentions a particular scene in *Ivanhoe* where "people are seated at night at the table of a castle hall when a stranger enters. Now it is perfectly all right for Scott to describe the stranger from his head downwards, how he looks and how he is dressed but it is a mistake to describe his feet, his shoes and his stockings. For if you are sitting at table in the evening and someone comes in, then you only see the upper part of his body. If I describe the feet, then daylight enters and the scene loses its nocturnal character" (to Eckermann, 11 March 1831). There was a lengthy discussion on 3 October 1828 between Goethe and Eckermann on *The Fair Maid of Perth:* "How it is made, what a hand!" said Goethe.

In the whole, a sure layout, and in the details, not one touch which does not lead toward the goal. And what detail, in the dialogue as well as in the descriptions, both of which are equally excellent! His scenes and situations are like paintings by Teniers, in the arrangement of the whole they show the highest art, the individual figures have striking truth [*sprechende Wahrheit*] and the execution extends with artistic fondness down to the smallest matters so that no single stroke is without significance.

The two men then went on to praise the individual, detailed touches in the action which give everything a basis of reality and therefore the conviction of truthfulness. "You will find everywhere in Walter Scott great sureness and thoroughness of depiction which comes from that wide knowledge of the real world which he has attained by lifelong study and observation and daily discussion of the most important conditions and relationships," said Goethe. "In *The Fair Maid of Perth* you will not find a single weak place where you feel that his knowledge and talent were insufficient. He has a thorough grasp of every ramification of his material" [*Stoff*].

Scott's attitude to the novel as a form had much about it that would necessarily find approval with Goethe. We have no evidence that Goethe read the *Essay on Romance* or any of Scott's other theoretical statements on the novel. But the way Scott integrated the supernatural into the realistic, his penchant for "marvellous and uncommon incidents" (to quote the *Essay on Romance*), the combination of the "idea" (in Goethe's sense) with the real, and the general transformation of disparate material through controlled form into meaningful content elicited his admiration. It is interesting that Goethe, in contrast to most of Scott's English contemporaries, praised the structure of Scott's novels. He was obviously not one bit disturbed by the contrivances of plot, the deviations into side issues, the sometimes expansive treatment of secondary personages and background. The most impressive thing about Scott was for Goethe his ability to turn great masses of material into real meaningful content.

Such "content" [*Gehalt*] in the sense of "ideal" content or idea-content he felt to be somewhat lacking however in *The Fair Maid of Perth*, despite its marvelous control of narrative and full use of every motif.[36] In 1823, moreover, after reading *The Black Dwarf* and *The Abbot*, he told Chancellor von Müller: "[I] now know what he is out after and what he can do. He would always entertain me but I cannot learn anything from him. I have time only for the best" [*das Vortrefflichste*].[37] It is difficult, in view of Goethe's various expressions of admiration for Scott, to interpret this remark. For he continued to read Scott and, as late as 1831, after reading *Ivanhoe*, he told Eckermann that Scott gave him a great deal to think about, and continued: "I find in him a whole new art which has its own laws."[38] Perhaps this was why he felt he could not learn from Scott. It was an admiration for an artistic achievement totally different from his own concerns as a novelist.

Adele Schopenhauer, sister of the philosopher, has left us an interesting report of a conversation with Goethe on 27 November 1821 on the subject of *Kenilworth*.[39] Goethe spoke of the skillful structure, the insight and the fine characters of the book. Adele Schopenhauer found the Queen vulgar: but Goethe defended this character on the grounds that the English demand historical truth and Scott was presenting the generally accepted view of Elizabeth as having a woman's body and a man's head—to which Adele replied that he could, however, have given her a more attractive, less coarse, man's head. Goethe granted her her views (possibly with one of his Olympian smiles?) but maintained that the character was that of a distinguished, dignified court lady. He himself could never have written this particular book, however, because he would not have been able to keep the poor heroine in such subjection and suffering for so long! Adele then suggested that we know almost nothing of Amy Robsart's previous life and how she got into this predicament; but Goethe disagreed, praising the way in which Scott by constant suggestions and hints filled in this necessary background, and observing that the book had a firm beginning with the wedding. He went on to pay tribute to such new creation from existing material [*Neuschaffen aus vorhandenem Stoff*], and also to the ability of English novelists to build on to an existing tradition of novel writing, whereas the German novelist was entirely dependent on himself. The Germans, said Adele Schopenhauer, were incapable of summoning up new things from out of existing beauty without falling into imitation, and she "introduced to Goethe his so-called twenty-four sons." Very gently he replied that it is usually later that time brings the harvest. Not a very original or profound remark, but testimony to the fact that Goethe in 1821 saw no tradition of the German novel, nor even any effect of his own novels on the genre.

When he was just beginning to read Scott's life of Napoleon, in November 1827, Goethe summed up Scott's qualities as clear comprehension of complex historical material [*Stoff*], penetration to significance of its content [*Gehalt*], facility in treatment and presentation, and the use of fictitious motifs to bring together the widely separated elements of historical material into a comprehensible whole.[40] This last point represents what constituted for Goethe that "new art" of Scott which he had referred to in talking to Eckermann after reading *Ivanhoe*. In his review, published in 1824, of Narcisse de Salvandy's novel *Don Alonso ou l'Espagne*, Goethe defined this new art, of which Scott was the master, as one which combined truthfully portrayed historical characters with other characters invented in accordance with the spirit of the historical moment portrayed in the novel, so that "the moral qualities and individuality of the chosen epoch are symbolized in individuals who, however, are maintained through all progress and change so that a great living mass of realities [*Wirklichkeiten*] combines and rounds itself into a credible, persuasive whole."[41]

The subtitle of Salvandy's book, which had been published in Paris in 1824, was "Histoire Contemporaine," and in his "Observations Préliminaires" to the novel the author asserted that his intention was to throw new light on a country that had always been a battlefield for the destiny of the world and was again in the throes of internal revolution, namely Spain. In this case the aristocracy was for change and the lower classes "in favor of fanaticism and enslavement."[42] Salvandy explained that he gave his work the form of a novel in order to avoid the dry brevity of historiography, because his contemporaries "were not interested in learning, they wanted to listen and see"; and also because the novel can embrace all subjects and styles. The genre of the novel defies all definition and all limitations, said Salvandy: "Its confines are no less than those of feeling and thought. The universe is its domain. Measuring its progress by the advance of civilization, modified by all that hastens or impedes this progress, it reflects the living image of civilization, the sovereign of the world: that is its true claim to glory." Since the novel follows the progress of civilization, the modern novel must conform to modern concerns. This, said Salvandy, Scott had demonstrated: "Sir Walter Scott seems to have taken on the mission of harmonizing the world of the novel with the world of society. . . . He teaches us how a hitherto bastard form, deceptive and disdained, could enrich and extend the domain of history instead of encroaching destructively on it." Salvandy set out to do the same.

Salvandy's novel deals with the history of Spain after the death of Charles III in 1788. The narrative structure is exceedingly complex, as is the plot. We are first given the contents of a manuscript written by a scion of a noble Spanish family, Don Alonso, which tells of the effects of the French Revolution on his childhood and then describes the subsequent degeneration of Spain, contrasting its institutions with those of England and America, emphasizing and demonstrating the increased despotism of church and state in the Napoleonic period, and expressing the hope that Spain may some day regain her ancient reputation, her *gloire*. This account is interrupted by the life-stories of various persons who later appear in the novel, and Alonso's brother, who has become a hermit, takes up the narration for a time. Alonso himself at one point immerses himself in Schiller: "like myself a martyr to the caprices of despotism, like myself dejected by the spectacle of servitude and iniquity, the poet applied his ardent and somber genius to the resolution of the great problem of the universe" [*martyr comme moi des caprices du despotisme, abattu, comme moi, par le spectacle de la servitude et de l'iniquité, le poëte appliquait son ardent et sombre génie à la solution du grand problème de l'univers*].[43] Different political attitudes to the national crisis are embodied in the various characters of the novel, but as the action gets ever more complicated, personal and political motives become closely intertwined. Extraordinary adventures and sensational coincidences dominate the plot-line, which is essentially that of the romance as Scott conceived it and Goethe approved it, and through the medium of these constant comings and goings a vast panorama is unfolded—a sort of earlier, and inferior, *War and Peace*. Alonso's friend Don Carlos takes up the narration with the events of 1810, which saw the collapse of the Spanish American Empire and the reintroduction into Spain of the *cortes*, which became centers of revolutionary activity working towards the introduction of a constitutional form of government. In the fifth and last volume of the novel Alonso broods on the alternative of monarchy or constitutional government and wishes for some fusion of the two. The period of the repressive *camarilla* (1814–1820) is then described in all its horrors, during which Alonso is sentenced to the galleys and Carlos imprisoned by the Inquisition. The year 1820 brings new hope. The King proclaims a new constitution and promises to summon the *cortes*. Those who had been banished now return, Carlos is freed but cannot find the whereabouts of his friend Alonso. It turns out that Alonso is living in the same village as the narrator. And the novel ends with an expression of hope that there must surely be some other possibility than either anarchy or despotism. Church and Throne must be preserved, says the narrator, and then "time, sanity, and God will do the rest" [*le temps, la raison publique, Dieu, feront le reste*].[44]

In his review Goethe maintains that the excellence of this novel lies in what he calls its "piety" [*Pietät*], by which he seems to mean something akin to Latin *pietas*. This piety, he says, is to be found "in the sense of the whole, in the mind and spirit of the author." He then elaborates on this concept of "piety":

> If certain phenomena in human nature, viewed from the standpoint of morality, compel us to ascribe to Nature a kind of radical evil, original sin, then other manifestations of human nature demand that we likewise ascribe to Nature original virtue, an innate goodness, righteousness and especially a tendency to reverence [*Ehrfurcht*]. This source [of virtue] which, when developed in man, also enters actively into public life, we call piety, as the ancients did.
>
> It is strong in parents toward children, weaker in children toward parents; its beneficial influence extends from [relations between] siblings to relations of blood, clan and race; it reveals itself toward princes, benefactors, teachers, patrons, friends, protectors, servants, serfs, animals and hence toward earth and soil, country and town; it embraces everything, and as the world belongs to it, so does it turn its highest and best toward Heaven: it alone counterbalances egotism; it would, if by a miracle it could appear forthwith in all men, cure the earth of all those evils which at the moment it suffers and which perhaps are incurable.[45]

In amplification Goethe quotes a passage from the review of Salvandy's novel in the *Journal des Débats* for 11 February 1824, which stresses the importance, especially for young people, of having something to respect, even to revere. The passage runs as follows: "La jeunesse a besoin de respecter quelque chose. Ce sentiment est le principe de toutes les actions vertueuses; il est le foyer d'une émulation sainte qui agrandit l'existence et qui l'élève. Quiconque entre dans la vie sans payer un tribut de vénération, la traversera toute entière sans en avoir reçu."[46] *Un tribut de vénération*, this is *Ehrfurcht*, reverence that one *owes*,

owes to life, and it is the tendency toward such reverence that constitutes man's natural virtue, from which proceeds that moral strength which alone may cure the world of its sickness. This piety includes love, community sense, national and local responsibility, and religion. Goethe then quotes some words of the hermit, Alonso's brother, in the novel, which assert that man's prime duty is to recognize limitations and accept them, even though this requires great moral strength: "Je crois qu'en effet le premier devoir de ce monde est de mesurer la carrière que le hasard nous a fixée, d'y borner nos vœux, de chercher la plus grande, la plus sûre des jouissances dans le charme des difficultés vaincues et des chagrins domptés: peut-être la dignité, le succès, le bonheur intime lui-même ne sont-ils qu'à ce prix. Mais pour arriver à cette résignation vertueuse, il faut de la force, une force immense."[47] The hermit's fault had been, as he himself admits, that he had not been willing to accept the limitations of his monastic existence and had plunged into the tumult of political life. This basic tension between the reflective and the active life, the need to accept limitation as a necessary condition for fruitful human endeavor, the importance of reverence and of "piety" in human relationships—all these considerations point toward the final version of *Wilhelm Meister's Journeymanship*, on which Goethe began to work in the year following the publication of his review of Salvandy's novel.

Sometime in 1826 or 1827 Goethe sketched out a survey of recent French literature, which he never finished and never published. In it he drew attention to the historical importance of Bernardin de Saint-Pierre's novel, *Paul et Virginie*, mentioning in particular its "reflections on Nature" [*Naturbetrachtungen*].[48] He was primarily interested in this book as an expression of the climate of opinion in France just before the revolution of 1789 (the novel was first published in 1787). He said it was more original than any other work that had appeared since those of Voltaire and Diderot, and that it, and not Chateaubriand's *Atala*,

marked the real beginning of the French Romantic movement.[49]
"This idyllic novel," he wrote, "had a great effect and it will
always give pleasure to the reader, even though after such a long
time [he was writing some forty years later] during which
things have radically changed. One can hardly say what it
brings and what it lacks." Its interest lay in its portrayal of
"that painful lack of coordination between nature and law,
feeling and tradition, aspirations and prejudices, which is so
fearful and frightening in the newest states and was even more
so in the past."[50] He did not therefore feel that the problems
raised in the book had been resolved, and he brought them into
relationship with the growth of new societies. (These same tensions were to figure largely in *Wilhelm Meister's Journeymanship*.) He went on to say that the book expressed everything
that was oppressing people in France at the time of its appearance, the same discontent that called together the notables, made
necessary the Estates General and finally caused the complete
downfall of the monarchy. It was a book written "in the best,
well-wishing sense . . . and this sense lasted for a long time
during the revolution in France." All this, we notice, deals with
content: there is nothing said about the form or art of this
novel, except the brief reference to the nature descriptions.

Goethe's attitude to Chateaubriand was ambiguous. Toward
the end of his life there is a diary entry: "Thought about
Chateaubriand. With the best will in the world I have never
learnt anything from him" (4 June 1831). This remark should
not, I think, be interpreted as a rejection of Chateaubriand. After
all Goethe had said much the same about Scott, and what he
surely meant was that, in each case, this was a type of novel
writing which he respected as something different from his own.
For in 1827 he had granted Chateaubriand "a very remarkable
. . . talent," though a special talent: "a rhetorical-poetic talent,
passionately seeking subjects in the external world, working himself up to [intensifying himself to, *sich steigernd zu*] religious
feelings, a really great physical-moral force, and appearing as

such in the political world."[51] In 1812 Goethe had read *Atala*, and the diaries for March and April of that year are full of references to *Le Génie du Christianisme*, to which he returned again in 1827 (when he was writing the sketch of French literature mentioned above). The *Génie du Christianisme* contains not only *Atala* but also *René*, that supreme expression of destructive, romantic melancholy. But nowhere in Goethe's whole work do we find any mention of *René*. It is difficult to believe that Goethe, in reading *Le Génie du Christianisme*, should have skipped over *René*. He must surely have looked at it—in which case he must have realized how much it owed to *Werther*. Indeed Chateaubriand himself had pointed this out, and it could well be that Goethe did not like being reminded of the fact. It is also significant that Goethe said nothing about Benjamin Constant's *Adolphe* (which he was reading in September 1816), on which *Werther* had also had its effect even though the whole tone of *Adolphe* and the characters of its two main personages are quite different from those of Goethe's novel. It could be that Goethe maintained silence on these two important and powerful novels because they reminded him of what he thought he had already put behind him.[52] And in the very same year that Goethe wrote his review of Salvandy's novel with its concern about active participation in affairs and its advocation of the importance of *Pietät*, he had written a poem, apostrophizing the shade of Werther, which still haunted him.

The exoticism of *Atala* and *Paul et Virginie* embodies a longing for a New World in which various tendencies of the eighteenth century—picturesque, sociologically critical, primitivistic and individualistic—converge. While fashioning the final version of *Wilhelm Meister's Journeymanship*, Goethe also turned to the novels of James Fenimore Cooper. In fact his work on the novel and his reading of Cooper went hand in hand. On 24 June 1827 Goethe recorded in his diary: "Thought about the *Journeymanship*, finished the first part of the English novel."[53] The "English novel" was *The Prairie*. Then, two days later, the diary notes:

"Evening with Professor Riemer. We went through the beginning of The Man of Fifty [a novella that figures in the *Journeymanship*]. Read the Cooper novel till almost the end and admired the rich material [*Stoff*] and the ingenious treatment. It
is not easy to carry through works like the Cooper novels with
such great consciousness and consequentialness" [*mit so grossem
Bewusstseyn und solcher Consequenz*]. But *The Prairie* was not
the only novel by Cooper that Goethe read. In the previous year
(1826) he had read *The Last of the Mohicans*, *The Pilot* and
The Pioneers. On 1 October 1826 the diary records that he was
reading *The Pioneers* for a second time, drawing up a list of the
characters, and observing the "art" of it [*das Kunstreiche daran*].
He was never specific about what he admired in Cooper, but the
terms of his appraisal are similar to those he used in connection
with Scott: richness of material, artistry in the handling, skillful
transformation into a meaningful, consequential whole. Cooper
was generally popular on the continent of Europe at this time,
but there must have been things about his work that especially
appealed to the Goethe who was struggling with *Wilhelm
Meister's Journeymanship:* the pioneer mentality, virgin land, the
mystique of a New World, wanderers in search of fulfillment.

On 25 July 1827 Goethe received a copy of Manzoni's novel
I Promessi Sposi and plunged into it immediately with eager
anticipation, for he was already familiar with Manzoni's poems
and dramas.[54] When he was almost through the first volume he
told Eckermann that it surpassed everything of its kind, and that
"the inner part [*das Innere*], all that proceeds from the soul of
the poet," was perfect and likewise the portrayal of external
localities.[55] We notice that once again Goethe is praising a work
for its fusion of the ideal—"all that proceeds from the soul of
the poet"—and the real. "Manzoni's inner culture [*innere Bildung*]
appears in this work at such a high level that it will be hard for
him to equal it—it delights us like a ripe fruit. And what clarity
in the treatment and portrayal of details, clarity like that of the

Italian sky itself." Three days later Goethe was already into the third volume and found that it stimulated "many new thoughts" in him: for instance, that Aristotle's assertion that tragedy should arouse fear applied also to other genres (for instance, the novel) and that this fear could be either anxiety [*Angst*] or trepidation [*Bangigkeit*], the distinction (in Goethe's mind) being that *Bangigkeit* "is aroused in us when we see moral evil advancing on and enveloping the characters, as for instance in *The Elective Affinities*," whereas *Angst* is aroused by the *physical* endangerment of the characters.[56] Manzoni's novel arouses *Angst* but by dissolving it into compassion [*Rührung*] he leads us into admiration [*Bewunderung*]. Four things seemed to Goethe to be noteworthy about Manzoni as a novelist: his great historical knowledge (which gives the novel *Würde und Tüchtigkeit*, which might perhaps be translated as "dignity (or seriousness) and competence (or thoroughness)," his Catholic faith ("from which many relationships of a poetic nature spring"), his personal experiences of revolutionary unrest and his first-hand acquaintance with the locale of the action of the novel.

But two days later, on 23 July, Goethe expressed some misgivings about this third volume of the novel: "In this third volume I find that the historian plays a nasty trick on the poet when Mr. Manzoni suddenly discards the mantle of the poet and stands there for quite a while as a naked historian. And this happens during the description of war, famine and pestilence—things which are repulsive in themselves and become intolerable in the elaborate detail of a dry, chronicle-like description."[57] In short, Manzoni had "as a historian too much respect for reality." But as soon as the main personages of the novel reappear, then "the poet stands there once again in full glory and compels again our accustomed admiration." On 26 October Goethe wrote to Karl Streckfuss, an experienced translator of Italian classics into German, that Manzoni's novel showed a conflict between historical narration and epic-dramatic presentation; and on 11 November he exclaimed to his artist friend Sulpiz Boisserée: "From an

aesthetic standpoint Alexander Manzoni's novel *I Promessi Sposi*
has been really epoch-making for me" [*machte . . . bey mir
wirklich Epoche*].[58]

So Goethe himself described the reading of this novel as a
milestone. One reason was that it was a particularly striking
example of the difficulty of reducing empirical forms to aesthetic
forms (to use Schiller's terms), of transforming the real into the
ideal (in Goethe's sense)—a difficulty inherent in the historical
novel (and, of course in historical drama) as such.[59] Goethe was
right: there is too much untransposed history in the latter part
of the novel. He saw the problem acutely. But nevertheless he
also admired the "inner culture" which permeated the novel and
which came "from the *soul* of the poet." This conversation
about Manzoni took place just a few months after that on his
own *Novella* (see above, p. 104) in which he had spoken of "the
ideal which proceeded from the *heart* of the poet." The rarefied
morality of Manzoni's novel is not dissimilar to that of Goethe's
Novella: it is based on the belief in the power of innocence, of
the pure and chaste soul encompassed by violence, danger and
suffering—a morality of pious, humble trust. In his essay on
Manzoni's novel, Hugo von Hofmannsthal says there is something reminiscent of antiquity about it: "an old-young humanity
as in antiquity, yet thoroughly immersed in the spirit of Catholic
Christianity."[60] Goethe may well have sensed this "antiquity" in
it. For the young lovers in the novel have a certain similarity
with those in Longus's *Daphnis and Chloe*, which was one of
Goethe's favorite books. Manzoni's young lovers, separated early
by force and finding each other again finally in the fearful shelter
of the fever-hospital, experience a train of adventures in the evil
toils of the world that is absolutely in the tradition of the romance. Even the remote rocky castle of the mysterious Unknown
One is straight out of Gothic fiction. But the violence of the
world pitted against these lovers, a world through which War,
Famine and Pestilence ride destructively, is counteracted by
what Goethe had called "piety" in the review of Salvandy's

novel. For this is a novel of faith and confidence. Renzo enters the *lazzeretto* in search of Lucia with fear but also with hope in his heart. The child at the end of Goethe's *Novella* descends unarmed and trusting into the lion's lair. Both emerge transfigured.

On 15 June 1831 Goethe finished reading the first part of Victor Hugo's *Notre Dame de Paris* and wrote that same day in his diary: "The excellent talent of Victor Hugo cannot escape from the wretched circle of the time, to combine what is most ugly with what is most beautiful—this is what men seem naturally [*in ihrem Elemente*] compelled toward." He sent the first part back to his Swiss friend Soret, saying that he did not want to see the second part of the novel, because he did not know why a man of his advanced age who had tried to maintain "a natural sense" [*natürlichen Sinn*, by which he presumably meant a judgment based on nature and therefore neither perverse nor unsound] should occupy himself with such abominations.[61] The diary records, however, that he did begin the second part of the novel on 20 June, and he comments: "Irritation at the puppets which the author pretends are humans, making them perform the absurdest gestures, whipping them, blustering, drivelling about them, and reducing us to despair. It is a repulsive, inhuman kind of composition." He never finished the second part, and returned it to Soret on 25 June with the comment: "Every trace of probability, natural state and event loses itself gradually in a chaos of abominations." His objection to the ugliness of the book seems to have been, therefore, that it was unnatural. On 18 June he had written to his friend Zelter that, in order to obtain immediate strong effect, French Romantic novelists load on to the reader the very opposite of all that might conceivably benefit him: "The ugly, the horrible, the cruel, the worthless, with all kinds of depravity—this they pour out on us in impossible amounts, this is their satanic business. One can and must indeed say 'business' [*Geschäft*], because a thorough study of past ages, their conditions, noteworthy complications and unlikely realities lies at the base of these works, which cannot therefore be termed empty or bad."[62] In other words: these novelists exploited ugliness for the sake of sensationalism, novelty and a quick return, despite the serious historical research behind their works. Ten days later Goethe wrote again to Zelter on the same subject, asserting this time that everything that is "true and aesthetic" has "removed itself" from this "literature of despair" [*Literatur der Verzweiflung*]. In this letter of 28 June he admitted that *Notre Dame de Paris* had a certain appeal because of its local color but he again repeated the charge that its characters were lifeless puppets which the author manipulates and twists into most unnatural positions; but, he continued, "all this happens with a definite historical-rhetorical talent to which one cannot deny a certain lively imagination without which he could never have produced such abominations."[63] The talent of Chateaubriand, we noticed, had been described by Goethe as "rhetorical-poetic"; Hugo's, we observe, is termed "historical-rhetorical." Both have talent, both have passionate imaginations, but both are rhetorical.[64] Soret reports that Goethe granted Hugo only great talent and imagination, but denied that he possessed genius.[65] The same was probably true, in Goethe's judgment, of Chateaubriand.

Of French Romantic novels other than *Notre Dame de Paris* and *Atala*, we know that Goethe tried twice (in March 1830 and again in July 1831) to read Vigny's *Cinq Mars*, but apparently abandoned all hope of getting through it.[66]

He did read *La Chronique du Règne de Charles IX* (in 1831) and in general liked Mérimée better than the French Romantics because although there were gruesome elements in his plays and poems, these did not touch the inner person of the poet: "he treats them with a certain objective distance, even with irony. He goes at it like an artist who thinks it fun to attempt something of this kind, but in doing so he denies his innermost self."[67] This, however, applies to Mérimée's *Théâtre de Clara Gazul* and *La Guzla* rather than to the *Chronique du Règne de Charles IX*.

Soret reports that Goethe liked "la vérité des tableaux" in Mérimée, and the fact that "his most horrible scenes can be read without ruffling the nerves."[68] What exactly this amounts to as a critical judgment it is indeed difficult to say.

In December 1830 Goethe read Stendhal's *Le Rouge et le Noir* and considered it the best of Stendhal's works.[69] *La Chartreuse de Parme* was, of course, not to appear until seven years after Goethe's death, but by the time he came to read *Le Rouge et le Noir* Goethe had read extracts from *Rome, Naples et Florence* and *Racine et Shakespeare*.[70] He was amused that Stendhal should have filched some traits from Goethe's own "memoirs" and reproduced them as his own.[71] The excerpts from *Rome, Naples et Florence* showed "his free and impudent manner, attractive and repellent, interesting and irritating—you can't shake him off."[72] We have two accounts of his views on *Le Rouge et le Noir*. Both Soret and Eckermann agree that Goethe considered it Stendhal's best work but that some of the female characters were—Soret says "a little too extraordinary (e.g. Mathilde)," Eckermann says "a little too romantic." But both report that Goethe thought these characters embodied great psychological observation, so that one could forgive the author for improbabilities in detail (Soret says "extravagances or improbabilities in details").[73]

The following year Goethe read Balzac's *La Peau de Chagrin* and noted in his diary for 11 October 1831, that it was "an excellent work of the newest kind, and especially distinguished by the fact that it moves with energy and taste between the impossible and the unbearable, uses the marvelous as a linking intermediary and presents with great consequentialness [*sehr consequent*] the strangest sentiments and events." Next day he compared it favorably with *Notre Dame de Paris* which, he said, portrayed the impossible and the unbearable without the intermediary of the marvelous to link them but instead tried to link them by a strange realism [*Realität*] which was persuasive only at moments. Soret reports a conversation on *La Peau de Chagrin* just a few weeks before Goethe died (in fact on 27 February 1832), in which Goethe said that one could attack every detail in the book, but despite all its structural flaws and extravagances it is "impossible not to recognize in it a work of more than ordinary talent and to read it without interest."[74]

We noted above that Goethe had singled out for praise the "consequentialness" of plot in Cooper's novels. In his review of Johanna Schopenhauer's novel *Gabriele* in 1823[75] he repeated this same point in a significant variation: "The novel should really be real life, but with a consequentialness lacking in life" [*Der Roman soll eigentlich das wahre Leben sein, nur folgerecht, was dem Leben abgeht*]. This is a novel of suffering and therefore, Goethe said, demands a woman for its protagonist. He was clearly attracted to the personality of this particular protagonist, Gabriele, admiring her "tenderness and grace" in intolerable suffering. The other characters, he said, are all victims of conflicts that proceed from the necessary or chance conditions of life, "the conflict of will, duty, passion, the law, desire and custom" [*Sitte*]. The general ethical content of this particular book, he went on, is embodied in the contrast of characters, in the conflict of physical and moral forces, and in the binding force of what one is accustomed to, in social and domestic conditions. Education consists of education to conditions, to those conditions under which one must live if one is to live in the world at all and especially in certain circles: but it is the unconditional that is represented as most interesting in this novel, "that boundless striving which drives us out of human society, out of the world, unconditional passion [*unbedingte Leidenschaft*] the only satisfaction of which, when faced with insuperable obstacles, is despair, and from which the only respite is death." Were *La Nouvelle Héloïse* and *Werther* in Goethe's mind when he wrote these words, one wonders. Or was he thinking of the Ottilie of *The Elective Affinities?* The words have an intense quality about them, as if this book had touched off something very important to him. It was the year of the *Marienbad Elegy*, a year when for many reasons, including his acquaintance with the eighteen-year-old Ulrike von Levetzow and their parting, he had had reason to look back on his own youth with its unconditional striving out of the world, its despair and . . . who knows what nearness to death. It was the year of Goethe's closest approach to Byron: it was in this year that Byron had planned to come to Weimar, it was in the next year that he died. Goethe tells us that he was reading *Gabriele* at Marienbad during the summer of 1822. It is a novel of renunciation.

The novel is not uninteresting despite a certain staginess. The central character, Gabriele, is indeed a tragic figure. Spiritually akin to her mother, whose real love was for someone other than her husband, Gabriele enters the novel in mourning for her recently dead mother and oppressed by an eccentric, morose father who has no love for her and sends her out into society. In her lonely unsophisticated sadness she is lost except for her admiration for Ottokar who, although belonging to the rather shallow society in which she finds herself, has aroused her interest by his kindness to a poor old woman. The story of her life is her love for three men, Ottokar, Adelbert and Hippolit, who enter her life at successive stages, the last two after her father, as a final act of revenge, has forced her into marriage with an older and totally unattractive cousin. She remains faithful to her husband, but also to her image of Ottokar, her first real love. Strengthened by this unsullied image, she is able to persuade Adelbert and Hippolit in succession to renounce their love for her and live fully developed lives. But she is unable to renounce her own love for Hippolit and, consumed by it, she dies just at the moment when the news of her husband's death might have allowed her to marry Hippolit. The interest of the book lies mainly in this central character, a passionate being whose whole nature is love, but whose purity, gentleness, grace and poise—all achieved by self-domination—invoke respect and affection from everyone—a beautiful, gifted, but essentially doomed young girl.

And this brings us to the second interesting thing about this novel: Gabriele is doomed largely because of the society in which she lives. It is an aristocratic world but an aristocracy which is breaking up because it has lost its social justification, a collection of dissatisfied and restless epigones, wounded, scarred, frustrated. They live abroad, they go to watering places in search of diversion, or they bury themselves in their ancestral castles, engaging in genealogy, alchemy or stargazing; they play *tableaux vivants;* one has no sense of their contact with the real needs of the world. Goethe appreciated this aspect of the novel too, as his comments show. He saw it both as a novel about a suffering character, and as a novel about the frustrating nature of a society where forms have become meaningless and degenerated into conditions.

Goethe thought that *Gabriele* was successful because it aroused emotion by simple means, leaving us not with pain and misery, but with a sense of pleasure produced by the "surprising truth of the conditions [described]." This was possible only because the author had freedom of spirit [*Freiheit des Gemütes*]. This quality had produced the facility of general arrangement in the novel, its clarity of style, its knowledge of life, its lack of *parti pris*, its general benevolence. Goethe admired its presentation of the praiseworthy and the blameworthy without comments of approval or disapproval by the author, the general nobility of thought and action in the book, its avoidance of the fantastic because the imaginative is always rationally connected with the real, and the way in which the problematic, though touching on improbability, was made to justify itself. It belonged, he wrote, to the genre of what one could term "tragic novels."

I mentioned, with reference to Goethe's comments on this novel, that various things seem to have reminded him in 1823 or thereabouts of the tragic mood of his own youth. Not the least of these reminders was the jubilee edition of *The Sorrows of Young Werther*, which was to appear in 1824, fifty years after its original publication. "Once more you venture forth into the daylight, o much lamented shade!" says Goethe in the poem apostrophizing his own hero. "I was bidden to stay, you to part; you went on ahead—and have not missed much." There is irony here, but the mood of the poem is deeply serious:

> You smile, my friend, with feeling, as is right,
> A fearful parting made you famous;
> We celebrated your wretched ill-fortune,
> You left us here to joy and pain;
> Then once again the uncertain course of passions
> Drew us on into its labyrinth;
> And we, devoured by repeated suffering,
> To parting finally—parting is death!
> How touching it sounds when the poet sings
> To escape that death which parting brings.
> Entrammelled by such torments, half deserved,
> May some god grant him to say what he suffers.[76]

In the apostrophe to Werther, despite its moments of smiling at himself, Goethe clearly looks back on this his novel as a tragic document—perhaps with more understanding than he had been able to muster for it during the intervening fifty years, and certainly with more affection. In suggesting that Johanna Schopenhauer's *Gabriele* could be termed a "tragic novel," Goethe demonstrated that he was now far from wishing to delimit tragedy from the novel, and that he could now envision the possibilities of the novel as a vehicle for expressing the tragic sense of life. In his essay entitled *Gleanings from Aristotle's Poetics* [*Nachlese zu Aristoteles' Poetik* (1826)] he speaks of "tragedies and tragic novels" in one breath, recognizing thereby that they belong together in some critical considerations.[77] And this means that he has advanced even one step further from the formulation of the distinction between tragedy and the novel in *Wilhelm Meister's Apprenticeship*. In fact very little is left of the seeming finality of that statement.

10

Archive into Novel

In the very year of the publication of *Wilhelm Meister's Apprenticeship* Goethe wrote to Schiller that he had the "idea and desire" for a continuation, and that he would have to consider to what extent the characters of the *Apprenticeship* should appear in its sequel. He recognized that there had to be connections "backwards," but he also wanted "to point forwards": "there must remain interlockings [*Verzahnungen*] which, like the plan itself, point toward a further continuation."[1] It would seem therefore that the original plan was for a series of three novels corresponding to the three grades in the medieval guilds: apprentice, journeyman, master. But the last element in the proposed triple structure apparently very soon dropped out of the picture. The question of how to structure the second stage, *Wilhelm Meister's Journeymanship*, was a big enough problem in itself.

Writing to the publisher Cotta, on 28 May 1798 Goethe listed various projects that were at that time either in composition or in his mind, among them one which he entitled "Letters of a traveler and his pupil, under romantic names, following on Wilhelm Meister."[2] This suggests a specific form—letters written on a journey, similar therefore as a structure to the *Lettres Persanes* or *Humphry Clinker*—but gives us no clue as to what the letters might be about or to whom they would be addressed. We can, however, assume that the "traveler and his pupil" were to be Wilhelm and Felix. There is no further mention of a plan for a sequel to the *Apprenticeship* until 17 May 1807 when Goethe recorded in his diary: "6:30 A.M., began to dictate the first

chapter of *Wilhelm Meister's Journeymanship*." By now, therefore, he has decided on a title, and got a beginning.

The novel is to begin (as it does in its final version) with the
story of a modern St. Joseph and his family, whom Wilhelm and
Felix encounter on their travels. This is a sort of novella, but
functions really as an image of the whole moral content of what
is to follow. It is one of several novellas that Goethe worked out
in 1807, all of which were ultimately to appear in the *Journeymanship*. Indeed there is some suggestion that another idea for
the structure of the sequel to the *Apprenticeship* was that of an
organized collection of novellas, what the Germans call a *Novel-
lenkranz*. Five of these novellas were published separately before
the first version of the novel appeared in 1821, and the beginning
of the novel was also published separately in 1809, to which
Goethe added the words: "In the original there follows at this
point a letter to Natalie which introduces the journeymanship
and connects up with the apprenticeship."[3] Natalie is thereby
identified as the recipient of the letters and as the link between
the two novels. But Goethe seems to have made slow progress
with the organization of this novel. It could be that he was
equally attracted to the idea of making it a travelogue and to
that of writing it as a novella-sequence and yet the two were
difficult to combine. Then there was the question of what the
letters written on the journey should be about. In Goethe's own
letters of 1809 and 1810 we find him inquiring about the manu-
facture of cotton. We also find statements that Wilhelm is to
encounter "earthly and heavenly saints" and "some lovely
children." There is also to be a "geological section."[4] The scope
of the novel seems to have grown progressively broader, and the
real problem was to find a satisfying narrative structure in which
to contain all that he wanted to be contained therein. In 1814 he
read through the *Apprenticeship* again and talked to Riemer
about the "generic" quality of his later works and the advantages of what he called a "rhapsodic" poetic structure divisible
into smaller autonomous elements and yet constituting a whole.[5]

The various parts of the novel were written at intervals between that time and 1821, when he published the small octavo
volume entitled *Wilhelm Meister's Journeymanship, or the Renunciants, A novel by Goethe, Part One.*[6] No "Part Two" ever
appeared. Instead this "first part" was reworked, expanded,
rearranged and reinterpreted in the final version of the novel,
published in 1829.

In the process it became a novel about the fullness of life, a
novel with perspectives that reach almost into infinity, a novel of
serene irony as well as of passionate anguish. It has a testamen-
tary quality about it, something of the nature of a summing-up
by one who has lived long, experienced widely and reflected
deeply. The central ethical thread running through it is the
necessity of renunciation, of *Entsagung*, of un-saying or dis-
saying—but this attitude is presented as a positive quality, as
achievement rather than deprivation. It is an "encyclopaedia" of
the inner and outer life of man such as the German Romantics
wished for from the novel as a genre, even though its content
and ethical position are in no wise Romantic. But as a structure
it not only absorbs into itself and fuses into one whole every
kind of experience and every form of communication—letters,
conversations, poems, stories, diaries and reflections—but seems
also to be Goethe's final resolution of the tensions of epic and
drama, novel and romance, prose sobriety and poetic boldness,
characters and sentiments, deeds and events, realism and the
marvelous—a novel concerned but also content with the fact of
being a novel.

Midway through the first version of the *Journeymanship* the
author addresses the reader and requests from him an unusual degree of cooperation. The fragmentary nature of the work is
emphasized and the reader is asked to fill in the gaps for himself,
to help toward the full realization of the work. Goethe speaks of
the great mass of material before him, of the necessity of select-
ing the best, and of recognizing that while some of the material

can be communicated in its original state, other parts cannot. There are, he says, also documents of a statistical and technical nature; there are anecdotes, stories and poems that are germane to the subject but difficult to place correctly; there are chapters which the reader himself is invited to develop in more detail.[7] From this passage it is clear that Goethe is not merely saying that some parts of the novel are not fully developed or properly integrated; he is saying that they cannot, indeed should not, be better developed or integrated, that this sketchiness and looseness is conscious, something that the author wants, just as he wants the disparateness of subject matter and forms of communication. The image behind this central passage is that of an archive containing a great deal of very disparate material in different forms and different degrees of articulation. The structure of the novel presents the fiction of consisting of communications from an archive—from the archive of life which is itself a portfolio of experiences, some coherent but some not, some self-explanatory but some in need of mediating commentary, some completed but others unfinished.[8]

The first "communications" are nine poems that may seem to have little to do with what follows, and yet belong to the same realm of thought and embody many of the same images: wandering, metals, journeys and pilgrimages, inheritance, time as a field to be tilled, longing as the heart's fool. The novel proper begins with a conversation between Wilhelm and Felix, which is followed by a letter to Natalie, and then the account of their meeting the "holy family" of father, mother and child and talking with the father, now called "St. Joseph the Second," and the father's recounting of his life-story. This is followed by a second letter to Natalie, then the account of the finding of a mysterious casket, the meeting with Jarno (who has changed his name to Montan) in the mountains, and a conversation between Wilhelm and Jarno on stones. This leads on to a conversation about education between Jarno and Wilhelm, which has specific reference to Felix but broadens out into remarks on education as a whole.

Father and son then take their leave of Jarno, and journey to the estate of the Uncle. This is followed by another (the third) letter from Wilhelm to Natalie, some letters of a group of young men and women associated with the Uncle—his two nieces, Juliette and Hersilie, and their cousin Lenardo—to each other and to their aunt Makarie, and the story of Lenardo's attempt to put right a wrong done in the past to a "nut-brown maid," an attempt that fails because he approaches the wrong woman. Then comes Wilhelm's offer to find the real nut-brown maid, and his visit to the house of the Collector [*der Sammler*], where he deposits the casket. This Collector directs Wilhelm to the "Pedagogic Province" where Felix is to be educated. These first nine chapters correspond to the first book of the final 1829 version (which has three books). All this material was included in the final version, but much was to be added to it.

Taken as a whole these first nine chapters of the 1821 version represent an alignment of disparate materials rather than an integrated structure. We notice the presence of sensational romance-type motifs (underground caverns, strange inscriptions à la *Magic Flute*, discovered objects, mysterious halls and palaces), and coincidental encounters which turn out to be of great significance (with Jarno and with the Collector) and which also derive from the tradition of the romance. These give the external action a particular tone and a certain unity. But inside this fairy-tale-like structure we have serious conversations on ideas such as would not naturally arise in such a structure but are nevertheless found in fantastic tales and novels of the eighteenth century—in *Rasselas*, for instance, in certain works by Wieland, and in the *contes* of Voltaire. We notice also in these first nine chapters the use of parallel but contrasting figures which are sufficiently similar to establish an idea or type but sufficiently different to bring out individual variations—such as the figures of "St. Joseph" and Lenardo who function as structural foils to Wilhelm (the first as a father, the second as a seeker, the first as seeming wanderer, the second as actual wanderer and future emigrant). The three letters to Natalie indicate that, despite the disparate nature of the materials included, the book does have a focus in Natalie who, though physically absent, is always ideally present as direction and directive. All three of these structural features —the use of mystery and coincidence, the presence of contrasting but connected figures, and the letters to Natalie—combine to point *beyond* the particular character or episode, either to supernatural forces, or to types of situations embodied in contrasting individual manifestations, or to an ethical focus lying *outside* the action of the book, namely Natalie.

The conversations move in the same way from specifics to fundamentals. And there is also the symbolic illumination of certain objects, such as the crucifix which the Collector had acquired part by part over a long period of time, or the mysterious casket that Felix finds and Wilhelm leaves unopened on the advice of the Collector. The casket, says the Collector, had been found through chance and should therefore be allowed to test Wilhelm's fortune: "For if you are born lucky [*wenn Sie glücklich geboren sind*], and if this casket means anything, then the key to it will be found some time or other and precisely where you would least expect to find it."[9] One is reminded of the reference at the end of the *Apprenticeship* to Saul finding a kingdom when he was actually seeking his father's asses. The Collector asserts that one should have faith in chance, and he tells the story of the crucifix to illustrate his point. Whether the casket has meaning for Wilhelm depends, according to the Collector, partly on chance and partly on whether one is born "lucky"—or, in the terms of Goethe's poem *Urworte Orphisch*, partly on one's *daimon*, and partly on *tyche*. But the crucifix is a sacred object, and so, presumably, is the casket. What we have here is the first intimation of Goethe's operating with symbolic structure. This is to become manifest in the final version, but in the first version it is purely incidental and only occasional, for the structural principle throughout remains that of the archive, the communication of disparate though related materials with no real indication of how they are related.

The Pedagogic Province section is a conglomeration of all sorts of contemporary ideas on education.[10] It is therefore itself an archive. It is not to be interpreted as dealing with an educational institution. This is not a school, but a province; and not *a* province but *the* Pedagogic Province—in other words a representation of the province of teaching and learning in life. Nothing could be more off the mark than to treat it realistically as a "model school" and dilate on its absurdly impractical nature. Here again Goethe is feeling his way toward the symbolic mode of the final version of the novel. In this first version the Pedagogic Province already has a basic structural principle, namely that of the Four Reverences. Reverence or respect [*Ehrfurcht*], we are told, is not something we are born with, it is something we have to acquire. We have to learn respect for what is below us, for what is above us, and for what is on a level of equality with us. These are the three Reverences, each expressed in a particular posture, which the Pedagogic Province imparts to its pupils. From these the pupil eventually learns respect for the self. The great ethical facts, including the religions, are presented as mysteries to the pupils of the Pedagogic Province, for there is nowhere any attempt at rationalistic demystification. "Mystery has great advantages," says the overseer in the Province, "for if you always tell someone right away what a thing means, then he will think there is nothing behind it."[11] Goethe consciously mystifies the reader in this first version of his novel. He is constantly leaving loose ends, promising to tell us something later and then not doing so, or breaking off his narration at an interesting point and saying that there is nothing more in the manuscript. The fiction of the archive is eminently suited to this technique, for technique it is, a technique that Goethe here indulged in not merely because it was novelistic but because it accounted for the apparent haphazard jumble of the archive of human experience.

After this first visit to the Pedagogic Province, the first version of the novel proceeds to communicate the tale of "The Man of Fifty," a tale of rivalry between father and son first for the affections of a young girl, Hilarie, and then for those of a somewhat older woman known as the Beautiful Widow. But the story is carried only up to the point where the Beautiful Widow, having been wooed by the Major on behalf of his son, begins to get interested in the Major himself—so that the novella here is essentially lighthearted, with none of the dark shadows that invade its conclusion in the second version of the novel. In the first version there follows an afterword by Hersilie (one of the nieces of the Uncle, who had given Wilhelm the story to read) in which she tells him that Hilarie and the Beautiful Widow are traveling in Italy. It is at this point that the author makes his direct appeal to the reader to flesh out the disjointed fragments of the work. But what follows is one of the most carefully constructed parts of the book: Wilhelm's sojourn with Hilarie and the Beautiful Widow on the Lago Maggiore, the landscape associated with Mignon. We will discuss this important section later, in the context of the final version, where it reappears virtually unchanged.

After this sojourn in Italy Wilhelm revisits the Pedagogic Province, and then is together again with Jarno at a mountain festival. No record survives of what they talked about, says the narrator. But he does find in the archive statements to the effect that Wilhelm at this time encountered "various old friends," and not merely Jarno, though the records are hazy on these meetings. But one mysterious experience that he has had with Natalie, a dreamlike encounter, is given us in Wilhelm's own words. He is standing one day on a high peak in the mountains, so narrow that there is only room for one person to stand there. He looks across to another peak right opposite and discerns several people standing there, mostly women, one of whom steps right up to the edge. Wilhelm is convinced that this is Natalie, and looks at her through a telescope, achieving thereby a "magical" union. He has a strange feeling of floating indeterminately between proximity and distance. And then suddenly the ladies catch sight of him, a white handkerchief is waved, and she, Natalie, now looks at him through her telescope, while he engages in gestures of affection and might have fallen into the abyss between them, had not a helping hand removed him "from danger and at the same time from the greatest bliss."[12]

We have heard nothing of Natalie since Wilhelm's third letter to her, but now suddenly here she is again, and physically present, though only through a telescope, not really in normal sight but in some kind of "magical" transfiguration, in a place difficult of access, and for one single observer, floating between near and far. It is a transcendental experience, Natalie representing once again the infinite potentiality of Wilhelm's finite reality. This passage, which is of great beauty and central to this version, was competely excised by Goethe when he was composing the second version of the novel. One can, I think, surmise why. Natalie's appearance in this dreamlike vision is too real to represent the ideal, for the white handkerchief (which in German has to be a *Schnupftuch!*) and the reference to her slender arms which had sympathetically embraced him in the past are too gross for the rarefied atmosphere of this mountaintop experience. Also: Wilhelm's vision of eternity was to take place, in the second version of the novel, in Makarie's observatory. Goethe decided that this important experience—a telescope experience in both versions of the novel—belonged rather in the house of Makarie. For in the final scheme of the novel he is careful not to confuse the values represented by Natalie and Makarie respectively.

In the first version this dream-vision is followed by Wilhelm's encounter with the *Bund*, a group of persons who have decided to spend their lives wandering. Lenardo is their leader, and among them is our old friend Friedrich. They do not intend to emigrate to another country, because, as Friedrich explains to Wilhelm, they are fully aware of the disappointments encountered by those who leave their native land in the hope of finding a better set of conditions.[13] By wandering in their own country this community of seekers (for that is what they are) are striving to learn how they may become more qualified to get the best out of life. Two novellas are incorporated into this section of the novel: a fairy tale of great subtlety and charm, "The New Melusina," and the tale of "The Foolish Pilgrim," the latter communicated by Friedrich from Lenardo's rich archive. The point of the latter story is to underscore the difference between wandering with a purpose and wandering from fixed prejudice; the idea in the Melusina story, which is also concerned with a casket, is that there are mysteries better left untouched and possibilities of existence better left unexplored.

The external action of the novel is now brought rapidly to a sort of conclusion. For although this 1821 version is described on the title page as "Part One," it does reach a conclusion and can be said to be complete in itself. Wilhelm finds the real nut-brown maid for Lenardo, Hersilie informs Wilhelm that the key has been found to the casket, Lenardo promises to give Wilhelm parts of his diary (but doesn't, for the moment!), Friedrich tells a lighthearted story—again taken from Lenardo's collection—about a stuffy young lover who does not have the guts to tell a girl that he has fallen out of love with her and therefore has to be taught a lesson by the girl herself. The last chapter contains Lenardo's speech to the assembled company, some of whom decide to "wander," but others to remain where they are, to stay put. And the novel ends with the song of the wanderers:

> Where we can enjoy the sunlight
> We are free from every care:
> That we may disperse within her
> Therefore is the world so great.[14]

Thematically the novel is concerned with wandering, and the song at the end and the picture of the "Holy Family" at the beginning are different manifestations of this same basic idea. Although its form is that of partial and separate revelations from an archive, there is a general progression in the work from aimless wanderlust at the beginning to purposeful wandering-as-seeking at the end, a progression in which various aspects of wandering are displayed as individual variations, and a tension between mobility and stability is established by the time we reach the Collector. "Every sheet in Lenardo's archive is in the sense of the whole," says Friedrich in the novel.[15] Goethe wrote similarly in a letter: "The coherence, goal and intention [*Zusammenhang, Ziel und Zweck*] lie inside the book itself; if it is not all of one piece, it is certainly all in one sense" [*ist es nicht aus Einem Stück, so ist es doch aus Einem Sinn*].[16]

This sense, *Sinn*, of the novel occupied him greatly, especially in view of the rather negative reception that the book had received. And so, as early as 1824, we find him engaged in a total revision of the work, which also involved considerable expansion. The passage from the diary that Lenardo had promised us is now included and becomes one of the most important parts of the final version. The tale of the nut-brown maid is now extended so as to find its conclusion in this passage from Lenardo's diary. The conversations with Montan are also extended, and now we *are* told what he and Wilhelm talked about at the mountain festival. The tale of "The Man of Fifty" is carried to its conclusion. Two series of maxims are worked into the texture of the novel. The *positive* aspect of emigration is now elaborated, and America enters into the thematic scheme of the novel. A speech by the leader of the non-wanderers is added, and now serves to balance the speech of Lenardo, which is retained intact. And the figure of Makarie—in the first version just a nice aunt to whom one writes letters—is developed into a major element in the structural pattern of ideas in the novel. On 11 September 1828 Eckermann reported that the *Journeymanship* was now to be a novel in three volumes, but was still far from finished:

The manuscript has blank spaces everywhere which need to be filled out. There are gaps in the exposition; sometimes a skillful transition must be found so that the reader will not have such a feeling that this is a collective work [*ein kollektives Werk*], sometimes there are fragments of great importance with no beginning, others with no end. And so in all three volumes there is still a great deal to be done, in order to make this important book both acceptable and pleasant.[17]

And so the very disconnectedness, the conscious withholding of transitions, the express cultivation of and emphasis on the un-explained which had apparently so much appealed to Goethe, was now removed by filling in gaps, providing transitions, be-ginnings and endings. The whole novel was thought through again and transformed from a collective work into a contra-puntal work.

11

Counterpoint in the Symbolic Mode

The counterpoint of the final *Journeymanship* is of various kinds: there are themes and counterthemes, there are primary subjects and secondary subjects, there is a main structure into which lesser and to a certain extent contrasting structures are introduced. The total effect is one of richness achieved by polar tensions, of tensions building one upon the other, progressively and yet not dialectically, for no synthesis is reached at the end.

The novel begins, as in the first version, with a conversation between Wilhelm and Felix in which the child's thirst for knowledge opens up the world to the father. This recapitulates a motif which had been announced toward the end of the *Apprenticeship* thus: "Wilhelm saw Nature through a new organ, and it was the child's curiosity and desire for knowledge that brought him to the realization of how feeble his interest had been in the things outside him and how little he knew."[1] Through Felix Wilhelm learns to see, and it is significant that the first important experience of his journeymanship should be a visual experience. It is, however, not just a question of seeing, but of perceiving and interpreting. The "Joseph family" becomes an idea, and at first he asks himself whether these are real people or merely phantom materializations of an idea in his head. But they are real enough and his interpretation of them turns out to be wrong, for although we have a mother, child and donkey, this is no Flight into Egypt. This family is not fleeing anything or anywhere; they are going home. Their home is indeed unusual, in that it consists of a disused monastery church; but it is nevertheless home and this family group represents a settled existence in contrast to the uncertain seeking of Wilhelm and Felix.² This polar tension between wandering and staying, between seeking and possessing, between mobility and stability pervades the whole novel and constitutes its most important thematic counterpoint.³

The first of the three books of the novel begins with this picture of the two real wanderers and the family of seeming wanderers, and closes with the conversation of the Wanderer Wilhelm with the Collector, the *Sammler*, whose whole being consists in *sammeln*, a verb which implies both collecting and collectedness. The Collector represents preservation in a world of change, the imparting of a degree of permanence to things which, without his attention, would fall into disuse and decay. His house symbolizes his concern:

a house, old and serious in character [*von alter, ernster Bauart*], but well preserved and clean in appearance. Opaque windowpanes, wondrously fitted together, gave rich splendor of colors to the inside. The inside did indeed correspond to the external appearance of the house. In clean rooms there were all sort of implements that had been used for several generations mixed in with little that was new. . . . The clocks had struck at many a birth and death, and everything else that was around showed that the past can survive into the present.⁴

The Collector insists on the importance of realizing the idea represented by his activity: "You can see here how long something can last, and one must see this as a counterweight to what changes so rapidly in the world." The idea represented by the house of the Collector is, however, not just that of a Preservation Society, for he asserts that *Beharrlichkeit auf dem Besitz*—concentration on what one possesses and persistence in it—imparts energy. His philosophy is therefore not passive antiquarianism but active transvaluation of the past into the present. In his conversation Wilhelm stresses that change is also valuable. The Collector agrees, but adds that "what preserves itself longest achieves most." From this remark it is clear that we are dealing here not with two mutually exclusive concepts but with a tension which is more fruitful than either element of the tension in isolation, because each element conditions and modifies the other.

This tension between movement and rest is sometimes made explicit, as when Montan, recalling an old legend, compares Wilhelm to a wanderer's staff which sprouts green leaves wherever one sets it down but never takes root anywhere.[5] The reference is to a pilgrim's staff, and the words "pilgrim" and "pilgrimage" are used throughout the novel to designate traveling towards a definite destination, whereas "wandering" seems to imply that no final destination is as yet decided upon. The Foolish Pilgrim in the novella of that name is an example of someone who believes she has a goal but is really just a wanderer with a mistaken and self-destructive *idée fixe*. Hersilie calls Lenardo a "crazy traveler" at one point.[6] He too thinks that he has a legitimate goal (to put right the wrong he did to Valerine, his "nut-brown maid"), but he is really operating from a false sense of scrupulousness, or "innate conscientiousness" as Makarie calls it.[7] This, uncontrolled as it is in Lenardo's case, results in the assertion of duties and demands which do not exist or apply. The fact that, for all his sense of guilt, he gets the girl's name wrong and goes after the wrong person (much to her surprise) is a sign that there is something foolish about Lenardo too at the beginning of the novel. It is also an example of that "high benevolent irony" which Goethe had so much admired in Goldsmith. For there is much good about Lenardo. He is a pioneer type, one naturally attracted to going back to beginnings, to *uranfängliche Zustände*, though not out of any antiquarian fervor, but in order to transform what survives, albeit in poor state, into something vital and creative for the future. Thus he wants to go to America, partly out of a reaction against sophistication and a desire to return to simpler things, partly out of a New Frontier spirit and because he is essentially a do-it-yourself-man, but also because, as he explicitly tells us, there is "over there" a neglected

piece of family property that he wishes to develop.[8] The desire
to return to origins is therefore connected with his "innate conscientiousness" toward inheritance. But whereas the Uncle
returns from America to Europe in order to maintain his cultural heritage in the environment from which it derived, Lenardo
wants to restore *his* cultural heritage in a land to which it was
transplanted and where it has been allowed to fall into neglect,
to restore it in a new, unencumbered environment to real power
and effectiveness, to transform the passive into the active, a
sterile, static anachronism into productive, vibrant presence.

In the structure of this first book of the novel the tension
between movement and rest does achieve some kind of envisioned resolution in the concept of "stable mobility" [*des
beharrlich Bewegten*] represented by Makarie. Overcome by the
sense of his insignificance in the face of the cosmos, Wilhelm
asks himself in Makarie's observatory how he can conceive of
his place in such a universe except by embodying that "stable
mobility circling around a clear midpoint" [*ein beharrlich Be-
wegtes, um einen reinen Mittelpunkt kreisend*] which he observes
in the heavens.[9] The important idea here is that the tension of
static and dynamic requires a "midpoint" (or center, or focus)
to be productive and to represent order, but that this center must
be within man himself, and must presumably be found by man
himself. The focus of Wilhelm's activity, in this *second* version
of the novel, is to lie not outside of himself in his potential as
represented by Natalie (as in the *first* version) but within himself, and is therefore to involve an act of self-discovery. This
is the important realization that comes to him in Makarie's observatory. This is why this scene corresponds to the mountain
vision of Natalie in the first version and replaces it. In both there
is a telescope, permitting more than normal vision.

A second thematic polarity in the novel is that between stones
and stars. As in the counterpoint of wandering and staying,
these appear first as opposites: Montan has a special relationship
to stones, Makarie to the stars. But as the novel proceeds we

come to realize that both are manifestations of one idea, namely
the relation of man to the supernatural. Montan has consciously
withdrawn from the world of man, and dwelling among the
mountain rocks, removed as it were from the incidentals of space
and time, he perceives only basic patterns:

It was a very fine day and Montan let them [Wilhelm and Felix]
observe the glorious view in every particular. Here and there were
several more mountaintops like that on which they were standing.
There was an intermediate range which seemed to be striving toward them but which never reached anything like the height at
which they were. Further off this became flatter and flatter although
there were still strangely projecting rock formations. And then in
the extreme distance lakes and rivers were visible, and a fruitful area
extended like a sea. If one's glance receded from this, then it fell into
the midst of shuddering depths in labyrinthine proximity to each
other with waterfalls thundering through them.[10]

The prose is exceedingly difficult to translate, but I have tried
to suggest the symbolic overtones of the words. *Schauderhafte
Tiefen,* chasms so deep that they make one shudder, *labyrinthisch
miteinander zusammenhängend,* connected in some sort of labyrinthine structure of dizzying obscurity. This area of dark uncertainty lies between the mountaintop on which they now so
firmly stand, and the fruitful area in the distance that is also the
future. The passage is typical of the symbolic landscapes of the
Journeymanship: mountains as the realm of thought, valleys and
plains as the sphere of action.[11]

Let us follow this first mountain conversation a little further.
Wilhelm observes that Montan does not always answer Felix's
questions truthfully. Montan replies that one should tell someone
only what he is able to understand, and with children one should
concentrate on how things are, rather than how they came to be
that way. Wilhelm counters this by saying that existence is so
complex and variegated that it is easier for children to ask
"Whence?" or "Whither?" This implies, of course, an avoidance
of the present in favor of the past or the future. Inability to size

up and live in the present has always been Wilhelm's problem. Montan declares that any such explanations addressed to children would necessarily be superficial: there is little they can really comprehend. But this is true of all men, says Wilhelm, and one longs for that happy time "when what is comprehensible seems trivial and foolish" [*jene herrliche Epoche, in der uns das Fassliche gemein und albern vorkommt*].[12] The point would seem to be that when one has acquired a sense of the incomprehensible, of what is not *fasslich*, a higher stage of understanding is reached. Montan calls such a state "halfway between despair and deification" [*Mittelzustand zwischen Verzweiflung und Vergötterung*], and is himself in such a state. In the *Apprenticeship*, as Jarno, he had been essentially a rationalist, devoted to *das Fassliche*: now as Montan in the *Journeymanship* he has passed beyond this, seeking what transcends it, what is both higher and deeper. He is not a *pater ecstaticus* however, but a geophilosopher, still essentially concerned with this world, with the earth, with metals —and with stones, "because these are at least not comprehensible,"[13] whereas men and women are all too easily comprehended. He talks about reading the alphabet of nature without someone's critical commentary; he has turned his back on mediation and confronts the unmediated directly. In the third book of the novel we encounter a strange female character, the "Stone-Feeler" [*Gesteinsfühlerin*], who can sense the presence of metals, coal and water beneath the surface of the ground. She is therefore in immediate and magical touch with the subterranean, the telluric, the elemental. She is associated with Montan and is one of the first to emigrate to America, where her powers will obviously be useful in virgin land. Goethe treats her ironically, as a foil to Montan's seriousness, saying that he tells about her so that scientists may be alerted to the existence of such persons.[14]

The polar contrast to the Stone-Feeler seems to be Makarie, whose relation to the stars is as immediate as that of the other woman to stones. Her relationship to the stars is very special and very individual, we are told; and it is prefigured in a dream of

Wilhelm's in which he sees her face as a star rising upwards into the celestial galaxy.[15] Her young companion Angela explains to Wilhelm that just as in a poet's mind the "elements of visible world" are latent and are gradually extrapolated by visual experiences, Makarie has an innate sense of the basic relationships of the solar system, and her actual, external experience of the solar system merely confirmed the truth of these presentiments. But Makarie not only *mirrors* the solar system; she is "spiritually an integrating part of it" and as such moves within it.[16] All this is communicated to the reader in the first Makarie chapter (Book One, Chapter Nine). In the second Makarie chapter (Book Three, Chapter Fifteen) we are told that since her childhood Makarie had pursued a spiral path around the sun which has resulted in her moving ever farther away from the center toward the outer regions. Corporeal beings strive toward the center, spiritual beings toward the periphery. Makarie is therefore the polar opposite to Montan, who is essentially centripetal, oriented towards the center of the earth. By the fact that Makarie both mirrors and figures in the cosmos, she represents the highest form of order presented in this novel, and indeed in all of Goethe's work.[17]

Which brings us to the third great thematic polarity of the novel: that of part and whole, narrow and broad, one-sided and many-sided. Montan declares in his first conversation with Wilhelm that many-sidedness provides the atmosphere, the "element" [*Element*], in which one-sidedness can operate. "Yes, now is the time of one-sidednesses [*Einseitigkeiten*]; it is a good thing that one should understand this and operate in this spirit [*in diesem Sinne*] for oneself and others."[18] In the *Apprenticeship* the word *Element* had been used to denote the raw material to be shaped: here the word is used specifically for what is shaped into *Bildung*, education or culture. The essential point is that one should start with a wide range of interests and out of this evolve a speciality. The speciality will be too narrow without the preceding wider activity, and real "one-sidedness" should mirror "many-sidedness"

[*Vielseitigkeit*]. "To know and execute one thing well gives more culture than halfness in a hundredfold" [*Eines recht wissen und ausüben gibt höhere Bildung als Halbheit im Hundertfälti-gen*] says the Collector.[19] This idea underlies the educational system of the Pedagogic Province, where every effort is made to discover the individual talent, the "one-sidedness" of every pupil and to develop this. Great stress is laid on handicraft as the basis from which art proceeds. After Wilhelm has decided to become a surgeon, he talks of his anatomical studies as combining technical and artistic aspirations, and in the big conversation with Friedrich in the third book he says that "what is now art must become craft [*Handwerk*], and what occurs in the particular must become possible in the general."[20] It is not clear whether "art" in this sentence is to be equated with "the particular" and "craft" with "the general," or whether Goethe is combining two quite distinct statements. But throughout the *Journeyman-ship* one does have the feeling that Goethe assigns more importance to craft than to art. Hence the detail with which certain crafts, such as spinning and weaving, are described.

The polarity of narrow and broad has combined with the opposition of one-sidedness and many-sidedness, and perhaps with that of art and craft, to develop a basic thematic counterpoint of particular and general. What Wilhelm learns on his journeying is to transform the general into the particular. And curiously enough it is Mignon who plays a leading part in this process.

It is Wilhelm Meister himself who describes his visit to the Lago Maggiore as a pious pilgrimage. Or at least seems to. For at the end of Chapter Six of Book Two of the *Journeymanship* he declares that he is about to embark on a *fromme Wallfahrt*, and in the next chapter he finds his way to the Lago Maggiore. We therefore assume that this journey represents the pilgrimage and that the Lago Maggiore was his intended destination, though we are never told either of these things. The nature of the "pilgrim-age," its purpose and the need for it, are not readily apparent:

Wilhelm speaks of it as something urgent, something which has
to be accomplished before he can return to his educative wanderings, but also as prerequisite for a new beginning in life, something that involves a finishing up, a sort of reckoning with the
past [*er, vor Beginn eines neuen Lebensganges, so manches
abzuschliessen gedachte*].[21] His journey eventually leads him to
the landscapes associated with Mignon. But why should a reckoning with Mignon be so urgently necessary before he can begin
a new life? Why should Mignon reappear at this point when
there had been so little mention of her since her death, and none
so far in the *Journeymanship?* And why is this a "pious pilgrimage"?

It is the painter he meets who leads him spiritually and geo-
graphically to Mignon. And after they have visited the localities
associated with her, we come, one third of the way through the
chapter, to this sentence: "Wilhelm himself felt that their express purpose [to see the localities of Mignon's early life] had
been achieved, but he could not deny the fact that his desire to
see Hilarie and the Beautiful Widow had to be satisfied, if he
were to leave these parts with an easy mind."[22] It may therefore
be that the goal of Wilhelm's sentimental journey, of his "pious
pilgrimage," was not Mignon but Hilarie and the Widow. This
makes much better sense: for as the center of the emotional conflict between the father and son of the novella "The Man of
Fifty," Hilarie forms an ironical parallel to Hersilie, toward
whom Wilhelm feels a dangerous attraction though she is really
destined for his son Felix. The finding of Hilarie and the Widow
will continue the interpolated novella of "The Man of Fifty,"
projecting its characters into the main framework by associating
them directly with Wilhelm. What have so far been fictional
characters for Wilhelm now become real acquaintances. We
should add that Mignon has so far been only a fictional character
for the painter, for his only knowledge of her, we are told, has
been gained from his reading of *Wilhelm Meister's Apprenticeship!*

This cross-fertilization of fiction and life is, however, much more than a bravura piece of Romantic irony, for by the complex mirrorings which it involves, this section of the novel is making an important statement about the relation between art and life. Wilhelm, like the painter, is checking fiction against life, imagination against reality. The painter is able, in his sketches, to render an imaginative vision in terms that move Wilhelm, open his eyes to nature—and, at the same time, reveal to Wilhelm that he himself will never succeed in being an artist. This is an important realization for Wilhelm to reach, and it happens in the atmosphere of Mignon. For this painter art is interpretation, not flight as it had been for Aurelie and, to a certain extent, for the Wilhelm of the *Apprenticeship*. Impelled by the image of Mignon, this painter incorporates that "formative force" [*bildende Kraft*] in reverence for which we were all beckoned back into life at Mignon's funeral, and he interprets her—and through her, life itself—in his pictures. He has drawn her many times, and there is one picture above all that impresses Wilhelm. It depicts the landscape of the last stanza of Mignon's famous song of longing, "Knowst Thou the Land," that landscape which *has* to be passed through: "Dahin geht unser Weg." But there are two additions and one reinterpretation. In the picture, the landscape is crowded with people—wild folk, gipsylike, inspiring neither fear nor trust—and, in the midst of them, Mignon herself, the lovable child, being led but not dragged, twice characterized as "graceful" [*anmutig*] and contrasted with the motley crowd and the grim, fierce landscape. Secondly, there is a bridge in this pictorial representation, a bridge which "indicates the possibility of connection with the rest of the world."[23] There was no such bridge in the song, with its desolate no-man's-land of deathly inevitability where dragons lurk in the caves. The painter has a cave in his picture, but instead of the firm statement: "In caverns dwell the ancient brood of dragons" [*In Höhlen wohnt der Drachen alte Brut*], we are told that the painter's cave can be considered *either* as a "nature-workshop

of mighty crystals" [*Naturwerkstatt mächtiger Kristalle*] *or* as
the dwelling place of mythical monsters [*Aufenthalt einer
fabelhaft-furchtbaren Drachenbrut*]. It all depends, obviously,
on what one chooses to make of it. In this rendition the deathly
terror is removed; the bridge to the world is there and Mignon
stands in the midst of pulsating life as ambiguous in potential as
nature's cave.

The next sentence reads: "It was with some degree of awe and
respect that the two friends visited the palace of the Marchese."
We are moving back through the song, taking the stanzas in
reverse order. Not much is said here about the house, the house
of the past in Mignon's song, that house where the statues had
asked her pityingly what life had done to the poor child [*Was
hat man dir, du armes Kind, getan?*]—perhaps because that question is now an embarrassing one for Wilhelm. And, rather
quickly, we move into the first stanza which, like the third, is
transfigured in the reliving. The lemons, oranges and laurel are
there—but the myrtle of girlhood is replaced by the cypress of
the dead. In addition we have mention of pomegranates, and the
oranges and lemons flower and fruit at the same time, so that
what had been a vague song of longing has now become a clear
picture of fertility. At the end of the *Apprenticeship* we were
told that Wilhelm's care for Mignon was *the* positive yield of
his past.[24] Now the memory, tinged perhaps with guilt, of her
unreturned virginal love, is to bear fruit as a "formative force."
Without Mignon, no vision: without the real experience afforded
by the journey, *only* vision. The effect on Wilhelm is to show
him that he must move from longing to achievement, without
ever losing the inspiration of longing. In other words all fulfillment proceeds from having had the experience of unfulfillment.
Wilhelm speaks of being "freed from doubts" regarding the
true colors of the landscape. Both he and the painter have attained a new certainty: they have come to terms with Mignon,
but not rejected her.

But there still remains the unfinished business of Hilarie and the Widow. The wish to see them must be satisfied if Wilhelm is to leave this district with a free mind, and the painter reserves a space for them in one of his drawings. Most of the traveling takes place on the uncertain element of water—image of mobility, of eros, and of escape from terra firma where Wilhelm has agreed not to stay in one place for more than three days. Here on the water time ceases, the world appears as "Paradise." Art and life join in this quartet of two real and two fictional characters. Their world, although blissful, is half-unreal, half-real: but the consequences will be real and dangerous if they yield entirely to their dreams and their longings.

The painter sings melancholy elegiac songs like those of the Venetian gondoliers which Goethe had admired so much, "*wundersam-klagend.*" To those on the land, he seems to be always close by because he sings louder as he moves further out into the lake. The image of longing remains constant to those who listen for it. Among those on the shore are the two ladies. But so enthusiastic is the singer that he goes on long after he is out of audible range. Ironic commentaries or interjections characterize the presentation from this point on in the chapter, and the irony is always directed towards the enthusiasts, in the name of reality. So wrapped up in emotion are they all, that what they see of the landscape is far less clear than what they see in the painter's pictures of it. So involved is the singer in his melancholy self-indulgence that he and Wilhelm would have forgotten to eat if the ladies had not sent provisions.

On the last evening these lovers—for that is what they all four ultimately are—sit on a terrace of the castle on the Isola Bella, musing on the supreme beauty of this sky, this water, this land where the sun shines stronger and the moon gleams milder—recognizing this "exclusively and lyrically" [*ausschliesslich und lyrisch*], says Goethe. It is now that the painter intones "Kennst du das Land . . . ," thereby completing the recollection in reverse order of every part of Mignon's song. He sings with too much passion and longing, we are told. And the effect of his song on the others shows him what he too has to renounce: the debilitating attachment to ideals which provoke dissatisfaction with the real everyday business of living. Twice falls the heavy phrase "departure from paradise." The ladies leave first, and for Wilhelm and his companion all is suddenly changed. They now see decay, neglect, dying and rotting all around. No self-centered hypochondriac could have been more sharp or jaundiced, says Goethe. There follows a letter from Lenardo to Wilhelm in which occur the words: "Longing disappears in creative activity" [*Die Sehnsucht verschwindet im Tun und Wirken*].[25]

It is clear that the Mignon chapter is of central importance in the structure of the novel.[26] In both versions it comes right in the middle of the book, followed by a pause of several years in the action. In the final version it is followed by the second visit to the Pedagogic Province and the important presentation of creative arts in a communal context, then by the mountain festival with the discussion on doing and thinking, and finally by Wilhelm's decision to become a surgeon. A reckoning with Mignon was crucial if Wilhelm was to find a firm place in society, for she represents the indeterminateness of undirected emotion, though also the desire for fulfillment. The memory of Mignon is transformed by the pilgrimage into *productive* inspiration. The thrust of this chapter is therefore, in my opinion, not quite so negative as some interpreters have asserted. Its theme is not the excision of longing, of the lyrical, from life, but rather its transmutation into a positive, inspiring force. The Renunciants in Goethe's novel are obligated, so we are told, not to speak of the past or the future and to occupy themselves solely with the present.[27] The sojourn on the Lago Maggiore had represented a temporary withdrawal from problems and obligations of the present. The return to these obligations at its conclusion is the hallmark of *Entsagung*, that Goethean form of renunciation which the novel embodies and which is a positive quality— not doing without, not *Entbehren*, but *saying* no, voluntarily dissociating oneself from something. Ideals, dreams and yearnings are not deprecated: they are still recognized as an important constituent in the total composition of meaningful living, but they must never become an obsession that distracts man from fruitful, though limited and maybe not totally satisfying, activity. Natalie remains the repository of Wilhelm's aspirations, and she is really the goal of his wanderings. It is significant that Wilhelm's turn toward productive activity, his deciding to become a surgeon, is communicated at the end of Book Two in a letter to Natalie, and in conjunction with his recounting to her the story of the fisher-boy's drowning which he had experienced in his youth—brooding, painful reflection leading now to resolute acceptance of activity. In this letter Wilhelm refers to the "great undertaking" Natalie is moving toward, in which he too wishes to take part as a "useful and necessary member of society."[28] This undertaking is the emigration to America, and we are told somewhat later that Natalie has gone ahead of Wilhelm, who is still in Europe at the end of the novel. With the end of Book Two, therefore, Wilhelm has found himself and his place in the scheme of things. His journeymanship would seem to be over, though Book Three shows that it is not, because of Felix. But as far as Natalie is concerned, her function in the general structure of the novel is fulfilled by the end of Book Two and she and Wilhelm are spiritually, if not actually, reunited.

It is time now for me to explain what I mean by speaking of the *Journeymanship* as a novel in the symbolic mode. We have already noticed the way in which landscapes figure symbolically in the novel, and I have already suggested that, in his encounter with the Joseph family, Wilhelm demonstrates the ability to see things meaningfully, which implies seeing things with relation to what they represent, seeing the particular with reference to something wider, perhaps to an idea. Goethe had a certain amount to say about this kind of visualization, and he formulated a distinction between allegory and symbolism. The distinction has not been accepted wholeheartedly by modern theoreticians, but whether it has general validity does not concern us here. The fact remains that Goethe's distinction between these two modes forms a useful approach to what he was consciously striving after in *Wilhelm Meister's Journeymanship*. The passage runs as follows:

Allegory transmutes a phenomenon into a concept, a concept into an image, but in such a way that the concept is always restricted and contained completely within the image and expressible by it; symbolism transmutes the phenomenon into an idea, the idea into an image, and in such a way that the idea remains always infinitely productive and inaccessible [*unendlich wirksam und unerreichbar*] in the image, and, even when expressed in all languages, yet remains inexpressible.[29]

Common to both modes is therefore their originating in the world of phenomena and the activity of transmuting this phenomenal world into images, but the intermediary in the process of transmutation is in the one case a concept, in the other an idea. The difference between the two is that the former is restricted and complete, and therefore expressible [*auszusprechen*], whereas the latter is "infinitely productive and inaccessible" (therefore unrestricted and, presumably, incomplete) and hence inexpressible [*unaussprechlich*]. Elsewhere Goethe distinguished between "concept" [*Begriff*] as the sum of experience, and "idea" [*Idee*] as the result of experience, the first belonging to the realm of the understanding [*Verstand*], the other to that of reason [*Vernunft*].[30] The evolution of concepts implies therefore the categorization of experience, whereas the establishment of an idea implies going beyond this in some interpretive, creative activity of the mind, for the idea is not contained within the sum of the experiences. A concept results from comprehensive classification and rubrication, an idea transcends these as an expression or intimation of some kind of more general order. The literary expression of this latter is the symbol, hence it is natural that in his use of the genre of the novel as man's search for order, Goethe should have moved gradually toward the symbolic mode, fully demonstrated in this final version of the *Journeymanship*. Goethe asserts that whereas allegory "seeks" [*sucht*] the particular example for the general concept, poetry "sees" [*schaut*] the general in the particular.[31] It does not *refer* the one to the other, it is not what we would nowadays call referential. In true symbolism, Goethe declared, the particular *represents* something more general, "not as a dream or shadow, but as a present, living revelation of the unfathomable" [*als lebendig-augenblickliche Offenbarung des Unerforschlichen*].[32] For Goethe a symbol must always have something undefinable and mysterious, something of that life of reflected truth which Faust referred to.[33] The symbol was also for Goethe always something that was constantly changing and growing in meaning, in contrast to the static nature of allegory. The symbolic mode meant therefore a continuing process of discovery, a process in which some mysteries were unravelled while others were revealed.

The most important symbol of the novel is America, and closely connected with this is the motif of emigration. In the first version of the novel emigration had been referred to as a whim (see above, p. 232f.), but now it has become a symbol of man's discovery of his true self by dissociation from what has always surrounded him. In a poem written in 1827 Goethe had apostrophized the United States as the land without ruined castles, useless memories and ghosts of the past.[34] Much has been written on Goethe's knowledge of America but most of it is irrelevant to the symbolic mode of this novel in which America is an "idea" in Goethe's sense.[35] We recall Lothario's words in the *Apprenticeship:* "Here or nowhere is America." For Lenardo the New World offers the possibility of building up from the ground, unimpeded by the weight of traditions but also unassisted by the strength of inherited culture. In contrast the uncle of the *Journeymanship* had returned to Europe because he felt he could better create a productive community within the limits established by history. In the third book of the novel it becomes clear that the Old World stands for limits and the New World for limitlessness, and that both represent obstacles to be overcome, for limits may produce narrowness and their absence may result in dispersion of efforts in too many directions. In his big conversation with Friedrich in the third chapter of the third book, Wilhelm clearly indicates that for him, a "New World" means the opportunity to do things *in new ways*, to escape from the treadmill of routine [*Schlendrian*], to begin anew. The trouble is, of course, that one can never begin completely anew, although Wilhelm does not recognize this fact. Why then America?

In Chapters Nine through Twelve of Book Three of the novel the advantages of the New World are set off against those of the Old. But everything is symbolic. When Lenardo begins his speech by acknowledging the value of *des festen Landes bewohnten Provinzen und Reiche*, it soon becomes clear that it is not the continent [*das Festland*] of Europe itself but what it represents, namely security of existence, *die Grundfeste alles Daseins*, which is uppermost in his thoughts, the advantages of living in an already established order. When he then turns to his advocation of mobility as more valuable than security, we have obviously left the realm of geographical opposition and are returning to the thematic counterpoint of wandering and staying which had characterized the opening of the novel. Yet not entirely: for mobility is presented as more plausible in the New World than in the Old, and emigration as an exercise and proof of mobility. The important thing is not to get lost, not to lose oneself, in the wide open spaces. But Lenardo recognizes the validity of aspirations, particularly in youth, toward a broader sphere of activity, toward what elsewhere in the novel is called *Weltfrömmigkeit*, "world-piety" (again in the sense of *pietas* used in Goethe's review of Salvandy's novel) as against "house-piety," *Hausfrömmigkeit*, productive reverence for work within and for a restricted community.[36] Lenardo's main concern is that man should not be dependent on time and place, but should be able to create from out of himself without external aids. This for him is the idea of America. But in order to find oneself in this way, man needs kindred spirits with like aspirations. This is the idea represented by the *Bund*, the community of renunciants that Lenardo heads.

Lenardo's speech is followed by that of Odoard, who seems to be an older man, more settled in his opinions. After Lenardo has finished speaking, a large portion of the assembled company leaves the hall. It is to those who remain, uncertain about the validity of Lenardo's arguments, that Odoard addresses his remarks: "These trusty-looking men who have quietly stayed behind here indicate by their remaining the clear wish and intention of continuing to belong to their native soil."[37] Odoard can offer them only "sufficient work, for several years." Lenardo's followers represent the ethos of wandering, Odoard's that of staying. The basic counterpoint of the novel is here expressed choreographically, with the one group leaving the hall and the other remaining firmly seated. And it is a true counterpoint, not a question of doing right versus doing nothing. In the eleventh chapter the ethos and the community aspirations of the wanderers are described in detail; in the twelfth chapter there is an equally rounded out description of the ethos and aspirations of the "remainders." It is therefore not exactly right to say that the final version of the *Journeymanship*, in contrast to the first version, has become a novel of emigration, for the other side is allowed to present its case, and its arguments have their own persuasiveness. The two sides are presented symbolically as representing the basic tension of movement and rest, of expansion and contraction.[38]

In the description of the new community to be established by the emigrants there is really little that is new. Their religion will remain Christian, because Christianity instills patience and teaches man how to accommodate himself to the inevitable. But the prevailing ethos is not to be quietist or passive. It will embody a respect for work which in turn will involve careful parcellation of one's time for activity while also leaving opportunity for reflection. Family life will be the center of communal life, and there will be a sort of police to ensure that "no one shall be trouble-some to anyone else," with a peripatetic higher authority enforc-ing laws for the benefit of the whole community. In a word, the main thing will be "to take over with us the advantages of civilization and leave its disadvantages behind."[39] What is being described here is not an actual political organization but an ideal moral community. The reason why such a community is en-visioned by Lenardo and his followers as being more possible in the New World, says Odoard, is that the idea of the New World seems to stand for expansion unimpeded by established institutions of inheritance and tradition; and because men feel that "bolts" are constantly being placed in the Old World on doors leading to what would seem to be better, they tend to transfer their aspirations for betterment into the idea of another world.[40] By "another" world he obviously means the idea of the New World, but he suggests that this is illusory and that emigra-tion is no answer to the problems of modern society. He him-self is neither despondent nor resigned, for he believes that the "century," by which he means the new (nineteenth) century, is working for the realization of organized communities of com-bined labor such as he plans in Europe, with each laborer as-signed his special task, all working for the good of the whole. The communities Odoard envisions are more tightly organized than Lenardo's, and he criticizes Lenardo as having to *create* a future, to evolve a great plan and to hope that others will accept it, whereas in Odoard's aspirations everyone knows *now* quite definitely what he has to do and what he has to leave undone. Lenardo is future-oriented, Odoard is present-oriented. That is the basic difference.

The idea of order is common to both these plans, and indeed so many different possible manifestations of order are advanced in *Wilhelm Meister's Journeymanship* that it can be called a novel of possibilities. Goethe once said to Eckermann that man was born not to solve the problems of the world, but to see where the problem lay and then keep within the bounds of what was comprehensible.⁴¹ During the mountain festival Montan presents various theories on the origin of the earth, adding that not truth but the problem itself lies in the middle, for all are plausible but none has final validity.⁴² This is true of the novel in general: possibilities are given us, but no final answers. In the same passage Montan asserts the relativity of all opinions and he advocates living according to one's own personal convictions, though always testing one's thoughts by one's actions and vice versa: "Thinking and Doing, Doing and Thinking, that is the sum of all wisdom. . . . Both must move through our life like breathing out and breathing in. Like Question and Answer the one should not exist without the other."

The device of the Band of Emigrants is *Ubi homines sunt modi sunt*, which is declared to mean that "when men gather together in society, the *manner in which they wish to be and remain together* immediately emerges."⁴³ This is an expansion rather than a translation of the Latin tag, and its message is that variety is tolerated when it coalesces into community. This community is a community of action, and in the song which its members intone (with Wilhelm's help), striving from "love" into a life of activity is praised:

> Und dein Streben, sei's in Liebe,
> Und dein Leben sei die Tat.

A second stanza describes the sorrowful severance from established ties and the anxious exposure to an uncertain future. But the third and final stanza extols the possibilities and hopes that await those with bold, adventurous spirits:

> Bleibe nicht am Boden heften,
> Frisch gewagt und frisch hinaus,
> Kopf und Arm mit heitern Kräften
> Überall sind sie zu Haus:
> Wo wir uns der Sonne freuen,
> Sind wir jede Sorge los:

Dass wir uns in ihr zerstreuen,
Darum ist die Welt so gross.

[Stay not on the ground affixed,
Fresh and bold let us go out,
Head and arm with cheerful spirit
Everywhere will feel at home:
Where we can enjoy the sunlight
We are free from every care:
That we may disperse within her,
Therefore is the world so great.]

The song of wandering has become a song of order: for the uncertainties that attend such a life are overcome by the ideal
which inspires the wanderers, the courageous search for circumstances that will satisfy the demand for a spiritual feeling of
home. This then is a sort of ordered existence, however tenuous
its order may seem, for there is an ordering principle to it, the midpoint that had been declared essential in the vision in Makarie's
observatory. It is an order based on the idea of "world-piety,"
whereas Odoard's vision is based on "house-piety." The American settlement is based on renouncing the Old World and beginning anew: the European settlement is based on acceptance of
the Old World but transforming it into something better. Later
in this third book we encounter a community of spinners and
weavers faced with the problem of whether to accept mecha-
nization or to begin a new life elsewhere. The same tension,
therefore, prevails here too. The Pedagogic Province is also a
representation of order—of education as progression toward an
ordered existence, in which the four reverences are the guiding
principle or midpoint, and the only religions that are accepted
are based on reverence: ethnic religion based on the first reverence (reverence for what is above us), Christian religion based
on the second reverence (reverence for what is below us), and
philosophic religion based on the third reverence (reverence for
what is our equal). Religion is therefore order, and the Band of
Emigrants accepts both the three reverences and the religions

based upon them. The fourth reverence—reverence for oneself—
is what they hope will ultimately emerge from their new community. Makarie represents the general concept of order which
both embraces and transcends the various manifestations of
order presented as viable possibilities within the novel.

But not all is order. Alongside its manifestations we have the
powerful presentation of disorder in the various novellas, and of
a not-yet-ordered existence in the poignant story of Hersilie and
Felix, which functions as countertheme to the main subject of
Wilhelm's journeymanship. This is a tale of young love with all
its anguish and uncertainties, its excitements and tribulations,
subtly and tenderly depicted by the masterly hand of the old
poet who never lost his understanding for the troubles of being
young. At its center is a symbol, the golden casket, which should
perhaps have functioned as an organizing midpoint, but actually
turns into an instrument of discord and disorder.

In the house of the Collector, Wilhelm had asked whether he
should try to open the casket, but he was advised to wait till he
finds the key, which he will if he is born lucky and if the casket
means anything. The casket has therefore been left for the time
being in the keeping of the Collector. The key, he told Wilhelm,
would probably turn up where least expected. But actually it is
Hersilie who finds the key, and not Wilhelm, for whom the
casket proves to have no meaning. She finds it in the jacket of the
boy Fitz who had been with Felix when he discovered the casket
in a subterranean cave. She feels therefore that she is in unlawful
possession of the key, expresses her sense of guilt to Wilhelm,
but also tells him that she will suppress this because of Felix and
that she longs to open the casket. The key has a peculiar shape:
it is like an arrow with a hook across it. Hersilie asks Wilhelm
to get the casket, but then admits that it really has nothing to do
with her and Wilhelm, for it belongs to Felix. This is an indirect
indication that the attraction growing between her and Wilhelm
should be curbed, for her love really belongs to Felix. The casket,
we are told, resembles in shape a book. It is the object of her

curiosity, of her urge to solve the mystery of the unknown. But it is also obviously connected with Felix and her love for him, and the key by its shape represents both the ardor and the pain of sexual desire. No Freud is needed to tell us that. Instead of standing for hidden knowledge, however, this central symbol of the Felix-Hersilie action develops into a representation of the impetuous desire for knowledge and the too eager demand for rapid fulfillment. Felix is impatient to see the casket and passionately desires, as he says, to "open Hersilie's heart," so that it may open up to him, come toward him, press him to itself and allow him to press it to his breast. The suggestion contained in his words is that Hersilie is still holding back, is still perhaps somewhat confused by her liking for Wilhelm, and anyway is not yet ready to abandon herself to Felix as completely as he would wish. The connection with the casket becomes clear when Felix tries to open it, forces the lock somewhat, and breaks the key. He then passionately embraces Hersilie, but she is still conscious of a void between them which only time will fill, and she pushes him angrily away. To which Felix replies: "Very well then! . . . I will ride out into the world until I perish."

The scene I have described marks the climax of this particular symbolic action and occurs in the penultimate chapter of the novel. Felix was too violently eager to open the casket, she assumes too readily that the key is irreparably broken and the casket will never be opened. In fact the key has a clean break and can easily be put together again, but the goldsmith whom they consult suggests that they had better leave the casket unopened. It is the old story—or what used to be the old story—of male aggressiveness and female defensiveness. Each of them goes too far in his or her direction, and the result is dislocation. To attain community they must learn to adjust to each other. Felix does not go to Makarie for advice as so many of the other characters do, including Hilarie and the Beautiful Widow. He has not yet learnt renunciation in the Goethean sense. But—and this is one of the great strengths of the novel—he is not rejected by

Goethe, for he has much that is positive about him—strength, fortitude and tenderness. This is why it is Felix who dominates the closing scene of the novel.

The close of the *Journeymanship* takes place in a highly symbolic landscape—midday sun with a cooling breeze playing over the gentle banks of a river flowing through rich cornfields, a boat gliding along it with Wilhelm in it. As Wilhelm looks up he sees a sturdy youth on a horse riding along. Suddenly the ground gives way beneath him, and Felix—for it is he—plunges headlong into the river. He seems to be dead when he is dragged to shore, but the father's acquired knowledge enables Wilhelm to bring his son back to life, and Felix then lies there naked in the sun on his father's out-stretched cloak and peacefully falls asleep. The master stands before the sleeping youth who is still in his years of apprenticeship: " 'And so you are always being born anew, glorious image of the Godhead,' cried Wilhelm, 'and you will always be hurt anew, wounded from within or from without.' " Felix's clothes are allowed to dry in the sun while he sleeps "so that when he awakened, he might be put once again into the socially most seemly condition" [*in den gesellig anständigsten Zustand*].

Such is the real ending of this novel, which was therefore to have closed with a scene balancing that of its opening: Wilhelm's conversation with the boy at the start and his rescue of the youth at the end, the sleeping child of the Joseph family at the beginning and the sleeping youth at the close, the comparison with the Holy Family at the beginning and the reference to man as created in God's image at the end. There is a reference to the Flight into Egypt at the beginning and a recognition of the dangers of flight at the end, and both at the beginning and at the end there is a statement, implied in the one case and explicit in the second, that man is both godlike and endangered. "Joseph," like Felix, had tried to bring about too quickly a permanent union with the woman he loved. Like Felix he has to learn to integrate his own passionate desires into the concerns of others. The idea of what constitutes real community is visually present in the Joseph family of the beginning, and in the impending reclothing of Felix at the end.

But in actual fact the novel, as published in 1829 and in most modern editions, does not end thus. After the scene I have just described, there follows a series of maxims, "From Makarie's Archive," and a poem entitled "In the Solemn Bone-House." The poem is a meditation on Schiller's skull and would seem to have nothing to do with the novel. The maxims can at best be related to the second Makarie chapter. The power of the last scene of the novel is thereby blunted.

The reasons why these things are there in the twenty-third volume of the last collected edition of Goethe's works published during his lifetime, the so-called *Ausgabe letzter Hand*, are curious. The maxims were originally intended, it seems, to come at the end of the *first* book of the novel, together with the poem (which talks about the lasting quality of things of the mind), but volume twenty-one of the edition (which contains the first book of the *Journeymanship*) was already printed when Goethe sent the maxims to the publisher. They were therefore placed, apparently with Goethe's approval, at the end of the third book.[44] This may seem like the result of an unlucky accident, and some readers of the novel have wished away the maxims, and, though accepting the solemn splendor of the poem, consider its position at the end of the novel to have been intended as only "temporary."[45] But we now know that it was Goethe's intention to include certain sets of maxims in the novel, a fact which emerges from various earlier drafts, particularly of the first Makarie chapter.[46] The poem is more of a problem. If Goethe indeed needed a "temporary" position for it, that is no reason why he should have put it here (there were plenty of other places where it might have gone); and if, as Eckermann suggests, the publisher found the volume a bit short and wanted it filled out, there were other things that could have been included.

Why, then, this particular poem? And what is the meaning of the words "to be continued" [*Ist fortzusetzen*] which follow it? Do these refer to the poem, or to the novel? Or is this a further indication that Goethe, aged eighty, planned to write a third Wilhelm Meister novel, a *Meisterjahre?* The problem has never been solved, though various answers have been suggested.[47] I find no ready answer. As for the poem on Schiller's skull, its presence here may be a reflection of Schiller's objection that the ideas behind the last books of the *Apprenticeship* were not sufficiently *explicitly* stated, for here the maxims from Makarie's archive are the distillation of central ideas of the novel, and the point of the poem, unfinished though it may be, is that "God-Nature" reveals to man that what is solid dissolves into spirit and what is of the spirit remains solidly:

> Was kann der Mensch im Leben mehr gewinnen,
> Als dass sich Gott-Natur ihm offenbare;
> Wie sie das Feste lässt zu Geist verrinnen,
> Wie sie das Geisterzeugte fest bewahre.

On completion of the second version of the *Journeymanship*, we find Goethe referring in various places to the "collective" nature of the work, to its combining "very disparate elements," of its being an "aggregate."[48] To one of his correspondents he suggested that one should look at the parts, and take what suited one. This particular correspondent, Rochlitz, replied that there was nevertheless a unifying concept in the novel, namely the portrayal of the "realistic" side of people and things "from an idealistic standpoint." Goethe objected, in a conversation with Chancellor von Müller, that this was too "systematic."[49] In all these utterances Goethe was not suggesting that the novel had no structure. He was, however, asserting that it did not have a *systematic* structure. It did not present a system, it was a "complex" like life itself and was therefore consciously "disparate" and "collective" in structure. Since a collective structure really knows no limits, the novel does indeed have "a kind of infinitude" [*eine Art von Unendlichkeit*] as he said in his reply to the systematizing correspondent referred to above, for it is never really complete, always pointing outwards. The disparate parts also reflect each other. Goethe once coined the phrase "repeated mirroring," and one critic has asserted that this is the real structural principle of the *Journeymanship:* the parts being not only complete in themselves but also, by mirroring each other, combining into a totality—and that this is nowhere more evident than in the insets of the novel.[50]

The most important of these insets are the various novellas.[51] Hersilie's letter to Wilhelm reporting the finding of the key to the casket is preceded by the exquisite fairy tale of "The New Melusina," in which another casket occupies the center of attention. A traveler encounters a beautiful woman, falls in love with her and dedicates himself to her service. She entrusts to him a casket, a key that opens all doors, and a bag of money that never becomes empty. He spends the money in careless gambling, is tempted to see what is in the casket and eventually discovers that she herself (who has frequently disappeared from his sight) is in miniature form living inside the casket. She discovers that he knows her secret, and when he scolds her for being but a dwarf, invites him to become a dwarf too and accompany her to her kingdom. This he does, but soon longs to be his normal size again, and finally leaves her and returns to earth. The casket of Melusina represents mystery and also demands respect for the mysterious. But our hero is uncomfortable in the lonely companionship of the casket, and hence seeks society at the gaming table. At one point he blames her for this, and urges upon her a more permanent relationship. The casket is always there beside them on the seat of the coach, however, and this disturbs him. He is unwilling to allow her her private mystery, but also unable to share the conditions of her life with her. Hersilie's letter about the golden casket precedes this story, and the story of Melusina illuminates the meaning of the casket in the main action. Both caskets signify not merely the inviolability of mystery but more specifically that of the private, individual heart.

The attraction which Wilhelm and Hersilie feel for each other is never directly referred to in the novel. But it is indirectly demonstrated by the story of "The Man of Fifty" which, in the first version of the novel, was given Wilhelm to read by Hersilie herself. There it was left uncompleted, however, whereas in the final version it is completed by its characters moving into the main action of the novel. This time the narrator communicates the story to the reader, not Hersilie to Wilhelm. The result of this change is that the reader, and not Wilhelm, is the one required to draw the right conclusions. Indeed he is the only person fully able to comprehend the story's connection with the main action. Externally the tale is connected with the main action by the fact that the Widow is a friend of Makarie and that Wilhelm goes to Italy in order to meet Hilarie and the Widow. On a deeper level the connection lies in the behavior of each of the four main characters at the end of the novella. The fifty-year-old Major finds out that his niece Hilarie, who he had intended should marry his son Flavio, is really in love with him. Flattered, he sets about rejuvenating his appearance with the aid of a cosmetic expert. When the time comes to explain the situation to Flavio, the Major learns that Flavio is greatly relieved because he has fallen madly in love with a Beautiful Widow. The Major meets the Widow, delights in her company, is flattered by her—and Flavio is rejected. His emotional disorder is so great that he becomes desperately ill, but the companionship of Hilarie restores peace to his battered mind. In this way, through suffering and concern, the two young people find their way to each other. One night as they are skating by full moon they see a dark figure approaching. It is the Major, who immediately senses what has happened. Hilarie declares that she is not ready to enter a lasting union with Flavio, and the Widow feels that she is responsible for the whole situation. At the end of the novella the Major sees that he must abandon all hope of a union with Hilarie, and the Widow is brought to a sense of what disaster can result from playing with other people's feelings. Flavio has recovered his self-respect to some extent, but neither he nor the "already wounded heart" of Hilarie is ready to launch into another all-absorbing relationship. Yet by the end of the *novel*— after a suitable period of healing time, and thanks to the influence of Makarie—Flavio marries Hilarie and the Major his Widow.

It is a marvelous piece of writing, delicate, penetrating, delightfully humorous and also deeply moving. It exposes both the absurdity and the dangers of playing with feelings. The father plays being a lover, and so does the son. The one is too old for Hilarie, the other too inexperienced for the Widow. The characters are constantly deceiving themselves, and often they are seduced into doing so by vanity. There is a casket in this story also, but it is a make-up box—not, therefore, a vessel of mystery but a box of tricks. What these characters have to learn is to divest themselves of the desire to be something different from what they really are, to find their way back to their true selves, accept limitations and pursue their paths through life with courage and composure. This is all full of meaning for Wilhelm, and Flavio has much in common with Felix. But only the reader can appreciate that.

A father-son relationship is the starting point of this story. Another such relationship is at the center of "The Foolish Pilgrim," the story that, in the second version of the novel, Hersilie gives Wilhelm to read soon after he arrives with Felix at the uncle's mansion. There is no casket in this story, but the heroine carries her secret sorrows with her and demands respect for her silence. The action begins with a gentleman (again a man in his fifties) taking into his home a beautiful young girl whom he finds wandering along the highway. There is a certain mystery about her. She stays two years but never reveals her secret, though from a ballad she sings one day it would seem that she is searching for a lover whom she had once caught in the act with another girl. She had removed his clothes so that he was publicly shamed into having to escape into the night, clad only in a cloak. Her "foolishness" consists in her belief that somewhere he will be mourning the loss of her love. Being "crazy from fidelity," she is interested in no other man. When both her host and his son fall in love with her, she evades the difficulties of the situation by coyly suggesting to the father that she is pregnant by the son. When the father reduces his son's inheritance to provide for the future "grandson," she is charged by the son with being in league with his father to support the as yet unborn child, which the son suggests is really his father's. She then tells him that the child is neither his nor his father's, and that he should be more respectful to women and "rely on his beloved's steadfastness and her silence."[52] The ethical center of this novella is therefore the demand for respect, as with "The New Melusina." Excessive eagerness for knowledge that invades another person's privacy, and overhasty wooing (as with "Joseph" and Flavio), are ironically castigated. The relation of all this to Felix and Wilhelm is clear, for Hersilie is indicating indirectly that every true association of one person to another—and especially of a man to a woman—must respect the hermetic identity of the other. This "pilgrim" is foolish because her goal is a *fata morgana*, but her outwitting of father and son is a warning from Hersilie that she will not allow herself to be desecrated.

The novella entitled "Who is the Betrayer?" is both humorous and sophisticated. It begins with young Lucidor expressing aloud to himself his disapproval of his father's choice of a bride for him. Lucidor is an impassioned youth like Flavio, like the son in "The Foolish Pilgrim," like the narrator of "The New Melusina," and like Felix. He has been educated to become a public servant and has displayed "sagacity and skill" in public affairs. But he is to show none of these qualities in his private affairs. The action is concerned with his attempts to tell various people that he is not in love with Julie, all of which are prevented by chance circumstances. Finally he tries to tell her sister Lucinde. But it is

Lucinde with whom he is really in love, so this attempt is not
exactly prudent. And it too is frustrated. In the end he is brought
to a confrontation with Julie—not, however, of his own making,
but because she forces him to it. In this highly ironic conversation Julie reproaches him with self-centeredness and with in-
sensitivity toward the feelings of women. She does not want
him, but she also does not want to be told so blatantly that he has
absolutely no interest in her, for his outcry at the beginning of
the story had been overheard. The trouble with Lucidor is that
he is too much concerned with himself, and too little with others.
Somehow he lacks courage. He shies away from real conversational interchanges, and prefers monologue to dialogue. Again
(as in "The Foolish Pilgrim") we have a girl putting a man in his
place. And this tale of the man educated to public life who is
nevertheless so incompetent in private life is a comment on Wilhelm's journeymanship as progress towards *savoir vivre*.

There are two other novellas of lesser importance. "The
Dangerous Wager" is described by the narrator of the *Journeymanship* as a "farce" [*Schwank*] and a relaxation from the
serious matters in the novel. It tells of a foolish prank, committed
out of youthful exuberance, which has unforeseen but disastrous
consequences, because someone inconsiderately blurts out something that should have been kept secret. This story is an advocation of tact in human relationships, whereas the inaction of
Lucidor had demonstrated the futility of too much tact. The
other novella, "Not Too Far," is about Odoard who, in the midst
of a successful career in public office, found himself relegated to
the governorship of a distant province because he was suspected
of a serious attraction toward the princess of the land, whom he
had celebrated in poems of his own composition as "Aurora."
His wife Albertine is bored in this provincial environment and
has made what she thinks is a serious attachment. As the story
opens Odoard is waiting with his children for Albertine to
return home, for it is her birthday and a festive board has been
prepared. But she does not come, and Odoard, leaving the sleep-

ing children, goes out into the night in search of his wife. Instead he encounters "Aurora." Meanwhile Albertine has discovered that the lover she thought to have secured for herself has betrayed her. And so she returns to the sleeping house, but to find Odoard not there. Albertine is bored because she needs society, Odoard is frustrated because he needs an ideal. One of the themes of the story is the difference between society and community. Each of these two needs real community and neither has it. Neither has in fact "renounced" those other desires that prevent such real community. No wonder that, in the main action of the novel, Odoard is to argue in favor of restriction, home soil, and building on to what one has, rather than roaming hopefully into the great wide distance of indeterminateness.

Another inset of great importance in the novel is the extract from Lenardo's diary with its description of the community of spinners and weavers.[53] This had been sent, so we are told, to Makarie (the center to which all roads in the novel somehow seem to lead) and is now communicated to Wilhelm. It tells of a journey undertaken by Lenardo at the request of the Band of Emigrants to find out whether any members of this alpine community would be suitable additions to the Band. In this way, and also because it completes the story of the nut-brown maid, it is connected with the main action, and ultimately with Makarie. It also portrays more extensively the character of Lenardo and bridges the gap between the rather foolish young dreamer that he appears to be at the beginning of the novel and the impressive leader and influential orator of the third book. As he sets out on his journey he is ill tempered and impatient, but when he reaches the settlement he is seeking, the warmth, composure and joy of these workers begin immediately to affect him. Their joy is their pleasure at their craft, a pleasure that is threatened, however, by the advance of the machine age. The whole process of spinning and weaving is then elaborately described—and not only elaborately but in the symbolic mode. For this section of the novel is

not merely a panegyric on handicraft and a paean to work, but
another, and this time very extensively developed, representation
of the idea of order. It is not fortuitous that, of all the crafts that
Goethe could have described here, he selected weaving, for
weaving had been and remained for him a particularly apposite
image of order, from the song of the Earth Spirit in *Faust*
(which had been composed sometime in the 1770s) right through
to this passage in the novel of 1829.

The very terminology used to denote the successive stages in
the process of weaving reveals the symbolic mode. Something is
being fashioned out of raw materials, something is being developed toward a desired end product. In the preparatory process of
spinning, impurities [*Unreinigkeiten*] are first removed, then
the fibers of the cotton are given "one direction" [*einerlei
Richtung*], and those doing the spinning move gracefully as they
work. The yarn is then starched—*gestärkt*, which in German
means both "starched" and "strengthened"—and wound on to
spools which are then put in the order [*Ordnung*] that the pattern [*Muster*] of the texture [*Gewebe*] will demand.[54] In weaving the threads must not be confused, everything must be kept
in perfect order. And so the process continues with joining,
winding, straightening, and so on. Goethe described this section
of his novel as being an "interweaving of what is strictly dry and
technical with aesthetic-sentimental events,"[55] using the term
"aesthetic-sentimental" in the same sense that he had used the
words "poetic" and "sentimental" in his letter to Schiller about
his Frankfurt journey in 1797 (see above, p. 100), that is, as
referring to objects arousing in him ideas whereby empirical
facts became aesthetic forms.

But this ordered world is threatened, or seems to be, by
machinery. Goethe uses the word *Maschinenwesen* which is
both more general and more symbolic than individual machines
or *Maschinen*. On the more obvious level this refers to the Industrial Revolution, but there is also a wider meaning here. The
point at issue is the decay of community sense through the deval-

uation of work as a force producing and sustaining a community. To suggest therefore that this passage indicates a "non-progressive" attitude in Goethe, or at least an ambiguous attitude toward the Industrial Revolution is to overlook the essentially symbolic nature of the concept *Maschinenwesen*, for the very word *Wesen* implies an essence rather than a specific historical manifestation. In the midst of this mentally, as well as economically, perplexed community we encounter the nut-brown maid of Lenardo's sentimental recollection, who has now become Frau Susanne, both good and beautiful, *die Gute-Schöne*, in whose opinion *das Maschinenwesen*, growing ever closer, threatens to destroy the community life that has been built up in these valleys. What she fears is an impoverishment of communal values through the incursion of mechanistic values.[56] What then is one to do? To stay and try to adjust, or to move on to new lands? The alternatives are basically the same as those represented by Odoard and Lenardo. The description of this community is therefore in no way an aesthetically unwarranted digression. It is perfectly integrated into the total thematic structure of the novel.

The first version of *Wilhelm Meister's Journeymanship* is an archive-novel, the second is a symbolic novel. Both versions are concerned with achieving breadth, with presenting fundamental attitudes to experience, with distillations of far-reaching vision and deep-reaching analysis. But whereas Goethe had demanded in the first version that the reader himself should see the novel as a collection of separate parts and either respect that or try to provide the connections himself, in the second version he has transformed the whole disparate collection into a highly complex, but nevertheless unitary, contrapuntal structure.

12

Conclusion

In the year before his death Goethe was talking one day with Eckermann about the old Greek novel *Daphnis and Chloe:*

"The work is so beautiful," said he [Goethe], "that it is not easy to retain one's impressions of it in the bad conditions in which we live, and one is amazed every time one rereads it. In it is the brightest day and one seems to see nothing but pictures of Herculaneum and these pictures work back on the book and help our imagination in reading."

There is, said I [Eckermann] a certain restrictedness [*Abgeschlossenheit*] about it which pleased me and in which everything is contained. There are hardly any outside references to lead us out of this happy circle. Of the deities only Pan and the nymphs play a part, hardly any other is mentioned, and one perceives that the shepherd's needs are fulfilled by these deities.

"And yet, with all this comparative restrictedness," said Goethe, "a whole world is revealed in it. We see shepherds of all kinds, tillers of the fields, gardeners, keepers of vineyards, boatmen, pirates, warriors and fine townsfolk, great lords and serfs."

We also see, said I, every stage in the life of man, from birth to old age; also all domestic circumstances as produced by the changing seasons.

"And then the landscape," said Goethe, "which is depicted with a few strokes so definitely that in the heights behind the characters we see vineyards, fields and orchards, and down below the pasturelands with the river and a touch of woodland with the expanse of the sea in the distance. And not a trace of gloomy days, of fog, clouds and dampness, but instead always the bluest, clearest sky, the most pleasing air, and ground that is always dry, so that one feels like lying down on it naked everywhere."

"The whole work," Goethe continued, "reveals the highest art and culture. It is so thought through that not one motif is faulty, all of them are of the fundamental and best kind, for instance that of the treasure by the stinking dolphin on the seashore. And taste and perfection and delicacy of feeling comparable to the best that has ever been written. Everything unpleasant which intrudes on the happy conditions of the work from outside, such as assault, robbery and war, is always dealt with quickly and leaves hardly a trace. And vice appears in the train of the townsfolk, and even there not in the main characters but in a subsidiary character of subordinate rank. It is all of the utmost beauty."

And then, I said, I was well pleased by the way in which the relations between masters and servants are expressed. The most humane treatment in the former and the greatest respect and endeavor to earn the master's favor, despite all naive frankness, in the latter. So the young townsman who has earned the disfavor of Daphnis by thoughts of unnatural love, tries to get back into his favor when he recognizes him as his master's son, by boldly rescuing Chloe from the oxherds and returning her to Daphnis.

"In all these things," said Goethe, "there is great understanding: as also that Chloe against the mutual desire of the lovers (who know no better) to lie naked together, retains her virginity to the end, which is so excellently and beautifully motivated that the greatest human matters are expressed thereby. One would have to write a whole book to give due respect to the great merits of this work, and one would do well to reread it every year in order to learn from it and to feel anew the effect of its great beauty."[1]

This was Goethe's most detailed analysis of a novel, and every word in it is important for the light that it throws on his attitude to the genre of the novel. The basic criterion was, as with all works of art, that the novel should be "beautiful," and this particular novel is beautiful both in form and in content. The general atmosphere of Longus's work is "the brightest day," "the bluest, clearest sky." We recall that Goethe had compared the clarity of presentation in *I Promessi Sposi* with the Italian sky itself, and in a conversation about the German Romantic writer Fouqué, who had dealt massively in murky pseudo-medievalism, Goethe had called for "clarity and brightening" in the dismal times in which they lived.[2] The implied contrast recalls also his comparison of the world of oriental poetry with the "cultivated, overcultivated, miscultivated, distorted" world in which Jean Paul had perforce to live and work (as had Goethe also). Not that Goethe ever wished artificially to beautify reality in the novel, for he acknowledges in the passage we have quoted that there is a good deal that is repulsive, violent and vicious in *Daphnis and Chloe*. But the point he makes is that this ugliness never becomes an end in itself, is not exploited for effect as, in his opinion, it had been in Victor Hugo's *Notre Dame de Paris*, but is subsumed into a wider order which is fundamentally humane and moral. He had recognized with approbation an ethical thread running through Jean Paul's work, in Goldsmith he had perceived a morality without sanctimoniousness or pedantry, and in Sterne he had discerned a moral equipoise despite the lewdness. The chasteness of Longus's novel was important to him, and his special mention of this reminds one of his love both for Manzoni's novel and for *Paul et Virginie*. Chloe retains her virginity and that, according to Goethe, shows her intelligence and also good motivation on the part of the author. By such a remark Goethe means not only psychologically credible motivation and not merely the felicitous selection and handling of individual motifs, although both these things are comprised within his statement. More generally he means the presentation of a basic essential through an individual particular "so that the greatest human matters are expressed thereby." With all its attention to real particulars, no novel should fail to achieve this too, for it is this—and this alone—that makes it great literature, *Dichtung* (poetry, if you like). *Daphnis and Chloe* is not about ideas. Indeed the presentation is so intensely realistic that one could lie down naked in any part of it. The world of this novel is restricted, but it is nevertheless a complete world. Perhaps it is complete because it is restricted and enclosed. It has relevance to other enclosed worlds, however. The world of *Daphnis and*

Chloe is not just a world of human beings; the landscape belongs to it, for landscape in this novel is a reality that conditions the activities of men. The unity that this novel represents is one that embraces art and culture, taste and refinement of feeling, for everything is thoroughly thought through and everything is transposed into beauty.

Longus's novel uses various means of narration: direct reporting of events, conversations, monologues, inset stories, and reflections. The general tone is idyllic, though pierced at times by violence, but the description of country pursuits is realistic and the treatment of sexuality in no way veiled. The change of the seasons accompanies the changing moods of the protagonists of the action, but much more objectively than in *Werther*, for in the world that Longus depicts the seasons actually condition the activities of the characters and therefore also their moods. The brightness of the work, that same brightness which Goethe had praised in Wieland and in Sterne, is not just climatic but also moral, for in the world of this novel, as in that of Manzoni's masterpiece, violence and vice never win out. As in *The Vicar of Wakefield* a "final triumph of good over evil" is attested. It is not difficult to understand why this tale of young love, this confirmation of goodness, piety and reverence, should have appealed so strongly to the old poet, the creator of Felix and Hersilie. And then there were plenty of novelistic elements in *Daphnis and Chloe*, and here, as in *The Vicar of Wakefield*, natural and strange elements—and ordinary and extraordinary circumstances, as in Scott—were happily combined.

Considerations similar to those just listed account for Goethe's interest in the three Chinese novels that he read. In a conversation with Eckermann, dated 31 January 1827, Goethe observed that the characters in these novels "think, act and feel almost as we do . . . except that with them everything is clearer, purer and more moral" [*nur dass bei ihnen alles klarer, reinlicher und sittlicher zugeht*].[3] Another difference is that "external nature lives its own life alongside these human figures." Goethe also praised the depiction of detail in these novels, the language being, as he said, rich in images and interwoven with legends oriented toward morality and propriety. We have evidence that Goethe read three Chinese novels: *Huan Chien Chi* (in an English translation published in 1824 under the title *Chinese Courtship*), *Han Kiou Choaan* (probably in the German translation by Christoph Gottlieb von Murr, published in 1766), and *Iu Kiao Li* (in a French translation, *Les deux cousines*, 1826).[4] All three are bright in general tone, like *Daphnis and Chloe*, but they also contain much that Goethe had described as "unpleasant" in his discussion of that work. *Chinese Courtship* deals with a conflict between love and decorum, between fidelity to the beloved and obedience to one's parents. But the two marriages which the hero concludes at the end of the novel are a cheerful solution to a seemingly tragic conflict, for thereby all parties are satisfied. This is also a moral solution. It is decreed by the Emperor, who is thereby recognizing the claims of filial decorum and the marriage arranged for the hero by his parents but also the purity and steadfastness of the hero's love for his chosen bride. The world of this novel is an ordered whole like that of *Daphnis and Chloe* and sustained by similar concepts of decorum and virtue. Both novels culminate in the victory of good over evil, and both contain characters who are basically chaste, reacting to the onsurge of passion with self-control and patient hope. Both suggest a relationship between human life and external nature which is real and not just the projection of heated human fancy. Both novels are full of novelistic motives, for both are essentially romances. In both we are transported into a closed world which nevertheless evokes wider perspectives in the reader. But there is one important difference. In the Chinese novel the ultimate moral authority lies not outside the finite world but within it at its social apex in the person of the Emperor, so that in this completely ordered world the highest social degree is identical with the highest moral degree.

Goethe objected to the Romantic mixing of genres, and he never confused them himself. A novel remained for him something basically different both in structure and in content from a novella, a drama or a poem. His novels are not extended novellas, and he never wrote a "dramatic" or a "lyric" novel. *The Elective Affinities* is not a drama and *Werther* is not a lyrical effusion. Goethe never considered for a moment making a novel out of the essentially dramatic confrontation of Tasso and Antonio, or Prometheus and Epimetheus, or Faust and Mephistopheles (though this last had been made into a novel by his contemporary, Friedrich Maximilian Klinger). He also never confused the novel with the epic, or suggested, as others had done, that the novel was the modern form of the epic. The epic, for Goethe, always presupposed an accepted moral and religious order, whereas his concern in his novels was to find order that would embrace what lay outside most accepted concepts of order, namely chance and the unfathomable, all that eluded rational categorization.

The plot of a Goethe novel is shaped with reference to this basic quest. The action is both external and internal, dealing simultaneously both with events and with sentiments, with *Begebenheiten* and *Gesinnungen*, to use Goethe's own terms. The events are often extraordinary and recall the sensational adventures in romances, because one of Goethe's concerns was to underscore the role of chance and the unexpected. The sentiments express the reactions of the characters to events, and also the general nature of a character's attitude to experience. To the sentiments belong also digressions, which start from either a particular event or a particular reaction to an event by one of the characters. The sentiments are multi-faceted and often embody alternative solutions, even polar oppositions, so that the final result is a richly woven texture of contrasting ideas. The essential progression of the plot is often one of ideas rather than of events, and that is why the structure may seem centrifugal in its determination to work in all directions and from all sides. But the basic quest for comprehensive order is centripetal, and gives each novel its coherence. This combination of a centrifugal and a centripetal tendency means that these novels have both a linear and a nonlinear plot-line, and are therefore simultaneously dia-chronic and synchronic in presentation. Goethe experimented with various forms of linear plot-line, beginning either at the beginning (the *Theatrical Mission*), or *in medias res* (the *Apprenticeship*) or at a critical point in a well-established relation-ship (*Werther; The Elective Affinities*). He also used various forms of synchronic presentation—the archive, the aggregate, and thematic and structural counterpoint. With Goethe, the mature novelist, the sentiments are therefore not "retarding" but pro-gressive, for they never slow down the external pace of events. Montan's speech about "thinking and doing" seems to represent a reflection of the novel on its own plot-line, as does Makarie's image of "stable mobility circling around a clear midpoint." Sentiments and events do not stand in a simple relation of cause and effect; they interpenetrate each other in a curious way, so that we have both the sense of a novel and the sense of a romance.

But not the sense of a romance which demonstrates *providentia*, for *fortuna* would seem to be the divinity that man has to accept and adjust to. But she is not a divinity that shapes our ends—or at least not entirely. It is ultimately the *daimon* in each of us that does this, though it interacts with events and circum-stances, which are often accidental. In a way, therefore, the interpenetration of sentiments and events in a Goethe novel parallels the interaction of *daimon* and *tychē* that was for Goethe the basic fact of all human progression.

But where do we progress to? These novels do not end with resolutions. The novelist, Goethe believed, should have a "free view of life," and his own novels, with the exception of *Werther*, present various attitudes and perspectives which do not confront each other, as in a drama, but complement each other. They are played off, sometimes even ironically, against each other. None triumphs in the end. Even in the *Journeymanship* there is the nonresignation of Felix asserting its claims alongside the "resignation," albeit a positive and active resignation, of Wilhelm. And although Charlotte orders that Eduard and Ottilie shall lie side by side in death, this does not prove that any one character has been vindicated over the others, or that the concept of elective affinities is to be respected or rejected. These novels do not give answers. They are open-ended in the sense that at the end we are left with much that is unconcluded. So considered, the last sentences of *The Elective Affinities* with their suggestion of peace take on even deeper meaning. The *Journeymanship* ends with sleep in the midday sun, the *Apprenticeship* with the sense of great good fortune—but in each case the end is only a pause before further progression. The fact that peace, sun or good fortune illuminates the end of these novels is paradigmatic, as is also the fact that the end of each novel points toward higher things—the *Apprenticeship* with its reference to the higher mission of Saul, *The Elective Affinities* with its hope of resurrection, the *Journeymanship* with its reminder of man created in God's image, and even *Werther* with its expression of the loneliness of the soul voyaging towards the unknown, but still going somewhere, continuing its journey: "No priest accompanied him." By such open-endedness the novels acquire what Goethe, in the somewhat more restricted context of his letter to Rochlitz on the *Journeymanship*, had termed "a kind of infinitude." For in each of these endings the novelist looks back on the order he has created in his novel, and looks forward beyond the limits of this order.

Notes

Goethe's works are quoted wherever possible from the so-called "Artemis Ausgabe" (*Gedenkausgabe der Werke, Briefe und Gespräche*, ed. Ernst Beutler, Artemis Verlag, Zurich and Stuttgart, 1948–1960, 24 volumes and an index volume) = AA. For works and letters not included in this edition, I quote from the larger Weimar Edition (*Goethes Werke*, Weimar, 1887–1919, 133 volumes) = WA. Conversations not included in AA are quoted from the new Artemis edition of the *Gespräche*, Zurich and Stuttgart, 1965–1972, ed. Wolfgang Herwig, 4 volumes = *Gespräche*. The diaries are quoted from the new Cotta Edition of Goethe's writings, vols. XI, XII and XIII, ed. Gerhart Baumann, Stuttgart, 1956–1968, the quotations being identified by date.

Abbreviations of titles used in the following notes are:

DVjs.   *Deutsche Vierteljahrsschrift für Literaturwissenschaft und Geistesgeschichte.*

EG   *Etudes Germaniques.*

Fests.   Festschrift.

Goethe-Jb.   *Goethe-Jahrbuch.*

Goethe   (A continuation of the *Goethe-Jb.*, 1914——)

GRM   *Germanisch-Romanische Monatschrift.*

HA   Hamburger Ausgabe von Goethes Werken.

Jb. d. dt. Schiller Ges.   *Jahrbuch der deutschen Schiller-Gesellschaft.*

Jb. d. fr. dt. Hochstifts   *Jahrbuch des freien deutschen Hochstifts.*

Jb. d. Goethe Ges.   *Jahrbuch der Goethe-Gesellschaft.*

MLN   *Modern Language Notes.*

PEGS   *Publications of the English Goethe Society.*

PMLA   *Publications of the Modern Language Association of America.*

ZfdPh.   *Zeitschrift für deutsche Philologie.*

Chapter 1. *Introduction*

1. There are only three lengthy treatments of Goethe's novels: Robert Riemann, *Goethes Romantechnik* (Leipzig, 1902) and Hans Reiss's two books *Goethes Romane* (Berne and Munich, 1963) and *Goethe's Novels* (London, 1969), the second of which is not a translation of his earlier book but a treatment that is differently accentuated and addressed to a general English-speaking public. Riemann concerns himself solely with structural questions in the individual novels (composition, characterization, dialogue), whereas Reiss goes further in that he also discusses the meaning and content of Goethe's novels in the context of all of Goethe's works. However, neither of the two deals in any detail with Goethe's statements about the form of the novel and neither has considered his evaluations of novels by other authors.

Shorter treatments of Goethe's achievement as a novelist are given in the essays of E. L. Stahl ("Goethe as Novelist" in *Essays on Goethe*, ed. William Rose, London, 1949) and Victor Lange ("Goethe's Craft of Fiction," *PEGS*, N.S. XXII [1952–1953]). Of these the more penetrating is the essay by Victor Lange, which ends with this comprehensive evaluation: "By bringing a poetic, a multiple, intelligence to bear upon the tangible world, and by illuminating the familiar figure or incident, he [Goethe] reveals something of their barely suspected complexity. With Goethe there begins the interest in the symbols of variety, of depth and incongruity, that concerns the modern novelists; but unlike them Goethe could still provide that perspective of symbolic depth without obliterating the realistic surface" (pp. 62f.).

Chapter 2. *Soliloquy in the Epistolary Mode*

1. "Fragment eines Romans in Briefen," AA IV, pp. 263–266.
2. Ernst Beutler, "Einführung zu *Werther*," AA IV, p. 1061.
3. AA X, p. 42. Goethe read *Télémaque* for the first time in Neukirch's translation. But he had managed to read the French original by 27 September 1766, for on that day he wrote in a letter to his sister that the style of this novel, though "magnifique" and "élevé," could not be used as a model for imitation. He remarked in his autobiography *Fiction and Truth* that the work had a pleasing and moral effect upon him (AA X, p. 42).
4. James Boyd, *Goethe's Knowledge of English Literature*, Oxford, 1932; Bertram Barnes, *Goethe's Knowledge of French Literature*, Oxford, 1937; Albert Fuchs, "Goethe et la littérature française," in *Goethe et l'esprit français (Actes du Colloque international de Strasbourg, 23–27 avril 1957)*, Paris, 1958. For knowledge of Wieland's works, see WA IV, 2, p. 188 and WA IV, 1, p. 179. On Sophie von La Roche, see AA X, p. 613.

5. AA XXII, p. 24.

6. Caroline Flachsland reports in a letter of May 1772 to Herder that Goethe read the story of Le Fever out of *Tristram Shandy* to a gathering *(Gespräche* I, p. 58). Goethe, also in a letter to Herder, talks of "Walter-Shandyish self-defenses" [*Walter-Shandyischen Notwehren*] (AA XVIII, p. 175). In a letter to Lavater, Goethe makes an allusion to Sterne's chapter on noses (January 1775; WA IV, 2, p. 227).

7. WA IV, 1, p. 192.

8. AA X, pp. 475f.

9. WA I, 26, pp. 380f.

10. WA I, 26, p. 352.

11. The two versions of *Werther* are printed face-to-face in the "Akademie" edition of Goethe's works (ed. Erna Merker, Berlin, 1954). They are also readily available in AA IV.

The various interpretations of *Werther* can be divided into three main groups. On one hand it is claimed that it is solely Werther's temperament that leads him to destruction, on the other that the inflexible forms of society drive him to his death. The third position holds that he comes to grief because of the opposition between his own inner world and outer reality.

According to Mme. de Staël, the novel deals with "les maladies de l'imagination dans notre siècle" *(De L'Allemagne,* Part Two, Chapter 28). Gerhard Storz holds similar views, seeing Werther's tragedy as growing out of an active but isolated imagination *(Goethe-Vigilien,* Stuttgart, 1953, p. 40). For Friedrich Gundolf, Werther is the cosmic, titanic man, the titan of sentiment [*Empfindung*] who sacrifices his love to his titanic stature *(Goethe,* 10th ed., Berlin, 1922, pp. 163, 169); the novel embodies the spiritual relationship of the divinely driven youth to ultimate experience [*zum schönen Augenblick*] (ibid., p. 164). Likewise, H. A. Korff suggests that the novel portrays the downfall of a divinely driven man who loves the very world which fails to come up to his great inner expectations *(Geist der Goethezeit,* I, 4th ed., Leipzig, 1957, pp. 295f.). For H. H. Borcherdt, Werther is a man who cannot compromise with outer reality, because for him the heart, and not the understanding, is the measure of all things *(Der Roman der Goethezeit,* Stuttgart, 1949, p. 17). In the introduction to his translation of *Werther* (New York, 1970), Harry Steinhauer writes (p. 110): "For Werther the outside world is but a reflection of his inner mental state. Things exist only in the meaning which he assigns to them. He is one of the first of those modern men whose attitude is summed up in the words of Schopenhauer: the world is my representation."

For Georg Lukács, Werther's tragedy is already the tragedy of bourgeois humanism, of "the insoluble conflict between the free and full development of the personality and bourgeois society itself" *(Goethe and his Age,* London, 1968, p. 45). It is society, according to Lukács, which thwarts such a development of the personality, not the nature of the individual himself. Arnold Hirsch emphasizes the influence of Rousseau on Goethe's novel, which can be seen in the hero's antagonistic isolation from society, although Goethe does not make his hero into any sort of Rousseauesque progressive thinker or revolutionary or reformer *("Die Leiden des jungen Werthers:* Ein bürgerliches Schicksal im absolutistischen Staat," *EG* XIII [1958], pp. 232f.). The novel relates the fate of an individual who suffers under the narrowness of bourgeois existence, but does not decide to take political action. Peter Müller claims that Werther's fate portrays the destruction of modern creative man by the feudal world; Goethe's novel depicts the transition from feudal social structures to a new bourgeois society *(Zeitkritik und Utopie in Goethes "Werther,"* Berlin, 1969, pp. 7f.).

One of the first interpreters to see Goethe's novel neither as a work about absolute subjectivity nor as a portrayal of the destructive power of social conditions but as an interplay between inner world and outer reality was George Sand. Goethe's novel seemed to her a masterly depiction of "passion contrariée dans son développement, c'est-à-dire, la lutte de l'homme contre les choses" *(Questions d'art et de littérature,* Paris, 1878, p. 25). Hans Reiss talks of Werther's persistence in a limited view of things, of his being destroyed by the opposition between outer and inner reality *(Goethes Romane,* pp. 25, 29). Hermann Blumenthal claims that *Werther* is the tragedy of a young man who decides to live for the sake of his own inner self, but cannot form or control his inner forces ("Ein neues Wertherbild?" in the periodical *Goethe,* N.S. V [Weimar, 1940], p. 319). He adds that this subjectivity can create for itself no "valid counterpart" in the real world. Erich Trunz is of the opinion that the novel describes the gradual abatement of the polar rhythm of self and world, inhalation and exhalation (HA VI, pp. 536, 544). Hildegard Emmel claims, however, that Werther does not appreciate the give-and-take of nature and human relationships *(Weltklage und Bild der Welt in der Dichtung Goethes,* Weimar, 1957, p. 31). Matthijs Jolles speaks of "Absonderung und hypochondrische[n] Vereinsamung," of an isolation where a dialogue is no longer possible *(Goethes Kunstanschauung,* Berne, 1957, p. 181). However, he does not deny the existence of an independent external reality in Goethe's novel. Klaus Scherpe's concept of the problem is close to my own: Werther tries to replace the outer world with his own inner reality, but it proves an inadequate substitute: "Die reine Innenwelt versagt jedoch als Ersatz für die reale Aussenwelt" *(Werther und Wertherwirkung,* Bad Homburg, 1970, p. 71).

Critics also differ widely in their attitude toward Werther's character. To Schiller he seemed "sentimental" (in the sense of "sentimental" given in his essay *On Naive and Sentimental Poetry),* to Korff he seems "divinely inspired" and "divinely driven," to Gundolf "titanic," to Peter Müller "Promethean" (in the sense of Goethe's poem *Prometheus*) and also crucified, to Ernst Feise ("Goethes Werther als nervöser Charakter," *GR* I [1926]) "nervous," to Ernst Beutler ("Wertherfragen," *Goethe*, N.S. V [1940], p. 151) completely moral (Werther kills himself in order to avoid evil). Victor Lange ("Goethe's Craft of Fiction," p. 37) believes that it was Goethe's intention "to describe the inadequacies of a world in which, not the mere sentimental 'man of feeling,' but the man of irresistible if irrational emotional energies cannot find his way," to give a portrait of an "eccentric in a world that has itself lost its center." Therefore Lange also believes that the "world" in this novel has an existence independent of Werther's consciousness.

In his more recent book, *Goethe's Novels*, Hans Reiss asserts that "in *Werther* we encounter two views of reality—that of Werther and that of the editor." Goethe speaks "with two voices which contradict one another" (ibid., pp. 48–49, taking up the view expressed by E. L. Stahl in his edition of the novel, Oxford, 1942). Reiss also believes that the novel "is a criticism of a man who thinks that he is a genius, but is not, and ruins his life by clinging to this mistaken belief" (ibid., p. 81).

12. This statement is by no means a "basic maxim," as Peter Müller claims (op. cit., p. 28), but rather a wishful dream.

13. On the image of the prison, compare the excellent presentation "Die Welt des Kerkers" by Hildegard Emmel in her *Weltklage und Bild der Welt in der Dichtung Goethes*. Like other interpreters, such as Trunz and Reiss, Miss Emmel emphasizes the motif of restriction [*Einschränkung*] in the novel, but adds that Werther knows that it is he himself who has made his world a prison (op. cit., p. 27).

14. AA IV, p. 279.

15. AA IV, p. 289.

16. The wanderer for Goethe represents the man who is not satisfied with an ordinary existence, but who feels pulled out into the world to search for something more (cf. *Wanderlied*, AA I, p. 498). He is the idealist, the striver. The hut represents a fixed orderly existence which is at home within the confines of society and human nature. The wanderer is often associated with images of turmoil, passion, sublimity, while the hut is defined by images of comfort, domesticity, stability. For more information on this, see L. A. Willoughby's article, "The Image of the 'Wanderer' and the 'Hut' in Goethe's Poetry," *EG* VI (1951).

17. Erich Trunz remarks that there is no greater contrast to Werther's tension-filled inner world than the world of children (HA VI, p. 548). But one should note that this contrast exists only for Werther, that there is no real contrast, for this "world of children" springs from out of his inner world and is a part of it.

18. On the conversation about suicide, see in particular Feise (op. cit.,

pp. 207f.), Herbert Schöffler (*"Die Leiden des jungen Werther": Ihr geistesgeschichtlicher Hintergrund*, Frankfurt am Main, 1938, pp. 25f.), Emil Staiger (*Goethe*, I, Zurich, 1952, pp. 166f.) and Peter Müller (op. cit., pp. 138–144). Erich Trunz claims that the book is original in its use of suicide as a theme, since at that time suicide seemed a monstrous thing that only simple people would contemplate (HA VI, p. 553). This, however, is not completely true: only in the minds of orthodox Christians and the simpler, more conservative people of the time was suicide really an atrocity. For the eighteenth century, particularly after Addison's *Cato*, the question of whether one had the moral right to take one's own life was an eminently debatable issue, and was indeed widely discussed. See, for example, the moral justification of suicide given in Montesquieu's *Lettres Persanes* (1721, Letter 76), or the sophisticated correspondence on this theme in *La Nouvelle Héloïse* (1761). In Goethe's portrayal in *Fiction and Truth* of the period in which he wrote *Werther*, Montesquieu's position on suicide is explicitly mentioned (AA X, p. 637). It was not Werther's suicide itself that people objected to when the novel first appeared, but rather the motive for the suicide, the fact that he killed himself because of an unhappy love.

For further information on the debate about suicide in the eighteenth century, see Lester G. Crocker, "The Discussion of Suicide in the Eighteenth Century," *Journal of the History of Ideas* XIII (1952), pp. 47–72.

19. AA IV, p. 329.

20. AA IV, pp. 343f. I do not believe that Werther's interest in Ossian can be explained by saying that he sees "a savagery and extravagance of feeling in Ossian's language which corresponds to his own feelings" (Reiss, *Goethe's Novels*, p. 35), for the feeling in Ossian is not particularly savage or extravagant. The important things are rather a certain sort of melancholy that characterizes the work, the godlessness of Ossian's world, and parallels in the work to Werther's own situation. See Staiger on the symbolic significance of Ossian in the novel (op. cit., I, pp. 170–171). Lukács is certainly wrong when he describes Ossian and Homer as being "for Werther and for young Goethe, . . . great popular poets, poetic reflections and expressions of the productive life that exists uniquely and alone among the working people" (op. cit., p. 43). For a contrast between the two authors is clearly intended. And what does Ossian have to do with the working people?

21. On Werther's "religious longing," see particularly Schöffler (op. cit.); J.-J. Anstett, "La crise religieuse de Werther," *EG* IV (1949), pp. 121–128; and Johanna Graefe, "Die Religion in den *Leiden des jungen Werther*," *Goethe*, N.S. XX (1958), pp. 72–98.

Schöffler interprets the novel as a religious work. He continually compares Werther with Christ, using, of course, the allusions in the text to the New Testament. However, he does not stop to consider that Werther, not Goethe, makes these comparisons, nor to wonder whether they have objective validity, and he overlooks Werther's particularly revealing comparison of himself with the prodigal son. Peter Müller, on the other hand, believes that the novel attacks the basic principles of Christian morality and encourages apostasy (op. cit., p. 36). Reiss asserts that Werther is a man who believes himself independent of God, but who still has very strong religious feelings, though it remains unclear what Reiss regards as "religious feelings" *(Goethes Romane*, p. 43). Borcherdt explains quite rightly that Werther's "God" exists only in his own speculations and in the intensity of his own feelings [*Fülle seines Herzens*] (op. cit., p. 20). Anstett on the other hand characterizes Werther as "une âme religieuse qui a besoin, dans son inquiétude, de se sentir assurée et portée par une force la dépassant" (op. cit., p. 121).

22. Ladislao Mittner, "Il 'Werther,' romanzo antiwertheriano," in his *La letteratura tedesca del Novecento e altri saggi*, Turin, 1960, p. 60: "Werther . . . è malato, perchè ama troppo sentirsi sano, perchè subisce troppo il fascino di ogni espressione di sanità."

23. Montesquieu, *Oeuvres Complètes* I, Bibliothèque de la Pléiade, Paris, 1949, p. 129.

24. Marmontel, *Oeuvres Complètes* X, Paris, 1819, pp. 342f.

25. "The nature of familiar letters, written, as it were, to the *moment* while the heart is agitated by hopes and fears, on events undecided, must plead an excuse for the bulk of a collection of this kind. Mere facts and characters might be comprised in a much smaller compass: but, would they be equally interesting?" Richardson, Preface to *Sir Charles Grandison*, London, 1753.

26. In Blanckenburg's view, the correspondents are "oft in zu grosser Bewegung, als dass sie in sich selbst zurück kehren, Wirkung und Ursach gegen einander abwiegen, und das *Wie* bey dem Entstehn ihrer Begebenheiten so aufklären könnten, wie wir es sehen wollen." *Versuch über den Roman*, Leipzig and Liegnitz, 1774, p. 285. (Blanckenburg's *Versuch* is readily available in a facsimile edition, ed. Eberhard Lämmert, Stuttgart, 1965.)

27. Ibid., p. 297.

28. Ibid., p. 412.

29. Blanckenburg's review is contained in the collection *Zeitgenössische Rezensionen und Urteile über Goethes "Götz" und "Werther,"* ed. Hermann Blumenthal, Berlin, 1935, pp. 75–99.

30. "Und eben so dichterisch schön sind die Eigenthümlichkeiten unsrer Sitten ins Werk hinein gewebt; sie werden zur *Ursache* von *Werthers* Verdrusse gebraucht . . . . Welche Schmach für die Feyerlichkeiten, und die Pendantereyen unsers deutschen Adels" (ibid., p. 87).

31. AA X, pp. 631–648.
32. AA X, pp. 631f.
33. Schiller, *Die Räuber*, Act I, Scene 2.
34. AA X, pp. 637f.
35. Ibid., pp. 630f.
36. Cf. Victor Lange, who holds that here an ironic contrast is intended between the monologic tone of the letters and the fact that they are indeed letters addressed to a very ordinary man ("Erzählformen im Roman des 18. Jahrhunderts," *Anglia* LXXVI [1958], p. 143).

Chapter 3. *The Fictive Editor*

1. This handwritten page is at present in the Weimar Goethe and Schiller Archives. The text is quoted from AA IV, p. 267.
2. AA IV, p. 1062.
3. See *Goethe und Werther*, ed. A. Kestner, Stuttgart and Tübingen, 1854, pp. 86–89. An abridged version of Kestner's account is easily accessible in HA VI, pp. 518–520.
4. Cf. Borcherdt (op. cit., p. 38), who believes that in the second version *Werther* almost became an "Antiwerther." A comparison of the two versions has been attempted by Gottfried Fittbogen ("Die Charaktere in den beiden Fassungen von Werthers Leiden," *Euphorion* XVII [1910], pp. 556–582), and Martin Lauterbach *(Das Verhältnis der zweiten zur ersten Ausgabe von Werthers Leiden,* Strassburg, 1910). Fittbogen examines the differing portrayals of Albert, Lotte and Werther in the two versions, but does not succeed in arriving at any clear understanding of the artistic purpose of the changes. Lauterbach mainly concerns himself with the verbal alterations, but also includes changes in content, which he sees as resulting from Goethe's relationship to the Kestners.
5. The function of the narrator in *Werther* has not been adequately studied in the critical literature. Moreover, the difference between the narrator sections of the two versions of the novel has never been examined with relation to their narrative voice. Reiss holds that it is the narrator's role to soften the tragic aspect of Werther's sufferings without lessening their total effect. And by introducing the narrator Goethe lets us see that he does not share Werther's view of reality, that another view is possible *(Goethes Romane,* p. 54). Trunz asserts a polar contrast between the language of the narrator section and that of Werther's letters (HA VI, p. 550). Staiger, in a position somewhat closer to my own, believes that the anonymous narrator is used to avoid the intrusion of some third person such as Albert or Wilhelm (op. cit., p. 149). Victor Lange has a very different view of this apparent break in the structure, believing that the narrator is introduced to save the relationship between reader and narrator, since he comes in at the point when

the reader's relationship to the primary narrator, Werther, is about to break down ("Erzählformen," pp. 135f.). Peter Müller states that the breaking off of first-person narration shows that Werther has lost the ability to think coherently about himself or his circumstances (op. cit., p. 183). Here we see a noteworthy confusion between author and central character, as if Werther himself gave up the narration and switched to a narrator!

6. Goethe remarks in a letter to Sophie von La Roche (19 January 1773) that the death of Jerusalem has deeply touched him: "der Bericht hat mich so oft innig gerührt, als ich sie las, und *das gewissenhafte Detail der Erzählung* nimmt ganz hin" (WA IV, 2, pp. 57f.; my italics).

7. For the biographical background and Goethe's relations with the Kestners, see Reiss, *Goethe's Novels*, pp. 10–17. I agree entirely with Reiss that this biographical material "tells us much about the gestation of the work and little, if anything at all, about the work itself" (ibid., p. 17).

8. Letter to Kestner of 2 May 1783: "Ich habe in ruhigen Stunden meinen Werther wieder vorgenommen, und denke, ohne die Hand an das zu legen was so viel Sensation gemacht hat, ihn noch einige Stufen höher zu schrauben" (AA XVIII, p. 732).

9. Thomas Mann, "Phantasie über Goethe," *Neue Studien*, Berlin and Frankfurt am Main, 1948, p. 71.

Chapter 4. *Uncertain Irony*

1. *Von und an Herder: Ungedruckte Briefe aus Herders Nachlass*, III, ed. Heinrich Düntzer and Ferdinand Gottfried von Herder, Leipzig, 1862, p. 10.

2. For more on Goethe and the theater, see W. H. Bruford, *Theatre, Drama and Audience in Goethe's Germany*, London, 1950; and Willi Flemming, *Goethe und das Theater seiner Zeit*, Stuttgart, 1968.

3. On the National Theater Movement, see Reiss, *Goethe's Novels*, p. 79, and Bruford, op. cit., *passim*.

4. Gundolf explains Goethe's choice of the theater as a subject by pointing out that the theater both reflects the stratification of society and works to change society *(Goethe*, pp. 340–342). Gundolf further claims that since actors lived a free life outside the ordered conventions of the day and yet still affected society, they were the suitable bearers of every new ideal that might transform society by introducing a new spirit of personal freedom. This seems to me hardly convincing, for the actors in Goethe's novel do not affect their society and have no such ideal. Gundolf is right, however, when he asserts that the theater background offers all the advantages of the picaresque and adventure novel as far as plot and entertainment value go. Borcherdt (op. cit., pp. 227–228) emphasizes that the theater occupied a central place in the aesthetics and

social ethics of the eighteenth century: the stage was considered not only a world of beautiful illusion, but also an educative influence, and all classes of society frequented the theater. Staiger regards the *Theatrical Mission* as the story of Goethe's dream of the founding of a German theater of high quality and educative influence. The novel for him embodies the fate of the hopes that Goethe's generation had for the theater, according to which it had to perform something of the function that was earlier fulfilled by the priest in the pulpit (op. cit., I, p. 429). Staiger further believes that the novel also shows the change in dramaturgical theories of the time, reflecting the move from the reception aesthetics of the Enlightenment to the individualist expressive ideal of Storm and Stress. The turning point in the novel, therefore, is for him the encounter with Shakespeare. In Staiger's view, the title is thus neither serious nor ironic, but poses the question of whether the theater does indeed have a "mission" and whether Wilhelm can fulfill it, a question to which Goethe hoped an answer would evolve as his novel progressed (p. 473). In order to support his contentions, Staiger refers to a letter of Goethe to Dalberg of 21 July 1779, written during the time the novel was being composed. However, this letter says nothing about any dreams for the theater such as Staiger mentions. Staiger also uses two references from Goethe's last decade, but these do not refer to any specific period of his life, and thus offer us no information about the inception of the *Theatrical Mission*.

5. *Der deutsche Merkur* I, Drittes Stück, p. 264.

6. Goethe mentions Cervantes in letters to Frau von Stein of 1780 and 1782 (WA IV, 4, p. 292; WA IV, 6, p. 35). He received the Spanish original of *Don Quixote* from Karl August for his birthday in 1783 (*Goethe-Handbuch*, I, 2d ed., ed. Alfred Zastrau, Stuttgart, 1961, p. 1610).

7. *Goethes Werke*, Festausgabe X, Leipzig, 1926, p. 345. See also Eduard Castle, "Der theatergeschichtliche und autobiographische Gehalt von *Wilhelm Meisters theatralischer Sendung*," *Wiener Goethe Verein* XXVII (1913), pp. 15–22; and Bernhard Seuffert, *Goethes Theaterroman*, Graz-Vienna-Leipzig, 1924. For the views of Gundolf and Staiger on the work as a theater novel, see note 4 above.

8. For a complete discussion of the various stages in the writing of the novel, see the exposition given by Oskar Walzel in the Festausgabe of Goethe's *Werke*.

9. The best modern edition of the Schulthess manuscript is to be found in the relevant volume in the Akademie Edition of Goethe's works (1957, ed. Renate Fischer-Lamberg). My references are to the Artemis Edition, but the Akademie Edition was used for comparison.

10. AA VIII, p. 525.

11. AA VIII, p. 530.

12. On the various interpretations of the *Theatrical Mission*, see the first part of Hans Reiss's essay, *"Wilhelm Meisters theatralische Sendung: Ernst oder Ironie?" Jb. d. dt. Schiller Ges.* XI (1967), and *Goethe's Novels*, p. 139, fn. 5. Reiss himself sees in the novel a conflict similar to that which he perceived in *Werther:* "a conflict between the two tones of the narrative, of which one is subjective, emotional and serious, the other detached, objective and ironic" *(Goethe's Novels*, p. 75). But "we should not conclude that Goethe was not sure of his style and therefore alternated continually from one level of writing to another. For the novel does not convey the impression of uncertainty in the author. Like the majority of the novels of the period, it belongs to the middle style . . . ." (p. 77).

13. Letter to Knebel (AA XVIII, p. 739).

14. Letter to Knebel of December 1783 (WA IV, 6, p. 230).

15. WA IV, 6, p. 384.

16. Letter of 27 June 1785 (AA XVIII, p. 856).

17. Gundolf says that Mignon and the Harper are introduced into the world of the theater in order to show its limitations and to point beyond it (op. cit., p. 351). These two figures represent for Gundolf the unfathomable elements of existence as sensed by Goethe (p. 345). Trunz claims that these characters represent an unlimited intensity of feeling that can lead only into death (HA VII, p. 622). For Borcherdt they embody the idea of fate, through which Wilhelm feels all his actions guided (op. cit., p. 236). Walter Wagner asserts that the purpose and function of Mignon is to be Wilhelm's "guardian angel" and to lead him into the rejuvenating land of art ("Goethes Mignon," *GRM* XXI [1933], pp. 401–415). This is, however, not true in my opinion, for it is not in the realm of art that Wilhelm is to be "rejuvenated."

The most complete analysis of the figure of Mignon is still Dorothea Flashar's study, *Bedeutung, Entwicklung und literarische Nachwirkung von Goethes Mignongestalt*, Berlin, 1929. In this work, Mignon is described as the essence of genius, who appears almost as a part of Wilhelm's own self: "Ihr Inneres fliesst in Wilhelms Seelenstruktur ein, sie fühlt seine Stimmungen aus ihm heraus, so dass sie nicht wie eine andere Person, sondern wie ein Teil seines Selbst erscheint" (p. 41). The Harper on the other hand embodies, according to this critic, the impulse of genius to expand itself *outward* into life. Both give Wilhelm a stronger faith in his artistic mission (p. 48). Whether Flashar's characterization of these figures is valid for the *Theatrical Mission* cannot be ascertained, since the work breaks off at a crisis point in Wilhelm's conception of his "mission," but it certainly does not hold true for *Wilhelm Meister's Apprenticeship*, as Flashar herself admits. In the *Apprenticeship*, says Flashar, Mignon obeys completely different laws, and loses all importance for Wilhelm once he enters on practical life. This is false, for

the continuing importance of Mignon for Wilhelm is emphasized again
and again in the last chapter of the *Apprenticeship*, and she reappears in
the *Journeymanship*, a further proof of her significance.

For more on these two figures see Eugen Wolff, *Mignon, ein Beitrag
zur Geschichte des Wilhelm Meister*, Munich, 1909; Gustav Cohen,
"Mignon," *Jb. d. Goethe Ges.* VII (1920), pp. 132–153; Julius Schiff,
"Mignon, Ottilie, Makarie im Lichte der Goetheschen Naturphilosophie," *Jb. d. Goethe Ges.* IX (1922), pp. 132–147; F. R. Lachmann,
"Goethes Mignon," *GRM* XV (1927), pp. 100–116; Paul Krauss, "Mignon, der Harfner, Sperata: Die Psychopathologie einer Sippe," *DVjs.*
XXII (1944), pp. 327–354; and Aivars Petritis, *Die Gestaltung der Personen in Goethes "Wilhelm Meisters Lehrjahren" und "Wilhelm Meisters Wanderjahren,"* Cologne, 1967 (Mignon, pp. 251–260; Harper, pp.
260–266).

On Philine, see Gundolf (op. cit., p. 349) and Storz (op. cit., p. 75).
Petritis observes that we are told almost nothing about Philine's past, and
that she is always portrayed in the present as a person who lives for
the present (op. cit., p. 243). Arthur Henkel ("Versuch über den *Wilhelm Meister*," in *Ruperto-Carola* XXXI [1962], p. 62) calls her "Virtuosin
der Gegenwart, höchst realistisch in der Gesinnung, aber als Gestalt von
einer schwebenden Poesie." Trunz perceptively comments that Philine
plays a larger part in Wilhelm's education than he realizes, by testing
whether he is or is not petty bourgeois: she is his "Probierstein der
Spiessbürgerlichkeit" (HA VII, p. 620).

18. AA VIII, p. 554.
19. AA VIII, p. 560.
20. AA VIII, p. 561.
21. AA VIII, p. 576.
22. AA VIII, p. 720.
23. On this turning point in the action, see Staiger (op. cit., I, p. 461).
He asks if it is still possible to take Wilhelm's theater plans seriously after
the Harper and Mignon appear. Can Wilhelm be willing to make the
necessary compromises with public opinion after he has seen the inner
integrity of feeling in Mignon, the high value the Harper places on art?
Staiger believes that the narrator loses interest after the chapters in
which these figures enter the novel, and a note of indifference and uncertainty invades the narrative: "Es wird schwierig sein, sich zurechtzu-
finden und dem fühlbar unmutigen Dichter auf seinen krummen Wegen
zu folgen." In answer to Staiger I would observe that uncertainty characterizes the whole novel, and does not just appear at this juncture; that
it is difficult to perceive any ill humor or *Unmut* in the author's tone,
albeit his uncertainty constantly increases; and that the appearance of
the Amazon lifts the novel to new heights.
24. Cf. Staiger, who remarks that while earlier Wilhelm was shamed

by false expectations of success, now he is ashamed that his efforts are
so successful—in the fifth book of the novel there appears "eine feinere
Ironie, die gegen Wilhelm Meister gerichtet ist: Bisher waren die
falschen Erwartungen grosser Erfolge beschämend für ihn. Jetzt ist es
beschämend, dass sein Bestreben so viel Anerkennung findet" (op. cit.,
p. 464).

25. AA VIII, p. 802.
26. AA VIII, pp. 798, 802.
27. AA VIII, p. 859.
28. AA VIII, p. 874.
29. Victor Lange uses a passage on Wilhelm Meister in Goethe's
Annals as proof that the *Theatrical Mission* was supposed to deal with
"disappointment, frustration and disillusionment" ("Goethe's Craft of
Fiction," p. 42). But this is not decisive, for the passage he quotes (AA
XI, p. 620) refers to the *Apprenticeship* and contains the comparison
with Saul which appears only in the *Apprenticeship*. Borcherdt supports
the opposite view, saying that there is no doubt that the novel was supposed to move toward the goal of establishing a national theater, for
there is nothing in this version that points to a way out of the sphere of
the theater. The Amazon, according to Borcherdt, was to lead Wilhelm
to a classical concept of the theater, "zu dem klassischen Theatergedan-
ken" (op. cit., pp. 230–231). This assertion, however, is not supported by
the text. Staiger wavers in his opinions. On the one hand he claims that
the novel points towards the foundation of the Weimar Theater (op.
cit., I, p. 427). On the other hand, he says that the ending of the novel
was unclear in those years, as was the ending of *Faust;* and that the
novel's perspectives shifted in the course of its composition (ibid., p. 472).
I see no reason to accept Hans Reiss's assertion that "it would be a gross
over-simplification to suggest that Goethe started out by sharing Wilhelm's enthusiasm but, on reaching the beginning of the seventh book,
abandoned the work because he had ceased to believe in the value of
the theatre and Wilhelm's creative power" *(Goethe's Novels,* p. 81).
Why not? All the evidence points in this direction, though the break
came *before* the seventh book, as I have tried to demonstrate.

30. AA VIII, p. 531.
31. AA VIII, p. 547.
32. Hildegard Emmel believes that the narrator of the *Theatrical
Mission* has a central position and positive value in the work: "der
Erzähler der *Theatralischen Sendung* ist durch den ganzen Roman hin
ständig gegenwärtig. Er ruckt alles zurecht, entscheidet über die Beleuch-
tung, erklärt das Unverständliche, begründet das Ueberraschende, lächelt
über Schwächen und zeigt dem Leser durch den Ton seiner Rede an,
wo er am besten gleichfalls lächeln sollte" *(Weltklage,* pp. 78f.). His
function, however, is not that constant, as I have shown above. Nor is

it always true that, as Staiger claims, the narrator looks at the hero and his world from a higher standpoint and sees things as they really are (op. cit., I, p. 431).

33. AA VIII, pp. 563–564.

Chapter 5. *Search for a Definition*

1. Goethe early voiced the intention of completing the *Theatrical Mission.* On 21 July 1788 he wrote to F. H. Jacobi that as soon as he had completed the eight volumes of his collected works, he would turn again to "Wilhelm," to whom, he added, he was very attached (AA XIX, p. 120). But he did not mention the work again until 1 January 1791, when he wrote to Knebel that he had taken up "Wilhelm Meister" again at the encouragement of the Dowager Duchess of Weimar (AA XIX, p. 176). The diaries for the first half of January 1791 reveal that Goethe was occupying himself almost daily with the novel. It was probably in these days that he revised his entire conception of the work. An entry for 6 January states explicitly that he is rethinking the "plan" of the novel. However, Goethe did not seriously undertake the working out of this plan until 1794. The first two books of the new novel were given to the publisher in September of that year. The third book was ready by the end of the year, the fourth by March of the following year. On 29 July 1795 Goethe announced to Schiller that the fifth book was written and the sixth would be finished in a few days (AA XX, p. 94). On 14 January 1796 he noted in his diary the completion of the seventh book. And on 26 June he wrote there: *Roman fertig,* "novel completed."

2. Cf. Hans Nicolai's chronology of Goethe's life and works (HA XIV, pp. 466, 469).

3. Book Five, Chapter Seven (AA VII, pp. 330f.). There is a passage in the *Theatrical Mission* which points forward to this, where Wilhelm states that deeds and movement are central to the drama; and that sentiments and feelings must be subordinated to them (AA VIII, pp. 614f.).

4. That the novel and the drama should be treated as equally valid genres might appear to us today to be a matter of course, but this was an issue open to debate in the eighteenth century. The novel was generally considered a lower form of literature, although it was widely read. Thus Choderlos de Laclos remarked in his review of Fanny Burney's *Cecilia* (in the *Mercure de France*, 17 April–15 May 1784): "De tous les genres d'Ouvrages que produit la Littérature, il en est peu de moins estimés que celui des Romans; mais il n'y en a aucun de plus généralement recherché et de plus avidement lu" *(Oeuvres Complètes,* Bibliothèque de la Pléiade, Paris, 1951, p. 499). Johann Karl Wezel had made the same observation in Germany a few years earlier in the

preface to his novel *Hermann und Ulrike* (see *Theorie und Technik des Romans im 17. und 18. Jahrhundert*, II, ed. Dieter Kimpel and Conrad Wiedemann, Tübingen, 1970, pp. 23–27). At the time at which Goethe was writing this passage, eleven years after Laclos had made the above statement, the reputation of the novel as a genre had risen, but was by no means assured. (Schiller, for one, had deep reservations about the form.) Theoretical discussions of the novel had done little to effect its recognition as a valid genre, but its image had been improved by the publication of a small number of important novels, such as *Clarissa, Tom Jones, Agathon, La Nouvelle Héloïse* and *The Sorrows of Young Werther*. Only with the appearance of *Wilhelm Meister's Apprenticeship* did the novel gain the recognition and acceptance in Germany which it had won years earlier in France and England.

In his acceptance of the novel as a genre with its own particular characteristics which were neither those of the drama nor those of the epic, Goethe stands outside the discussions in the eighteenth century on whether the novel was essentially "dramatic" or essentially "epic" in structure. Blanckenburg in his *Versuch über den Roman* demands of the novel that it approximate itself to the drama. The novelist should not only make wide use of dialogue, but should also concern himself primarily with characters in conflict with external circumstances, as does the dramatist, and should seek to achieve that inevitability of cause and effect which is the essence of drama. Wezel in his preface to *Hermann und Ulrike* describes the novel as close to the classical idea of the epic. He defines the novel as a "bourgeois epic" [*wahre bürgerliche Epopee*] which follows or should follow the rules of epic poetry, even though the novel deals with the basically human and conveys the atmosphere of real life, whereas the classical epic is completely poetic in tone and concerns itself with the ideal. Both have an element of the marvelous in their composition, which is found in the actual characters and events of the epic, whereas it appears in the novel in unusual combinations of otherwise ordinary elements.

For more on the eighteenth-century debate about whether the novel is "epic" or "dramatic" in nature, see J. Warshaw, "The Epic-Drama Conception of the Novel," *MLN* XXXV (1920), pp. 269–279; and Walter F. Greiner, *Entstehung der englischen Romantheorie an der Wende zum 18. Jahrhundert*, Tübingen, 1969.

5. For information on Goethe's knowledge of Aristotle's *Poetics*, see Karl Schlechta, *Goethe in seinem Verhältnis zu Aristoteles*, Frankfurt am Main, 1938.

6. S. H. Butcher, *Aristotle's Theory of Poetry and Fine Art*, 4th ed., New York, 1951, pp. 340, 342f.

7. *Aristotle's Poetics: A Translation and Commentary for Students of*

Literature, trans. Leon Golden, commentary by O. B. Hardison, Englewood Cliffs, N.J., 1968, pp. 125f.

8. "Les mœurs sont ce qui marque les qualitez de ceux agissent; & les sentiments sont les discours, par lesquels ils font connoître quelque action ou découvrent leur pensée" *(La Poétique d'Aristote traduite en françois*, Paris, 1692).

9. AA IX, p. 605.

10. Letter to Jacobi of 6 January 1813 (AA XIX, p. 688).

11. Boswell, *Life of Johnson* II, ed. G. B. Hill, Oxford, 1887, p. 175.

12. Scott defines the novel itself as "a fictitious narrative, differing from the Romance, because the events are accommodated to the ordinary train of human events, and the modern state of society." This definition of the novel and that of the romance are found in Scott's *Essay on Romance* (1824), here quoted from *Scott's Miscellaneous Prose Works*, IV, Edinburgh and London, 1827, pp. 155–156. For more on Scott's attitude toward the novel, see Ioan Williams, ed., *Sir Walter Scott on Novelists and Fiction*, London and New York, 1968.

13. AA I, p. 669.

14. Friedrich Schlegel, "Charakteristiken und Kritiken I, 1796–1802," *Kritische Friedrich Schlegel Ausgabe*, II, ed. Hans Eichner, Munich-Paderborn-Vienna, 1967, p. 338.

15. Goethe declared in a letter to Charlotte von Stein of 9 May 1782: "Mama hat mir die neue schöne Genfer Edition von Rousseau geschenkt, die Confessions sind dabei. Nur ein Paar Blätter die ich drinne gesehen habe, sind wie leuchtende Sterne, dencke dir so einige Bände! Welch ein Himmel voll! Welch ein Geschenk für die Menschheit ist ein edler Mensch" (AA XVIII, p. 664).

16. *Gespräche* I, p. 267.

17. "[Goethe] sagte: so schöne Dinge, so viel grosser herrlicher Sinn auch darin sei, so könne er nun einmal für sich das, was man den *Geruch dieses Buchs* nennen möchte (anders wisse er sich nicht auszudrücken) nicht leiden" *(Gespräche* I, p. 276: Johanna Schlosser's emphasis).

18. "The Novels of F. H. Jacobi and Goethe's early Classicism," *PEGS*, N.S. XVI (1947), p. 58.

19. *Ibid.*, p. 86.

20. WA I, 17, p. 80.

21. AA X, pp. 24f.

22. AA XII, p. 387.

23. AA XIV, p. 521.

24. AA XIX, pp. 42f.

25. WA IV, 8, p. 102. On the relationship between Moritz and the *Theatrical Mission*, see E. L. Stahl, "Goethe as Novelist," p. 56. For more on Goethe and *Anton Reiser*, see Hans Berendt, *Goethes "Wil-*

helm Meister": *Ein Beitrag zur Entstehungsgeschichte*, Bonn, 1911; Rudolf Lehmann, "Anton Reiser und die Entstehung des *Wilhelm Meister*" in *Jb. d. Goethe Ges.* III (1916), pp. 116–134; and Hildegard Emmel, *Geschichte des deutschen Romans*, I, Berne, 1972, pp. 196–202.

26. AA XVIII, p. 788.

27. AA XX, p. 138.

28. Diderot, *Oeuvres Romanesques*, ed. Henri Bénac, Editions Garnier Frères, Paris, 1962, pp. 868f.

29. AA XVIII, p. 492. See also *Diaries*, entry for 3 April 1780. Fielding used almost exactly the same metaphor in the very first chapter of *Tom Jones*, which is entitled "The Introduction to the Work, or bill of fare for the feast."

30. AA XV, p. 1056.

31. AA XI, p. 741. For more on Goethe's relationship to Diderot, see Herbert Dieckmann, "Goethe und Diderot," *DVjs.* X (1932), pp. 478–503 (also in H. D., *Diderot und die Aufklärung*, Stuttgart, 1972); and Roland Mortier, *Diderot en Allemagne*, Paris, 1954.

32. Mortier, op. cit., p. 222.

33. *Romanciers du dix-huitième siècle*, I, ed. Etiemble, Bibliothèque de la Pléiade, Paris, 1960, p. 1522.

34. AA XX, p. 90.

35. Mme. de Staël, *Essai sur les fictions*, included in *Recueil de Morceaux détachés* 1795, pp. 335f. (see F.-C. Lonchamp, *L'Oeuvre imprimé de Mme. Germaine de Staël*, Geneva, 1949). I have used the text as reprinted in her *Oeuvres Complètes*, I, Paris, 1861, pp. 62–72.

36. Staël, p. 63. Goethe: AA XV, p. 337.

37. Staël, p. 64. Goethe: AA XV, p. 339.

38. Staël, p. 67. Goethe: AA XV, p. 346.

39. AA XV, p. 349 (Staël, p. 68).

40. Staël, p. 68. Goethe: AA XV, p. 349.

41. Staël, p. 68. Goethe: AA XV, p. 350.

42. Staël, pp. 68–70. Goethe: AA XV, pp. 351–353.

43. Staël, p. 70. Goethe: AA XV, p. 355.

44. Staël, p. 72. Goethe: AA XV, p. 361.

45. Staël, p. 67. Goethe: AA XV, p. 348.

46. In an essay on didactic poetry, Goethe remarks that all literature should be educative, and yet its didactic purpose should not be explicitly stated, but rather implicit in the material so that the reader may deduce it: "Alle Poesie soll belehrend sein, aber unmerklich: sie soll den Menschen aufmerksam machen, wovon sich zu belehren wert wäre; er muss die Lehre selbst daraus ziehen, wie aus dem Leben" ("Über das Lehrgedicht," published in 1827 in *Kunst und Altertum*, AA XIV, p. 370). In a letter to Nicolai Borchardt of 1 May 1828, Goethe comments in a similar vein: "Ich bin in meinen Arbeiten nicht leicht didaktisch

geworden: eine poetische Darstellung der Zustände, theils wirklicher, theils ideeller, schien mir immer das Vorteilhafteste, damit ein sinniger Leser sich in den Bildern bespiegeln und die mannichfaltigsten Resultate bei wachsender Erfahrung selbst herausfinden möge" (WA IV, 44, p. 79).

47. AA XX, pp. 114f.
48. AA XX, pp. 394f.
49. AA XX, pp. 416ff.
50. AA XX, pp. 422f.
51. AA XX, p. 333.
52. AA XXIV, p. 202.
53. Conversation with Eckermann of 29 January 1827 (AA XXIV, p. 225).
54. AA XXIV, p. 213.
55. AA XX, pp. 443–444.
56. Reiss, for example, declares: "Goethe found the genre of the novel inadequate. He knew that perfection could not be expected from it. Perfecting the novel technically by smoothness of language, organic relationship of images, consistency of intention and so on, was not enough. The form of the novel itself was 'impure'; it contained foreign elements, so to speak, such as lyrical poetry. It could not therefore stand comparison with dramatic form" *(Goethe's Novels*, p. 135).

Rasch, in an otherwise interesting essay on Goethe's narrative art, also claims that Goethe saw the novel as an inferior art form, and relates his views to the general eighteenth-century disdain for the novel. Rasch points out that Schiller saw the novelist as only the "half brother" of the poet, and that Goethe, even as late as 1806, described the novelist as a "kind of poetaster" [*eine Art von Poeten*] (Wolfdietrich Rasch, "Die klassische Erzählkunst Goethes," in *Formkräfte der deutschen Dichtung vom Barock bis zur Gegenwart*, ed. Hans Steffen, Göttingen, 1963, pp. 81–99). There is much that can be said in answer to these assertions. First of all, Schiller's description of the novelist is by no means as negative as Rasch assumes: Schiller is saying that the novelist, though not equal in stature to the poet, is nonetheless related to him. Secondly, one must object to Rasch's interpretation of the phrase *Art von Poeten* as a derogatory description of the novelist, since the word *Poet* did not have the same negative connotations in Goethe's time as it has today, and was indeed much closer in meaning to its simple English cognate, "poet," than to the word used above to convey Rasch's reading of it ("poetaster"). The passage in Goethe's writings from which Rasch takes this phrase certainly does not use the word negatively, as is evident from the context (AA XIV, p. 241). (For other clearly positive uses of *Poet*, see AA XX, p. 840; and AA XXIV, p. 161.) Further, if Goethe had indeed rejected the value of the novel as a form by using this phrase, as

Rasch claims, then it is astonishing that he would enthusiastically set to work on another novel two years later, in 1808.

Victor Lange's interpretation of Goethe's statement on the "impure" form of the novel seems to me to come closest to the truth of the matter: "Goethe's reply [to Schiller] suggests . . . his awareness of the almost crippling difficulties offered by the 'impure' form of fiction . . . . Yet he remained convinced that the narrator's freedom of movement, the blending of seemingly discrepant imaginative elements, offered advantages that he was not willing to sacrifice to any traditional view of epic consistency" ("Goethe's Craft of Fiction," p. 49).

57. AA XIV, p. 369.

58. AA XX, pp. 472ff.

59. AA XX, p. 476.

60. Lieselotte E. Kurth points out that one should not blandly read the excursus as a statement of Goethe's views on the novel: "Jeder Satz dieser Zusammenfassung [bedürfte] eigentlich einer sorgfältigen Analyse, ehe man sie—wie das fast ohne Ausnahme bisher geschehen ist—als Goethes eigenen Beitrag zur Romantheorie betrachtet" ("Formen der Romankritik im achtzehnten Jahrhundert," *MLN* LXXXIII, 1968, p. 686).

Chapter 6. *Fate and Chance*

1. The Countess is briefly mentioned in the *Theatrical Mission*, but her character is not elaborated.

2. Marianne Thalman, *Der Trivialroman des 18. Jahrhunderts und der romantische Roman*, Berlin, 1923; Hildegard Emmel, *Was Goethe vom Roman der Zeitgenossen nahm*, Berne, 1972. On the Ghost, see Emmel, pp. 24–34.

3. I do not think that we can agree with Lukács when he says that "hatred of 'fate,' of any fatalistic resignation, is constantly preached in the novel [the *Apprenticeship*]" (op. cit., p. 57). On the dialectic between fate and chance in the novel, see Max Wundt, *Goethes "Wilhelm Meister" und die Entwicklung des modernen Lebensideals*, 2d ed., Berlin and Leipzig, 1932, pp. 281–284; and Karl Schlechta, *Goethes "Wilhelm Meister*," Frankfurt am Main, 1953, pp. 47–51; although neither of the two offers a thorough study of this thematic pattern.

4. The various interpretations of the *Apprenticeship* differ according to the answers that they give to two fundamental questions: whether Wilhelm really attains to some form of culture or education, and what this culture or education consists in. Max Wundt gave the classic formulation of the *Apprenticeship* as a *Bildungsroman;* embodying the ideal of *Humanität* (op. cit., p. 169). He interprets the novel as consisting of a successive and rising series of various forms of *Humanität* which replace

the theater as a cultural goal. These are, according to Wundt, first "religiöse Humanität" (the *schöne Seele)*, "ästhetische Humanität" (the Uncle), and finally "sittliche Humanität" (moral humanism; Natalie). Korff follows a similar line of interpretation, but the final ideal reached in the novel has for him the quality of balance and is therefore aesthetic in character. Korff and others point to the fact that Wilhelm's *Bildung* at the end of the novel is not something achieved but something envisioned (op. cit., II, p. 336). Lukács characterizes the content of the novel as "the education of man for [i.e., to] the practical understanding of reality" (op. cit., p. 59). Reiss remarks in the same vein that "the whole tendency of the novel is directed against those who are unable to find a practical attitude to life, but also against those who completely succumb to practical activity" *(Goethe's Novels,* p. 126). Jürgen Rausch ("Lebensstufen in Goethes *Wilhelm Meister,*" *DVjs.* XX, 1942) and Joachim Müller ("Phasen der Bildungsidee im *Wilhelm Meister,*" *Goethe,* N.S. XXIV [1962], pp. 55–80) assume a progressive linear development in the concept of *Bildung* throughout the *Apprenticeship* and the *Journeymanship.* The goal of this entire progression is the development of the whole man in contrast to development of individual sides of him (Rausch, pp. 113f.). Müller is mainly concerned with the tension between egocentricity and selflessness. In his opinion the basic paradox of the *Apprenticeship* is that self-knowledge is achieved only by selfless action. Lukács is of the opinion that the *Apprenticeship* is concerned not merely with the development of the individual but also with "the tragic crisis of bourgeois humanist ideals and the beginning of their growth—temporarily utopian—beyond the framework of bourgeois society" (op. cit., p. 64). *Wilhelm Meister's Apprenticeship* is therefore for Lukács not just a *Bildungsroman* but also a social novel. Victor Lange asserts that "what Goethe here intended to achieve was the education, not of Wilhelm, but of the reader, and instead of representing a body of society, he hoped, by this novel, to create one" ("Goethe's Craft of Fiction," p. 45).

   Different as these interpretations are, there is one thing common to all of them, namely that the novel shows a progressive linear development toward some kind of perfection. But not all critics have held this view. Günther Müller, for instance, in his important book *Gestaltung – Umgestaltung in "Wilhelm Meisters Lehrjahren"* (Halle, 1948) rejects the idea that the novel shows a linear progression towards an ideal and instead asserts that it represents a series of metamorphoses, none of which corrects any of the previous stages. Kurt May in *"Wilhelm Meisters Lehrjahre,* ein Bildungsroman?" *DVjs.* XXXI (1957), pp. 1–39, questions the general assumption that a harmonious balance between the individual and the world is achieved at the end of the novel. He sees no concretization of harmony and totality there, but rather an advocation of limitation, and contraction instead of totality. In fact, he sees in the novel's close a submerged criticism of those very ideals of harmonious and total development which critics such as Korff and Wundt had declared to be present in the novel.

Karl Schlechta in his somewhat perverse study of the novel goes so far as to assert that it shows a gradual but steady impoverishment of Wilhelm's poetic vision and a corresponding victory of the secret society of the Tower, which Schlechta accuses of rigid empty formalism. The novel therefore becomes for Schlechta a tragic work that portrays the loss of youth, love and poetry and shows a steady downward progression from the relationship with Mariane, in which Wilhelm had experienced the utmost that was possible for him. Arthur Henkel ("Versuch über den *Wilhelm Meister*," pp. 59–67) also concerns himself with the problem of whether Wilhelm's development represents a steady moral progression. His answer is that Wilhelm has learned something, but has received his new understanding as a *gift:* "Dass er am Schluss freier ist, die Welt und sich darin besser versteht, ist freilich der gefeierte Gewinn seiner Jugend,—aber als Geschenk. Oder gilt auch im Bereich der goethesch verstandenen Bildung, dass Gnade die Natur voraussetzt und vollendet?" (p. 60). In the course of his presentation Henkel rightly asserts that in this novel the eighteenth-century faith in the power of reason, its optimism, its naïve trust in the educability of man are questioned (p. 65).

5. AA XX, p. 443.

6. AA VII, p. 37.

7. AA VII, p. 76.

8. AA VII, pp. 88f.

9. AA VII, p. 85.

10. AA VII, p. 108.

11. AA VII, p. 198.

12. AA VII, p. 205.

13. AA VII, p. 208. Gundolf says of Jarno that he is a man of superior intelligence [*Mann des überlegenen Verstandes*], and belongs to the series of Mephistophelian characters, who are characterized more by their emphasis on reason to the exclusion of other faculties and by a certain uncharitableness than by a truly evil or satanic nature (op. cit., p. 361).

14. AA VII, p. 223.

15. AA VII, p. 258.

16. AA VII, p. 265.

17. AA VII, p. 263.

18. AA VII, p. 259.

19. Cf. William Diamond, "Wilhelm Meister's Interpretation of *Hamlet*," *Modern Philology* XXIII (1925–1926), pp. 89–101. Diamond rightly points out that "Wilhelm Meister's picture of Hamlet . . . resembles

more strikingly Wilhelm Meister himself than Shakespeare's Prince of Denmark" (p. 92), but he does not examine the significance of this identification in the total structure of the novel.

Gundolf observes correctly that one should not regard the conversations about Hamlet as an autonomous "interpretation" of Hamlet: these conversations are part of the composition and plot of the novel, and are modulated in theme and tone to harmonize with the context in which they occur *(Shakespeare und der deutsche Geist,* 11th ed., Berlin, 1959, p. 277).

20. AA VII, p. 469.
21. AA VII, pp. 277, 526.
22. AA VII, p. 20.
23. AA VII, p. 367.
24. AA VII, p. 252.
25. AA VII, p. 557.
26. AA VII, p. 301.
27. AA VII, pp. 311–314.
28. AA VII, p. 39.
29. AA VII, p. 290.
30. AA VII, pp. 317ff.
31. AA VII, p. 366.
32. Wundt (p. 206) claims that Aurelie is destroyed by the decline of the theater she and Serlo had established, and that her fate symbolizes the destiny of the theater and with it the end of the predominance of art in Wilhelm's life. Gundolf characterizes her as a born actress [*die geboren schauspielerische Seele*], and suggests that the stage offers natures such as hers a place where they can discharge, at least symbolically, some of their inner tensions (*Goethe,* p. 350). Henkel sees in Aurelie the great aesthetic educator of Wilhelm: "Ihr verschwimmen . . . die Bereiche des Scheins und des Wirklichen. Alles ist ihr Rolle, und sie verwechselt sie leicht" ("Versuch über den *Wilhelm Meister*," p. 64). The deepest analysis of this character is to be found in an essay by Gerhard Storz (op. cit., pp. 126–135). Storz describes her as a sister of Werther, a female Narcissus who, like him, is doomed to the fate of being destroyed by the intensity of her own self-absorption.
33. Robert Hering (*"Wilhelm Meister" und "Faust,"* Frankfurt am Main, 1952, pp. 137ff.) deals extensively with the relationship between Goethe's sixth book and the documents on the life of Susanne von Klettenberg, who is often thought to have been the model for the *schöne Seele.* Frederick J. Beharriell has also examined the relationship between this book and the "sources" in his recent important article "The Hidden Meaning of Goethe's *Bekenntnisse einer schönen Seele*" (*Lebendige Form,* Fests. for Heinrich E. K. Henel, Munich, 1970, pp. 37–62), in which he has expanded and corrected many of Hering's assertions.

34. For various interpretations of the function of the "Confessions of a Beautiful Soul" within the total structure of the novel, see Gundolf, *Goethe*, p. 515, Kurt May, op. cit., p. 25, Erich Trunz, HA VII, p. 637, Gerhard Storz, op. cit., pp. 87–92, Hanno Beriger, *Goethe und der Roman: Studien zu "Wilhelm Meisters Lehrjahre,"* Zurich, 1955, pp. 54–74, Petritis, op. cit., p. 292, Beharriell, *passim* and Stefan Fleischer, *"Bekenntnisse einer schönen Seele:* Figural Representation in *Wilhelm Meisters Lehrjahre,"* MLN LXXXIII (1968), pp. 807–820. Wundt refers to Hegel's characterization of the *schöne Seele* as both high point and end of a purely self-oriented system of morality (op. cit., p. 220).

Lukács underscores the irony in this section of the novel, and adds, "This subjectivist quest which takes refuge in pure inwardness forms there the relatively, but only relatively justified counterpart of the empty and fragmented pragmatism of Werner, Laertes, and even Serlo" (op. cit., pp. 57f.). Beharriell asserts that in portraying the *schöne Seele*, Goethe wished to combine two simultaneous but divergent purposes: first, "to show, through a sympathetic portrait of the heroine, how ascetic piety may present itself as one possible and attractive life-style," and secondly, "to expose, through ironic insights, what he had come to believe were the hidden roots of religiosity in sickness, neurosis and fear" (op. cit., p. 37).

35. AA VII, p. 464.

36. On 5 November 1796 Christian Gottfried Körner wrote to Schiller that none of the Society's preparations were effective in achieving Wilhelm's full development: "alle diese Anstalten waren zu Meister's Bildung nicht hinlänglich. Was sie [die Bildung] vollendete, war ein Kind—ein lieblicher und höchst wahrer Gedanke." The debate on the role and importance of the Society of the Tower in the total structure of the novel began immediately with the publication of the work and has continued ever since.

In a letter of 8 July 1796 Schiller described the Society of the Tower as "ein verborgen wirkender hoher Verstand" ("a higher reason working in secret"; AA XX, p. 202), suggesting thereby a relationship with the gods of Greek tragedy. Schiller was not very happy with this element in the novel, and wished that Goethe had made the meaning of this machinery and its necessary relationship to the inner core of the work more apparent to the reader. Many readers, he feared, would see in it merely a theatrical game and a device to complicate the plot further and create surprises and the like (ibid., p. 203).

Staiger considers the Tower a rationalistic motif embodying the idea of Providence as foreknowledge, overview, "Vorwalten des oberen Leitenden" (op. cit., II, p. 153). Storz expressly calls it a secular analogue to Providence (op. cit., p. 86). Hering speaks of it as embodying natural religion in contrast to the revealed religion of the *schöne Seele*, and as representing a movement in the direction of *Humanitätsreligion* (op. cit., pp. 189f). But critics have also drawn attention to the unreliability or limited validity of the tenets of the Tower, among them Staiger, who expressly states that the authority of the Society of the Tower is not unquestionable (op. cit., II, p. 153). Trunz points out that it is not the Tower, but Natalie who has the last word in the novel (HA VII, p. 621) —which is not strictly true, for if anybody has the last word, then it is literally Wilhelm, but actually Friedrich. Schlechta's interpretation of the Tower as a retreat into a position of opposition to a free life ("man hat sich aus dem freien Felde des Lebens in die starre Verteidigung zurückgezogen"; *Goethes 'Wilhelm Meister'*, p. 46), and Beriger's assertion that its educative function fails when it is not dealing with a character innately in sympathy with its ideals (op. cit., p. 33) may well be overstated, but it is nevertheless true that the Tower does not represent any absolute and final court of appeal. Henkel writes perceptively that the Tower has validity as a rational corrective, but that its limitations are revealed by the figure of Natalie. "Der Turm ist auch die gestaltgewordene Korrektur der Vernunft am Unmittelbaren des Lebens, in Affekt, Stimmung, Gefühl. Dass der Dichter diese Korrektur nicht absolut will gelten lassen, hat er in der deutlichen Kritik Nataliens verlautbart. Sie, die ja auch als Erzieherin wirkt, entwickelt andere Grundsätze. Ihr ist die Liebe das Mittel, den zerbrochenen Lebensring wiederherzustellen und das Klima, in dem allein Erziehung möglich ist" (op. cit., p. 66).

37. AA VII, pp. 570f.

38. "Paesaggi Italiani di Goethe," *Atti dell' Istituto Veneto di Scienze, Lettere ed Arti*, Venice, CXVI (1958), pp. 365–366; reprinted in extended form in Mittner, *La letteratura tedesca del Novecento e altri saggi*, pp. 91–137.

39. The problem of irony in the *Apprenticeship* is dealt with extensively by Reiss *(Goethes Romane*, pp. 90–97; *Goethe's Novels*, pp. 100–103); Schlechta *(Goethes 'Wilhelm Meister,'* pp. 153–169 and pp. 203–220); Hans Joachim Schrimpf *(Das Weltbild des späten Goethe*, Stuttgart, 1956, esp. pp. 115–117) and Gerda Röder *(Glück und glückliches Ende im deutschen Bildungsroman: Eine Studie zu Goethes "Wilhelm Meister,"* Munich, 1968). Schrimpf distinguishes between different sorts of irony used by the later Goethe, and believes that in the *Apprenticeship* a kind of irony predominates which Günther Müller had called "morphological irony." Schrimpf characterizes this sort of irony as the attitude of a developing personality toward former states of its development (op. cit., pp. 115f.). He comments generally that Goethe's use of irony does not signal a Romantic triumph of self over world, but the contrary: "Ironie ist . . . für ihn eine Funktion des Geistes, mit der nicht das Ich über die Welt und seine eigenen Erzeugnisse desillusion-

ierend triumphiert, sondern umgekehrt, und auch hier verrät Goethe seinen Abstand von der Romantik, eine demütige Unterwerfung des subjektiven Geistes unter der Sinnfülle der Gegenstände" (p. 73), which appears to me to be an excellent formulation of a correct observation.

Chapter 7. *The Novel as Poetry*

1. *Kritische Friedrich Schlegel Ausgabe,* II (1967) p. 335.
2. Cf. Clemens Heselhaus, "Die Wilhelm Meister-Kritik der Romantiker und die romantische Romantheorie," in *Nachahmung und Illusion,* ed. H. R. Jauss, Munich, 1964, pp. 113–127.
3. See Gerhard Schulz, "Die Poetik des Romans bei Novalis" (first published in *Jb. d. fr. dt. Hochstifts,* 1964), in *Deutsche Romantheorien,* ed. Reinhold Grimm, Frankfurt am Main and Bonn, 1968, pp. 81–110.
4. Novalis, *Schriften,* III, 2d rev ed. by Richard Samuel and Paul Kluckhohn, Stuttgart, 1960, pp. 638f.
5. Ibid., pp. 280f.
6. Ibid., p. 558.
7. Ibid., pp. 639f., 649, 668.
8. "Über Goethes Meister" (first published in the *Athenäum,* 1798), *Kritische Friedrich Schlegel Ausgabe,* II, pp. 126–146.
9. Ibid., p. 129.
10. *Literary Notebooks* 1797–1801, ed. Hans Eichner, Toronto, 1957, p. 58, no. 434.
11. *Kritische Friedrich Schlegel Ausgabe,* II, p. 156; p. 149: "In diese liberale Form [socratic dialogue] hat sich die Lebensweisheit von der Schulweisheit geflüchtet."
12. *Literary Notebooks,* p. 177, no. 1771.
13. *F. W. J. Schellings Sämtliche Werke,* ed. K. F. A. Schelling, Stuttgart, 1859, Section I, Vol. 5, p. 683: "nicht Welt- sondern Sittengemälde."
14. "Indem ich dem Gemeinen einen hohen Sinn, dem Gewöhnlichen ein geheimnisvolles Ansehen, dem Bekannten die Würde des Unbekannten, dem Endlichen einen unendlichen Schein gebe, so romantisiere ich es.— Umgekehrt ist die Operation für das Höhere, Unbekannte, Mystische, Unendliche—dies wird durch diese Verknüpfung logarithmisiert —Es bekommt einen geläufigen Ausdruck. Romantische Philosophie. Lingua romana, Wechselerhöhung und Erniedrigung" *(Schriften,* II, p. 545).
15. *Kritische Friedrich Schlegel Ausgabe,* II, pp. 318f. See Walter Bausch, *Theorien des epischen Erzählens in der deutschen Frühromantik,* Bonn, 1964, pp. 118–133; and Karl Polheim, *Die Arabeske,* Paderborn, 1966, pp. 128f.
16. On this "center," Bausch says: "Ein Maximum von Subjektivität

wird aus dem einfachen Grunde, dass das Zentrum des Subjekts am Allgemeinmenschlichen teilhat, zugleich ein Maximum von Objektivität, wird eine über den Einzelfall hinausweisende allegorische Wahrheit" (op. cit., p. 61).

17. Goethe seems to have had a fairly favorable opinion of the *Athenäum* Fragments. Schiller wrote to Goethe in July 1798 to ask him what he thought of the Fragments and at the same time expressed his own distaste for them: "Mir macht diese naseweise, entscheidende, schneidende und einseitige Manier physisch wehe" (AA XX, p. 604). Goethe replied that he thought the work of the Schlegel brothers was a good addition to the otherwise mediocre output of German journals, and added "Bei allem, was Ihnen daran mit Recht missfällt, kann man denn doch den Verfassern einen gewissen Ernst, eine gewisse Tiefe und von der andern Seite Liberalität nicht leugnen" (AA XX, p. 605). A few days later he remarked to Schiller that he would like to go through the Fragments with him: "als Veranlassung zum interessanten Gespräch werden sie gewiss sehr dienen, selbst indem sie zum Widerspruch aufregen" (AA XX, p. 609).

Caroline Schlegel wrote to her brother-in-law Friedrich that Goethe was very satisfied with the essay on *Wilhelm Meister*, and had "die belobte Ironie darin gefasst" *(Caroline: Briefe aus der Frühromantik*, I, ed. Georg Waitz and Erich Schmidt, reprint Berne, 1970, p. 393).

18. See AA XII, p. 451; AA XVIII, p. 525; AA XXIII, p. 236; and Werner Brüggemann, *Cervantes und die Figur des Don Quixote in Kunstanschauung und Dichtung der deutschen Romantik*, Münster, 1958, pp. 155–165.

19. *Gespräche* III/1, pp. 98f. "Solange sich der Held Illusionen macht, ist er romantisch, sobald er bloss gefoppt und mystifiziert wird, hört das wahre Interesse auf."

20. AA XIV, p. 508.

21. AA X, p. 526.

22. In an unfinished fantasy, *Reise der Söhne des Megaprazon* (AA IX, pp. 465–480), Megaprazon being the great-grandson of Pantagruel.

23. AA XV, p. 1032.

24. In a letter to Schiller, dated 20 April 1805, Goethe spoke appreciatively of Scarron's jocularity [*den Spässen des Scarron*], in which "one does not sense the gout pains," a reference to Scarron's courage in the face of years of suffering from a painful disease. But this does not tell us anything about his work, and indeed, we have no specific evidence that Goethe ever read the *Roman Comique*. That Goethe read Fénelon's *Télémaque* very early in his life has already been noted above (p. 19; see note 3 to Chapter 2).

25. On 23 September 1825 Goethe noted in his diary that he was reading the "Oeuvres Complètes de Madame de la Fayette et de Tencin."

The edition he was referring to appeared first in Paris in 1804 and had been reprinted both in 1820 and 1825. It contained, of course, *La Princesse de Clèves*.

26. Goethe noted briefly "Romanhaftes des 17ten. Jahrhunderts. Ist abenteuerlich, und soll durchaus bedeutende Motive haben. Abenteuerliches des 30 jährigen Krieges, Simplicissimus . . ." (WA I, 27, pp. 388f.).

27. ". . . er [Simplicissimus] sei in der Anlage tüchtiger und lieblicher als der Gilblas. Nur können sie kein Ende finden, Verleger und Publikum, daher es zuletzt kollektiv werde" *(Gespräche* II, p. 490).

28. See entries in the diaries for 4–10 August 1807.

29. WA I, 36, p. 388.

30. AA XXII, p. 723.

31. AA XXIV, p. 445.

32. Albert Fuchs (op. cit., p. 16) claims that Goethe read de Sade in the period 1788–1805, but gives no specific references or concrete evidence to support this assertion. Hippolyte Loiseau, in his thorough examination of Goethe's French reading, makes no mention of de Sade *(Goethe et la France*, Paris, 1930).

33. AA XX, pp. 482f.

34. "C'est donc un roman que je vous donne, honorable Lecteur; mais soyez sûr de n'y trouver que des faits véritables, consignés dans des lettres véritablement écrites. Je n'ai pas besoin de rien inventer; ma vie fut pleine d'événements capables d'intéresser, parce que je fus toujours exempt de trois vices, qui consument et abrutissent les autres hommes, le vin et la table, le jeu, l'indolence. Tous mes instants ont été remplis par le travail et par la plus noble des passions, la seule véritablement intéressante, l'amour. J'aimai mes parents, la vertu, la vérité, quelquefois trop le plaisir; jamais le vice".

35. *Goethes Briefwechsel mit den Gebrüdern von Humboldt*, ed. F. Th. Bratranek, Leipzig, 1876, pp. 67f.

36. AA XIX, p. 375.

37. WA IV, 16, p. 328.

38. Heinrich Voss reported in 1804 that "Er [Goethe] erkennt die Delphine als ein geistreiches Werk, tadelt vieles daran, was auf Rechnung der Französin fällt, aber lobt doch mehr. Einen Mittag sprach er darüber und sagte, einige Darstellungen . . . hätten ihn beinahe ausser sich gesetzt und wäre das Ganze diesen gleich, so müsste die ganze Welt davor auf den Knien liegen" (AA XXII, p. 335). According to Böttiger, Goethe said that *Delphine* did honor to the age *(Gespräche* I, p. 902).

39. See, for example, AA XX, pp. 282 and 602.

40. AA XI, p. 983.

41. AA XIV, pp. 232–243.

42. AA XIV, p. 232.

43. *Bekenntnisse einer schönen Seele—von ihr selbst geschrieben*, Berlin, 1806, no author given.

44. Ibid., pp. 281f.

45. Ibid., pp. 319f.

46. Ibid., p. 268.

47. AA XIV, p. 239.

48. Karoline Paulus (pseud. Eleutherie Holberg), *Wilhelm Dumont*, Lübeck, 1805, pp. 85ff.

49. Ibid., p. 196.

50. AA XIV, pp. 240f.

51. AA XX, p. 83.

52. AA XX, p. 87.

53. AA I, p. 354.

54. AA XXII, p. 478. In 1809 Goethe read Jean Paul's *Doktor Katzenbergers Badereise*, but it drew no more favorable reaction from him than *Hesperus*. "Alle Welt schimpft hier auf Katzenbergers Badereise, selbst Goethe, der den Verfasser überhaupt nicht liebt" *(Gespräche* II, pp. 447f.). Evidence that Goethe later changed, or at least modified, his opinion of Jean Paul will be presented below in Chapter 9.

55. AA XIX, p. 347.

56. AA XIV, pp. 186f.

57. Ludwig Tieck, *Franz Sternbalds Wanderungen* (first version), ed. Alfred Anger, Stuttgart, 1966, p. 41.

58. Ibid., p. 43.

59. Caroline Schlegel reported a similar comment by Goethe on the first part of the novel: "Sollte es ein Künstlerroman sein, so müsste doch ganz viel anders von der Kunst darin sein, er vermisste da den rechten Gehalt, und das Künstlerische käme als eine falsche Tendenz hinaus" (letter to Friedrich Schlegel of 14 October 1798 in *Caroline: Briefe aus der Frühromantik*, I, op. cit., p. 459).

60. There is evidence that Goethe read Dorothea Schlegel's novel *Florentin*. He commented in a letter to Schiller of 18 March 1801: "Obgleich Florentin als ein Erdgeborener auftritt, so liesse sich doch recht gut seine Stammtafel machen, es können durch diese Filiationen noch wunderliche Geschöpfe entstehen. Ich habe ohngefähr hundert Seiten gelesen und konformiere mich mit Ihrem Urteil. Einige Situationen sind gut angelegt, ich bin neugierig, ob sie die Verfasserin in der Folge zu nutzen weiss" (AA XX, p. 846). Schiller had said (letter of 16 March 1801, AA XX, p. 846): "Sie werden darin auch die Gespenster alter Bekannten spuken sehen. Indessen hat mir dieser Roman, der eine seltsame Fratze ist, doch eine bessere Vorstellung von der Verfasserin gegeben, und er ist ein neuer Beweis, wie weit die Dilettanterei wenigstens in dem Mechanischen und in der hohlen Form kommen kann."

61. AA III, p. 461.

62. AA XIX, p. 566.

63. "Das Romantische ist kein Natürliches, Ursprüngliches, sondern ein Gemachtes, ein Gesuchtes, Gesteigertes, Übertriebenes, Bizarres, bis ins Fratzenhafte und Karikaturartige. Kommt vor wie ein Redoutenwesen, eine Maskerade, grelle Lichterbeleuchtung. Ist humoristisch (das heisst ironisch, vergleiche Ariost, Cervantes; daher ans Komische grenzend und selbst komisch) oder wird es augenblicklich, sobald der Verstand sich daran macht, sonst ist es absurd und phantastisch. Das Antike ist noch bedingt (wahrscheinlich, menschlich), das Moderne willkürlich, unmöglich" (AA XXII, p. 500).

64. See the diary entry for 25 July 1808.

Chapter 8. *Novella into Novel*

1. Goethe remarked in a diary entry for 11 April 1808: "An den kleinen Erzählungen schematisiert, besonders den 'Wahlverwandtschaften' und dem 'Mann von fünfzig Jahren'," and in the *Annals* for 1807: "Die bereits zum öftern genannten kleinen Erzählungen beschäftigten mich in heitern Stunden, und auch die Wahlverwandtschaften sollten in der Art kurz behandelt werden. Allein sie dehnten sich bald aus; der Stoff war allzu bedeutend, und zu tief in mir gewurzelt, als dass ich ihn auf eine so leichte Weise hätte beseitigen können" (AA XI, p. 822). Hans M. Wolff attempted to reconstruct the original novella structure of the novel *(Goethe in der Periode der "Wahlverwandtschaften,"* Berne, 1951, pp. 203–213). Paul Hankamer describes the special structure of the finished work as growing out of the tension between the expansive tendencies characteristic of a novel and the swift and inexorable plot-movement that is characteristic of a novella *(Spiel der Mächte*, 5th ed., Stuttgart, 1960, p. 243).

2. The mere fact that Goethe was working on *The Elective Affinities* and "The Man of Fifty" at the same time (see note 1, above) is no certain proof that the former was originally intended to be part of *Wilhelm Meister's Journeymanship.*

3. A treatise entitled *De attractionibus electivis* by the Swedish chemist Torbern Bergmann had been published in 1775 and was translated into German in 1785 by Heinrich Tabor. Tabor did not use the word *Wahlverwandtschaft*, but it appears in Christian Ehrenfried Weigel's translation of Bergmann's preface to the chemical lectures of G. T. Scheffer, published at Greifswald in 1779 (see Grimm, *Deutsches Wörterbuch*, under *Wahlverwandtschaft).* Goethe wrote to Schiller in October 1799 about the "zarte chemische Verwandtschaft, wodurch sie [the passions] sich anziehen und abstossen, vereinigen, neutralisieren, sich wieder scheiden und herstellen" (AA XX, p. 768). On this matter

see also Oskar Walzel, "Goethes *Wahlverwandtschaften* im Rahmen ihrer Zeit," *Goethe-Jb.* XXVII (1906) and Paul Hankamer, "Zur Genesis von Goethes *Wahlverwandtschaften,*" *Fests. für Berthold Litzmann,* Bonn, 1920, pp. 36–62.

4. AA XXIV, p. 225.

5. On the question whether fate or chance is predominant in *The Elective Affinities,* see H. B. Nisbet, *"Die Wahlverwandtschaften* : Explanation and its Limits," *DVjs.* XLIII (1969), pp. 472 ff. There was already a divergence of opinion on this matter in Goethe's lifetime: Jung-Stilling, for instance, thought that the novel presented a fatalistic view of life, whereas Wilhelm von Humboldt declared that he missed any sense of "Schicksal und innere Notwendigkeit."

Nisbet declares that the characters of the novel are often themselves unable to distinguish between fate and chance, or do not wish to, and "there is never any conclusive evidence that fate, as opposed to chance and natural causes, is responsible" (p. 476). The critics who consider the work as concerned with fate include André François-Poncet *(Les Affinités Electives de Goethe,* Paris, 1910), Walter Benjamin ("Goethes *Wahlverwandtschaften,*" 1924/5, quoted from W. B., *Schriften,* I, Frankfurt am Main, 1955), Kurt May *("Die Wahlverwandtschaften* als tragischer Roman," *Jb. d. fr. dt. Hochstifts* 1936) and Paul Hankamer *(Spiel der Mächte),* but Hankamer also deals with the chain of coincidences in the novel. Besides these, the most important interpretations of the novel are those by Grete Schaeder ("Die Idee der Wahlverwandtschaften," in the periodical *Goethe,* N.S. VI [1941], revised ed. in G. S., *Gott und Welt,* Hamelin, 1947); Paul Stöcklein ("Stil und Geist der *Wahlverwandtschaften,*" *ZfdPh* LXXI [1951]); Hildegard Emmel *(Weltklage);* H. G. Geerdts *(Goethes Roman "Die Wahlverwandtschaften,"* Weimar, 1958); F. J. Stopp ("Ein wahrer Narziss," *PEGS,* N.S. XXIX [1960], and "Ottilie und das innere Licht" in *German Studies presented to Walter H. Bruford,* London, 1962); Peter Ammann *(Schicksal und Liebe in Goethes "Wahlverwandtschaften,"* Berne, 1962); Werner Danckert *(Offenes und geschlossenes Leben,* Bonn, 1963); H. G. Barnes *(Goethe's Die* Wahlverwandtschaften: *A Literary Interpretation,* Oxford, 1967, and various articles, see Bibliography); Paul Böckmann ("Naturgesetz und Symbolik in Goethes *Wahlverwandtschaften,*" *Jb. d. fr. dt. Hochstifts,* 1968); and G.-L. Fink ("Les *Wahlverwandtschaften* de Goethe," *Recherches Germaniques* I [1971]).

Staiger in the relevant chapter (which is excellent) of his Goethe book underscores the romantic aspects of the novel, whereas Stöcklein describes it as an "Agon mit der Romantik" *(Wege zum späten Goethe,* Hamburg, 1949, p. 46). Borcherdt (op. cit., p. 487) sees in it a tension between classical life-style (Charlotte and the Captain) and romanticism (Eduard and Ottilie), which would seem to be too simplistic a view.

Both Benjamin and Danckert emphasize the mythic element in the novel. Benjamin characterizes the novel as "ein mythisches Schattenspiel in Kostümen des Goetheschen Zeitalters" *(Schriften*, I, p. 72), the fable of renunciation but at the same time the attempt to escape the terrors of the daemonic. Danckert interprets the novel as systole and diastole, as a conflict between "open and closed existence" [*der Widerstreit des offenen und geschlossenen Daseins*] (op. cit., p. 75). The older interpretation of the novel as representing the conflict between moral order and passion (Walzel, Korff) is now generally discounted as being too simplistic, and it is preeminently the ambiguity and multi-levelled meaning of the work that is underscored (Reiss, H. G. Barnes, Nisbet; especially Reiss in his article "Mehrdeutigkeit in Goethes *Wahlverwandtschaften*," *Jb. d. dt. Schiller Ges.* XIV [1970], and Barnes in his article "Ambiguity in *Die Wahlverwandtschaften*," in *The Era of Goethe*, Oxford, 1959). The role of the daemonic in the novel is emphasized by May, Ammann, Hankamer, Fink and Grete Schaeder.

6. Hildegard Emmel remarks: "Die beiden Gespräche zwischen Eduard und Charlotte im ersten und zweiten Kapitel des Werkes führen vor Augen, wie zerbrechlich das Glück, nach dem beide strebten, schon erscheint, noch ehe sie recht damit begonnen" *(Weltklage*, p. 275). Fink comments similarly: "il n'y a pas de réelle communauté entre les époux . . . . Ils . . . coulent l'expression de leurs sentiments dans le moule d'un langage respectueusement conventionnel. Pas de spontanéité dans leurs rapports, pas de noms tendres ni de mots d'amour non plus" (op. cit., p. 65).

7. H. G. Barnes remarks similarly: "[Charlotte] is given to uttering generalizing, sententious statements which her niece reserves for her Journal" *(Goethe's* Wahlverwandtschaften, p. 162).

8. On Charlotte's society-oriented ethic, see the fifth chapter of H. G. Barnes's book, particularly pp. 179–181.

9. Stöcklein was the first to draw attention to the curious role of the narrator in the novel (see his "Stil und Geist der *Wahlverwandtschaften*"). The analysis and interpretation of this role is one of the main concerns of H. G. Barnes in his book. He speaks of the "contrast between the attitudes of the narrator and the tendency of the fable," the novel being "a romantic story in the mouth of an un-romantic narrator, [who] casts doubt on the absolute value of life by raising conventional or worldly objections to what might be termed the message of the novel" (op. cit., p. 4). Reiss has a radically different view of the narrator's function. He sees the narrator as observant and perceptive, "concerned not only with describing the individual case but with discovering the general in the specific, and with discerning its symbolic value" *(Goethe's Novels*, pp. 155–159). Reiss maintains that this narrator provides a certain distinguished distancing. In *Goethes Romane* Reiss speaks repeatedly

of the "superiority" [*Überlegenheit*] of the narrator, a view which seems to me quite unfounded.

10. For more on the figure of Mittler, see Reiss, *Goethe's Novels*, pp. 185–187. Reiss summarizes his view of Mittler as follows: "Incapable of deeper insight, he states only truisms, though they may sound impres-- sive" (ibid., p. 186). According to Geerdts, Mittler embodies the petty bourgeois both sociologically and morally (op. cit., p. 57). Fink characterizes him as "ce pasteur sécularisé, très fin XVIIIe siècle, auquel la morale sociale tient lieu de religion" (op. cit., p. 63).

11. AA IX, pp. 25–26.

12. On this conversation, cf. H. G. Barnes: "The function of the discussion is not the elucidation of a system of natural philosophy, and no strict analogy is established between the workings of human sympathy and the chemical process of separation and combination. The discussion serves to heighten the ambiguity of the action and to foreshadow in ironic fashion later phases of the plot. It also deepens the characterization" (*Goethe's* Wahlverwandtschaften, p. 31). Grete Schaeder interprets Charlotte's words as the voice of the poet warning against treating nature too much as if it were human (*Gott und Welt*, p. 289). Hildegard Emmel points out quite rightly that the reader is deluding himself if he thinks that the chemical analogy will account for the events of the novel (*Geschichte des deutschen Romans*, I, p. 323). One might also ask whether the narrator is not deluding the reader into such a delusion.

13. See Benjamin, op. cit., I, p. 71, and Esther Schelling-Schär, *Die Gestalt der Ottilie*, Zurich, 1969, p. 46, and Danckert, op. cit., p. 57. Schelling-Schär points to the "Mühlenerotik der Volkslieder," Danckert wonders whether Goethe knew that the mill was a place of initiation, where in ancient times "sich die erste entschiedene Ablösung der Jugendlichen vom Elternbilde vollzog, womöglich verbunden mit Einweihung in die Geheimnisse von Liebe und Tod (Kornmysterien)." Benjamin considers the scene a symbolic descent to the underworld and a prefiguration of the death of the two lovers.

14. On this conversation, see the excellent analysis by Hildegard Emmel in *Weltklage* (pp. 300–310).

15. AA IX, p. 130.

16. Goethe wrote to Reinhard on 21 February 1810 that Eduard was "inestimable" [*unschätzbar*], because his love was unbounded [*weil er unbedingt liebt*]; AA XIX, p. 597.

17. AA IX, pp. 134f.

18. AA IX, p. 135.

19. H. G. Barnes, *Goethe's* Wahlverwandtschaften, pp. 135ff.

20. AA IX, p. 145.

21. See Stopp, "Ottilie and das innere Licht," pp. 117–122.

22. AA IX, p. 174.

23. "Es schien ihr [Ottilie] in der Welt nichts mehr unzusammenhängend, wenn sie an den geliebten Mann dachte, und sie begriff nicht, wie ohne ihn noch irgend etwas zusammenhängen könne" (AA IX, p. 194).

24. AA IX, p. 205.

25. AA IX, p. 207.

26. AA IX, p. 245.

27. AA IX, p. 260.

28. AA IX, p. 268. Staiger's claim that Ottilie intends to die on Eduard's birthday (op. cit., II, p. 507) seems to me unfounded. H. G. Barnes observes, to my mind correctly, that "the belief that Ottilie seeks her death is the *communis opinio*, but in the text itself there is no reason for this supposition" (*Goethe's* Wahlverwandtschaften, p. 23).

29. "gefühls-höflich und unverbindlich schnörkelhaft," and "konzilianten Schnörkel" *(Gesammelte Werke*, IX, Oldenburg, 1960, pp. 339 and 743).

30. In a letter to Louise Colet (Flaubert, *Oeuvres Complètes*, Paris, Conard, Vol. XVII, p. 398).

31. *Goethe's Novels*, p. 200.

32. Thus R. J. Hollingdale (London, 1971), and Elizabeth Mayer and Louise Bogan (Chicago, 1936).

33. "Vor dem fünfzigsten Jahre kann man est kaum völlig würdigen, aber es gehört ebensowohl zum Fluch als zum Segen des Gereiftseins, dass man es kann" *(Sämtliche Werke*, III, ed. Peter Frank and Karl Pörnbacher, Munich, 1964, p. 775). Goethe was of course past his fiftieth year when he composed the novel, and it is significant that he was working on "The Man of Fifty" at the same time. Eduard himself once comments that "Wer in einem gewissen Alter frühere Jugendwünsche und Hoffnungen realisieren will, betrügt sich immer: denn jedes Jahrzehnt des Menschen hat sein eigenes Glück, seine eigenen Hoffnungen und Aussichten. Wehe dem Menschen, der vorwärts und rückwärts zu greifen, durch Umstände und durch Wahn veranlasst wird" (AA IX, p. 230). He nevertheless persists in the error that he here so clearly signalizes.

34. Op. cit., II, pp. 509f.

35. Ludwig Kahn, "Erlebte Rede in Goethes *Wahlverwandtschaften*," *PMLA* LXXXIX (1974), pp. 268–277.

Chapter 9. *Subjective Epic and Tragic Novel*

1. AA IX, pp. 511, 632.

2. AA XII, p. 694.

3. AA X, pp. 297–299; AA XII, pp. 693–716.

4. AA VIII, p. 511.

5. AA X, p. 634.

6. AA XII, p. 709.

7. AA XII, p. 711.

8. AA X, p. 390.

9. AA XXI, p. 884.

10. AA VIII, p. 513.

11. Goethe remarked to Eckermann in October 1825: "Die Frau von Genlis hat daher vollkommen Recht, wenn sie sich gegen die Freiheiten und Frechheiten von Voltaire auflegte. Denn im Grunde, so geistreich alles sein mag, ist der Welt doch nichts damit gedient; es lässt sich nichts darauf gründen. Ja es kann sogar von der grössten Schädlichkeit sein, indem es die Menschen verwirrt und ihnen den nötigen Halt nimmt" (AA XXIV, pp. 163f.).

12. AA III, pp. 476–477.

13. As I stated earlier, it is difficult to assess Goethe's opinion of the novels of Fielding, for he said very little about him. We have the bald mention of *Tom Jones* in the passage on novel and drama in the *Apprenticeship*, and the general statement to Eckermann in 1824: "Our novels, our tragedies, where do we get them from but Goldsmith, Fielding, and Shakespeare," which does not tell us much. See also my article, "Goethe's Silences," in *Geist und Zeichen:* Fests. for Arthur Henkel, Heidelberg, 1976.

14. Blanckenburg, op. cit., pp. 196, 236, 240n.

15. L. M. Price, *Die Aufnahme englischer Literatur in Deutschland*, Berne, 1961, p. 199.

16. AA XI, p. 693.

17. AA XXIV, p. 254.

18. But compare the diary entry for 22 August 1825.

19. Bertrand H. Bronson, ed., *Rasselas, Poems, and Selected Prose by Samuel Johnson*, Rinehart Editions, San Francisco, 1971, p. xx.

20. AA X, pp. 468f. On Goethe's relationship to Goldsmith see S. Levy, "Goethe und Oliver Goldsmith," *Goethe-Jb.* VI (1885), pp. 281f.; L. M. Price, *The Reception of English Literature in Germany*, Berkeley, 1932; and C. Hammer, "Goethe's Estimate of Oliver Goldsmith," *Journal of English and Germanic Philology* XLIV (1945), pp. 131–138.

21. AA X, p. 512.

22. AA XXI, p. 884.

23. AA XIV, pp. 380f.

24. AA XIV, pp. 917f.

25. AA XII, p. 381.

26. AA VIII, pp. 517–518.

27. AA XVIII, p. 175 (letter of 1775); AA II, p. 74 (poem of 1780); AA VIII, p. 517 (definition of shandyism).

28. "[Ich las] . . . Zuletzt in Tristram Shandy und bewunderte aber-

und abermal die Freiheit, zu der sich Sterne zu seiner Zeit emporgehoben hatte, begriff auch seine Einwirkung auf unsre Jugend. Er war der erste, der sich und uns aus Pedanterei und Philisterei emporhob" (Diary for 1 October 1830).

29. AA XXI, p. 935.

30. AA VIII, pp. 517–518. For more on Goethe's relationship to Sterne, see W. R. R. Pinger, *Laurence Sterne and Goethe*, Berkeley, 1920; Gisbert Klingemann, *Goethes Verhältnis zu Laurence Sterne*, Marburg, 1929; and Victor Lange, "Goethe's Craft of Fiction," pp. 38f.

31. AA X, p. 555.

32. Letter of 6 December 1765 (AA XVIII, pp. 21f.).

33. AA X, p. 253.

34. AA X, p. 620.

35. AA XI, p. 937. James Boyd *(Goethe's Knowledge of English Literature)* and G. H. Needler *(Goethe and Scott*, Toronto, 1950) discuss Goethe's relationship to Scott, but neither gives much consideration to Scott's significance in relation to Goethe's own approach to the novel.

36. AA XXIV, p. 281.

37. AA XXIII, p. 311.

38. AA XXIV, p. 471.

39. AA XXIII, pp. 192–194.

40. AA XIV, pp. 924–925.

41. AA XIV, p. 855.

42. *Don Alonso*, 3rd ed., in five volumes, Paris, 1824.

43. Ibid., II, p. 176.

44. Ibid., V, p. 230.

45. AA XIV, pp. 860f.

46. Goethe quotes this passage as though it were to be found in the novel itself. But this is not the case.

47. *Don Alonso*, IV, p. 209.

48. "Bei Betrachtung der französischen, besonders poetischen Literatur des neunzehnten Jahrhunderts muss man zurückgehen bis auf Bernardin de Saint-Pierre, Paul et Virginie 1789" (AA XIV, p. 898). Goethe makes a mistake here: Bernardin de Saint-Pierre's novel appeared in 1787.

49. AA XXIII, p. 637. See Bertram Barnes, *Goethe's Knowledge of French Literature*, p. 103.

50. AA XIV, p. 899.

51. AA XIV, p. 898.

52. See my article "Goethe's Silences."

53. On the afternoon of the same day, Goethe notes in his diary, "Zweyter Theil der Prairies" [*sic*], and on the next day remarks, "Den 2. Theil der Prairies geendigt." No one has ever made a thorough study of Goethe's relationship to Cooper.

54. Goethe read the first version of Manzoni's *I Promessi Sposi*, which

appeared in three volumes from 1825 to 1827 (the final version of the novel did not appear until 1840). The original version is easily accessible in the second volume of the edition of Manzoni's works published by Mondadore in 1954. On Goethe's relationship to Manzoni, see in particular Jean F. Beaumont, "Manzoni and Goethe," *Italian Studies*, II, Manchester, 1939, pp. 129–140; and Emmy Rosenfeld, "Goethe und Manzoni," *Literaturwissenschaftliches Jahrbuch*, N.S. I (1960), pp. 91–116.

55. AA XXIV, p. 263.

56. AA XXIV, p. 264.

57. AA XXIV, p. 266.

58. WA IV, 43, pp. 135f. (letter to Streckfuss); AA XXI, p. 772 (letter to Boisserée).

59. Goethe was disturbed by the way in which Manzoni chose to transmute history into literature. The nature of the problem was suggested by Manzoni's division of the characters of his drama *Il conte di Carmagnola* into "historical" [*istorici*] and "ideal" [*ideali*] personages. Goethe observed that no character used in literature is ever really "historical": "Für den Dichter ist keine Person historisch, es beliebt ihm seine sittliche Welt darzustellen, und er erweist zu diesem Zweck gewissen Personen aus der Geschichte die Ehre, ihren Namen seinen Geschöpfen zu leihen" (AA XIV, p. 822). Manzoni replied with the assertion that he was led to this division of characters by a scrupulous respect for historical fact. Goethe then explained in his comments on Manzoni's *Adelchi* (AA XIV, pp. 837–844) that Manzoni was striving to harmonize the morally and aesthetically apposite with things as they actually were ("das sittlich-ästhetisch Geforderte mit dem wirklich-unausweichlich Gegebenen völlig in Einklang zu bringen"), and that this was the source of his uniqueness. But, Goethe added, a poet has the right to mold history to his purposes, "die Mythologie nach Belieben umzubilden, die Geschichte in Mythologie zu verwandeln" (AA XIV, p. 838).

60. Hugo von Hofmannsthal, "Manzonis *Promessi Sposi*," *Gesammelte Werke: Prosa*, IV, ed. Herbert Steiner, Frankfurt, 1955, pp. 417f. This essay was first published in 1927.

61. WA IV, 48, p. 248.

62. AA XXI, p. 987.

63. AA XXI, p. 991.

64. Albert Fuchs asserts that when Goethe characterizes Chateaubriand as "rhetorical," he does not use this word to imply hollowness but rather breadth and energy [*Schwung*] (*Goethe-Handbuch*, I, 2d. ed., Stuttgart, 1961, p. 1622).

65. AA XXIII, p. 757.

66. Goethe remarked in his diary on 25 March 1830, "Ich las in dem

Roman *Cinq-Mars*"; and on 31 July 1831 "Ich machte einen Versuch, Cinq-Mars von Alfred de Vigny zu lesen."

67. AA XXIV, p. 728.
68. AA XXIII, p. 757.
69. AA XXIV, p. 755.
70. WA IV, 29, p. 80; WA IV, 37, p. 151.
71. AA XXIII, p. 637.
72. WA IV, 29, p. 80.
73. AA XXIV, p. 755 (Eckermann); *Gespräche* III/2, p. 747 (Soret). For more on Goethe and Stendhal, see Henry H. H. Remak, "Goethe on Stendhal: Development and Significance of his Attitude," *Goethe Bicentennial Studies*, ed. H. J. Meessen, Bloomington, Ind., 1950, pp. 207–234.
74. AA XXIII, p. 846.
75. AA XIV, pp. 319–322.
76. AA I, pp. 474–475.
77. AA XIV, pp. 709–712.

Chapter 10. *Archive into Novel*

1. AA XX, p. 217.
2. "Briefe eines Reisenden und seines Zöglings unter romantischen Namen, sich an Wilhelm Meister anschliessend" (AA XIX, p. 340).
3. See Hans Gerhard Graef, ed., *Goethe über seine Dichtungen*, Frankfurt, 1901–1914, Part I, Vol. II, p. 899. The five novellas published separately were: "Die pilgernde Törin," 1808; "Sankt Joseph der Zweite," 1809; "Das nussbraune Mädchen," 1815; "Die neue Melusine," 1816; "Der Mann von fünfzig Jahren," 1817. All five were published in Cotta's *Taschenbuch für Damen*, as was the beginning of the novel.
4. For references, see Graef, op. cit., Part I, Vol. II, pp. 903 and 910–913.
5. AA XXII, pp. 721f.; *Gespräche* II, p. 890. The point about rhapsodic structure had been made with reference to the epic in the essay *Über epische und dramatische Dichtung* (AA XIV, p. 369).
6. *Wilhelm Meisters Wanderjahre oder Die Entsagenden, Teil 1*, Stuttgart and Tübingen, Cotta, 1821. The text of this first version is not now readily available though it was reprinted by Max Hecker in 1921 and in the thirty-fourth volume of the Propyläen-Ausgabe in 1926. Some recent editions (for instance the new Cotta edition) give the differences between the two versions as "variants" of the text, without recognizing that this first version is a totally different novel from the final one. To evaluate the first version on its own terms one must either use one of the two reprints listed above (which are both now out of print) or, as

I have done, go back to the original edition of 1821. I have used the copy
in the Cornell University Library.

   7. The passage, to be found on pp. 254–257 of the original edition,
runs as follows:

> Dass eine gewisse Lücke, vielleicht in kurzem fühlbar, im Ganzen
> hie und da bemerklich und doch nicht zu vermeiden seyn werde,
> sprechen wir lieber selbst aus, ohne Furcht, den Genuss unserer
> Leser dadurch zu kränken. Bey der gegenwärtigen, zwar mit Vor-
> bedacht und Muth unternommenen Redaction stossen wir doch
> auf alle die Unbequemlichkeiten, welche die Herausgabe dieser
> Bändchen seit zwanzig Jahren verspäteten. Diese Zeit hat daran
> nichts verbessert. Wir sehen uns noch immer auf mehr als eine
> Weise gehindert und, an dieser oder jener Stelle, mit irgend einer
> Stockung bedroht. Denn wir haben die bedenkliche Aufgabe zu
> lösen, aus den mannigfaltigsten Papieren das Wertheste und Wich-
> tigste auszusuchen, wie es denkenden und gebildeten Gemüthern
> erfreulich seyn und sie, auf mancher Stufe des Lebens, erquicken
> und fördern könnte. Da liegen nun aber vor uns Tagebücher,
> mehr oder weniger ausführlich, bald ohne Anstand mittheilbar,
> bald wegen unbedeutenden, auch allzubedeutenden Inhalts un-
> räthlich einzuschalten.
>
> Sogar fehlt es nicht an Heften der wirklichen Welt gewidmet,
> statistischen, technischen, und sonst realen Inhalts. Diese als unge-
> hörig abzusondern fällt schwer, da Leben und Neigung, Erkennt-
> niss und Leidenschaft, sich wunderbar vereinigend, im engsten
> Bunde mit einander fortschreiten.
>
> Alsdann begegnen uns Entwürfe, mit guter Einsicht und zu
> herrlichen Zwecken geschrieben, aber nicht so folgerecht und
> durchgreifend, dass man sie völlig billigen oder aber in der neuen,
> so weit vorgeschrittenen Zeit für lesbar und wirksam halten
> könnte.
>
> Eben so begegnen wir kleinen Anecdoten ohne Zusammenhang,
> schwer unter Rubriken zu bringen, manche, genau besehen, nicht
> ganz unverfänglich. Hie und da treffen wir auf ausgebildetere
> Erzählungen, deren manche schon bekannt, dennoch hier noth-
> wendig einen Platz verlangen und zugleich Auflösung und Ab-
> schluss fordern. Auch an Gedichten ist kein Mangel und doch lässt
> sich nicht leicht, nicht immer entscheiden, wo sie eingeschaltet
> werden dürften, um der wahren Stimmung nachzuhelfen, welche
> gar leicht gestört und umgewendet wird. Wenn wir also nicht,
> wie schon oft seit vielen Jahren, in diesem Geschäft abermals
> stocken sollen, so bleibt uns nichts übrig, als zu überliefern was
> wir besitzen, mitzutheilen was sich erhalten hat. Und so geben
> wir daher einige Kapitel, deren Ausführung wohl wünschenswerth

gewesen, nur in vorüber eilender Gestalt, damit der Leser nicht
nur fühle, dass hier etwas ermangelt, sondern dass er von dem
Mangelnden näher unterrichtet sey und sich dasjenige selbst
ausbilde, was, theils der Natur des Gegenstandes nach, theils den
eintretenden Umständen gemäss, nicht vollkommen ausgebildet
oder mit allen Belegen gekräftiget ihm entgegen treten kann.

Eberhard Sarter says of this address to the reader that in it everything
which hindered the completion of the *Journeymanship* is related under
the guise of fiction *(Zur Technik von "Wilhelm Meisters Wanderjahren,"* Berlin, 1914, p. 13). Sarter has recognized the central importance
of this address to the reader, but has misunderstood it, for Goethe has
not hidden his substance "under the guise of fiction," but has transformed it into fiction, into the fiction of the archive novel.

    8. For analyses, different from mine, of the first version of the *Jour-
neymanship*, see Eugen Wolff, "Die ursprüngliche Gestalt von *Wilhelm
Meisters Wanderjahren,"* *Goethe-Jb.* XXXIV (1913), pp. 162–172; Gerhard Küntzel, "*Wilhelm Meisters Wanderjahre* in der ersten Fassung
1821," *Goethe*, N.S. III (1938), pp. 3–39; Hans Reiss, "*Wilhelm Meisters
Wanderjahre.* Der Weg von der ersten zur zweiten Fassung," *DVjs.*
XXXIV (1965), pp. 34–57.

    9. First version, p. 150; cf. AA VIII, p. 160.

    10. For a list of secondary literature on the "Pedagogic Province,"
see Bernd Peschken, *Entsagung in "Wilhelm Meisters Wanderjahren,"*
Bonn, 1968, pp. 92f. The older critics frequently concerned themselves
with whether the educational system of the Province was feasible and
could be instituted, or whether it was Utopian and impracticable. Christian Hartmut Schädel thinks this question is unimportant, for in Goethe's
Pedagogic Province the objects of learning are secondary, and the real
concern is inner development, not "education" in the usual sense *(Metamorphose und Erscheinungsformen des Menschseins in "Wilhelm Meisters Wanderjahren,"* Marburg, 1969). The Province is "pedagogic" only
in the sense that it brings about a heightening of human nature through
cultivation of the natural talents of its students and creation of an atmosphere of reverence (ibid., p. 66). Thus it is to be interpreted symbolically
rather than pedagogically. August Raabe believes that the educational
system of the Province is directed in all its aspects toward fighting the
opposing tendencies of the demonic ("Das Dämonische in den *Wanderjahren,"* *Goethe* N.S. I [1936], p. 124), whereas Schrimpf (op. cit., p.
277) interprets it as a representation of the idea of authority enabling
Felix to avoid the painful process of trial and error that his father had
had to undergo. Anneliese Klingenberg *(Goethes Roman "Wilhelm
Meisters Wanderjahre oder die Entsagenden": Quellen und Composition,* Berlin and Weimar, 1972, pp. 49–70) examines in great detail the

relation of this section of the novel to contemporary ideas on educational reform and contemporary "new" educational institutions, with special reference to Fellenberg's institute in Switzerland and to the ideas on educational reform bruited by a group of Prussian state officials close to Freiherr von Stein, with whom Goethe had various contacts. She also mentions Goethe's opposition to the ideas and operations of Pestalozzi, an opposition based on the belief that Pestalozzi gave his pupils formal instruction without the necessary accompaniment of "religious, moral and philosophic maxims" (conversation reported by Sulpiz Boisserée, 5 August 1815; AA XXII, p. 808). Jane K. Brown *(Goethe's Cyclical Narratives*, Chapel Hill, N. C., 1975, pp. 87–97) believes that this section of the novel was intended as a parody of Basedow, and (like Eichendorff decades earlier) she finds it difficult to take it entirely seriously. It seems to me that Goethe here concentrates on what he told Boisserée was lacking in Pestalozzi, namely basic ideas, and that these are a matter of the utmost seriousness and are presented as such.

11. "Ausserdem hat das Geheimnis sehr grosse Vortheile: denn wenn man dem Menschen gleich und immer sagt worauf alles ankommt, so denkt er, es sey nichts dahinter" (First version, p. 159; AA VIII, p. 165).

12. Since the passage referred to is little known, and is one of the most interesting sections of the first version of the *Journeymanship*, I will quote it in full. It appears on pp. 333–336 of the original edition. Wilhelm is speaking.

> "Wenn wir uns bisher in dem metallreichen Gebirge aufgehalten, welches oben sanft und keineswegs wild anzusehen ist, geleitete man mich nun durch schroffe, kaum zu ersteigende Schluchten und Felsen; zuletzt gelangt' ich ganz oben auf eine Klippe, deren Gipfel nur einem einzigen Stehenden Raum gab, welcher, in die greuliche Tiefe hinabschauend, gewaltsame Bergströme durch schwarze Klüfte schäumen sah. Diessmal blickt' ich ohne Schwindel und Schauder hinab, es war mir leicht zu Muthe; nun aber richtete sich meine Aufmerksamkeit auf gegenüberstehende gleich gähstotzige Felsen, deren Gipfel jedoch grössere Flächen und Räume darboten. Obschon durch eine ungeheuere Kluft getrennt drängten sich doch die gewaltigen Massen so nah heran, dass ich mit blossen Augen ganz deutlich mehrere Personen oben versammelt erblicken konnte. Es waren meist Frauenzimmer, deren eine bis an den Rand hervortretend mich doppelt und dreyfach für sie besorgt machte, als die völlige Ueberzeugung in mir aufging, es sey Natalie selbst. Die Gefahr eines solch unerwarteten Wiedersehens wuchs mit jedem Augenblick; gränzenlos aber, als mir ein Fernrohr vors Auge kam, das mir sie völlig heran, mich zu ihr völlig hinüber brachte. Sehrohre haben durchaus etwas Magisches. Wären wir nicht von Jugend auf gewohnt hindurch zu schauen,

wir würden jedesmal wenn wir sie vors Auge nehmen schaudern und erschrecken. Wir sind es die erblicken und sind es nicht, ein Wesen ists, dessen Organe auf höhere Stufe gehoben, dessen Beschränktheit aufgelöst, das ins Unendliche zu reichen berechtigt ward.

Belauschen wir z.B. Weitentfernte durch ein solches Mittel, sehen wir sie harmlos-unschuldig vor sich hin, als einsam unbeobachtet handeln, so kann es uns wirklich bange werden, sie möchten uns entdecken und wegen verrätherischer Zudringlichkeit beleidigt zürnen.

Und so bedrängte mich gleichfalls ein seltsam Gefühl zwischen Näh und Ferne zu schwanken und von Augenblick zu Augenblick beydes zu verwechseln.

Auch jene waren uns gewahr worden, woran das Zeichen mit einem weissen Schnupftuch nicht zweifeln liess. Einen Augenblick säumt' ich es zu erwiedern, denn ich fand mich ganz in der Nähe des angebeteten Wesens. Diess ist ihre reine, holde Gestalt, ihre schlanken Arme, die mir einst so hülfreich erschienen und mich, nach unseligen Leiden und Verworrenheiten, endlich doch, wenn auch nur für Augenblicke, theilnehmend umfassten.

Ich bemerkte ganz deutlich, dass auch sie ein Sehrohr hielt und zu mir herüberschaute; da verfehlt' ich denn nicht, durch Zeichen, wie sie mir bereit waren, den Ausdruck einer treuen und herzlichen Anhänglichkeit auszusprechen.

Und wie die Erfahrung giebt, dass ferne Gegenstände, die wir durch ein Sehrohr deutlich erkannt, sich auch nachher dem blossen Auge als in deutlicher Nähe bestimmt offenbaren, es sey nun dass genauere Kenntniss den Sinn geschärft, oder dass Einbildungskraft was ihm abgeht ersetze; genug, die Theure sah ich so genau und deutlich als zu erreichen, ob ich gleich ihre Gesellschaft noch nicht zu erkennen vermochte. Indem ich mich nun auch hierum bemühte, und mich nach ihr um destomehr bestrebte, da drohte der Abgrund mich zu verschlingen, hätte nicht eine hülfreiche Hand mich ergriffen und zugleich der Gefahr, wie dem schönsten Glück entrissen."

13. First version, pp. 415–417 (not in the second version). Friedrich is speaking:

"Die Grille des Auswanderns, hiess es, kann in einem beengten kümmerlichen Zustand den Menschen gar wohl ergreifen, sie wird, wenn einzelne Fälle durch glücklichen Erfolg begünstigt werden, im Ganzen sich als Leidenschaft hervorthun, wie wir gesehn haben, noch sehen und dabey nicht läugnen, dass wir selbst von einem solchen Wahne bethört gewesen.

Das Auswandern geschieht in betrüglicher Hoffnung eines bes-

sern Zustandes, doch sie wird beym erfolgenden Einwandern gar
oft enttäuscht, weil man sich, wohin man auch gelange, immer
wieder in einer bedingten Welt befindet und, wenn man auch
nicht zu einer abermaligen Auswanderung genöthigt wird, den-
noch den Wunsch darnach im Stillen zu gehen geneigt ist.

   Wir haben uns daher verbündet auf alles Auswandern Verzicht
zu thun und uns dem Wandern zu ergeben. Hier kehrt man nicht
dem Vaterlande auf immer den Rücken, sondern man hofft, auch
auf dem grössten Umweg, wieder dahin zu gelangen; reicher,
verständiger, geschickter, besser, und was aus einem solchen
Lebenswandel Vortheilhaftes hervorgehen mag. Nun aber ist in
Gesellschaft alles leichter und glücklicher zu vollbringen als einem
Einzelnen gelänge, und in diesem Sinne betrachte, mein Freund,
was du hier bemerkst: denn was Du auch siehst, alles und jedes
befördert ein grosses, mobiles Verhältniss tüchtiger und thätiger
Menschen aller Klassen."

14. "Wo wir uns der Sonne freuen,
     Sind wir jede Sorge los.
     Dass wir uns in ihr zerstreuen
     Darum ist die Welt so gross."
15. "Jedes Blatt in Lenardos Archiv ist im Sinne des Ganzen" (first
version, p. 461).
16. Letter of 7 September 1821 (AA XXI, p. 461).
17. AA XXIV, p. 277.

Chapter 11. *Counterpoint in the Symbolic Mode*

1. AA VII, p. 535.
2. Cf. Trunz, HA VIII, pp. 607ff. He summarizes thus: "Bevor in den
späteren Kapiteln Bilder der Leidenschaft, Masslosigkeit und Verwirrung
folgen, steht hier das Gesunde." A totally different view is presented by
Anneliese Klingenberg (op. cit., pp. 31–38), who interprets the Joseph
sequence as a negative example of the confusion of *Kunstwahrheit* and
Vernunftwahrheit, and sees in it an ironic presentation of dilettantism
and of the dangers of an uncontrolled drive to imitate. One must, I think,
recognize that there are elements of falseness (and even of absurdity)
in the story; but one must also distinguish between what the Joseph
family now presents to Wilhelm (which is what Trunz is describing)
and Joseph's errors in the past (as described by Klingenberg).
3. For a summary of the more important interpretations of the final
version of the *Journeymanship,* see the book by Peschken, op. cit., pp.
2–9. Peschken himself emphasizes the polarity of separation and union
in the novel. He takes issue, both in his book and in his earlier essay,
"Das 'Blatt' in den *Wanderjahren*" *(Goethe* N.S. XXVII [1965], pp.

205–230), with Henkel's interpretation of the work as a novel of *Entsa-gung*, asserting that there is also the complementary ideal of *Erhebung*. Henkel would surely be the last to disagree with this, for *Entsagung*, if properly understood, surely implies *Erhebung*. The weakness of Pesch-ken's interpretation is that he does not take the novellas and the aphor-isms sufficiently into consideration. Since Peschken, the most important studies of the novel have been those of Manfred Karnick (*"Wilhelm Meisters Wanderjahre" oder die Kunst des Mittelbaren*, Munich, 1968), Christian Hartmut Schädel, Heidi Gidion (*Zur Darstellungsweise von Goethes "Wilhelm Meisters Wanderjahren*," Göttingen, 1969), Anneliese Klingenberg, and Jane K. Brown.

Karnick interprets the novel as a statement about the possibilities and limits of "communication" [*Mitteilung*] in the broadest sense of the word, comprising not merely verbal communication but all contact with beings and things outside of oneself. The really important and essential things are inaccessible by direct communication, the novel tells us. Schädel tries to interpret the novel in terms of Goethe's scientific thought, and, building on Günther Müller's earlier studies, presents a morphological interpretation of the work. *Entsagung*, he says, is meta-morphosis under another name. The four main characters are (for Schädel) Makarie, Montan, Lenardo and Wilhelm, and these, he thinks, represent "metamorphosische Erscheinungsstufen der ideellen Einheit des urbildlichen Menschen" and each embodies one of the four rever-ences of the Pedagogic Province (op. cit., p. 109). The weakness of this schematic interpretation is that it relegates Felix and Hersilie to second place. Heidi Gidion takes up Reiss's objection to those critics who as-sume too readily (following Goethe's own words, or misinterpreting them) that the novel has thematic and structural continuity. She asserts that it has a consciously *discontinuous* structure, partly integrating but also partly dissociating (op. cit., pp. 140ff.). Anneliese Klingenberg presents an intelligent and very interesting interpretation from a Marxist approach. In her view the work presents a combination of "Weltanschauung des 18. Jahrhunderts, Weltanschauung der vorrevolutionären Zeit, in der das Bürgertum noch im Namen der Menschheit und um ein glückliches Leben für alle zu kämpfen wähnte" with "Wirklichkeit des 19. Jahrhun-derts." Jane K. Brown asserts that the hope of a harmonious society which was raised in the *Apprenticeship* has now "completely evapo-rated," society being now viewed as having a tragic basis, and the future as consisting of a "continuous tumult of struggle and strife" which, however, is affirmed as being uniquely human (op. cit., pp. 132–134). This critic examines the structure of the novel with reference to its use of irony (meaning thereby conscious discrepancies between disparate points of view) and parody (in the sense of parallelism in contrast). Klingenberg rejects Gidion's assertion that the novel has a consciously discontinuous structure, and declares that the structure is dialectically progressive, embodying Goethe's concepts of *Polarität* and *Steigerung*. The goal of this dialectical upward movement is, according to Klingenberg, "die vernünftig geordnete menschliche Gesellschaft" (op. cit., p. 152). I would quarrel with the adverb *vernünftig;* for the novel, like all Goethe's novels, attempts to include in its evolving concept of order that which is not *vernünftig geordnet.*

4. AA VIII, p. 158.
5. AA VIII, pp. 46f.
6. AA VIII, p. 78.
7. AA VIII, p. 140.
8. AA VIII, pp. 155f.
9. AA VIII, p. 131.
10. AA VIII, p. 38.
11. For discussions of symbolic landscapes in the *Journeymanship*, see André Gilg, *"Wilhelm Meisters Wanderjahre" und ihre Symbole*, Zurich, 1954; and Joachim Müller, op cit., p. 70.
12. AA VIII, p. 38.
13. AA VIII, p. 40.
14. AA VIII, p. 485. For more on this figure see Trunz, HA VIII, pp. 713f.; and Peschken, *Entsagung*, p. 141.
15. AA VIII, p. 134.
16. AA VIII, p. 481. This is very similar to Leibniz's conception of the monads, which are part of the universe and also mirror the whole.
17. Trunz offers a diagrammatic statement of the various stages in the presentation of Makarie in the novel (HA VIII, pp. 710f.). Robert Hering believes that Makarie represents a completion of the idea of the Pedagogic Province in that she is the embodiment of man in his relation to the supernatural (op. cit., pp. 308f.): she symbolizes the union of revelation and nature (ibid., p. 432). Hering thus interprets the figure of Makarie in primarily religious terms. Karnick does likewise, asserting a difference between the "holy" nature of Makarie and the limitations of ordinary people (op. cit., pp. 114f.). Schädel, on the other hand, believes that Makarie does not represent an exceptional or more-than-human mode of existence, but rather a metamorphic possibility completely in accordance with natural laws, which grows out of devotion to and reverence for that which is above us (op. cit., p. 46). Anneliese Klingenberg interprets Makarie as the embodiment of Goethe's belief in the unity of inner intuition and external organization, the interdependence of mind and nature (op. cit., pp. 95–100). Jane Brown rejects all this and views her ironically (op. cit., pp. 69–75). In this she has support from Ehrhard Bahr *(Die Ironie im Spätwerk Goethes*, Berlin, 1972). Both of these critics are mistaken, I believe, in taking the narrator's begging pardon for the "ätherische Dichtung" of the second Makarie chapter as undercutting its serious intent.

18. AA VIII, p. 43.
19. AA VIII, p. 162.
20. AA VIII, p. 357.
21. AA VIII, p. 246.
22. AA VIII, p. 250.
23. AA VIII, p. 248.
24. AA VII, p. 636.
25. AA VIII, p. 262.
26. Though almost everyone has recognized the crucial importance of this chapter, interpretations of it have differed. Schrimpf considers the experience of art as central to it (op. cit., p. 199), but he also asserts that the scene reveals the danger involved in a "purely inner experience of art." Küntzel interprets the scene as a regression to immaturity, as a critique of sentimentality and of excessive emphasis on the heart (op. cit., pp. 24f.). Wilhelm Emrich characterizes the whole episode as "sehnsüchtige Mignon*beschwörung*" (my italics), meaningfully placed before the return from enthusiasm to craftsmanship in the Pedagogic Province. The associating of Hilarie and the Widow with Mignon, says Emrich, relates the emotional tangles of the novel to the demonic aspect of Mignon ("Das Problem der Symbolinterpretation in Hinblick auf Goethes *Wanderjahre*," *DVjs*. XXVI [1952], reprinted in W. E., *Protest und Verheissung*, Frankfurt am Main, 1960, pp. 344f.). Staiger asserts that the sojourn on the island in the Lago Maggiore becomes a catharsis of the darker feelings (op. cit., III, p. 157). Benno von Wiese interprets the whole episode as a variation on the theme of "The Man of Fifty," which he considers to be "endangerment through Eros," and characterizes the theme of this incident as the powerful dionysian attraction of Eros [*dionysische Lebensüsse des Eros*], which can be borne only by "highest Apollonian dignity" ("Der Mann von fünfzig Jahren," in B. v. W., ed., *Die deutsche Novelle von Goethe bis Kafka*, II, Düsseldorf, 1962, pp. 49f.). Henkel, on the other hand, emphasizes the irony of the narrative stance, and says: "in dieser Szene wird dem Lyrischen und seiner 'schmelzenden' Wirkung kaum mehr ein kathartischer Wert . . . zugebilligt, eher erscheint es als eine unerlaubte Debauche des Gefühls" (*Entsagung. Eine Studie zu Goethes Altersroman*, Tübingen, 1954, p. 102).
27. "Nun aber gehörte zu den sonderbaren Verpflichtungen der Entsagenden, auch die: dass sie, zusammentreffend, weder vom Vergangenen noch Künftigen sprechen durften, nur das Gegenwärtige sollte sie beschäftigen" (AA VIII, p. 44).
28. AA VIII, p. 306.
29. "Die Allegorie verwandelt die Erscheinung in einen Begriff, den Begriff in ein Bild, doch so, dass der Begriff im Bilde immer noch

begrenzt und vollständig zu halten und zu haben und an demselben auszusprechen sei.

Die Symbolik verwandelt die Erscheinung in Idee, die Idee in ein Bild, und so, dass die Idee im Bild immer unendlich wirksam und unerreichbar bleibt und, selbst in allen Sprachen ausgesprochen, doch unaussprechlich bliebe" (AA IX, p. 639).

30. AA IX, p. 643.
31. AA IX, p. 529.
32. AA IX, p. 532.
33. At the beginning of *Faust, Part Two,* Faust decides to turn his back on the sun, to cease in his direct striving for the absolute, and declares: "Am farbigen Abglanz haben wir das Leben" (AA V, p. 294).
34. *Den Vereinigten Staaten*
Amerika, du hast es besser
Als unser Kontinent, das alte,
Hast keine verfallene Schlösser
Und keine Basalte.

Dich stört nicht im Innern,
Zu lebendiger Zeit,
Unnützes Erinnern
Und vergeblicher Streit.

Benutzt die Gegenwart mit Glück!
Und wenn nun eure Kinder dichten,
Bewahre sie ein gut Geschick
Vor Ritter- Räuber- und Gespenstergeschichten.
(AA II, pp. 405f.)
35. On Goethe's knowledge of America, see Walter Wadepuhl, *Goethe's Interest in the New World,* Jena, 1934; Ernst Beutler, "Von der Ilm zum Susquehanna: Goethe und Amerika," *Goethe-Kalender,* 1935, pp. 86–153 (reprinted in E. B., *Essays um Goethe,* I, Leipzig, 1941); and Johannes Urzidil, *Das Glück der Gegenwart: Goethes Amerikabild,* Zurich and Stuttgart, 1958. Schädel (op. cit., p. 381) does mention the symbolic aspect of the idea of America in the *Journeymanship:* "Amerika ist das Symbol für die Möglichkeit, ein geschichtlich voraussetzungsloses Sozialwesen nach Massgabe urbildlicher Gesetzmässigkeiten zu verwirklichen," but my interpretation goes farther.
36. AA VIII, pp. 263f., 413f.; AA XIV, p. 860.
37. AA VIII, p. 421.
38. Küntzel sees the opposition between "world-piety" and "house-piety" as a polarity of systole and diastole (op. cit., p. 23). Both Hans Reiss ("*Wilhelm Meisters Wanderjahre:* Der Weg von der ersten zur zweiten Fassung," p. 47) and Staiger (op cit., III, p. 131) express the view that whereas the first version of the novel has wandering as its

theme, the final version is about emigration. Staiger goes further and asserts that the transformation of the idea of wandering into a concern with emigration violates the real theme of the novel, an opinion with which I cannot agree.

39. AA VIII, p. 437.

40. AA VIII, p. 439.

41. "Der Mensch ist nicht geboren, die Probleme der Welt zu lösen, wohl aber zu suchen, wo das Problem angeht, und sich sodann in der Grenze des Begreiflichen zu halten" (AA XXIV, p. 164).

42. AA VIII, p. 285.

43. AA VIII, p. 335.

44. See Wundt, *Goethes "Wilhelm Meister,"* pp. 493–500, and "Aus Makariens Archiv," *GRM* VII (1915), pp. 177–184.

45. Thus Eduard von der Hellen in the *Jubiläumsausgabe* of Goethe's works (I, p. 371).

46. Wundt and Julius Petersen indicated that even the early plan no. 17 for the novel spoke of a "Heft mit Auszug aus den Collectaneen" ("volume with excerpts from the collectanea"). See Wundt, *Goethes "Wilhelm Meister,"* pp. 493f.; and Julius Petersen, *Die Entstehung der Eckermannschen Gespräche und ihre Glaubwürdigkeit,* 2d ed., Frankfurt, 1925, pp. 6f. Wundt pointed out that not only plan 17, but also certain hand-written drafts of the first Makarie chapter prove that the collection of aphorisms was conceived from the start in relation to this chapter.

47. See especially the articles by Karl Viëtor ("Goethes Gedicht auf Schillers Schädel," *PMLA* LIX [1944], pp. 142–183) and Franz Mautner (" 'Ist fortzusetzen': Zu Goethes Gedicht auf Schillers Schädel," *PMLA* LIX [1944], pp. 1156–1162). Both discuss the meaning of the words "Ist fortzusetzen," but neither deals with the problem of why this particular poem is put in this particular place.

48. Goethe wrote to Rochlitz in July 1829: "Eine Arbeit wie diese, die sich selbst als kollectiv ankündigt, indem sie gewissermassen nur zum Verband der disparatesten Einzelheiten unternommen zu sein scheint, erlaubt, ja fordert mehr als eine andere, dass jeder sich zueigne was ihm gemäss ist, was in seiner Lage zur Beherzigung aufrief und sich harmonisch wohltätig erweisen mochte (AA XXI, p. 864). He wrote to Boisserée a couple of months later that the new version of the *Journeymanship* was his second attempt to unite such disparate elements (WA IV, 46, p. 66). In November, he wrote to Rochlitz again:

> Mit solchem Büchlein aber ist es wie mit dem Leben selbst: es findet sich in dem Komplex des Ganzen Notwendiges und Zufälliges, Vorgesetztes und Angeschlossenes, bald gelungen, bald vereitelt, wodurch es eine Art von Unendlichkeit erhält, die sich in verständige und vernünftige Worte nicht durchaus fassen, noch

einschliessen lässt. Wohin ich aber die Aufmerksamkeit meiner
Freunde gerne lenke und auch die Ihrige gern gerichtet sähe,
sind die verschiedenen, sich von einander absondernden Einzelnheiten, die doch, besonders im gegenwärtigen Falle, den Werth
des Buches entscheiden. . . . Das Büchlein verleugnet seinen kol-
lektiven Ursprung nicht, erlaubt und fordert mehr als jedes andere
die Teilnahme an hervortretenden Einzelnheiten.

(AA XXI, p. 880.)

49. AA XXIII, p. 667.

50. Emrich, "Symbolinterpretation," DVjs. XXVI 1952), p. 350.

51. On the novellas in the *Journeymanship*, see Myra R. Jessen, "Spannungsgefüge und Stilisierung in den Goetheschen Novellen," *PMLA* LV
(1940), pp. 445–471; and Ernst Friedrich von Monroy, "Zur Form der
Novelle in *Wilhelm Meisters Wanderjahren*," *GRM* XXXI (1943), pp.
1–19. On the relationship of the novellas to the main action, see Deli
Fischer-Hartmann, *Goethes Altersroman. Studien über die innere Einheit
von "Wilhelm Meisters Wanderjahren*," Halle, 1971; Eberhard Sarter,
op. cit.; Trunz, HA VIII, pp. 600f.; and Schädel, op. cit., pp. 159–162.
Trunz asserts that in the overall structure of the work, the framing
story is the realm of those who have already learned renunciation, while
the novellas form the realm of those who have still to acquire it or
have just learnt it. Schädel tries to prove that the formal qualities of the
novellas correspond to the respective phases of the framing action in
each of the three books of the novel. The novellas in the first book
(with the significant exception of "The Nut-Brown Maid") display a
strictly closed form, reflecting the closed worlds of Montan, the Uncle,
the Collector and Makarie. In the second book, which, according to
Schädel, portrays various processes of development and education that
mirror and reflect each other, stands "The Man of Fifty," which is
itself about education and development, and mounts to a climax that only
Makarie can resolve. The third book leads us into a world of fruitful
activity that is open-ended and directed toward the future; thus, the
novellas it contains display an open form. Anneliese Klingenberg has
recently taken a fresh look at the novellas of the *Journeymanship*, asserting that the six stories represent three complementary pairs which
mirror but at the same time answer each other (op. cit., pp. 126–142).
Jane Brown considers the novellas in great detail and in the light of her
concepts of irony and parody. She has an excellent discussion of "Saint
Joseph" and "Who is the Betrayer?" as dealing with problems of correspondence and perspective (op. cit., pp. 33–53), an illuminating comparison of "The Foolish Pilgrim" with its French original (pp. 53–58)
and interesting speculations on the possibility that some of the other
stories are parodistic variations (or even counterings) of stories by other
authors.

52. AA VIII, p. 72.

53. Goethe wrote a text of Lenardo's diary expressly for the novel in 1821, but it was not included in the first version (see Graef, op. cit., Part I, Vol. II, p. 956).

54. AA VIII, pp. 371f.

55. "Verflechtung des streng-trocknen Technischen mit ästhetisch-sentimentalen Ereignissen" (letter to Göttling of 17 January 1829; WA IV, 45, p. 128).

56. Or, in Anneliese Klingenberg's terms, the triumph of social and industrial advancement over humane values and life, over the eighteenth-century ideal of *Humanität*. Gustav Radbruch in an essay "Wilhelm Meisters sozialpolitische Sendung," published in 1919 (*Logos* VIII, pp. 152–162), and reprinted with the title "Wilhelm Meisters sozialistische Sendung" in G. R., *Gestalten und Gedanken*, Leipzig, 1944, asserts that there is a progression from individualistic thinking in the *Apprenticeship* to socialistic thinking in the *Journeymanship*. Pierre-Paul Sagave describes the structure of the *Journeymanship* as presenting "l'évolution de l'homme qui va, sans rupture, du capitalisme de l'Oncle jusqu'à l'économie technocratique des Voyageurs" ("L'économie et l'homme dans *Les Années de Voyage de Wilhelm Meister*," in *Recherches sur le roman social en Allemagne*, Aix-en-Provence, 1960, p. 28). Klingenberg considers this too simplistic, and rejects Sagave's assertion that the economic ideas behind the novel come from the Physiocrats and primarily from Charles Dupin, asserting instead that they derive from Goethe's reading of Adam Smith's ideal of the confluence of individual and communal values in a capitalistically ordered society.

Chapter 12. *Conclusion*

1. AA XXIV, pp. 482–484.

2. "Der Mensch wird überhaupt genug durch seine Leidenschaften und Schicksale verdüstert, als dass er es nötig hätte, dieses noch durch die Dunkelheiten einer barbarischen Vorzeit zu tun. Er bedarf der Klarheit und der Aufheiterung, und es tut ihm not, dass er sich zu solchen Kunst- und Literaturepochen wende, in denen vorzügliche Menschen zu vollendeter Bildung gelangten, so dass es ihnen selber wohl war, und sie die Seligkeit ihrer Kultur wieder auf andere auszugiessen imstande sind" (AA XXIV, p. 280).

3. AA XXIV, pp. 227f.

4. For further details on these Chinese novels and Goethe's comments on them, see my article "Goethe and the Chinese Novel," in *The Discontinuous Tradition: Studies in German Literature in Honour of*

E. L. Stahl, Oxford, 1971, pp. 29–53. Stuart Atkins has recently pointed out that the Chinese novels I discuss in my article all belong to the category of the romance (Stuart Atkins, *"Wilhelm Meisters Lehrjahre:* Novel or Romance?"* in *Essays on European Literature. In Honor of Liselotte Dieckmann,* St. Louis, 1972, p. 52).

Bibliography

Secondary Literature referred to in the Notes.

For explanation of the abbreviations used in this list, see above, page 279.

Ammann, Peter. *Schicksal und Liebe in Goethes "Wahlverwandtschaften."* Berne, 1962.

Anstett, J.-J. "La crise religieuse de Werther." *EG* IV (1949).

Atkins, Stuart Pratt. *"Wilhelm Meisters Lehrjahre:* Novel or Romance?" In *Essays on European Literature. In Honor of Liselotte Dieckmann.* St. Louis, 1972.

Bahr, Ehrhard. *Die Ironie im Spätwerk Goethes.* Berlin, 1972.

Barnes, Bertram. *Goethe's Knowledge of French Literature.* Oxford, 1937.

Barnes, H. G. "Ambiguity in *Die Wahlverwandtschaften.*" In *The Era of Goethe: Essays presented to James Boyd.* Oxford, 1959.

——. "Bildhafte Darstellung in den *Wahlverwandtschaften.*" *DVjs.* XXX (1956).

——. *Goethe's* Die Wahlverwandtschaften: *A Literary Intrepretation.* Oxford, 1967.

Bausch, Walter. *Theorien des epischen Erzählens in der deutschen Frühromantik.* Bonn, 1964.

Beaumont, Jean F. "Manzoni and Goethe." *Italian Studies II.* Manchester, 1939.

Beharriell, Frederick J. "The Hidden Meaning of Goethe's *Bekenntnisse einer schönen Seele.*" In *Lebendige Form,* Fests. for Heinrich E. K. Henel. Munich, 1970.

Benjamin, Walter. "Goethes *Wahlverwandtschaften.*" In W. B., *Schriften,* I. Frankfurt am Main, 1955.

Berendt, Hans. *Goethes "Wilhelm Meister": Ein Beitrag zur Entstehungsgeschichte.* Bonn, 1911.

Beriger, Hanno. *Goethe und der Roman. Studien zu "Wilhelm Meisters Lehrjahre."* Zurich, 1955.

329

Beutler, Ernst. "Einführung zu *Werther*," in AA IV.
——. "Von der Ilm zum Susquehanna: Goethe und Amerika." In *Goethe-Kalender*, 1935. Reprinted in E. B., *Essays um Goethe*, I. Leipzig, 1941.
——. "Wertherfragen." *Goethe*, N.S. V (1940).
Blackall, Eric A. "Goethe and the Chinese Novel." In *The Discontinuous Tradition: Studies in German Literature in honour of Ernest Ludwig Stahl*. Edited by P. F. Ganz. Oxford, 1971.
——. "Goethe's Silences." In *Geist und Zeichen*, Fests. for Arthur Henkel. Heidelberg, 1976.
Blanckenburg, Friedrich von. *Versuch über den Roman*. Facsimile of the orig. ed. of 1774. Edited by Eberhard Lämmert. Stuttgart, 1965.
Blumenthal, Hermann. "Ein neues Wertherbild?" *Goethe*, N.S. V (1940).
Blumenthal, Hermann, ed. *Zeitgenössische Rezensionen und Urteile über Goethes "Götz" und "Werther."* Berlin, 1935.
Böckmann, Paul. "Naturgesetz und Symbolik in Goethes *Wahlverwandtschaften*." *Jb. d. fr. dt. Hochstifts*, 1968.
Borcherdt, Hans Heinrich. *Der Roman der Goethezeit*. Urach and Stuttgart, 1949.
Boyd, James. *Goethe's Knowledge of English Literature*. Oxford, 1932.
Brown, Jane K. *Goethe's Cyclical Narratives "Die Unterhaltungen deutscher Ausgewanderten" and "Wilhelm Meisters Wanderjahre."* Chapel Hill, N.C., 1975.
Bruford, W. H. *Theatre, Drama and Audience in Goethe's Germany*. London, 1950.
Brüggemann, Werner. *Cervantes und die Figur des Don Quixote in Kunstanschauung und Dichtung der deutschen Romantik*. Münster, 1958.
Butcher, S. H. *Aristotle's Theory of Poetry and Fine Art*. 4th ed. New York, 1951.
Castle, Eduard. "Der theatergeschichtliche und autobiographische Gehalt von *Wilhelm Meisters Theatralische Sendung*." In E. C., *In Goethes Geist*. Vienna and Leipzig, 1926. Also in *Wiener Goethe Verein* XXVII (1913).
Cohen, Gustav. "Mignon." *Jb. d. Goethe Ges.* VII (1920).
Crocker, Lester G. "The Discussion of Suicide in the Eighteenth Century." *Journal of the History of Ideas* XIII (1952).
Danckert, Werner. *Offenes und geschlossenes Leben*. Bonn, 1963.
Diamond, William. "Wilhelm Meister's Interpretation of *Hamlet*." *Modern Philology*, XXIII (1925–1926).
Dieckmann, Herbert. *Diderot und die Aufklärung. Aufsätze zur europäischen Literatur des 18. Jahrhunderts*. Stuttgart, 1972.
——. "Goethe und Diderot." *DVjs.* X (1932).

Emmel, Hildegard. *Geschichte des deutschen Romans*, I. Berne and Munich, 1972.

——. *Was Goethe vom Roman der Zeitgenossen nahm.* Berne, 1972.

——. *Weltklage und Bild der Welt in der Dichtung Goethes.* Weimar, 1957.

Emrich, Wilhelm. "Das Problem der Symbolinterpretation in Hinblick auf Goethes *Wanderjahre.*" *DVjs.* XXVI (1952). Reprinted in W. E., *Protest und Verheissung.* Frankfurt am Main, 1960.

Feise, Ernst. "Goethes Werther als nervöser Charakter." *GR* I (1926).

Fink, Gonthier-Louis. "Les *Wahlverwandtschaften* de Goethe: Structure du roman et aspects du temps." *Recherches Germaniques* I (1971).

Fischer-Hartmann, Deli. *Goethes Altersroman: Studien über die innere Einheit von "Wilhelm Meisters Wanderjahren."* Halle, 1971.

Fittbogen, Gottfried. "Die Charaktere in den beiden Fassungen von Werthers Leiden." *Euphorion* XVII (1910).

Flashar, Dorothea. *Bedeutung, Entwicklung und literarische Nachwirkung von Goethes Mignongestalt.* Berlin, 1929.

Fleischer, Stefan. " 'Bekenntnisse einer schönen Seele': Figural Representation in *Wilhelm Meisters Lehrjahre.*" *MLN* LXXXIII (1968).

Flemming, Willi. *Goethe und das Theater seiner Zeit.* Stuttgart, 1968.

François-Poncet, André. *Les Affinités Electives de Goethe: Essai de commentaire critique.* Paris, 1910. German trans., Mainz, 1951.

Fuchs, Albert. "Goethe et la littérature française." In *Goethe et l'esprit français (Actes du Colloque international de Strasbourg, 23-27 avril 1957),* Paris, 1958.

Geerdts, Hans Jürgen. *Goethes Roman "Die Wahlverwandtschaften": Eine Analyse seiner künstlerischen Struktur, seiner historischen Bezogenheiten und seines Ideengehaltes.* Weimar, 1958.

Gidion, Heidi. *Zur Darstellungsweise von Goethes "Wilhelm Meisters Wanderjahren."* Göttingen, 1969.

Gilg, André. *"Wilhelm Meisters Wanderjahre" und ihre Symbole.* Zurich, 1954.

Goethe-Handbuch. 2d ed., ed. Alfred Zastrau, Stuttgart, 1961. Only the first volume has appeared.

Graef, Hans Gerhard, ed. *Goethe über seine Dichtungen.* 9 vols. Frankfurt, 1901–1914.

Graefe, Johanna. "Die Religion in den *Leiden des jungen Werther:* Eine Untersuchung auf Grund des Wortbestandes." *Goethe,* N.S. XX (1958).

Greiner, Walter F. *Studien zur Entstehung der englischen Romantheorie an der Wende zum 18. Jahrhundert.* Tübingen, 1969.

Grimm, Reinhold, ed. *Deutsche Romantheorien.* Frankfurt am Main and Bonn, 1968.

Gundolf, Friedrich. *Goethe.* 10th ed., Berlin, 1922.

———. *Shakespeare und der deutsche Geist.* Quoted according to the 11th ed., Berlin, 1959.

Hammer, Carl. "Goethe's Estimate of Oliver Goldsmith." *Journal of English and Germanic Philology* XLIV (1945).

Hankamer, Paul. *Spiel der Mächte. Ein Kapitel aus Goethes Leben und Goethes Welt.* Tübingen, 1943. 5th ed. Stuttgart, 1960.

———. "Zur Genesis von Goethes *Wahlverwandtschaften.*" In *Fests. für Berthold Litzmann.* Bonn, 1920.

Hardison, O. B. Commentary to *Aristotle's Poetics,* translation by Leon Golden. Englewood Cliffs, N.J., 1968.

Hellen, Eduard von der. Introduction to Vol. I of the *Jubiläumsausgabe* of Goethe's works. Stuttgart and Berlin, 1902.

Henkel, Arthur. *Entsagung. Eine Studie zu Goethes Altersroman.* Tübingen, 1954.

———. "Versuch über den *Wilhelm Meister.*" *Ruperto-Carola* XXXI (1962).

Hering, Robert. *"Wilhelm Meister" und "Faust" und ihre Gestaltung im Zeichen der Gottesidee.* Frankfurt am Main, 1952.

Heselhaus, Clemens. "Die Wilhelm Meister-Kritik der Romantiker und die romantische Romantheorie." *Nachahmung und Illusion.* Edited by H. R. Jauss. Munich, 1964.

Hirsch, Arnold. *"Die Leiden des jungen Werthers:* Ein bürgerliches Schicksal im absolutistischen Staat." *EG* XIII (1958).

Hofmannsthal, Hugo von. "Manzonis *Promessi Sposi.*" In *Prosa* IV. Frankfurt, 1955.

Jessen, Myra R. "Spannungsgefüge und Stilisierung in den Goetheschen Novellen." *PMLA* LV (1940).

Jolles, Matthijs. *Goethes Kunstanschauung.* Berne, 1957.

Kahn, Ludwig W. "Erlebte Rede in Goethes *Wahlverwandtschaften.*" *PMLA* LXXXIX (1974).

Karnick, Manfred. *"Wilhelm Meisters Wanderjahre" oder die Kunst des Mittelbaren. Studien zum Problem der Verständigung in Goethes Altersepoche.* Munich, 1968.

Kestner, A., ed. *Goethe und Werther.* Stuttgart and Tübingen, 1854.

Kimpel, Dieter and Conrad Wiedemann, eds. *Theorie und Technik des Romans im 17. und 18. Jahrhundert.* 2 vols. Tübingen, 1970.

Klingemann, Gisbert. *Goethes Verhältnis zu Laurence Sterne.* Marburg, 1929.

Klingenberg, Anneliese. *Goethes Roman "Wilhelm Meisters Wanderjahre oder die Entsagenden": Quellen und Composition.* Berlin and Weimar, 1972.

Korff, H. A. *Geist der Goethezeit.* 5 vols. Quoted according to the 4th ed., Leipzig, 1957–1958.

Krauss, Paul. "Mignon, der Harfner, Sperata: Die Psychopathologie einer Sippe." *DVjs.* XXII (1944).

Küntzel, Gerhard. *"Wilhelm Meisters Wanderjahre* in der ersten Fassung 1821." *Goethe,* N.S. III (1938).

Kurth, Lieselotte E. "Formen der Romankritik im achtzehnten Jahrhundert." *MLN* LXXXIII (1968).

Lachmann, F. R. "Goethes Mignon." *GRM* XV, 1927.

Lange, Victor. "Erzählformen im Roman des achtzehnten Jahrhunderts." *Anglia* LXXVI (1958).

——. "Goethe's Craft of Fiction." *PEGS,* N.S. XXII (1952–1953).

Lauterbach, Martin. *Das Verhältnis der zweiten zur ersten Ausgabe von Werthers Leiden.* Strassburg, 1910.

Lehmann, Rudolf. "Anton Reiser und die Entstehung des *Wilhelm Meister.*" *Jb. d. Goethe Ges.* III (1916).

Levy, Siegmund. "Goethe und Oliver Goldsmith." *Goethe-Jb.* VI (1885).

Loiseau, Hippolyte. *Goethe et la France.* Paris, 1930.

Lonchamp, F.-C. *L'Oeuvre imprimé de Mme. Germaine de Staël.* Geneva, 1949.

Lukács, Georg. *Goethe and his Age.* London, 1968.

Mann, Thomas. "Phantasie über Goethe." In *Neue Studien,* Berlin and Frankfurt am Main, 1948.

——. "Zu Goethes *Wahlverwandtschaften.*" In *Gesammelte Werke* IX. Oldenburg, 1960.

Mautner, Franz. " 'Ist fortzusetzen': Zu Goethes Gedicht auf Schillers Schädel." *PMLA* LIX (1944).

May, Kurt. *"Die Wahlverwandtschaften* als tragischer Roman." *Jb. d. fr. dt. Hochstifts,* 1936.

——. *"Wilhelm Meisters Lehrjahre,* ein Bildungsroman?" *DVjs* XXXI (1957).

Mittner, Ladislao. "Il 'Werther,' romanzo antiwertheriano." In L. M., *La letteratura tedesca del Novecento e altri saggi.* Turin, 1960.

——. "Paesaggi italiani di Goethe." In L. M., *La letteratura tedesca del Novecento* etc. Turin, 1960.

Monroy, Ernst Friedrich von. "Zur Form der Novelle in *Wilhelm Meisters Wanderjahren.*" *GRM* XXXI (1943).

Mortier, Roland. *Diderot en Allemagne.* Paris, 1954.

Müller, Günther. *Gestaltung – Umgestaltung in "Wilhelm Meisters Lehrjahren."* Halle, 1948.

Müller, Joachim. "Phasen der Bildungsidee im *Wilhelm Meister.*" *Goethe,* N.S. XXIV (1962).

Müller, Peter. *Zeitkritik und Utopie in Goethes "Werther."* Berlin, 1969.

Needler, G. H. *Goethe and Scott.* Toronto, 1950.

Nisbet, H. B. "*Die Wahlverwandtschaften:* Explanation and its limits."
DVjs. XLIII (1969).

Pascal, Roy. "The Novels of F. H. Jacobi and Goethe's early Classicism." *PEGS*, N.S. XVI (1947).

Peschken, Bernd. "Das 'Blatt' in den *Wanderjahren.*" *Goethe*, N.S.
XXVII (1965).

———. *Entsagung in "Wilhelm Meisters Wanderjahren."* Bonn, 1968.

Petersen, Julius. *Die Entstehung der Eckermannschen Gespräche und
ihre Glaubwürdigkeit.* 2d ed. Frankfurt, 1925.

Petritis, Aivars. *Die Gestaltung der Personen in Goethes "Wilhelm
Meisters Lehrjahren" und "Wilhelm Meisters Wanderjahren."* Cologne, 1967.

Pinger, W. R. R. *Laurence Sterne and Goethe.* Berkeley, Cal., 1920.

Polheim, Karl. *Die Arabeske.* Paderborn, 1966.

Price, Lawrence Marsden. *The Reception of English Literature in Germany.* Berkeley, Cal., 1932.

———. *Die Aufnahme englischer Literatur in Deutschland.* Berne, 1961 (a
revised and expanded version of the English text).

Raabe, August. "Das Dämonische in den *Wanderjahren.*" *Goethe* I
(1936).

Radbruch, Gustav. "Wilhelm Meisters sozialistische Sendung." In G. R.,
Gestalten und Gedanken. Leipzig, 1944.

Rasch, Wolfdietrich. "Die klassische Erzählkunst Goethes." In *Formkräfte der deutschen Dichtung vom Barock bis zur Gegenwart.* Edited
by Hans Steffen. Göttingen, 1963.

Rausch, Jürgen. "Lebensstufen in Goethes *Wilhelm Meister.*" *DVjs.* XX
(1942).

Reiss, Hans. *Goethes Romane.* Berne, 1963.

———. *Goethe's Novels.* London, 1969.

———. "Mehrdeutigkeit in Goethes *Wahlverwandtschaften.*" *Jb. d. dt.
Schiller Ges.* XIV (1970).

———. "*Wilhelm Meisters theatralische Sendung:* Ernst oder Ironie."
Jb. d. dt. Schiller Ges. XI (1967).

———. "*Wilhelm Meisters Wanderjahre:* Der Weg von der ersten zur
zweiten Fassung." *DVjs.* XXXIV (1965).

Remak, Henry H. H. "Goethe on Stendhal: Development and Significance of His Attitude." In *Goethe Bicentennial Studies.* Edited by
H. J. Meessen, Bloomington, Ind., 1950.

Riemann, Robert. *Goethes Romantechnik.* Leipzig, 1902.

Röder, Gerda. *Glück und glückliches Ende im deutschen Bildungsroman: Eine Studie zu Goethes "Wilhelm Meister."* Munich, 1968.

Rosenfeld, Emmy. "Goethe und Manzoni." *Literaturwissenschaftliches
Jahrbuch*, N.S. I, 1960.

Sagave, Pierre-Paul. "L'économie et l'homme dans *Les Années de voyage de Wilhelm Meister.*" *EG* VII (1952). Reprinted in P.-P. S., *Recherches sur le roman social en Allemagne*. Aix-en-Provence, 1960.

Sarter, Eberhard. *Zur Technik von "Wilhelm Meisters Wanderjahren."* Berlin, 1914.

Schaeder, Grete. "Die Idee der Wahlverwandtschaften." *Goethe*, N.S. VI (1941). Revised ed. in G. S., *Gott und Welt*. Hamelin, 1947.

Schädel, Christian Hartmut. *Metamorphose und Erscheinungsformen des Menschseins in "Wilhelm Meisters Wanderjahren": Zur geistigen und künstlerischen Einheit des Goetheschen Romans*. Marburg, 1969.

Schelling-Schär, Esther. *Die Gestalt der Ottilie: zu Goethes "Wahlverwandtschaften."* Zurich, 1969.

Scherpe, Klaus. *Werther und Wertherwirkung. Zum Syndrom bürgerlicher Gesellschaftsordnung im 18. Jahrhundert*. Bad Homburg, 1970.

Schiff, Julius. "Mignon, Ottilie, Makarie im Lichte der Goetheschen Naturphilosophie." *Jb. d. Goethe Ges.* IX (1922).

Schlechta, Karl. *Goethe in seinem Verhältnis zu Aristoteles*. Frankfurt, am Main, 1938.

——. *Goethes "Wilhelm Meister."* Frankfurt am Main, 1953.

Schöffler, Herbert. *"Die Leiden des jungen Werther": Ihr geistesgeschichtlicher Hintergrund*. Frankfurt am Main, 1938.

Schrimpf, Hans Joachim. *Das Weltbild des späten Goethe*. Stuttgart, 1956.

Schulz, Gerhard. "Die Poetik des Romans bei Novalis." *Jb. d. fr. dt. Hochstifts*, 1964. Reprinted in *Deutsche Romantheorien*. Edited by Reinhold Grimm. Frankfurt am Main and Bonn, 1968.

Seuffert, Bernhard. *Goethes Theaterroman*. Graz-Vienna-Leipzig, 1924.

Stahl, E. L. "Goethe as Novelist." In *Essays on Goethe*. Edited by William Rose. London, 1949.

——. Introduction to *Die Leiden des jungen Werthers*. Oxford, 1942.

Staiger, Emil. *Goethe*. 3 vols. Zurich, 1952–1959.

Steinhauer, Harry, trans. *The Sufferings of Young Werther*. New York, 1970.

Stöcklein, Paul. "Stil und Geist der *Wahlverwandtschaften*." *ZfdPh.* LXXI (1951).

——. *Wege zum späten Goethe*. Hamburg, 1949.

Stopp, F. J. "Ein wahrer Narziss: Reflections on the Eduard-Ottilie Relationship in Goethe's *Wahlverwandtschaften*." *PEGS*, N.S. XXIX (1960).

——. "Ottilie and das innere Licht." In *German Studies presented to Walter H. Bruford*. London, 1962.

Storz, Gerhard. *Goethe-Vigilien*. Stuttgart, 1953.

Thalmann, Marianne. *Der Trivialroman des 18. Jahrhunderts und der romantische Roman*. Berlin, 1923.

Trunz, Erich. "Anmerkungen" to *Werther*, in HA VI. "Anmerkungen" to the *Lehrjahre,* in HA VII. "Anmerkungen" to the *Wanderjahre,* in HA VIII.

Urzidil, Johannes. *Das Glück der Gegenwart: Goethes Amerikabild.* Zurich and Stuttgart, 1958.

Viëtor, Karl. "Goethes Gedicht auf Schillers Schädel." *PMLA* LIX (1944).

Wadepuhl, Walter. *Goethe's Interest in the New World.* Jena, 1934.

Wagner, Walter. "Goethes Mignon." *GRM* XXI (1933).

Walzel, Oskar. Introductions to Goethe's novels in the "Festausgabe": *Werther,* Vol. IX; *Theatralische Sendung,* Vol. X; *Lehrjahre,* Vol. XI; *Wanderjahre,* Vol. XII; *Wahlverwandtschaften,* Vol. XIII. Leipzig, 1926.

——. "Goethes *Wahlverwandtschaften* im Rahmen ihrer Zeit." *Goethe-Jb.* XXVII (1906). Reprinted in O. W., *Vom Geistesleben des 18. und 19. Jahrhunderts.* Leipzig, 1911.

Warshaw, J. "The Epic-Drama Conception of the Novel." *MLN* XXXV (1920).

Wiese, Benno von. "Der Mann von fünfzig Jahren." In B. v. W., ed., *Die deutsche Novelle von Goethe bis Kafka,* II. Düsseldorf, 1962.

Williams, Ioan, ed. *Sir Walter Scott on Novelists and Fiction.* London and New York, 1968.

Willoughby, L. A. "The Image of the 'Wanderer' and the 'Hut' in Goethe's Poetry." *EG* VI (1951).

Wolff, Eugen. "Die ursprüngliche Gestalt von *Wilhelm Meisters Wanderjahren.*" *Goethe-Jb.* XXXIV (1913).

——. *Mignon: ein Beitrag zur Geschichte des Wilhelm Meister.* Munich, 1909.

Wolff, Hans M. *Goethe in der Periode der "Wahlverwandtschaften."* Berne, 1951.

Wundt, Max. "Aus Makariens Archiv: Zur Entstehung der Aphorismensammlung." *GRM* VII (1915).

——. *Goethes "Wilhelm Meister" und die Entwicklung des modernen Lebensideals.* Berlin and Leipzig, 1913. 2d ed., Berlin and Leipzig, 1932.

Index

337